DORA BIRTLES was born [...]
1903, and educated at The W[...] [...], Sydney, and Sydney
University. Fascinated by the sea and a keen sailor from an early age,
in 1932 she joined the crew of the cutter *Skaga* on an eight-month
voyage from Newcastle to Singapore – the first such journey to
include women from Australia, and one keenly followed by the press
at the time. She and the other women on board wrote regularly for
various newspapers throughout the voyage as a means of financing
the venture; *North-West by North*, a much more complete account of
shipboard life, was not published until 1935. In it she describes not
only the sailor's day-to-day experiences of exhilaration and danger,
discomfort and tedium, but also the extraordinary psychological
pressures of physical confinement: along with the thrill of adventures
shared come personal rivalries and misunderstandings; close friends
on shore do not necessarily live together happily within the space of a
thirty-four-foot yacht.

When *Skaga*'s journey ended in Singapore, Dora Birtles spent
several years abroad with her journalist husband, and was active on
the Women's Committee Against War and Fascism in London
before the Second World War. She also continued to write, and has
published two books of children's fiction as well as works of adult
fiction and non-fiction, among them *The Overlanders*, also a successful
film. She still lives in Sydney and, with her husband and two sons,
remains active in the yachting world.

THE voyage from Sydney to Singapore described in this book was made in 1932. The account is a personal one based on diaries written at the time. The journey of five thousand miles took almost eight months and it was accomplished in a cutter thirty-four feet long. No engine was used. The book is a record of feelings as well as of adventures and impressions, and the object in writing it was to set everything down as truly as possible.

A JOURNAL OF A VOYAGE

NORTH-WEST
BY NORTH

DORA BIRTLES

With a New Introduction by the Author

Published by VIRAGO PRESS Limited 1985
41 William IV Street, London WC2N 4DB

First published in Great Britain by Jonathan Cape Ltd 1935

British Library Cataloguing in Publication Data
Birtles, Dora
    North-West by North.
    1. Skaga (*Ship*)   2. Voyages and travels
    3. South Pacific Ocean
    I. Title
    910'.091647   DU22
    ISBN 0-86068-644-7

Printed in Great Britain by Anchor Brendon Ltd
at Tiptree, Essex

The cover shows a detail of 'Sydney Harbour, 1913'
by Elioth Gruner 1882-1939, Australian.
Oil on canvas
54.6 × 64.7 cm
Purchased 1970
Reproduced by permission of
the National Gallery of Victoria, Melbourne.
Author's photograph by Catriona Moore.

CONTENTS

CONTENTS

ILLUSTRATIONS

Between pages 160 and 161

Between pages 192 and 193

INTRODUCTION

It is more than fifty years since I made the voyage described in *North-West by North*. Since the book was first published in 1935 and the catharsis of writing it is over, I have thought of it with a sort of amused humour and the up-dated wisdom of the '80s as contrasted with the scarifying mortifications of the '30s. I write of the difference in time as well as with whatever wisdom age has. That voyage is now only one of the significant periods of my life.

When I was eighteen a dearly loved maiden aunt who wrote poetry said to me, 'I am eighty, Dora, but inside me I feel just the same as if I were still eighteen.' Now *Dora* is eighty-one and I feel much the same too.

Yesterday I went sailing with our second son Kanga, his wife, her parents, my husband and our little one-year-old grand-daughter. 'Take the tiller Mum?' Kanga asked. 'I don't trust myself,' I replied, but glad that he had asked me. Kanga makes yachts. This one had been designed for handicap racing, Sydney to Hobart, thirty feet long and a mast over sixty feet high and an even newer variation in keel. Not my style with the wind gusty and changeable from the hills around Sydney Harbour where we live, the waves breaking on the rocks below our windows.

When I re-read *North-West by North* places and people spring to life for me. Now it is history. Life was so different in those untouristed times. It was 1932. The worst year of the world Depression.

The idea was mine, the first money put down was mine; by chance my husband, a journalist, found *Skaga*. It was not the idea of being heroines, the first women to undertake such a thing in Australia, but just the cheapest and easiest way of travelling in a floating home and seeing the world en route to London, a more shining beacon for all of us than any Samarkand.

We women were school and university friends. Ruth and Joan were cousins. We had gone on camps and walking tours together and knew some of each others' most private secrets, but our backgrounds were different. Ruth's father was a headmaster and religious; Joan's an eminent and talented Commonwealth official. They were Sydney, I was Newcastle.

I had grown up on Throsby Creek, flowing into Newcastle Harbour, New South Wales. Turbaned or shirt-tail-flapping Indians trudged past our house every day. Chinese market gardeners grew their vegetables near a swamp not half a mile away. A frightening, enormous negro called Shanghai Jack stood outside one of the hotels in the main street of Newcastle near the Post Office. He shanghaied drunken sailors, who found themselves on the road to Rio in a four-master full of coal when they had just returned from India delivering grain or a draft of horses from the Upper Hunter River. Among other things our horses, employees and menfolk pulled railway trucks of coal night or day under the cranes on Carrington wharves.

When I was small my grandfather took me to visit his friends, Welsh captains of tied-up sailing ships waiting at Stockton for berths and cargoes. I had a bo'sun's whistle round my neck. I knew the names of all the masts and rigging. I had to be able to recite the difference between a barque and a barquentine. I saw the goat for'ard for milk for the captain's wife and children; the hens in their coops; the pig aft in his sty. For me the sea was a homely world. I spent a lot of time on the mud flats gathering shells and watching crabs. The pelicans, fishing, were bigger than I was. When I was about six I let my little brother, Fred, bend forward and topple off a wall we were sitting on into a high tide. I fished him out and got scolded. At eight I was supremely happy paddling someone else's canoe at Belmont. At nine and ten I sailed with my six boy cousins at Killaben Bay on Lake Macquarie. We shouted and squabbled, cut out and sewed our own chaff-bag sails for a retired lifeboat that would never capsize however hard we rolled it. Why chaff bag? Uncle Will knew that the wind blew through it as well as against it. He kept his own sails locked up.

INTRODUCTION

In my teens I sailed with my elder brother, Victor, in various craft he had. A big one called *The Ark*, *Storm*, *Frolic*. Later he built *Ruthean* of Huon pine, still beautiful and still sailing. He was a foundation member of the Lake Macquarie Yacht Club and through him *Skaga* got the Club's burgee, which gave us the privilege of enjoying the hospitalities of being a yacht. Sven kept the burgee under his mattress, but Henery never wanted it flown. It was one of his little snobbisms. Poor chap, I believe he died in Singapore when the Japs took that city.

In 1932 I had just worked out my five-year student's bond which was required by the Department of Education, NSW. The Education Department was going to sack married women teachers – the young ones, not the oldies, who could demand heavy superannuation. I got leave of absence from the Department. Ruth had, some time before, given up her teaching job for other reasons. Joan had had no job I knew of but had written a detective story. Henery had 'something in the city' his father-in-law told me loftily. Before that he had been a jackaroo; after the *Skaga*'s adventure he became a news photographer.

The three of them worked on *Skaga* with one of the former owners, a Swede. In Sydney the diesel engine was taken out, sold and a small outboard purchased. 'That may push your old tub to an anchorage, that's all,' my brother Victor said. Actually the men couldn't ever get it to go. The Swede pulled out and married a nice widow. I had only met him once, and after one brief question I knew it was a very sensible thing for him to do.

Secretly I deplored the girls' handiwork – thick white enamel paint in waves everywhere. To repay for their labours they made a trial trip to Melbourne where the General resided. They had a professional sailor as navigator, and he wrote an article in *Truth* newspaper which said 'Sailors Beware, Sailors Take Care Of "The Skaga's" Adventure'. It was a vengeance article, oddly paradoxical. He must have learnt that we proposed to make money by writing articles on the trip – Joan's idea – and he got in first and very nastily. Even I who knew nothing about him was mentioned un-named but as a married woman sailing without her husband. A nasty innuendo at that time. My people swallowed it without mention but my mother took me to a fortune-teller who said, firmly, that I should never die by drowning. That relieved her a lot. I never saw her after we left Newcastle. She died in 1935 when Bert and I were in Greece.

It was true that Bert did not want to come with us. He had practical reasons as well as instinctive ones. He was brilliant at his job and wanted to improve and nurse it in the Depression. We also had our new attractive house to pay off. Privately he told me he did not wish to sail with my friends. No reasons. I did not ask for any. I thought we would be separated for a year. It turned out to be three.

The invalid wife of a sub-editor whom we very much respected tried, vaguely, to warn me of 'risks'. I was so naïve and foolish then as not to know these included distance, waiting, poor communications, loneliness, poverty, bitterness, infidelity, grog, sheer misery or plain illness. The robust Bert got bad pleurisy while I was away. To keep him always in mind I put up in *Skaga* a reproduction of a pencil sketch B. E. Minns had made of him; I could see it from my bunk. I did not ask permission from my shipmates. It was my one assertion. I needed it.

When *Skaga* came to Newcastle Sven had already come aboard in Melbourne. I think the General had vetted him and chosen wisely. Years afterwards Sven told me he had paid for his keep, something I did not know.

Sven was a professional sailor. He had his first mate's and was going for his captain's ticket. Of Swedish descent, he had from boyhood sailed in the last commercial sailing ships from South Australia to Tasmania carrying grain. He had been around Cape Horn and still is a member of the Cape Horner's tradition. He married Emmy, the girl he had known before the *Skaga* adventure.

INTRODUCTION

We are still good friends. Like us they have two sons and a few grandchildren. In the Second World War Emmy stayed with us while Sven was at sea. They visit us when they come to Sydney. We saw them in Christmas 1984.

Joan died last year. I never saw her after that last glimpse in Singapore, December 1932. Once my husband met her and her elder sister in Melbourne. It was in the Post Office where he was sending a press telegram. He took them to afternoon tea! That did astonish me.

During the Second World War when I was writing *Other People's Lives*, billed as 'Articles of Social Significance', and the novel *The Overlanders*, she was writing about feeding infants and bringing up children in *The Tribune*, the Communist newspaper. She was, I believe, childless. Not so long ago I taxed the then editor with it. He defended himself: 'I had to keep her off the front page,' he said.

It was quite different with Ruth. We saw a lot of each other in London in 1933. Then she went off to Russia and for a while got a job as an archivist. Later in life she married happily. We met in the same bus once coming from Palm Beach. I had our two boys with me. She was the same old Ruth, beaming with pleasure. 'I bet they keep your hands full,' she said. She told me about her life then. I managed to get a portrait of her father, painted by Dahl Collings, back to her, but we have lost touch since. I have forgotten her married name.

That is some of what happened to us later. It is not often readers get such an epilogue. Only Sven and I had the sea in our blood, if that sort of thing has any meaning. My maiden name was a Viking one from Devonshire. All my family have lived by the sea. I wrote *Miss Toll of Strete* from instinct – and my Aunt Polly. Curiously my husband's mother was a Grenfell – from Penzance!

When I came back from China and Japan in 1933 there was only one person to greet me. The Norwegian who had towed us into Singapore and given us hospitality, he was there. He told me that

Skaga was sold, that he had been given my expensive fishing gear subscribed for by Newcastle friends; that my horse-hair mattress, given me by the Major, had gone with the boat; that he did not know where my summer clothes or books or other possessions were. I swapped the fishing gear for a portable typewriter he had and went back to the YWCA. It was only chance that let me catch Henery, Joan and her sister driving a car in the street. Presumably the cash was in their pockets or the bank. It never occurred to me to ask for a hand-out, or where *Skaga* was, or my things. There was no time. I was just genuinely pleased to see them. Singapore had liberated me, and other people liked me. I gave them the locality of an Australian-run government rest house and the name of a courteous English rubber planter who had shown me his plantation and taken me out crocodile shooting with the local Commissioner and driven me to Malacca. They used the introduction to the full and I had to blush for them later.

Back in Australia years afterwards I got a lengthy financial statement. I think the General, for legal reasons, made them do it. It was very funny and I kept it.

> 'That is the way the world ends,
> not with a bang but a whimper.'

If I ended *North-West by North* with a poem, you must pardon me. I still believe in what the poem says. I also remember how John Curtin answered my journalist husband's shrewd question about how the war-time Prime Minister of Australia felt about an old split in the Labor Party. John Curtin said, '*One can forgive, but only a fool forgets*'. The sea has its own truth.

I am too old to remember any more.

I hope you enjoy reading *North-West by North*.

Dora Birtles,
January 1985.

CHAPTER I

THE DEPARTURE FROM NEWCASTLE

FOUR men stood in the rowing boat and waved to me. The little boat rocked violently and yet they managed to stand upright, four black streaks making a pattern like a broken fence against the grey of the distant wharf on which I could see a knot of people, a bundle of confused gesticulations; Father, mother, many friends. Four men waving good-bye; two brothers, a husband, and one a stranger, curious at it all, a journalist. How tall Fred was and how solid Vic, and that other, with a white face and the sun reflected from his spectacles, waving most determinedly of all, waving as if I must never forget him and the moving compassion of his arms, that was Kim.

We came about. I could see them no longer. This then was good-bye – for a long time. Ten o'clock in the morning and the voyage had begun. In my throat grew a large hard lump big as a pigeon's egg that I could not swallow. It felt as if my Adam's apple had slipped and was choking me. Impossible that I was going to cry. Of course not. Ruth looked friendly. She sat down very close beside me and I knew she had done it because she knew . . . Gradually the Adam's apple melted, the terrible constriction of the throat passed.

I was aware of the boat, of Sven at the tiller, Joan beside him, Henery moving about for'ard, and Byron Cooper, the advertised-for sixth man, crouching by the gunwale. We were to see how he shaped, he might be coming all the way with us. We were moving out along the breakwater, Nobbys was lifting its small bald head at us, the polished glass of the lighthouse winking like a monocle in the sunshine; the flat brown water of the Hunter River was changing to a flurry of green waves beyond the bar. I could see the houses high on the hill behind the city, the red-brown mass of the cathedral dominating them; below, close to the wharves, were the railway and the power-station; to the north-west the tall chimneys of the steel-works. They stood out, the strategic points of the town. A haze dulled the suburbs beyond. I had never seen my home city so significantly before.

'Dona B——, a native of Newcastle.' How odd. The epitaph of going. Yet I did belong here; the school on the hill, the local library, the beaches where I had played, the house I had built, the bushy hills behind it, the lagoon and the roads leading out of the town, they were all curiously part of me at this moment. Long association had made them mine and I was leaving them. To encourage this new perspective I thought of Cook, out at sea, naming the headland 'Nobbys' from a distance, of Oxley creeping in and exploring what he named Coal River, of the convicts in Governor King's time mining coal from the open seam below the fort and making their vegetable gardens and pigsties where the great commercial banks now stand. Deliberately I used this trick of the historical imagination.

It is a fine device. I was more normal now, free to wonder about the boat, the acute agitation of leave-taking subsided.

Though I was supposed to be going round the world in the *Skaga* I had never been for a sail in it before, a little manœuvring for a film in Sydney, that was all, and the disastrous experience of yesterday when we had hoisted the sails and made a couple of boards for the sake of a camera-man who wanted to get a picture of the boat under sail for his newspaper. Disastrous because the feeling between Henery and Sven had been suddenly revealed to me, the mismanagement of a simple operation, the violence of their disagreement, the sullen unspokenness about it afterwards.

I had been used to sailing with my uncle, or with my brother, skippers in their own boats, men who knew what they wanted to do and how they intended to do it, who gave a steady command and cursed a laggard, who didn't mince matters if one muffed a gybe or tried to be lady-like and keep the tail of one's trousers dry.

14

I had known the tearing strain of a hand-held sheet and the thrill of hanging out with only a toe under the foot-strap, one's whole body strained out over the water. I understood the light skimming of sixteen- and eighteen-footers and the graceful flight of bigger yachts under immense spreads of canvas. I knew the joy of running under spinnaker and balloony, the risk of a capsize, the camaraderie and the doubtful jokes of the sailing fraternity. We had sailed on Lake Macquarie since childhood.

Skaga was different. A solid, stolid, thirty-four-foot ship with a comparatively small sail area, clumsy heavy gear, a delayed re-action to the tiller. The irritation of the men had been different too. It was a frightening prospect, Sven with his way of doing things, Henery with his, and the difficulties of an indeterminate command. The other two girls had taken it so calmly. Had it happened before? Apparently. It had opened an abysm before me and I was careful not to mention the episode to anybody, not even to Kim. Relatives and friends were worried enough about the trip already and over-critical besides of the actions of the other members of the party. There had been Major's gloomy prophecies and Vic's forthright condemnation of the out-board motor, our only engine. 'It might come in handy on the dinghy, running you to and from a jetty, but that's all. You can't expect it to push that tub of yours along.' There had been Kim's insistence on a qualified navigator.

Then, before we were a mile beyond the heads, the wind changed, leaped upon us; the waves curled high; from the land we were lost to sight between them and I was helping to reef down clumsily, inexpertly, wet to the skin. I remembered that it was the wrong day of the month to have started an adventure upon. The boat was riding the seas well, but one had to hold tight, sitting or moving. I thought the motion gallant but I had not expected to sail so rapidly into adventure, into such a wind. Our light yachts could never have faced it, they would have been running for home by now. Not so *Skaga*. This was her weather, she was built for storms. She was Swedish, and had been in the

North Sea pilot service for twenty-odd years, a boat unique in Australian waters. Two men had sailed her out from Sweden via Panama the year before. The voyage had taken them ten months. Then we had clubbed together to buy her and we hoped to sail to England by way of the Dutch East Indies, Singapore, the Indian Ocean, and the Cape of Good Hope. Henery had estimated the voyage at from ten to fourteen months, winds favourable.

Seasickness! Should I be seasick? On the trial trip to Melbourne the others had suffered terribly. Ruth had written me a letter about it, a Dante's Inferno description of maritime dyspepsia with no discomfort concealed. It had put adventure on a real, if sordid, basis; yet I had a sanguine expectation that seasickness would not happen to me. I had often been wave-tossed but never seasick; the family is a strong-stomached crowd; what we have, we hold. But I was cold, I had a wet cotton singlet under my woollen sweater and it hung in clammy folds about me. The wind was piercing, I should have to go below and change. Yet I hung back, I had an aversion to going below. Joan and Ruth had, and now Joan came back, calm, but with a strangely-tinted face, like a sunset after storm, yellows and greens.

I stayed on deck a little longer. It was getting really rough with the deck continually half-buried and exhilarating dashes of spray going right over the boat. Sven and Henery were shouting amicably to each other, talking about reefing the staysail as well as the mainsail. They decided not to. I was glad. I like 'having a go for it', as Vic calls it; but I was also shivering. The men were waterproofed and warm. 'You'll catch your death of cold,' said Sven, 'put a coat on.' They were the first words he had ever said to me that mattered. I had only met him a few times before. He had joined the adventure in Melbourne, as navigator. The vessel was ours but the sailing experience his; the arrangement was that he was to share equally with us in the travelling expenses.

Reluctantly I stepped below, into a close, hot, keroseney vileness of air and was instantly, unexpectedly, ignominiously and generously seasick. Fresh persimmons and bacon and egg with emotion to follow had been rather an unusual mixture to go to sea on.

'Sorry,' I apologized, and began to mop up the mess. Joan gave me the first thing that came handy. It was one of my new towels, a big rough kind, imported from Ireland, something special. It hurt my thrifty soul to throw it overboard, but I did, and after it a bouquet that my sister-in-law had placed lovingly on my pillow. It floated like a wreath after the towel. Sea burial!

I could hear Joan up for'ard by the lavatory. Ruth was couchant on her bunk, a pad over her eyes. There were all sorts of things strewn about the cabin. 'Lie down,' said she, wells of sympathy for both of us in her voice. 'It's the only way to feel at all comfortable.' I was just then feeling extraordinarily well, lightened, at peace with the ocean, but damnably cold. I simply must get something warm on. I rooted in my locker. I had given a lot of thought to my luggage and I had packed the locker tôo tightly, with evening and port dresses in cardboard boxes enveloped in waterproof cloth, a cylindrical shoe bag, a little flat case of medicines and toilet paraphernalia, books, writing materials, a pair of sea boots, fishing tackle, a big box labelled pompously 'S.U.' (silk underwear), and at the last moment all the gifts people had given me; a diary, a twelve-pound fruit cake in a tin, chocolates, chewing-gum, cigarettes, brandy, a camera and films. Now I wanted nothing in the world but a dry pair of shorts, that old cream sweater, and a towel to dry my soaking hair.

The locker was deep and dark as pitch, a coffin with a door in the small end. To get at it I had to stretch across my bunk and fumble, bringing object after impossible object into the half-light of the cabin. The box of underwear got wedged in the narrow locker doorway and would neither pull out nor push in. Where in God's name was the electric torch? If only I could see or feel a familiar garment! This bending and stretching was breaking me in two; the boat was pitching; it was like clinging to a diabolical merry-go-round that functioned without regularity or music.

Henery came along. He had two battens and he banged them in cross-wise between our bunks, Ruth's and mine. 'What for?' I asked.

'So the pressure inside on the sides of the water tanks when she rolls won't bust them open,' he replied wisely. 'They're not too strong.' What did he mean? We had had those water tanks built especially. Off he went, leaving behind him the spectre of them 'busting' at any minute. I had got a bang on the knee, and now it was impossible, because of the batten, to stand wedged between the table and the bunk and peer into that coffin of a locker.

Crash! A horrible roll that one. She must have buried her gunwale pretty deeply that time. Both my funny-bones were shrieking. Waves of hot and cold swept over me, surges of changing temperature. There was nothing for it but to go to bed as Ruth had said. I could see Byron Cooper tucked in on the bilge bunk, face to the wall, saying and doing nothing. I had managed to get out a travelling-rug and a blanket and there on a box below the table was somebody's white woolly sweater, a grand fleecy sweater, made for the Arctic, like a polar bear's skin.

Joan rolled an eye at me from the little aperture near the mast – it was a kind of window between her bunk and mine. 'All right?' she asked. She was lying low.

'Cold, I can't find a warm thing,' I moaned. The eye disappeared, she offered no advice. It decided me. I should appropriate the magnificent sweater. I struggled out of my wet clothes, keeping a watch on the back of Byron Cooper's head. What a damnsilly thing a muslin chemise with roses and lace on it was. On with the sweater. Its warmth was comforting. I unlaced my deck shoes and trampled my sodden khaki shorts underfoot. The sweater did not come far enough and I was not decent. Never mind, the rug would hide me. I scrambled on the bunk, it was high and narrow, not so much a bed as a picture moulding. The door of the locker would not shut because the horsehair mattress Major had given me was too fat for it to slide or be pushed over it. I curled myself round the open door and lay facing the shaft of light that passed between the deck and the sliding hatch, while the camera and the diary, the tin of cocoa and the chewing-gum nestled beside me.

Heaven! Heaven to lie flat. Glory to be straight-extended with the possibility of getting warm. I lay wrapped in the bliss of immobility, clinging to my ledge of a bunk, braced against the tossing of the sea. Presently I should get up and see if I could help them, but not just now—no, emphatically, not just now.

Time passed. It grew late afternoon, at least the oblong of light was a greenish grey. They had put up the slide above the combing of the hatch, like the barrier that stands at the doors of cottages to keep the babies from falling out. A good deal of water was coming aboard and spilling through even the small aperture that remained, so now they pulled the sliding hatch entirely shut and fastened down the canvas hatch-cover over it. There was no more air or light for us, nor afternoon nor evening either, no sense of minutes passing, just a long time-dragging black-green night.

What a night! A night of strange noises, incredible nerve-racking new noises, watery noises most of them. The snarl of the water slapping on the deck exactly four inches above my nose, the hiss of its indrawn breath serpentining alongside us, the funny little squeaks of the timbers of the boat 'talking' to each other—though they had been twenty years together they still found something to say. All good vessels 'talk' like this, the Swede who had sold *Skaga* to us had said. There was the rattle and strain of the tackle and ominous creaking from the mast. Was it safe, that mast? A spruce mast. The natural crack in it was very wide. Every now and then came the crashing immediately on top of me of the heavy block through which the staysail sheet ran. The reverberation below of that horrible impact was a Vulcan's hammer descending. Ruth told me what it was, she was shuddering at it too. 'I had it once on my side,' she said, 'it was awful.' She complained of it to Henery on one of his frequent passages past us, but he said it did not matter, and that they could not fix it. She and I thought it would pound the deck to pieces.

Sometimes there was a tremendous wallop as an extra big sea jolted the bow, the ocean giving her a straight left on the nose, and I wondered how the shipwrights managed to fit timbers to the stempost that they stood it at all. The blows on the ship were as merciless as those on the horse being flogged to death in *The Brothers Karamazov*, almost as unendurable to those lying within. Irresistibly one's sympathies became identified with the little vessel. Would she stand that one? She did. Brave, brave *Skaga!*

Once or twice Sven came down from the tiller and consulted a chart. Water was streaming from him, it was raining up there. His eye-sockets were red with salt; he manipulated the parallel rulers, measured, and twirled the dividers about. We were going to run in for shelter. I noticed his short blunt fingers, everything he touched he left wet, his hands were cracked and blackened from the ropes and the sea. He had lit the small kerosene lamp; its smoky glare shut us all in tightly, a little close world of light in a roaring chaos of water and wind outside. He took no notice of Ruth or me, said nothing at all, but rose from the table and swung up out of the high hatch, giving us for a moment an eddy of fresh air.

From *inside* the boat there had been a steady lap, lap, lap in the darkness, exactly the kind of lapping a slobbering big dog makes when he drinks thirstily. Now I leaned over, peered down the steep side of the bunk and saw in the lamplight that the floor of the cabin was gone and in its place was a slopping lake of viscid black: greasy, slimy, and with strange objects, bits of cork and paper and the poor unwritten-in diary, floating about in it. As *Skaga* rolled this noxious liquid slapped and splashed viciously up the sides of the water tanks on top of which were our two bunks, one on each side of the cabin. It was the bilge that had risen, augmented by frequent cascades of sea water down the steering cockpit aft. The black colour came from the preparation the bilges had been painted with, terrible stuff.

I wanted to help, desperately I wanted to help. I felt quite well; I had been sick once more, but was better. If I couldn't help in managing the boat, and obviously I could not do that in this storm, at least I ought to get the men something to eat, something hot to drink. I am the kind of person who in the face of difficulties always thinks of something to eat or drink. It is a limitation. If I were recruited to an army they would put me in the cook-house and not the command. I should have liked something hot to drink myself. In fact I craved for a hot drink.

I put out a foot in tentative endeavour. It looked very white against the black greasy bilge and I hesitated, thinking the situation over before committing the member to that sink of iniquity below. I was not adequately clothed, I should have to trail my blanket with me and it would certainly get wet. I had only just got warm and in any case I had not the faintest idea how primuses worked; my only recollections of them were of fierce hissings and sudden upflarings. I had never lived on board like the others and knew nothing of domestic procedure. I blamed myself for being an unprepared, inadequate ignoramus and . . . drew in the foot.

While I was worrying and deriding myself there was a sudden sideways lurch and the lighted lamp sprang from the table to my pillow and went out. I expected an explosion, but nothing happened. A smear of warm oil spread over my cheek and kerosene saturated the bedclothes, that was all. I groped for the lamp and found the metal bowl which I managed to fit back again; the glass chimney I found next day tucked in beside me, unbroken.

When Henery came by next time the lamp, not unnaturally, refused to light and he asked for the torch. I sat up, fumbled in the depths of that noisome locker and by a miracle found it, but the effort left me perspiring, weak, and the conclusion was obvious, I was still seasick. However, as well as the torch I had located a bag of buns and the fruit cake. The men ate the buns and great chunks of the cake. It was good to see them eat; they had been battling away on deck in this tumult of wind and water without any food since breakfast of the day before. The simple act of finding those buns relieved my conscience, I felt more cheerful and my fancy began to work.

It was a new situation for me. I had never felt the presence of so much water, for so long and so close to me before. The ocean pressed in on us, it weighted the air in the cabin, there was a watery pressure in every breath we took, the timbers of the *Skaga* strained outward resisting it; it possessed a limitless force that it had not yet exerted fully, there was always behind it the hint of further power held in reserve. The ocean would never tire; it might give up, but it would not tire. The water washed over the deck just above my head, I could almost feel the waves break round my pillow, every little noise was so close; from the water tank below me came animal gurglings with every change of level, it was only half full and every roll sent it shifting. A few planks and then the depths of the sea. They sucked at us; the wonder was that we kept on floating. Similes teased me. We were six salty little sardines jammed tight in a floating tin and the bilge was the oil; *Skaga* was a Swedish matchbox with five red-nosed wet matches inside it and one outside steering, striking a way on the foam. Stupid conceits, but time passed.

A running pat-a-pat of water came from the sliding hatch on to the foot of my bed, the mattress was quite soaked there. Another drip ran along a beam and at irregular intervals would come splash on my chest. I used to squirm so that it should not come on my face. From the shut porthole above my head came an intermittent spatter of drops, wetting the pillow. Into every tiny crevice the water forced a way. The others had similar leaks about them, we were a wet ship.

For a long time the smell of petrol had been in the air. Opposite the wash basin for'ard we had a fifty-gallon tank of oil and petrol, prepared ready for the engine. The fumes had been getting worse and worse. They were sickening and mixed with them was the odour of kerosene, heavy and sweet. Four gallons of kerosene had emptied themselves from the drum aft into the bilges. The tap had been knocked ajar. The risen bilge had a separate peculiar stink of its own. Besides that the four of us had been shut down and breathing the same limited amount of air for sixteen hours. The atmosphere was indescribably fetid. Came a voice from Joan's bunk in serious inquiry, 'Do you think petrol fumes can asphyxiate?'

'Certainly,' I replied with terrible promptness and conviction. I had been thinking of nothing else for the previous quarter of an hour. 'But an explosion would be more likely.'

Ruth confessed next day that I had given her 'the horrors'. Every time Henery or Sven bent down in the steering cockpit and struck a match out of the wind, and they did so a number of times for the binnacle lamp kept going out, she thought 'we should all go sky-high'.

When morning came with the sea settled to a moderate gale and a grey light coming through the slightly slid-back hatch, I got up and explored the mysteries of Ajax. I emerged perspiring, bruised, but oh the relief of it! The triumph of being well and able to get about. Floating in the cabin was an apple. I was hungry, my middle felt like two sheets of brown paper flapping together. I picked the apple up and wiped it. It was impregnated with kerosene to the core. I ate it all. 'If that doesn't make me sick, nothing will,' I thought. Nothing happened, so out came the plum cake. For breakfast we had slabs of it with a cold drink of limejuice cordial. I was not, except on one historic occasion, to suffer another seasick qualm.

I found a pair of flannel shorts and my waterproof cape and poked my head through the hatch and took the air. It was marvellous. There was hardly any sky. Spray spun overhead. We were in a new country where the waves were a procession of mountain ranges tumultuous and majestic. Sven pumped the bilge and cleaned up the cabin floor, the residuum on it was filthy, the water had been nearly six inches deep. He began to wipe the primuses, Byron Cooper roused himself to help him — Byron had a flair for primuses. Ruth got up and investigated the food box under the table, separating the spoilt goods from the unspoilt with many a groan. She had bought them in Newcastle and had been too sick to attend to them. They were mostly spoilt. We had strong sweet coffee. It was good.

My first twenty-four hours at sea. Nobody had slept. It had been a noisy, smelly, anxious nightmare. But it was over. I was never again to experience that desolate amalgamation of incompetence and seasickness. I was proud, too, secretly. An inward self said, 'It was bad luck getting such a storm right away, but you weren't frightened, not really; you were anxious and uncomfortable but you weren't cowardly, you weren't afraid for your miserable skin'.

I had had confidence somehow, a blind confidence in *Skaga* as she strained and her timbers talked and she kept pushing on, defying the gale; confidence in Sven as he had sat in the lamplight, bleary-eyed, his blunt fingers tapping on the table, thinking, not seeing anybody. I felt intensely grateful to him and to Henery for their strenuous labours of the day and night that everyone had accepted in a taken-for-granted way. I had not presupposed those labours and I felt the same kind of adoring hospital gratitude for them as when one is seriously ill and the night nurse has brought one drugged respite.

The pity of it was that strong emotions don't last. Soon I was wiping up the dishes and complaining of my bruises.

CHAPTER II

AFTER THE STORM:
CAPE HAWKE AND DRIFTING

THE next days, April 29th to May 2nd, were strange. We were anchored off Cape Hawke waiting for the storm to die down before going north. I did not realize that it was still sufficiently stormy outside to excuse us from going on, I irked at the delay and wanted to use the favourable wind and hurry to Brisbane. 'Waiting for kerosene', had been Henery's spoken reason for remaining, we had about half a gallon left for cooking and the lamps. I chafed at it and only on the third day, when a small coasting steamer going south came into the bay for shelter, did I understand that we, too, were sheltering and, what was more important for him, giving the crew a chance to get over their buffeting. Such ignorance sounds incredible, but it was the kind of silence among us about boat policy that time did not improve.

Sven was very glum. He sat on deck most of the day fishing. From time to time I fished, too, but the cold and the rain, it rained in heavy squalls about every twenty minutes, usually drove me down. Almost every warm garment I had was wet. Things flapped about on the rigging trying to dry and wore themselves out in the wind as they twirled and cavorted, and I did not care. I did not care about anything except keeping warm. It was a cold and cheerless time. My only excitement was when I caught a three-foot fiddler shark shaped like a frying-pan with wavy brown markings on the back and two stings where the handle joins the pan. Sven cut it up for bait and continued fishing. I learnt later that he had tried to urge Henery to push on with the good wind and had gone into his shell when his advice was rebuffed.

The monotony was frightful. There was a heavy swell that made reading practicably impossible, we were all cooped up together, wet and antagonistic, in sight of land but unable to reach it because of the heavy surf that beat on the shore and over the shallow bar. Strange how antagonism blossomed in those three idle uncomfortable days. Cooper talked most. His conversation bristled with 'jolly's', 'good-oh's', and 'by Jove's'. He was tall and good-looking in a stagy kind of way. Every night before he slept he wrote up his diary, a methodical habit that I admired and might have emulated except that my diary had been drowned in the bilge, but his reason for writing it up struck me as funny. He wanted to keep a record of where he had been and what he had done every day so that if challenged under any circumstances whatever he could produce evidence to the contrary! I liked his naivety, his public schoolboy adolescence at a mature age. If one got tired of his chatter one could always shut one's ears to it or shut him up. He did not mind being told to stop talking and through long hours in crowded staff-rooms I had acquired the habit of not attending too seriously to gossip.

He had brought copious supplies of limejuice on board with him and blushed scarlet when Ruth asked innocently, 'Why do you drink so much limejuice when it is so awfully cold?' He took it like medicine. We drank it, too; its bitterness was palatable after all the bread and jam and cocoa that was our staple diet at this time.

Sven and Henery made an unsuccessful excursion through the surf to the shore for kerosene and tobacco. Sven said it was madness to try but he went all the same, both of them glad to do something to break the wretchedness of inactivity.

I spent the three days learning to use the domestic machinery, first the galley with its two primuses. Lighting them was a complicated dirty task because we had no methylated spirits to start them and had to fountain the kerosene, then release the pressure and start again. There was something wrong with each of them in turn, they were blocked and needed certain parts renewing, one had to pump furiously and keep on pumping to get any pressure at all.

Then there was Ajax, christened so in memory of the Elizabethan masterpiece concerning the first of all water-closets, 'The Metamorphoses of Ajax'. He had a system of a ring that wound clockwise and counter-clockwise, a knob that swung over on a short lever and a pump, and all of these had to be manipulated properly to make the valve work and the water flow. A noisy business, embarrassing, too, in such close quarters. The usual procedure was to keep up a strenuous pumping, a stiff and watery concerto, the whole time. It did more to develop the muscles of the right arm than any other nautical exercise. Crawling through the little doorway into that dark stuffy little den and crouching down was a sort of return to the womb without the safety device of an umbilical cord. The principal objection to a former shipmate taken on the trial trip was, I gathered from the other girls, that he was too bulky to squeeze in, or if in, ever to get out!

The third member of the pumping trio was the bilge. During this first heavy weather it had to be pumped often, but as we voyaged on it became a less frequent, and, as the bilges got cleaner, a more pleasant exercise.

Because I was taller than the other girls I could not stand upright in the cabin and I kept forgetting it. Also I was quite unused to the angles of the boat and boat furniture; for instance, there was a step to be negotiated while creeping along through the rabbit-like tunnel that led from the main cabin past the big lockers on one side and Joan and Henery's bunk on the other, and there were three heavy overhead beams in the darkness above, while progressing galleywards was like taking the hurdles in an obstacle race. As I was emphatically the novice the possibilities for bumping oneself became, with me, almost infinite. The sharp corners of the cabin table seemed to take a fiendish delight in coming into sudden contact with my hip-bones. Jumping down from the deck into the cabin I missed the water tank that did duty as step and cooking table and scraped my shins and strained my shoulders. Going up I got an awful knock because someone pulled the overhead slide along; once a bigger wave than usual caught the boat, unsteadied me, and I sat plomp in the basin of water I had placed ready to wash in, while the back of my head split on the combing of the hatch, and then I shot forward and skinned my nose on the petrol tank. I got a lump the size of half an egg on my forehead from some other bump. In three days I was a mass of bruises and cuts and so sore that I could not find a sound place on which either to lie or sit. Six weeks later when Ruth took a photo of me bathing I was still a patchwork of sinister-coloured bruises in the drowned rainbow stage of development. It was like being in a mad Luna-park mechanism, an erratic and joyless imitation moon. After a few weeks on board I got used, as the others had, to the snares of *Skaga*'s carpentry and slid round them and my companions as if I had always lived like one of a number of fish in an aquarium.

It was perhaps inconceivable to the others that anyone could go on hurting herself so consistently as I did. 'Clumsy brute,' I could hear Joan thinking, 'What a fuss to make over a trifle.' I think she had a theory of not being 'soft' and that if one got hurt one ought to be noble and silent about it, and that to throw me a morsel or two of sympathy would be encouraging me to get hurt. I could feel the clouds of her disapproval growing, so that whenever I added to my knowledge of *Skaga*'s timbers I would invariably apologize after my first exclamation of pain and this possibly made the offence worse. I began to realize that to progress in Joan's estimation was to walk on a right line without a hair's breadth of deviation. I began to pick my steps along the knife-edge of her regard and falter as I did so. I was no longer myself but someone who had to please. I tried not to complain too much, but on the other hand I was restless and mentally excited and moved about a lot, popping up on deck and back again, not used to the confinement and cramped quarters. Because of my own state of mind I could not understand the lethargy of the other two girls. I thought them inactive and lazy when they were merely seasick.

I thought they were 'soft', but it seems that with some there is a nausea that persists long after the actual throwing-up is over. I was enlightened months afterwards by Ruth, who, with Joan, was always miserable for three or four days after any calm anchorage or short stay on shore. At the time I did not realize quite how lucky I was to miss this left-handed gift of the sea. My health and my chatter must have been hateful to the lassitudinous two. No wonder the air of the cabin bristled with antagonisms.

Henery and I weren't getting on very well either. My people had confided my safe-keeping to Sven and had pointed out to him that if anything went wrong he was the man with the certificate who would carry the nautical responsibility. On the other hand Joan's people and Ruth's had reposed their daughters in Henery's charge, which was only natural, for Joan was married to Henery and Ruth was her cousin. I did not want to be entrusted to anybody particularly; one of my reasons for going away was to have a chance to be quite independent, for the first time in my life to be quite responsible for myself. I did not know Henery very well and I was irritated by his nervous mannerisms and the painful slowness of his speech. I always kept wanting to put the words into his mouth.

One day I came to lunch and laid aside my book of modern verse, rather 'precious' in the literary sense, the only book of poems I had brought with me, a good edition, a gift. We were eating fried fish and bread and butter, there was a lot of grease about. Henery reached over without apology, opened the book haphazardly and read a passage aloud. He sneered. It was the kind of poetry that lent itself to sneering. I hated him for sneering and I feared for the cleanliness of the first edition. 'Put it down while we're eating, Hen,' I enjoined, not so mildly. He turned sideways and held it farther from me as if I might snatch it; there was the attitude of the schoolboy tease in his manner, taunting me. He went on reading, but silently, flicking over the pages quickly. Then I saw his greasy thumb go down. A long-forgotten rebellion against teasing flared in me. 'Take your dirty paw off it!' I said angrily and took the book. He looked surprised. I was surprised at myself too. Surprised and ashamed. Joan's eyes snapped. She rose and left her plate of fish. Her silence was as final as a funeral pall. The rest of the meal was awkwardly casual.

Next day he happened to drop overboard a fishing gaff that my younger brother had fashioned for me and that in a spasm of foolish brotherliness he had badged with my name in burnt-in over-large letters along the side. I had been embarrassed by that sprawling name, but my brother had never in his life *made* me anything before and that big signboard of private property had only meant, 'For Dona, from Fred'. I did not mind the gaff going, it was too short and heavy, but Henery left me to find out the loss, and I thought he did so on purpose; we were both rather overt and childish in our dislike.

So it was a relief to everyone when on May 2nd we left Cape Hawke and set out Brisbanewards again. We had been at sea a day and had not gone far when the wind fell altogether. After another day we were floating in a flat calm far out at sea. The sun came out and it was warm and pleasant. We pulled out of our lockers clothes and packages that the bilge had inundated during the storm. I got my bedding, blankets and most of my warm clothes dry. I lined the locker with canvas and re-stowed it with more acumen. I read voraciously and kept quiet. For me it was a fairly happy time, a respite; I even managed to sleep for an hour or two. The sudden change in my way of living had made rest impossible for me, my mind agitated itself beyond endurance, it beat itself out worrying about myself and the situation, the boat and the crew.

At night there were the stars above, no moon but the large reflected stars glowing up from the black water with wriggling golden star tracks like snakes going from them. The water was flatly placid and there was a feeling of indescribable softness about everything, as if the night and the sky and the water were melting away together and yet were so close that they might be grasped. We were afloat in Time as well as in Space. Existence was so tenuous that only happiness mattered and . . . we were unhappy. There was about this bubbleless sea some of the subtle magic that hangs over and transfigures still lakes, soothing and relaxing the senses. When we flashed the torch into the thick water that by daylight had gleamed dully blue, striped with bands of colour as if there were a meniscus of oil upon it, it went suddenly transparent, a shop-window glass, and fish, attracted by the glare, swam in it, displayed for a moment or two, ghosts of fish with a flicker of phosphorescence about them, their colour abstracted by the electric brightness. They had been round us by day, kingfish about three feet long, beautifully marked, on each side patches of vivid blue, like wings, that as they moved to lower depths changed to luminous green, to copper-burning flames lit in the sea.

We gossiped on the deckhouse, Sven, Cooper, Ruth and I, arguing about the cartwheel of the zodiac and being flippant at the expense of the constellations. Sven pointed them out to us, the Twins, the Scorpion, the Ship and the Balance. We stared, squinted, held our heads upside down till the sky went dizzy in spangles. Sven guffawed at our landlubberliness, they were so plain to him. I was very gay and in the mood when it was fun to draw Cooper out and hear him arguing about first causes with Ruth, and I enjoyed making subtle discoveries about this shy and aloof sea-creature, Sven.

It was a time of amnesty for dislikes, superficially at any rate; with the fine weather we had added a new stratum, the tiny and cumbered deck, to our living quarters. It was possible to lie about, to read and enjoy oneself. But just as beneath the tranquil surface of the water ran a six-knot current hurrying *Skaga*, though we could neither feel nor perceive any motion, a hundred miles or more south and fifty miles out to sea, so underneath this smooth exterior were uneasy currents; all the time I sensed that Joan was disapproving of me, disapproving of the sound of my voice, of my light and foolish laughter, disapproving that I encouraged Cooper in his follies and did not snub him on every possible occasion as she did, not that he was always aware of the snubbing, but it existed nevertheless. I did not know what was the matter with her; I had known her quiet before without being morose, brusque without being rude. Now she kept making me feel a worm. She was insolently aloof, as if I had come into a railway carriage and wanted the windows up when she wanted them down. Icy draughts whistled about her. Nothing was friendly. I knew I had done something wrong, that in fact everything about me was wrong. I could not find out what it was and I was not brave enough to ask. I admired Joan. I had always thought of her standards as being exacting, sometimes wrong in theory, but in personal behaviour lofty and to be aspired to. I had expected to be treated as an equal, as a comrade; instead it was as if she had suddenly discovered that I didn't measure up to her standards, as if there was too much ordinary human clay about me; as if my every action had a bad smell. I felt a clod. I felt miserable.

Then I turned and resented, resisted this crushing weight of the silent and superior judgment acting upon me. Frivolity was my only escape. It wasn't fair. She hadn't given me a chance. A few days and the friendliness of years swept overboard.

I began to itemize the reasons for her discontent, to go over the long months of planning for this voyage. I saw things through her eyes and made excuses for her, condemning myself; but it did not mend matters, whenever I tried to interest her she retired; did I enter a conversation it ceased as if she had shut a door in my face.

I realized that through the time of preparation she had borne the strain of breaking up her first home, selling with considerable business acumen piece by piece newly-acquired furniture to make the necessary financial weight. She had not been married long; I could understand that hurt, it had happened to me, too, once. I knew that she had idealized the labour of preparation that had fallen to her enthusiastic lot. I had been a hundred miles away and whenever I had come down in week-ends to help had not felt one of the initiates in the sacred cause baptized by weeks of painful chiselling and scraping. I had thought a lot of their labour waste pains, a little silly and badly done, but our numerous long dis-

cussions of plans and ways and means had always been amicable.
I had always fallen in with their wishes and with the changes in
their wishes. It had been taken for granted that my absence was
inevitable and also that the trip to Melbourne was to be a reward
for Joan and Henery as well as a trial of *Skaga*. In Newcastle,
where they called to pick me up, there had been, as in Sydney,
this uneasy tension, 'The relative strain' I had dubbed it to Kim,
but my relatives this time.

I had anticipated that the unexpected cloud on the horizon of
our friendship would melt away when we were actually off and
adventure-bound together, the worries of the past months behind
us; instead in a few days it had grown rapidly as a yeast ferment,
pervading every sentence and action, nebulous and spongy with
disillusion.

Joan had had her months of feeling that this was her home, her
boat. She had loved it, tired of it, hated it and lived in it and now
she had to share it with someone she found she disliked and had
a grudge against. It was not pleasant, not for either of us. The
volcano of her repressions flamed subterraneously and sullenly; she
hardly spoke, her politeness had the acid of malice in it. Her
ignoring was deliberate, a magnificent piece of work. I admired it
even while suffering from it. It was like tragic acting.

Ruth was being drawn in, she was changing, growing strange,
feeling unhappy. She sensed the conflict to come. Her loyalties
were divided between us. She imagined she could see where we
were each wrong and each right, but her ultimate allegiance
would always be to Joan. Joan, not I, had persuaded her into the
scheme. They had played together as children and had many
infantile recollections in common. Though Joan had been the
younger she had always been the dominant character; she had
had a different kind of home and some family prestige about
her. Her father was a general.

There is a certain entrancing Peter Pan quality about Ruth.
Somehow she has never quite managed to grow up. She is
capable of asking the bluntest *enfant terrible* questions; of betraying

33

lamentable gaps in the ordinary everyday stock of knowledge or in awareness of the emotion of others; of propounding seriously fairy-tale schemes that would be alluring if their propounder had not overlooked the alphabet of fact. She is so odd that her friends keep expecting some work of genius from her and have a tenderness for her, yet on occasion she can be ruthlessly practical, militant, even hard. Her father was a successful headmaster, her mother other-worldly, and between them Ruth, nearly thirty, still had the dew of innocence upon her. We had known each other at secondary school and when I followed her to the university she directed my awe-stricken footsteps. At college she had already got, without seeking it, a kind of notoriety. She won the English professor's prize, climbed trees in the college grounds and invented a new undergarment. On moonlit nights we had sneaked out together and danced barefoot on the lawn under the shadows of the trees, a most unconventional proceeding under the circumstances; Ruth is essentially an original.

At this time, I was about seventeen, I remember long discussions with her on the Phaedrus and on ideals of friendship, but neither of us had ever heard of homosexuality or Lesbianism. We took friendship very seriously in those days. I was always tortured because I could not achieve Ruth's levels in the matter. She had more definite ideas on the subject and a better command of dialectic than I. Joan was always the symbol to her of this mystic relationship and for a long time before I met her I had admired her through Ruth's eyes.

When I did meet her there was fear tinged with my admiration, a fear that other women have confessed to sharing. Joan had about her an air of aloof reserve, of incommunicable pride, of a rather formidable integrity. She had a devastating power of being able to wither by an apt silence, disconcerting to anyone mercurial or volatile, as I am. She had a reputation, too, for ability . . . we were in the same year. Both Ruth and I admired the heavy severity of her beauty, a beauty that our acquaintances could not or would not see, her high-bridged nose, the clear olive of her complexion, her thick straight hair that was almost black, her delicate fastidious hands. Even her inherited family blemish, a drooping eyelid, was attractive to us.

There was a period of walking tours and camps that paradoxically made us know each other less, but I recall long gossipy botanical walks with Ruth over heathy North Shore uplands. Then precociously at nineteen I fell in love, defied authorities and parents and Joan stood by me loyally when I needed support. She could not understand the new, confused and bewildering points of view that I had acquired along with the grand passion and was sceptical about it all, yet, never fond of needlework, she embroidered a couple of camisoles as a wedding gift. It was the fashion for girls to give camisoles in those days. Characteristically, they were well done; I treasured them for ages.

We drifted apart. On crucial occasions we chanced to rub the seams of our lives together. Then some years later Joan married; we met again and I found her changed in outlook, thawed out, delightfully human, mature in my sense. My husband and I were both apparently interesting to her. Laughingly, over my dinner-table, the *Skaga* adventure was proposed and the *Skaga* mentioned. The idea was mine, Henery had the inclination, Joan the will. Joan put the ballast of 'Why not?' to my bubble of 'Let's'. I was ready to go, I had been married eight years and had no children. I had begun to fear the smugness of happiness and the rut of existence: I should be leaving a lot, security, pleasure, love, but it should make no difference to us. He could not come; he had estimated pretty shrewdly just what he would not be able to stand on the trip.

I had only heard occasionally of Ruth. She was teaching and did not like it. When we met again it was on the old friendly confidential terms.

The three of us had behind us this long-stretching background of intimacy – complex, shadowed, variable. It explains the nature and importance of the crisis that followed. We each of us possessed very private illuminating bits of knowledge about our past

35

histories, that threw up into monstrous forms our present individual actions and reactions, like immense shadows cast on a blank hoarding by figures stalking before powerful arc lights. I know of no similar sailing trip in a small boat on which several women went. The spiritual success of the venture depended largely on us, the women; we had known each other the longest, we had trusted in planning the adventure to the rope of friendship and goodwill that had always bound us, and now, before the first strain, it had broken, or was not there, was non-existent—there was no handrail to guide us.

While we drifted imperceptibly farther from land and farther south porpoises, or more properly dolphins, came by us. They leaped and cavorted playfully. By leaning over the bows we could discern clearly their piglike snouts, their small eyes and traps of mouths, the barnacles on their coarse skins, their individual markings. One had a piece torn out of his left flipper. They came up blowing about us, making snorting noises like contemptuous old men in a public library when they read what they consider nonsense. They revelled and paraded before us, they leapt, they swam in fours, they curved in watery arcs and cut capers together; a trained ballet sparkling with joy in life, they teased us, stuck still, with their mobility.

Henery leaned over and tickled old Lop-fin with a piece of wood and Lop-fin considered his dignity insulted and instantly flipped with his tail, sending a retaliatory shower of spray. They were so graceful, so sportive, so sociable in their little group that we all envied them, Ruth most of all. For them, not for us, was the freedom of the seas. They provided an object lesson that we could not follow; our antagonisms were accumulating in their intensities, driving us to the wreckage of our social group.

CHAPTER III

STILL TRYING TO GO NORTH

RUTH was on watch one morning at 6.30. The tiller was lashed, any occasional light air that blew did no more than tickle the sail. We had bucket baths on deck. Ruth showed me how to throw the bucket down so that it hit the water sideways and filled and how to bring it up without spilling any of the water. It was jolly, splashing each other and getting soapy, making rude remarks, an easy friendliness between us. We reminded each other of the walking trip at Bobbin Head, years before, when, hot and dusty, we had come to an inlet that looked secure enough from sharks and been lured, bathing-suitless, into the water. From modesty we had worn our tunics in, but from prudence, as the water deepened, we raised them and finally hung them on some mangroves that grew on a sandspit in the middle of the bay. While we were swimming some boys, in a similar state of nudity, had come walking round from the other side of the mangroves! How disturbed she had been, lest perhaps they had come from father's school and father get to hear of it! Then, emerging hastily, the tunics slipping downwards this time, we had looked up and seen high on the scrub-covered hills that made a deep loop about the bay a big red bus and passengers leaning out admiring – the view.

She had rebuked my levity then and she did now. 'Hush,' she said, 'Mustn't wake Joan and Henery,' and added, a little sentimentally I thought, 'They do love their mornings in bed, you can never get them up.' Which was true enough, and I was glad. It made a little time-cave in the day into which I could always crawl.

Not yet had we learnt to be unselfconscious of the publicness in this way of living; we both confessed to agonies of shame in the operation of Ajax, and at night there were all the sounds, intimate or unpleasant, of the other sleepers, the perpetual closeness of each other, the awareness of movements, of bodily turnings, of mental restlessness beneath willed stillness, of physical presence, and shufflings. It was amusing to find that we all, except Sven whom we never caught, despised and despising alike, had the common failing of snoring, some more, some less, some in concert and others singly, but all of us, thank Heaven, only occasionally. Living on *Skaga* was an exceedingly close-fitting, multiple, marriage of inconvenience and it took time to get used to it.

There were canvas curtains that we rolled up and down, one on the alleyway leading for'ard to the double bunk and another above the transverse water tank beneath the main hatch; this separated the cabin from the galley aft, on either side of which were the bunks for the two men. The enclosed space between the curtains was about seven feet long by six wide. Seldom were the curtains down, they had to be up for convenience, ventilation and light. Ruth's bunk was tucked away in a recess made by the curve of the boat and behind the fixed seat in the cabin. A snug berth. In the centre of the cabin was the table, a foot-wide piece of board with two side flaps. When these flaps were up a thin person could just squeeze himself along between table and seat up to the fore part of the boat. If anyone sat working at the table on that side, nobody else could go for'ard by the cabin route without disturbing him, consequently my side was popular for anyone who wished to sit and work or read. There was less room on this side and no seat. One balanced on top of the bunk, shoulders pushed forward by the right angle formed by the junction of deck and deckhouse and knees wedged under or on a level with the table. To get out or stand was an effort, but the occupier gained because, once installed, he was undisturbed. So someone was always sitting on my bed, and when in bed I lay half in and half out of the cabin. There was little privacy for Sven or Ruth or me.

During the day of light airs that followed the two days of be-calming we played drawing sequences, a parlour game. One person drew the head and turned the paper down, the next drew the body and a third the legs. Some of the results were piquant, a haloed saint with pussy-cat club feet, a disagreeable long thin fellow with striped legs who looked virtuous and smirked unpleasantly, he had a distinct resemblance to Byron Cooper, and on another Ruth drew a priest's hat and face, Henery added the body of a nude woman and Joan a pair of high buttoned boots. In the last one Sven, whom we deemed unimaginative, put a mermaid's tail to a figure that Ruth had topped with the head of a dictator wearing a Napoleon hat. Symbolism! Call it Psychopathia Sexualis! The game ended in laughter; it was the only game all of us ever joined in on board.

Ruth had brought an old microscope with her. She fished up samples of sea water and rhapsodized over the strange forms in them; but, since nobody knew or could find out what the creatures were, their functions or life histories, after the moment of wonder there was, for the rest of us, nothing further to be interested in. A hobby to be satisfactory must have a basis of knowledge; and a little science, it seemed to us, was a dangerous thing. Joan spent hours composing a letter in French; consciously in this two-day idleness we sought amusements and they were not altogether satisfactory. Yet we were destined, when matters were much worse between us, to survive a similar period of nearly two months. I found amusement in writing.

'That your diary?' asked Ruth brightly. 'Let's have a look.'

'It's a letter,' I answered slowly. Letters are so fortunately private. It had only been one of Ruth's *enfant terrible* remarks and my reply had been snubbing. I was shocked. Was nothing to be private? Could one have nothing of one's own except a toothbrush on board? What a possessive kind of creature I was discovering myself to be; I had hated the book of poems being dirtied, I wanted the torch put back in its special pocket in the tidy by the head of my bunk so that I knew exactly where to find it in the darkness, and I wanted my corner of the boat and the book I was reading to myself.

This business of living together is difficult. 'The property of friends is common, the property of friends is common,' says an adage in a typewriting copybook. Is it? Perhaps the mutual respect of what one doesn't want to share is the best basis of most persons getting on together. It is so easy to share the things that are not important, like clothes and entertainment, but it is harder to share what one really values, the elements of comfort, ideas, spiritual values. I was shut out of sharing on the higher levels, out of the common contact of friendliness with Joan and out of sympathy with the ideas of Ruth, and I reacted by wanting to assert myself in the matter of bunk space and cake-eating. I thought we had been greedy; we had eaten that big cake up in two or three days and I had envisaged it lasting us for more weeks, one or two slices a day. Henery brought this possessive attitude home to me in the grand row we had. During that first fortnight his 'I' and my 'my' had clashed with the fury of the drums and trumpets in a nursery brawl.

Thinking it over at night I regretted that I had not shown Ruth most of my letter, it might have brought us together, it was innocuous and amusing and the parts that every lover is shy of a third person seeing could have been skipped. But the opportunity was gone. The trouble was that private property and privacy were, in circumstances like ours, bound up together. The most private property one can own are one's thoughts and by the peculiarity of it one cannot be sure of keeping them to oneself. A judgment becomes a feeling, is drowned in it; in companionship one works by feeling, reason has little to do with it, and in a confined space our close neighbours sense our thoughts, they can do more, by intuition they can know our sub-conscious gropings, which we are not aware of ourselves.

At sunset on the second day of the calm Sven predicted wind. Midday had been clouded, he had not been able to get a sight but he feared from his estimation of the current that we were south of Newcastle. We were inclined to disbelieve him. It seemed impossible. But an hour after sunset a strong south wind sprang up and we tore along, leaving a glittering wake. Wave after wave came rippling over the starboard bow, breaking in a white smother of foam lit up by the incandescence of myriads of little globules of light from the animalculae that switched off and on every moment like so many tiny electric bulbs in the water. Then as each wave curled warm over my bare feet the fairy lights went out and the water sweeping away through the port scuppers was a plain black curded with flakes of white. It was as if old *Skaga* as she rushed onwards kept throwing a scintillating scarf over her deck, a translucent fabric shot with diamonds and fringed with a lather of pearls.

How refreshing it was after the days of oily calm. Time had started again with an exhilarating rush of stars above and stars in the water below and the clean strong wind in our sails. We reefed down to the second row of points and sailed north-west nearer the land. Before midnight a great loom of light showed up on the north-western horizon and a smaller one far to the south. We could see Sydney and were eighteen miles south of Newcastle! Ten days from home and south of it after sailing northward all the time! This topsy-turvy, Luna-park, moon-mechanized world of our adventuring.

It was arranged that I should take my turn at the tiller that night. I was anxious to learn to manage the boat. Owing to the storm and the calm I had not had an opportunity so far and I was sceptical of my ability. I asked Henery to show me, but he said shortly, 'Sven will look after you', and the reference did not penetrate my thick head.

I was below trying to sleep and thinking poignantly of ordinary things that the lights of my home suburb on the horizon had raised in me, of fires burning, of the dry furriness underfoot of bedroom carpets, of my cat, what a scallywag he was, always trespassing on my neighbour's beds of seedlings, miaowing furiously for his milk in the mornings, never indoors except after dinner at night when he always turned up to complete the domestic picture. I was, in short, having a debauch of homesickness when I was called up to take my first turn at the tiller.

Under such a strong wind the swell had grown very heavy and
the waves high; the *Skaga* rolled a little with the cross-wise seas;
it was thrilling to watch her breasting the long ocean surge and
rising, bowsprit in air ready to spear the stars and then rushing
down the long glissade of water ahead with a black mountain,
foam-crested, menacing behind, and then to feel her soar again
with a froth of water smothering the bows. The sails were no
longer white, they were black fins against the midnight blue of
the sky; from the binnacle lamp with its pyramid-shaped metal
hat that threw a radiance down on the flickering compass card
came a steady if smoky yellow light and the odour of warm tin.
On the blackness of the sea the wave-tops glistened, breaking and
tossing in a confusion to which only the steady drone of the wind
gave any meaning. This was no storm, this was fine sailing; the
army of advancing wave mountains were regular troops to be
conquered and overcome, to be skilfully out-manœuvred and
scrutinized for any hostile flank movements, to be surmounted
and left behind on the battleground of the sea. The *Skaga* was not
fighting desperately against but using the enemy forces, steadily
winning her way along, singing, it seemed, a sea saga of her own;
'Shaking', as Sven said, 'the bone in her teeth.'

He talked quietly to me, explaining things. I was very nervous,
the tiller hard and obstinate. He showed me the trick of easing
her down the long slopes and how to keep a certain star, Vega it
was, just to port of the mast. I wanted to keep staring at the
lubber-line. I had never sailed a compass course before and was
frightened of getting off it and unwilling to trust to a far-away star.
I felt a typical academic with the black mountains of sea behind
laughing at me in nature's gigantic grin, the tongues of foam on
their tops lolling forward ready to lick down and poop us. Sven's
hand was behind mine on the tiller. I was glad of it, in ten
minutes of this steering my arm was aching from palm to shoulder;
I was thankful to relinquish the tiller and sit on the combing of
the cock-pit, a wide parapet about four inches high, my big
macintosh cape over me like a tent, 'the corpse-cover' Henery

had called it, and I had not liked him for calling it that. It seemed an invitation to the Fates and Destinies to do their worst and it evoked in me old night-horrors of war-time, when I had been a child and my brother dead at the Front.

The wind was cold, ear-tingling. Sven had on the heavy cream sweater that had befriended me on my first night out and a big furry conical white woollen cap. It looked the kind of cap one could face a blizzard in, and he told me he had bought it in Yokohama and that it had seen a blizzard or two. Casually he said it, as a woman might mention a certain brand of sheeting wore well. The remark opened before me a new vista of our part of the world with Japan at the end of a sea corridor from Sydney, of a Pacific ringed about with real countries having real people in them and shops where sailormen walked in and bought caps and then walked out and faced blizzards wearing them. I was in a new world. As an Australian who had never left home, the rest of the world had never seemed actual to me before, just so much cable news on the inside page of the newspaper, the theatre of political events and theories as remote as text-book history.

In some way Joan had managed to stun my personality, to devaluate it completely, and it had not yet recovered consciousness from the blow. Into this lacuna the hitherto distant world came with a sudden pictorial shock. The atlas was now more real than myself, it had emerged from the fiction of the schoolroom into an overwhelming reality of place. I think it was the geography vision of this night that took me later, without much reason, to Japan. I fell silent before such world travel as Sven had had and took another turn or two at the tiller, holding it with both hands, for it was heavy, and wondering if I too should ever get to strange lands and talk to strange foreign people.

Two hours is a long time, on watch, when one is not used to it. I was tiring rapidly and took longer rests, my soul, or whatever it is that dwells most inwardly in us, flung out of myself by the night and the new experience and crying a little nakedly in the cold desolation of loneliness. It seemed to me as I sat there a

43

profoundly sorrowful thing that peoples should be so remote from each other, engaged in wars, national rivalries, senseless bickering; intolerably sad that everybody should be bowed down in his economic chains with so little possibility of escape for anybody, when we all ultimately have the same common denominator of pleasure and pain, work and relaxation, and when time and the sea and the mocking vault of the sky are so infinitely omnipotent; mankind such a transitory phenomenon.

In my aloneness I felt a cessation of my individual reality, as if my ego had escaped down a long lighted passage and left its habitation like a detached shadow behind. At the same time, or immediately afterwards, I felt a conviction of the eternal absolute of one's own being that has no possibility of knowledge outside itself, of the futility of trying ever to know anyone else. A curious apathy followed, an emptiness of emotion, a negation, as of having lost myself and the world with it.

I always doubt the word 'cosmic'. I doubt any printed declaration of it, I have thought writers pretend to the awareness of it too easily; I have despised poets who used it too glibly; it has been for me a secret word, a hearing-the-world-turning kind of word and I would never apply it in my life to any experience but this, and now I approach it humbly, for I think it is the only word that fits.

Looking back on what I did then I see a long train of associations, but at the time I felt only an impulse, an inchoate apprehension that I should perish if I did not obtain release, if I did not manage to break this numbness, to establish contact with an outside world and in doing so recover my own reality that was slipping away.

What I did do was to stretch over and put the tip of my right forefinger lightly on the back of Sven's shut hand as it rested on the combing. He must have been surprised, it was long since either of us had spoken. He said nothing, but slowly, oh so slowly, turned his hand over and grasped the finger tightly, holding it clenched as a key fits into and is held by a keyhole. For a few minutes it stayed there, externalized from me, bright in the binnacle light, while the night and the fear and the aloneness became something shared and passed away. Then immediately a ridiculous symbolization of that finger and shut hand seized me, became comic; I drew the finger away.

That seeming absurd incident meant a great deal to us; for me a salvation as if I had been spiritually drowning; for Sven it illumined the future. I was no longer to him an intellectually daring, irresponsible somebody else's wife, the kind of person he had never met before nor thought existed, but a very human being who had been afraid and miserable and who needed him. For me it was the close of powerful emotions connected with my leaving home, it ended there; but for him it was a hope, a beginning. In a wretched moment in the time ahead he blamed me for that finger, and indeed I take the blame.

Neither of us referred to it for months afterwards; then, when I found that it had been terrifically significant to him also and because the impression of my own state of mind at the time had been so strong and lasting, I tried to analyse the nature of that peculiar and unmeditated movement of mine. I think I have found the causes of it. I had been regretting that I had not brought with me a pencil sketch of my husband to put up opposite my bunk because Ruth had pasted up in the cabin two prints, 'Bacchus and his Pards' and da Vinci's 'Creation of the World'. Both have the interest concentrated on the pointing finger that must touch or the continuity of life, its pleasure in one case and creation in the other, be shattered. Now I wanted two things on this voyage, the happiness of freedom and the creative desire. The connection between my mood and action, is, for me, determined by this unconscious association, though I fear to the outsider the episode and the explanation may sound very grandiloquent.

CHAPTER IV

PRELUDE TO SOMETHING UNPLEASANT

OUR new course brought us closer to the land and, by keeping well in to avoid the current that had been our downdrift before, we found ourselves in the lee of Sugarloaf Point. The feeling of being close to land again and of seeing it from a new angle was exciting. It rose abruptly from the water as if it had been cut through by a carving knife, one could see the strata in layers, sharp sloping faults striking the water-line at an acute angle. The sea was very rough but with the wind south to south-west we were making good progress. For four days we streaked along, glorious sailing.

It was cold and often raining, we were practically out of kerosene and out of necessary commodities like tea, fat, biscuits, bread or fresh provisions. We lived on tomato stews and bully beef. We had a number of luxury goods, but without essential ingredients or using much heat it was hard to make a menu. We took it in turns to cook. My turn was last, a Sunday, and I determined to do my best, which was bully-beef fritters, thick, substantial, thoroughly cooked and very filling. I was proud of them, a lot of ingenuity had gone to their making and nobody suspected that the pan had been greased with a large lump of paraffin wax, used for proofing canvas, that I had come across. Everyone was pleased at having something solid to eat and I felt that at last I had managed to do my bit, something that nobody else had thought of doing; that I definitely 'belonged' and was, as far as work went, one of the gang.

At the tiller too I was more competent. I had had practice in daylight watches, my muscles were becoming used to the new strains they were called upon to endure, the blisters on the palms of my hands had broken and were changing into corny little pads and the tiller was easier as the wind blew itself out.

I had had another memorable night watch with Sven, a supremely happy occasion. I had come with a headache from the smoky, frowsy cabin, where the light was too poor to read by unless one was on top of it and where the five of us had sat jammed up, noses nearly meeting over our books, elbows continually rebuked by their neighbours should they spread themselves, and an uncomfortable discontent and moroseness about everybody, to the rain-washed purity of sea air.

Sven was cheerful, he had been looking forward to this watch, he called Henery up to point out a light they had been expecting to see and they made some alteration to the sails. I was proud to be left alone at the tiller and anxious not to have a flying gybe as Cooper had the night before when the backstay had carried away with a report like a pistol shot. It was tricky steering with the steep following seas, the wind a little too far to the beam for comfort and the kicking strap out to its limit. Henery sat on the deckhouse smoking and yarning, while Sven and I sat on opposite sides of the cockpit, our feet dangling down and the tiller between and behind us.

I liked Henery then. The respect I had felt for him on the day and night of the big storm came back to me, the petty grievances I held against him sank into their places as trivialities not worth bothering about. I listened modestly; they were talking about the wind, the quick trip of the past three days and of the entrance to Moreton Bay into which the Brisbane River flows. They were discussing the probable time of our arrival. It was a relief to hear them talking pleasantly and openly about what was going to happen, for Sven had complained to me about his position on board and his share of locker and stowage space. That night Henery was just sufficiently deferential to Sven's experience and Sven was feeling pleased with himself, perhaps because I was there. After half an hour Henery went below, hesitating, a little reluctant, for we had all been enjoying the serenity of this night sailing. Standing on the water tank, his head out of the hatch, he turned and said to me jokingly, a little envious of our quiet expected intimacy, 'Don't spoil Sven, Dona'.

I laughed back, lightly, happily, because this was the first personal thing that had been said to me for days and to me it seemed as if God was in his heaven and all suddenly well with the world, as if Henery approved of our friendliness. 'No fear, he's a shell-back.'

Left to ourselves we talked easily, about Japan and the ships he had been in, since boyhood, and, with some glee, of a sailor's miserable life. The steering devolved more and more on Sven; for me it was unadulterated joy to be alive, going somewhere, taking oneself there with the hiss of the water past the bows and a wake like a comet pearling the darkness behind, to have all the thrill of continuous surf-boat riding with an added sense of security and the knowledge that it was going to last like this for months. Months! Enough to make a seasoned misanthrope happy. A stray recollection of my youth came back to me, of a black mood when my sister, disgusted at my churlishness over having to tag on in the institution of little sister chaperonage, had said to her fiancé, 'Oh, let's take her out sailing and half drown her, the little brute's only happy then', and how right she had been about it. I had sat in the bows and glowered till I got spray-soaked and in spite of myself the grievances had vanished. The episode had became a brother-in-law joke.

After a while Sven sang, song after song, sailor's songs that I heard for the first time, merry heartless songs without a thought behind them. 'Oh whisky for my Johnnie', 'When we are out-ward bound', 'Bound for Rio'; chanties, 'Blow the man down', 'What shall we do with a drunken sailor?'; amusing songs, 'The Rugabug Barque', 'Can she pake a cherry pie, Pilly Poy, Pilly Poy'; waltzes that he had learnt in Sweden the year before; a naughty song, 'In Amsterdam there dwelt a maid', appropriately censored for my benefit, he told me with a grin. He would not sing it unexpurgated. He sang in a flat rather monotonous way that

48

was pleasant, he admitted to having been a chorister once. He enunciated his words clearly, for he liked the ballads perhaps better than the tunes and he had a prodigious word memory. Last of all he sang a very sentimental song, I have forgotten what it was, I only heard it the once, but he sang it for me with great feeling and the setting was romantic enough, who but would not have been flattered? I was.

Most things on the *Skaga* had an anti-climax. In the high pitch of the moment he forgot to watch the steering closely and she got off her course and for a moment it looked ugly, as if we were going to gybe, but he saved us. 'Two points on the wrong side,' he impressed on me, 'that is as bad as four points off, and I've never been guilty of that, but then,' he paused, 'I've never had a watch like this one before.' And he added, 'Go on down, you must be tired. I'll take the rest of the watch, my turn's next, anyway.'

I went down smiling, a detractor might have said smirking, feeling very happy because it had been so natural, so spontaneous, that Sven, this shy, song-singing Sven, had not misinterpreted my weakness of the night before. He was not going to force a situation, he only wanted to talk freely, to expand, and I was a sympathetic listener; his world of the sea was a new world and his sort of life and its interests strange to me. I found it fascinating.

Ruth was still up reading. It was almost one o'clock. 'You look pleased with yourself,' she said, curious and not pleased.

'I enjoyed it,' I answered. 'It's lovely on deck. Did you hear Sven singing?' It was a reply too transparently innocent to be taken at its own value. Though it was true it sounded, even to me, highly artificial.

We rolled down the blind, washed and got ready for bed, and when we had almost finished I noticed that we were between the light and the blind and that the resulting shadow show was irresistibly comic. Ruth fussed altering the light. She laughed too and yet was distressed. 'Trust you to notice a thing like that,' she said. I had a low reputation with her. 'I've changed in the cabin

49

scores of times and not thought about it.' Finally we put it out, it seemed the only way.

I find it hard to sleep with a light in the room, an old failing. Ruth managed well enough in the semi-obscurity of her bunk, but I could not, the lamp stood a few inches from my pillow. One midnight Joan was still writing. I moved restlessly. She wrote on. She was determined that the light should not go out till she wanted it to. At 1 a.m. I changed myself round, putting the pillow next the wooden division that separated Sven's bunk from mine; still the light stared derisively at me. It was a tussle of wills and the state of our relationships was such that no comment could be made about it. Joan won. At 2 a.m. she retired with dignity to her own dark cubby-hole.

Time solved the lamp problem. In the tropics it was often possible to take one's blanket on deck and sleep there. Also circumstances taught us consideration. It became tacitly a convenient thing to put the light out at about ten for the sake of those with watches at 1 a.m. to 3 a.m., or from 3 a.m. to 5.30 a.m. and these watches came to all of us in our turn.

Insomnia troubled me. Altogether I did not sleep more than four or five hours in that first fortnight travelling to Brisbane. In vain I conjured up images of my shore bedroom, its space, its shuttered dimness, its benevolent silence. I tried every sleep-provoking device and still I was wakeful, unrested. I felt frayed as a piece of old rope weathered by existence.

The strain was finding us all out. Cooper sang and sang. He sang for hours; he sang in the wind on his watches till he got hoarse, and then he had no mercy but sang on. He sang every latest song of the moment, the most worthless dance-hall song with its sickly spread of emotion over platitude and syncopation to match; the lowest vulgarization of sentiment was sweet to him. He crooned. His repertoire was astonishing. To do him credit he knew the words of the verses as well as those of the choruses, and he had just come back from Fiji with some choice specimens. Ruth and I had fits of giggles listening to him. Joan loathed them. During one of our nights of becalming she had played on the gramophone 'Old Man River', sung by Robeson, and now Cooper 'Ole Man Ribbered' her to the point of exasperation; he always wanted her to play it again and she kept putting him off successfully. She could be inflexible in resolution. I think he spoilt it for her for all time; she gave it away in Macassar without a qualm.

Even Sven bristled at Cooper, who did not like getting wet. There was a rainbow and Cooper said facetiously, foolishly, 'This boat should be a jolly old rainbow. You ought to call her *The Rainbow*, we've had nothing but rain since we left'.

A damning silence all round; then Sven, 'You ought to be the rainbow'. Pause, everybody wondering. 'You always come out after the rain.'

Ruth and I had become estranged, subtly, for no obvious reason. I asked Sven if she were vexed with me over him. There were a lot of unknown quantities on this boat. They had been together almost two months before I came on board, perhaps they cherished tender feelings for each other? 'Good Lord, no,' said Sven with a vigour which I thought a pity. Joan and I before the trip began had nursed hopes on Ruth's behalf. Ruth drew away from Joan as well as from me. She created for herself a world of her own, I never knew her to be further from everyday life than in these few last days. She existed within herself and was satisfied, wanting nothing more. I envied her. For my part I was conscious every moment of the boat and of my fellow travellers, of the motivation of most actions and remarks, including my own.

Ruth and Henery had their own troubles, secret resentments, artistic prejudices, unuttered judgments of character; the strain was observable in tones of voice, in the matter of sharing the boat camera. When faced with this fundamental difficulty Joan backed into her natural reserve, out of the strife. Ruth became more irresponsible. She dropped over two buckets and then, I think it was she, a large dish, all in a short space of time and, to my annoyance, did not seem to think it mattered in the least bit, as indeed to a philosophic mind it ought not, there is no come-back for a bucket dropped in mid-ocean.

Then there was the food question. I like drinking tea. It is a necessity for me. There was none on board. Ruth, responsible for the provisioning in Newcastle, had forgotten it, and I had been a fortnight without tea. I bore her a grudge over that because she thought that that too didn't really matter. Then she liked porridge, thick coarse wheat porridge; we ground the wheat ourselves till I thought I should go clucky. I hated that porridge and we seemed to have little else to eat. Moreover she conned *aloud* pamphlets from the school of dieticians who won't use salt in cooking because it hardens the arteries, and who think that any sugar but brown is rank poison. She was serious about vitamins, could distinguish them, their effects on the human system and remember the foods from which each was derived, while I from the disagreeableness of my porridge-plastered stomach thought it the height of absurdity, an insult added to injury, that in this time of dearth she should set herself up as the authority on food values and talk of oranges and cheese, eggs and unpolished rice when there was not an attractive crumb in the larder. I fancied myself as a housewife, I had years of it behind me. She had none. Do not think these are small matters. If you insist on thinking so go to sea in a cutter and find out.

My retaliation was to commence a poem in which she, in the guise of Princess Rhodope with an egg-yolked austerity, walked the tightrope of hard common sense. At the time I was probably confused with the tradition of walking the plank. I never finished that poem, nobody ever saw it, it is destroyed.

My feelings for Joan could not be so readily expressed. Occasionally, usually at meal times, I would sparkle. There is an irresistible charm for me in a certain kind of imaginative wittiness, for me ideas always dress themselves up in pretty words and act out a conversational action on a stage of their own, perhaps that is why I never look on them as belonging to me and I should always be tempted to sacrifice truth to give them a good curtain.

I effervesce easily, I like being flippant, but it is difficult ever to get Joan in the mood for this kind of intellectual banter. She listens and listens, and then sometimes, rarely, she will smile, a delicious slow smile of enjoyment that is like a benediction and one is satisfied that one's efforts have not been wasted, that here at last is the right kind of appreciation. Now she never smiled. Her silence froze gaiety as elemental truth might rebuke a false imagination. Sometimes I felt her heavy eyes on me as I talked and then she would rise solemnly and go to her cubby-hole and scratch in her big black book and I would think, 'Bother, she won't reciprocate or be gay herself, she thinks, "To be observed, stored and put away for use".' The effervescence would fizz out of me. My clearest visualization of her at this time is of her getting up and going away.

Lying awake, unable to sleep, I used to wonder about *Skaga* and the men who for twenty years had lived in her, the kinds of men they were and their passions. I speculated on whether they had infused into the wood of the boat itself the strangest and most primitive emotions, fear and hatred, along with their slow hard northern drabness, their powers of endurance, and whether the sea had salted down those qualities, preserving them as long as the wood should last and the *Skaga* hold together. Was there any emanation of mistrust from them? I thought of the two men who had brought her out from Sweden, how the more sensitive of the two could hardly endure to be in the presence of the other, even for a business interview, after the trip was over. Joan was more enduring, more solid than I. When I had been longer in the presence of this boat spirit, this obstinate and wooden vitality, should I too be able to endure, to conquer the hare-spirit in me, to hold on?

The last painful incident of my unhappy probation came next afternoon, the fourth day of the wind, the eleventh day out. Ruth was at the tiller, the wind strong but the mountainous seas subsided to a brisk swell. I stripped, took the only bucket that remained to us, twisted the short lanyard attached to it round my left hand several times and got up a couple of half-bucketfuls, spilling most of the water. We were travelling at six knots over the ground in spite of the adverse current, and the water sizzled by. The deck pitched like a razzle-dazzle at a fair. At one moment the surge was slopping through the scuppers, at the next it was far below, the rope on the bucket too short to allow it to reach the surface. I steadied myself, shins pressed against the low bulwark, and with both hands threw the bucket down as Ruth had shown me so that it would fill quickly. It did so too successfully, filling and holding like a sea anchor; before I could attempt to lift it I was hurled to the deck, bent back, my left arm stretched unendurably, the rope cutting into my hand, my body dragged down and back by the weight of the sea and flung against a ring, against a stanchion, against the steel wire of the stays and pinned there. I held on to the bucket, that last bucket, I had one idea, not to let it go. I screamed. Sven sprang to the tiller, Ruth rushed along and took the bucket, released me, helped me up. I glimpsed Henery's head out of the hatchway. Slowly Ruth went back to the tiller, Sven below.

I sat recovering, moving myself to find out breakages, none . . . some ribs perhaps. I put on a garment or two; Ruth was white, she had been badly scared, I might have been pulled over had the stays not caught me. Sven gave us both a lecture afterwards, I should have held on with one hand, 'One hand for yourself and one for the ship' was the motto for us. Attempting to rescue me might have risked all of us, so be careful next time. It had been dangerous to try to bucket in such a sea. As for Ruth, he had been able to come up when she called, but what one ought to do in such an emergency was to put *Skaga's* head into the wind and throw the lifebuoy, it was difficult to see a man overboard in the hollows of a windy sea, particularly from a low deck like ours. We did not forget that lesson.

I got below; I was cold and shivering. Joan did not look up from the book she was reading but she said, and it was the last blow, 'Really you ought to be hardened off by now'. Her tone was one of disgust. She did not move.

I turned my face to the wall and wept, the first tears of the trip, wept bitterly, silently, under the ignominy of knowing that she might hear. I was sick into the towel, and then lay still. This then was our vaunted friendship, Joan sitting there deliberately taking no notice. I had not thought it possible she could be so hard. I had not known her.

I stopped crying. I was cold, my feet numb, any movement painful. 'Shock,' I told myself, 'Shock, that's all. People always go cold with shock.' It seemed very long, more than half an hour, when Sven approached with an air of guilt, as if he were assuming wrongfully a prerogative of tending. Joan was lying on her bunk, Henery beside her. Sven asked if I should like anything. Yes I should. I should like brandy and blankets. He got both and piled the coverings on. I was still cold. He chafed my feet and drew on them some woollen socks of his own. The brandy steadied me. I got warm and he went away.

'Idiot,' Self told myself, 'Idiot to cry,' and 'You deserved this. You called "Wolf, Wolf" often enough over your little hurts. You were careless, you deserved this.'

'No, I didn't,' Idiot replied, 'Not in humanity, not from a friend, not from Joan.' It was a kind of internal bleeding, this wail, 'Not from Joan'.

Then Self raged, mortified, sorry for Self, fingering its ribs, 'I could not have done it . . . as Skipper's wife it was her *duty* . . . She would have the title "Skipper" for Henery, she wouldn't let Sven have it . . . What can I hope from her now? If I broke my leg . . . To leave me to a man . . . a comparative stranger. . . .' Thousands of surburban wives talk like that, in parlour italics.

Friendship is elastic and when it is strained beyond its limits of stretch it breaks with a snap or does not break but is worthless all the same, a piece of chewed string. It never goes back, never quite the same, resilient over trifles, gripping a situation, enduring.

The row was imminent. The clouds had been lowering long enough, it only wanted the lightning to flash.

CHAPTER V

THE ROW

THE row broke before we made Brisbane. I have waited more than two years and perhaps it is not in perspective yet. It seemed for a long time as if I would never get it to scale in the proportion of my life. Whenever I thought of it the bilge rose in me bringing its taste of soured happiness. But yesterday I made a discovery. I read again, since I had to write about it, a long catharsis I had written within a few weeks to a friend, a physician, who had prescribed it, and in that terrible truth-telling account there were details, accusations, incidents, a fury of indignation, an intensity of outrage, provocations – what a selfish unmannerly lot we can become, we civilized, educated people – and, this was my yesterday's discovery – I had forgotten. I had forgotten some things I had imagined at the time I should never be able to forget. I had forgotten – but it is not meet to uncover old rudenesses.

Perhaps we might never have quarrelled if the weather had been kinder to us, if we had not run into a storm and then a calm and out of our ordinary comforts. If perhaps we had been better prepared. But on sailing trips something always happens. I know a devoted group of two sisters and two brothers out of a large family who hired a yacht and went for a holiday, it was something they had looked forward to for years. It rained all the time and they have never been the same since, four days disrupted twenty years of affectionate association.

I did not like writing this book because of the row. I would so infinitely rather have written an account of a joyous co-operative venture that succeeded. The especially painful part to me was that the row should have come so soon, and since the book tries to be a wholly truthful if subjective account of the adventure, that it should have to be got over at the very beginning of the journal. It would have been so much easier not to have written about it. Yet it had to be written about. The whole experience could never have been settled for me until that was done. I have been incompetent to do anything else properly for two years because of it. On the other hand though our Odyssey was disrupted by the row I think that the voyage itself accumulated a wonder and interest that should be written about. And I have not lost faith in my original premises. I still think such a trip could be done, and in harmony. It needed only just a little more to have been the perfect group experience. Furthermore these small boat adventures are still going on. They have become fashionable. Recently a party of six Germans, all men, set out. Where, and how, will they arrive? Two men have taken over *Skaga;* her travels are not yet done. I should like this book to help the adventurous. Perhaps they can see more clearly than I why we failed.

Sven had pampered me since the accident, making me warm drinks, anticipating my needs at the table, following my movements with his eyes, looking at me. It was embarrassing yet in a way I liked it. Discomfort has since taught me what a petted safe life I had had till the outbreak of the *Skaga* adventure. I had been swaddled in the trappings of loyalty and consideration. This first stage of the voyage was one of those progressions in human relationships with the sigma of circumstances forcing six unpredictable quantities into an arbitrary cycle of co-existence without possibility either of solution or summation. Already I had experienced discomfort, neglect, disillusion, and, if Sven will pardon the comparison, here was Man Friday ready to serve a female Crusoe.

Joan was strong enough to keep the steel of her dislike away from the flint of her indignation, but I was not, the two struck sparks in me. So I wrote down my grievances. Yes, I wrote them down and made a letter of them with a list of suggestions, and I handed it across the silent table like an ultimatum of war. I kept a duplicate. Reading it now makes me shudder, the requests were so reasonable and mild and the setting out of them so stiff. To look at it is to feel again the atmosphere of that cabin, emotionally rancid, unwholesome, like the stale reek of tobacco smoke on one's clothes after a protracted sitting the night before in a café.

The matter of the ultimatum concerned a financial statement, long overdue, organization, food and medical supplies, the overhauling or disposal of the engine, relations between Henery and Sven. But the row went much deeper and on more painful matters.

Joan and Henery considered it all day and then broke the storm when Sven was on deck on watch. It might have been better had he been in it for it concerned him. Cooper stayed on his bunk, overhearing but discounted. I sat on my bunk, Ruth lay on hers, sitting beside her Joan and Henery. They launched a counter attack, it hardly mentioned the points of the ultimatum but concentrated on my chief fault, the 'spoiling' of Sven, a new point of view to me, Henery's phrase had turned serious. 'Ruined a good man,' he said now. He said it in his admiral's voice.

Rows are funny things. I don't know now why I should have had to bear the brunt of a long dissertation on Sven's character, why Henery and he couldn't have had it out there and then, but at the time we four were still 'the family' aboard and Sven and Cooper not. Sven had been testy over the indefiniteness of his position, the very way Henery said 'man' indicated the reason. There were other matters that worried him, finance, equipment. I denied responsibility for Sven, I believe with justice, but a scapegoat was needed for the breakdown in relationships and I already bore a burden of guilt because in some mysterious way I had failed to please Joan, whom I wanted above all to please, whose judgments I feared, whose strength and stability I wished to cleave to and imitate. On the trial trip a scapegoat had been easier to find and he had been bitter about it and retaliated in the press, a full page interview, 'Sailors Beware, Sailors Take Care, of the *Skaga* Adventure'. I had hitherto accepted Henery's point of view about that casting out into the wilderness but now I felt that the scapegoat might have had a thing or two to say in his favour.

I had been wrong on the question of food values, said Ruth, and not kind over what she had done in the matter of provisioning. On the Sven issue she was, on the whole, with Henery, who wore at this stage the shield of male superiority and the air of being, modestly, a champion in the lists of honour against a ferocious adversary, me. Joan had nothing to say. He was saying it for her. She sat like the heavy reinforcements. Looking back on it it seems curious and absurd and muddled, that row. We argued it out in a mist of emotions, old scores were brought up, home-truths pointed out. I felt out-numbered and right in spite of being put so adroitly in the wrong. The row lasted and lasted. All our feelings went crescendo; I began to feel that what I was saying was convincing when the surprise came from Joan. She wanted to bring the argument to a conclusion; she had now no reason, her passivity, her poise, her envied poise, dropped. 'I shall never like you again,' she cried, 'I didn't know you before, staying with each other was different, but living with you . . .' Her contempt cut me. She said it with passion, with fury, it was not dislike, it was hate, and I knew, that moment, that coming from Joan, it meant – forever.

The dreaded judgment come down like a guillotine. And I – I howled, I cried hysterically. I had no argument against this amputation. Yet I hated being the weak one. In the midst of my weeping I raged mentally against my mother for letting me grow up a cry-baby. My sobs were those of anger, of defeat, of exhaustion, of a protest I was not wise enough nor clever enough to articulate.

Money was mentioned, as if money could buy back the old things, and all pretences had gone now. 'What do I care about money? Don't you think I've looked forward to it too? Just like you? The adventure, the sailing, the . . . the . . .' But friendship was a drowned word, it had died.

Henery was moved, this sincerity had touched bottom; my

suffering distressed him, it was as if he too knew the shame of being weak, the cry-baby, the despised of the loftily-minded. Or perhaps he thought they had gone too far. At any rate, he said impulsively, 'Let's forget it, let's start all over again'. He held out his hand and urged. I hesitated, this was more than a shaking hands matter. Then I took it and he and I forgave each other many things.

The row was over, melodramatically. But Joan got up. We did not shake hands. In such circumstances she could never have cried, no more than an Indian papoose cries. She probably thought my crying mere tactics. She and I could never regain the easiness of other times. Friendship was the stretched elastic between us and the tension had broken me and left her, implacable.

The storm of my emotion subsided slowly as the body of a dead snake goes on twitching for hours. It convulsed me from time to time in an agony. I had not had such a bath of grief since childhood; all my adult troubles were nothing to this. Ruth tried to comfort me. I had taken up my book of poems and was reading aimlessly, a mere seeing of words. She asked me to read to her as one might ask a child to show its doll to distract it. But her sympathy meant more than that. It meant that she was sorry as I was sorry; that she wanted again to try to understand the things I was interested in; that we should be friends again. I tried to read to her and failed. The row had been a devastating business.

Very late that night we were again alone. Sleeping sounds came from the other side of the curtain. We talked for a long time softly. I learnt many things. I learnt how fierce and maternal a certain kind of wifely regard can be. I learnt some of Ruth's fears. It was father again. She could not endure the thought of public criticism of us, though there had been much already, nor could she understand that whatever happened gossip would credit us with vices and mésalliances according to its fancy and the permutation of our numbers. She kept talking of the impossibility of the 'normal consummation' of any affair on board. It obsessed her.

I had left home partly to escape the net of bondages being long-married implies, to find an individual freedom for a little time, and now I found how humiliatingly unfree 'free' people could be and how much heavier than the bondage of affection was the bondage of hatred.

Arguing discreetly with Ruth so as not to shock her lifted me out of the morass of my emotions. Sven had not even kissed me, though no doubt he might in the future, and here were Ruth and I talking pedantically of 'normal consummations'. Her phrase. Sven would have been startled could he have heard us. It was unique in my experience, fantastic.

When she had finished talking she drew out a little blue book belonging to a tenpenny series. It was called *Love and Marriage in Soviet Russia*. Ruth was by way of being a communist, but the prospect of a little free love at close quarters was undoubtedly very disturbing. The sight of that title restored my wounded feelings. I cannot withstand the ridiculous. The whole thing was ridiculous. Kim. The breach with Ruth was bridged.

CHAPTER VI

IN BRISBANE. PROVISIONING

WE made the shelter inside the Moreton Bay lighthouse about 3 a.m. one black night a fortnight after leaving Newcastle. That first port-making was interesting, the tense readiness of the men, the importance of the chart as they pored over its currents and shoals, the signalling about an anchorage to the lighthouse-keeper. The anchorage made, I slept for an hour or two in the unaccustomed silence, and at dawn went on deck and found calm clear still water and land, sunlit, beautiful, at peace with itself, spread with the comfort, the order, the repose of one's bedroom after a bad dream.

The shore was soft, soft natural tumuli of sand rising in a series of dunes to a headland and cut sharply away on the water's edge as the hard rock had been at Sugarloaf Point, as the bank on the inner bend of a quick-flowing river is cut away. That slice of sand revealed a deep yellow, an orange that was almost red in sovereign strata at the base and on this gold standard rested a black band, coaly, it suggested economics and industry, above that was pure glistening white and it could symbolize any spiritual quality you cared to give it, but the three were strictly separated, there was no mixing, which was strange for they were all of sand. It looked as if an artist had got up early and painted stripes of clean colour on the prepared palette of the earth. Covering the dunes was long bluish sand grass, it rustled in a wind that blew on the top of the tumuli but did not touch us where we lay in shelter. Away in a cleft between two hills was the whitewashed lighthouse round which we had come the night before. The sunlight was gentle, the earth colours glowed with a subdued radiance, the rounded curves of the dunes were satisfyingly harmonious. I wanted to go ashore and run barefoot on that splendid sand and trickle it through my fingers as a miser counts gold. Ruth, up early with me, wanted to do so too. Greatly daring we swam round the boat once. We could have swum ashore but we were frightened of sharks, it looked a sharky kind of place. It was; at least we were told afterwards that sharks by the dozen had been seen there a few days before. We contented ourselves with jumping up and down on the bobstay.

Soon Sven got up and talked of unlashing the dinghy and going ashore to feel the land underfoot and touch that wealth of golden sand, but Henery was not up and we three did not feel the freedom to follow our own desires. It was always like that. It ended in having a late breakfast and then making our way, beating against the wind, to Sandgate, a favourite swimming resort for Brisbane people. It took us all that day to do so, and at midday Henery brought out some whisky to celebrate our safe arrival in the Brisbane River. I was lying on my bunk in the splendid isolation of assumed slumber. They called on Sven to give the toast and he did so, in Swedish: 'Nin skäl, din skäl, alla vakra flickers skäl'. They all drank and then asked what it meant.

'To all the pretty girls', translated Sven quietly. A sailor's toast reaching port. It let the ordinary daylight of sexual attraction into the murk of our confused and abnormal emotions. I was merry at it, but nobody laughed. This Sven was not so simple as he had appeared, or if he were simple his simplicity was of the right order. His and my merrymaking had been natural, proper to our situation; grave reserve, pretentious aspiration, fear of public opinion were things that could be rebuked by a sailor's toast.

We came to Sandgate in the late afternoon. It was cold and windy and had been raining, the kind of afternoon in a summer resort when pleasure-seekers cower over novels and cards. Cooper and I went for provisions. We had a wet row to a jetty and scrambled with difficulty on to it for it was ebb tide and steps non-existent below the high-water level. The dinghy we secured by two ropes to the barnacled pier posts. We feared that it would be bashed to pieces against the piles for the water was rough and the wind boisterous. Exulting in being on land we ran along the planked jetty and ashore through a little park. The path undulated like a snake under our feet. I rolled, said Cooper, as if I were drunk, and he begged me to walk straight, for from shop doors spectators were watching us and he was very self-conscious. We were certainly odd enough, I had no shoes on, my khaki shorts were wet behind and salt-stained in front, our sweaters were grubby and our hair wild, we grinned idiotically at everything and our feet flapped on the ground as if we expected it, like the deck, to do half the work of walking and rise underneath them. I told him he was as erratic in his movements as I, but he did not believe me until he tripped on the kerbing of the first footpath we met and almost went sprawling. Then I lurched into a veranda post that I simply had not seen, and we both came to our senses and walked as sedately as possible to make purchases; bread, butter, cheese, tea, potatoes, onions, dripping, kerosene, a cabbage, pineapples and bananas, and then separately, he to the barber's, and I to the post office to send telegrams. After that I got several pounds of steak and some chocolate. We met again laden with bags and bundles. 'Beer,' I proposed; there was an hotel opposite.

Cooper hesitated; 'Ruth doesn't like it.' The purchases were to come out of boat funds.

'On Kim,' said I, and he got some bottles.

It was awkward getting ourselves and the goods into the dinghy which was leaking and half-full of water. Some fishermen on the jetty above helped us. They approved of the beer and wanted to share it. In their efforts not to shatter the bottles against the piles they almost dropped the bread and the other precious dry things in the water. By this time it was past sunset and had begun to rain again. I cowered over the bread trying to keep it dry and held the other things out of the wet while Cooper sweated with the exertion of getting us to the *Skaga* before the dinghy foundered.

Sven was cook that day. He scolded us for the way we had

moored the dinghy to the jetty, but forgave us when he looked inside the parcels. Soon the cabin was blue with smoke, noisy with the hiss of primuses and ambrosial with the fumes of frying. We enjoyed a preliminary snack of bread and cheese and beer. Luxuries. Such a change from sloppy tinned tomatoes and salt beef. Everybody approved of everything. We ate enormously. Sven suddenly looked up from his acreage of steak with its heavy crop of potatoes. He beamed genially on every one and on me particularly. 'You are a sensible woman,' his glance said, and I thought with complacency, 'All men are the same,' and went on chewing. Not for nothing had I navigated matrimonial seas. In our shut-in closeness the scene was cave-like, safe, and – it might have been the pervading aroma of meat – in some way prehistoric.

Next day, Saturday, May 14th, the secretary of the Yacht Club came to pilot us up the river to our anchorage, and when he came on board so did deception, for unanimously, without consultation, we presented the united front that we subsequently brought to every social encounter. Getting the few miles up the river took all day, we ought to have tried out the engine but Henery had the idea of sailing 'every inch of the way to England'. Cooper went home. He lived in Brisbane.

I was distressed. The row had upset me physically, an alarming thing. I spent the next two days very sorry for myself, and my accumulation of woes resulted in a flat reaction against the preceding fortnight of high tension. So on Monday morning I dressed myself in clean lounge pyjamas; all the others were going ashore and at my own wish I was to mind the boat and get some rest. But first I rowed Henery and Sven ashore. On coming back to the *Skaga* I shipped the oars and got aboard. There was a strong ebb current running and as I went to hitch the mooring rope round the hawse aft, I dropped the end of the wet rope and away spun the released dinghy bobbing like a cork.

I called to Ruth, she came up blinking. She had been getting her clothes ready to go ashore. The dinghy was already about thirty yards away, I could see it drifting out to sea and it had cost us £5, so, since Ruth did not dive in as I had half-hoped she might, for she knew my plight, I did myself, all frilled pyjama legs and ornamental coat. I managed to catch the dinghy in about fifty or sixty yards and scrambled in without sinking it. We drifted past a point of land. I had no oars and wondered if I should jump out and swim for it, towing the dinghy. I recalled that there was a meat works not far away and that a child had been snatched from its parents' hands while bathing in this very stretch the summer before. While I hesitated a man at the power station saw me and shouted that he would come. His skiff was in a little basin quite handy and it did not take him long to reach me, but the current was so fierce that it took half an hour to row back against it. A press photographer happened to be on the bank and he got a good story and a funny wet picture of me with my hair snaky like the Gorgon's head, so that in our subsequent Australian ports of call I was recognized as 'The lady who went after the dinghy'.

My day of rest was not a peaceful one. There were many callers, reporters, salesmen, curious people, including one Palomela, a powerful Dane, a riverman who rowed up with the remark: 'This boat I tink come from my countree'. I could not convince him that *Skaga* was Swedish not Danish and he talked for an hour or more, patting *Skaga*, stroking her, and full of mysterious hints as to how we might make a fortune by sailing round the world, he was going to do it himself when he could build the right kind of boat. He coveted *Skaga*, the sight of her made him homesick. He began to talk, but in sad tones, of why Brisbane was better than Denmark; he showed me his references and sailor's discharges that he carried in a dirty bundle round his neck and from the fullness of his heart he insisted on me accepting a pound of sausages that he had with him.

The next day I fell in the water again, this time no heroine, but a fool who paid for her folly with a soiled passport, ruined 'best' dress and a watch to be overhauled. We were anchored off New Farm and had no landing but a steep bank of slippery rocks. Ruth in

the bow had her hold wrenched away by the strong current while
I, caught in the moment of disembarking, arms full of bundles,
one foot on shore and the other in the dinghy, straddled a wider
and wider gulf until the inevitable occurred: I only saved the
crown of my hat from the water and came up mud to the teeth.
It had been arranged that I help Ruth with the ship's laundry
while Joan minded ship; we had a great many dirty garments,
ideas of economy and the loan of a laundry ashore. A fine scheme,
but it had flaws. To begin with, washing clothes in bulk is an art.
It needs an attention to detail, a scrupulosity over trifles, practice,
an acquired knack and a cheerful heart. I had none of these.

When we set out the morning was already late. To get breakfast,
wash and dress on *Skaga* took about five times as long as the same
processes would have done on shore. There was the waiting for
each other, the pumping of water, the crawling round with the
little wash basin, taking turns, finding shore clothes and getting
into them in the cabin that was not so free as the inside of a piano
case, and then the final arrangements, instructions and the ferry-
ing across. It always took ages. Because of my immersion I
had to go through it again, so Ruth, with Sven to help carry the
sea bags of dirty clothing, did not wait but set off for the house of
her cousin who was away on holidays but whose husband had
left the key of the house somewhere and the laundry at our
disposal. A complicated arrangement. It might have been
satisfactory except that Ruth had told me the wrong number of
the house and I only knew the cousin's Christian name!

So I wandered up and down a long street in a fashionable
suburb, ringing first at the front doors and then, with more sense,
at the back, and asking if Miss W—— were washing here please.
Everybody seemed very astonished at a lady who was so vague
about where her comrade char was doing a day's laundering. By
this time it was afternoon, the outlying suburb had taken a long
time to get to from our anchorage, and on the way I had stopped
to phone an old acquaintance who had invited me to dinner that
evening.

Despair emboldened me; I ventured into all back premises that looked promising and scanned any washing hanging on the lines, alas without a glimpse of any familiar garments. The Brisbane houses stand on piles for coolness and have beautiful gardens; it seemed to be siesta hour, only the dogs were wide awake. Had it not been for the thought of Ruth surrounded by sacks and suit-cases of soiled clothes I should have given up the search. In one house I found a sympathetic girl. I outlined my position and gave my only clue, the cousin's Christian name. It worked like a charm. 'Oh, you mean Mrs. M——. She lives next door.'

'But I have been there. There is nothing on the line, nobody about.'

'Try again. As a matter of fact, your friend is there, she asked me the time through the fence.'

So I tried again and Ruth emerged from the laundry in the trellised-in basement of the house. I told my tale. She told hers, of the prodigious effort she and an appointment-smitten Sven had made to get all the bags and bundles on and off trams and of how at the appearance of every tradesman or handbill hawker down the garden path she had fled to the inmost recesses beneath the piles of the house – for shame's sake. Thus we had missed each other.

We began to wash. She already had the copper on and some clothes in it and had been out to buy soap, washing powders, and ammonia. We washed furiously. The first garments might have been well done but towards the end! A mysterious brown stain appeared on all the white things afterwards, something had 'run'. Heavy woollen shirts and sweaters and coarse sea-faring shorts were hard to do and we broke our nails over them. There were towels and sheets . . . I began to add up the possessions of other people and to reckon how much this 'economy' was costing me. How wise the common-sense Sven had been to send most of his things to the laundry round the corner from the ship. Touched by the irony of this business I amused myself rubbing and scrubbing at Henery's shirts, taking out my animosity along with the dirt. But it didn't quite work; between collars I brooded on the stupid tasks so-called intelligent women let themselves in for.

At dusk we were still 'pegging out', the clothes lines were filled, the lawns and bushes draped with garments. Puddles of coloured water dripped from the wet clothes, our combined efforts at wringing had grown progressively weaker. My friend had asked me to dine at Brisbane's smartest hotel and now I should be late for the appointment, we could not find any lights in the house to dress by and my hands were wrinkled puffy horrors. The incongruities of this day. I had to take a long taxi ride because I was late, I helped eat a dinner that probably cost a great deal, subsequently I paid the dry-cleaner and the watch-mender thirty-five shillings, the price of falling in the river, I had made my soiled clothes half-clean, used up a lot of energy and saved – a few shillings.

Then some friends of my husband came to visit me on board. They were dears, and shocked at the confinement of the cabin and the state of my health carried me off to an old and typically Brisbane home with verandas, hanging baskets of fern, trees, shrubberies, pets, flower beds, regular meals . . . I revived within twenty-four hours.

Each day I went to the boat or to the town on business. We had the primuses fixed and bought spare parts for them; we bought provisions for six months and medical supplies, I had a horror of our ignorance should any serious illness or accident befall us, particularly since the bucketing incident did I realize the risk of suffering and permanent disability should one of us break a limb.

We were all vaccinated against smallpox and the specialist who did it was a mine of amusing travel stories and useful information; I still have his recipes for the curing and storing of shoals of fish, for ways of mixing and sprouting cereals and concocting energy restorers, for first-aid makeshifts and many tropical do's and don'ts beside. His dictum that only the tenderfoot travels in discomfort pleased me, the spartan and ascetic sides of life which Joan exalted could be overrated as qualities in themselves I thought; any more unnecessary discomfort would be folly. We cut and cut his list of what should be in the medicine cupboard till the barest essentials remained. The most expensive items were some capsules for putting in the tanks containing our drinking water, for some reason chlorate of lime was not suitable. Joan put the capsules away with the care appropriate to their cost until the time when they should be needed. Months later a sticky gelatinous mess in one of the lockers puzzled us till we remembered – the water preservatives.

Ruth and I had taken on the job of provisioning and visited business men and got wholesale rates in biscuits, medicines, bacon and cheese. The cost of foodstuffs was higher in Brisbane than in Sydney. We spent hours checking and re-checking requirements and prices, arguing about vitamins and consulting likes and dislikes. We went to a theatre or two. Joan and I called on the acting governor of the state and his wife; she dubbed us 'brave young women', it was a phrase we were to get used to, it always made me feel like a veteran with medals on my chest. I wrote a couple of personality articles about ourselves and our plans. We were frightfully keen on making some money, we seemed to be spending such a lot. In between work I went to some dances, a picnic and a ball and flirted outrageously, trying by means of the conventional good time to establish a case-hardened untouchable ego ready for the next stage of the voyage.

We met a party of English yachtsmen who had every comfort money could buy and who were sailing round the world. In their engine-room was a motor to start an engine that started the big engine! At first we were all sick with envy and inferiority feelings and then an Australian kind of pride rose in us and we would not have changed our old sea-whiskered *Skaga* for their grand boat and all its engines. I fancied that they too with space, agreeable fittings, and wealth had their irritations. One can't be sure of these things. We met one of the partners in the *Amyrillis* adventure and he scrutinized us closely, with interest; he knew this elbow-rubbing long distance sailing.

Then there was Cooper. The rest of us had agreed that we should do better without him though his financial co-operation would be an asset that ought to be considered. I met him in town. He was undecided. I pretended we still wanted him to come and at the same time gave him such a picture of our temperamental complexities that he was convinced all of us or some of us would either go mad or commit murder on the way. Incidentally in my gloomiest moments after the row I had dwelt at length on ways of exploding the petrol tank and drowning us all, but murder, committed mentally, is a safety valve, fortunately there is a big gap between imagination and execution. Eventually he decided not to come.

The Specialist was interested in us as a crew. He told me a curious story of how as a younger man he had set out on a long tramp, weeks in duration, in desert country outback, with one male companion, a person than whom he could not have found anyone more suitable, whose tastes were his tastes, whose brain was brilliant and conversation stimulating and whose acquaintanceship had the interest of novelty, the perfect companion. In a fortnight they had talked each other out and there was nothing more to say. The way grew more monotonous and for three days absolutely deserted as it can be between Adelaide, South Australia, and Bourke, N.S.W. There came a day when the two of them did not speak at all, a long hot day with a dry wind blowing; dust, a day of fatigue and sullen not-thinking when the mind of the Specialist had nothing in it but hatred of the big boots of the man walking on the camel pad ahead of him. That night at the evening meal, still without speaking, they made two camps and two camp-fires and two dampers, within sight of each other but separate, these two friends sleeping apart in the wilderness with a dry dust of hatred in their hearts, a hatred that had arisen as do the willy-willys, the whirlwinds of the western plains, out of nothing, out of the unstirred air of too great a perfection. The next night, fortunately, they fell in with some drovers who built one big campfire and after that they were able to finish the journey, but they never wanted to see each other again.

He was shrewd that doctor, sensitive, and . . . curious. He

had sailed a lot himself in tropic seas. He had detected in our reserve or in our united social front the awareness of the need for it. 'Which of you,' he shot at me after telling this story, 'in your opinion is the most neurotic?'

I answered immediately and the word split itself out of my mind without thinking, without consciousness almost: 'Sven'. As surely as the most unexpected, the most ordinary person in the detective story must necessarily be the villain, so the most seeming simple, unconfused and straightforward of us was, as by a divination, pronounced the most difficult, the most bewildered.

The inquisitor was respectful, he agreed, but why had I thought so? How did I know? I only partly knew my reasons then, that the four of us were aware, or becoming aware of ourselves, and were for good or evil more or less psychologically fixed and would come ultimately to no harm, but Sven who had lived by doing instead of thinking was bound to come off worst in an adventure that was to be outwardly one of doing and in reality a most profoundly psychic one. Then too he was guilt-conscious and the emancipation from guilt is a slow one.

I was fearful of this. We all of us must maintain stable relations for so long if our setting out again without affection but with new knowledge was to be successful. The duelling interplay of motives between the four of us would have the stability of foils crossed in a fencing match, parry and thrust and locked purposes, antagonism behind the steel, but play, masks on and no bleeding allowed. Was Sven safe in such an encounter, not only safe for himself but safe for me? The Specialist said yes.

The day after this talk we went up the river to beach and copper paint the boat on a sandy stretch. The work was interesting, not very hard. We did one side one day and the other the following day. In the night in between Ruth spoke of making a wheat damper ashore. She was to mix the dough while Sven and I collected fuel. I love making fires out of doors. We got a great blaze going and still she did not come. Sven went for her, she had changed her mind. Perhaps she was really tired, perhaps there had been a conference on board. At her request I had hardly seen Sven in Brisbane and now she was literally forcing me into his arms. We had to watch the fire burn itself out. We were both constrained, awkward. Then the moon rose, a marvellous crimson with black clouds like horned devils drifting across it. It changed to molten gold with a broad yellow pavement across the water like a swift by-pass to the Celestial City while the trees rustled softly, the sentimental kind of barcarole that makes old maids melt. Everything seemed easier, simpler. Sven took me in his arms and for the first time kissed me. We talked. We talked for a long time, for the first time freely.

There was so much to be said, intimate things, ideas, habits. We explained our pasts, made confessions, agreed to the attitude we should adopt in the future, the straight and narrow path we should have to walk because of the boat situation. We fixed up a *modus vivendi*, a defensive alliance, a half-way liberation for each of us. I worked out my conception of fidelity, I was much influenced by D. H. Lawrence's 'slow hard jewel' poem. Then as the big fire died away he tapped out in Morse code through the thin silk of my blouse the words, 'Jag elskar dig'. But it wasn't so, I said, it couldn't be, it was nothing but a quaint conceit to write it like that, an amusing trick. So women, since Eve, have always tried to slide round difficulties.

I had been doubting whether I ought to go on. I wanted to but we had smashed so much since we left; we had done all the things that ordinary, insensitive, prosaic, evil-wishing people had said we should. We had quarrelled over money, we had flown into senseless rages, we had been frightened of each other and jealous of amities and irritated to murder. We had made affection between the sexes illicit and we had made plain-speaking impossible.

Yet there had been compensations, beauties of sea and wind and sky, anticipations of untrammelled adventuring, moments of beauty. It was worth going on. Sven would be a friend, though all friendship was a tattered banner. Three days later we sailed.

CHAPTER VII

BRIBIE ISLAND

On the last day of our stay in Brisbane Joan had handed me the financial statement for the expenses of the past six months. It had now no significance for me. The planning for adventure was over. We had a boatload of provisions and about £10 in boat funds and the possibility of raising more by articles. I had said that I should be leaving at Singapore because time, though it did not matter to the others, did to me. I had leave of absence from my job and some work to do in London on account of it. Ruth, Sven and I had about £50 each for incidental expenses and travelling. Money no longer interested us except as a horizon problem. For weeks at a time we were to live without need of touching coinage. We certainly had to write some articles to pay off an advance we had received from a newspaper and we were to feel the lack of money in some ports, but living to the daily accompaniment of account rendered, change madam, fares please and salary received was over. We had passed out of it. I was on holiday at last.

The sense of holiday began at Bribie Island, the twenty-mile-long morsel of land held in the northern jaw of the wide-open mouth of Moreton Bay.

We were weather-bound there for three days and the first day we made a picnic of it, going for a walk to the seaward beach of the island. It had been raining, the sandy ground had soaked up the water, the sky had been washed clean, was pale blue and damp, streaked with white clouds, like the face of an Australian wild violet dewy in the early morning. Every twig and moisture-holding bract of the scrubby foliage was vital with the rain, was expanding and soaking it up, storing it. Little birds moved swiftly in the thickets, honey-eaters and tits. They penetrated the thorny fastnesses of the grevillia and the twiggy ambushes of the ti-tree like sharp-pointed arrows, like coloured shuttles flying. It seemed surely that the next moment one or another would be impaled, spiked through its feathered breast, but no, their twittering and cheeping continued, was of the earth joyous. We walked talking of wayside things; or not talking and enjoying the quietness, the expanse of space, the straight red road with its puddles, the tall bracken under which one expected to see large rabbits, like domestic cats, sitting up and delicately washing their faces. Except for the road the bush looked untouched as if it were in the same half-receptive, half-antagonistic condition as when Flinders first set foot there.

It was he who had named the point off which we lay Skirmish Point; his sloop, the *Norfolk*, was leaking badly and he had beached it up the Bribie channel and caulked it. Flinder had found the Bribie Island blacks, notorious cannibals, unattractive. He writes, 'One had more the appearance of a baboon than of a human being. He was covered with oily soot; his hair matted with filth, his visage even among his fellows, uncommonly ferocious; and his very large mouth beset with teeth of every hue between black, white, green and yellow, sometimes presented a smile which might make anyone shudder.'

Both Englishmen and aboriginals were alien to the emptiness of this rain-washed morning on Bribie Island. The Englishmen had gone away, their ghosts would never trouble the thin soil. The ghosts of the native Bribie Islanders were otherwhither but they would come back, for here was their habitat. On moonlight nights they would glide, the shadows of shadows, behind the spotted gums and move more quietly than the wind past the ti-trees.

We walked in the edge of the surf. The water was cold and dirty with scraps of black pumice, river wreckage and jetsam floating in the yellow soiled foam. There was a fierce undercurrent, the waves slapped up out of deep water and hooped hollowly down with a hiss like so many serpents holding their tails in their mouths. We built a fire and had lunch. A black vagrant dog nosed about us. He was attractive but hunger had made him over-friendly and cowardly at the same time. It came on to rain again and we sheltered under the veranda of a shack, somebody's holiday residence. Then, when the shower was over, we set out again for the boat, home – we were a family going home. We had not meant to do anything with this day but enjoy ourselves, we had been lazy though pretending to bursts of energy and occasionally running for fifty yards or so. Altogether we had walked not more than eight miles yet somehow we had accomplished vaguely that intangible thing, happiness, or, for it was perhaps not so radiant as happiness, content. There was the picnic feeling about us. We had not had to appear before any outsiders and like a family we did not feel that we were bound to please each other. We were all separate and a bit hard enjoying ourselves.

There was the inevitability of going on about us and the memory besides of other walks, many just such pointless all-day bush rambles. We breathed the same familiar aromatic quick scents of the bush, the tang of bottle-brush and wild honeysuckle, young gum leaves and bracken. They were held in under the heavy cover of salt air that swept in on the storm breeze from the ocean.

Sven was brown-legged, bare-footed, wearing a big grass hat and swinging a bush stick as he walked. He swaggered. The night before the fire seemed remote, as if it had not been. He knew I had flirted and prevaricated and put him off, that I had lost interest in him on shore and that I had thoroughly enjoyed the fuss that was made of me. He had understood that. Now he showed me how inadequate women were in throwing stones, running, making grass-whistles, calling a dog to heel, and every time he beat me he grinned, the superior grin of the showing-off male, eldest and strongest of a large family, lots of them sisters.

I retaliated, jeering at his feet. I told him my first impression of them, 'Like a gorilla's'. They had indeed been hardly human.

77

Weeks of being shoeless on deck had made his naturally short, broad foot splay out till the big toe became a grasping unit and the sole calloused iron hard. The sun had blackened the upper sides and the continued action of sea water had cracked and scaled the skin till it was tough as crocodile hide and leprous as a cast snake-skin. He had bought new shoes in Brisbane but how he had managed to get his feet into any shoes had been a puzzle.

Presently we came to the Novelty Gardens that all the people on this empty holiday-making island had told us to be sure to see. An old man had turned hundreds of cypress pines into railway carriages, peacocks, coats of arms, letters of the alphabet. It had been a laborious process of years, slow, unbeautiful, useless. By the tormented trees was a sea eagle chained. There was the odour of caged animals and birds. I wanted to get away. Visions of the schoolrooms I had left came over me, the rows of bent backs, the immovably clamped down desks and seats, the heads dutifully bent over composition books, the fingers that ought to have been catching balls and making things stiffening on pens in laborious unnecessary writing, the shoulders hunched forwards by sitting still, lopsided through carrying heavy school-bags; the harsh light streaming through bare ugly windows, and always, day after day, those two ogres of mass education, perpetual tidiness and perpetually enforced quiet. I was guilty. I had cracked the whip of discipline with its lash of punishments over those bent backs. That was why I wanted to get away.

The cypress pines were the old man's slaves; they would never toss their branches in the wind or nod their plumy tops at dawn, for them would never be the exultant resistance of planted strength against moving force; the utmost limits of their freedom would be a constrained trembling, a painful shivering, while about them rose the untrammelled bush. I wanted to apologize to them for the brutality of mankind; they made me ashamed to have been a slave-driver of children, beneficent but a slave-driver.

While we deplored his taste we could not but admire the old

78

man's ingenuity of stake, pruning and wire. He was an octo-
genarian wit. 'Here is Tutankhamen, the chap with the gold
teeth. He had forty wives, eh boy!' At this point a lewd nudge in
Henery's ribs. Or, 'I've been three years getting that bunch of
flowers there and now Mr. Punch will always carry a nosegay.'

Before we went he and his wife and daughter sang us Welsh
hymns and the national anthem. There is always an association
for me between revival hymns and the punishment of children,
due perhaps to a Welsh grandfather and hours of long leg-dangling
sermon times. So, for me, this singing farewell rounded off the
visit with a peculiar completeness. My visions of children in
school had not been so inapt after all, the Welsh gardener had had
the revival zeal, he had been a blind missionary, his converts trees.
By the door was a big collection box.

Next day in order to avoid the swell we moved *Skaga* nearer the
back channel, just off the Talbot Point Post Office. The weather
was still squally with occasional showers of rain. Some week-end
fishermen came down and anchored near us and Sven and Henery
went across to fraternize. Pleading an article that I had under-
taken to do I went ashore, waterproofed and with a rug and a
bottle of ink. There was only the one house, grey, iron-roofed,
high on its piles like an elevated bee-hive; in front of it a large
boat-shed with the timbers of a broken jetty running out and the
stakes of an oyster lease. The wooded flats, the distant blue hills,
the water a muddy green and the sky grey with the presage of
rain made a scene dolorous as a harp accompaniment to an old
song. I plunged away from the house through the long sword
grass to a lair under some she-oaks and lay idly watching two
herons that had come down to fish. It was a delight to rest, to
be alone, to do nothing. It began to rain, gently, beading the
needles of the she-oaks, dewing my coat and cap with moisture,
shining on the grass and running in thin trickles down the folds
of the waterproof. A wind cold and cheerless came over the water.

I huddled myself inside the rug and commenced a long letter.
How pleasant it was to be writing to someone beloved, writing

intimately. I struggled to express my longing for the return of dear things, the sudden flash of a smile, the softening of a glance, the exquisite exactness of a gesture like a cadence of music; the serenity of the secure, the well-known mode of living. Yet I went on to laud the newly-acquired sense of independence, the freedom, the marvellous freedom of not having to go to work punctually at nine with the bells ringing, the feeling of being an entity on one's own, not half of a social duo; even if one made mistakes and fell down and was disappointed and elated unreasonably there was the intoxication of responsibility. I wrote my aspirations, solemnly. I was not to be hurt by random shots, I was to cultivate an insensibility to trifles instead of letting them lacerate me, to concentrate on external things. There was a lot in it too of effort, of overcoming laziness, babbling and shallowness, of becoming silent, quiet-thinking, as I thought Joyce was.

Oh these strivings for the ideal self, the substitution of new Will for old Conscience, a substitution that is like nothing else but a change of ministry in the government with all the machinery of bureaucracy functioning just the same, fears and habits and old disappointments. The aspirations and guilts that lead the same tortured 'I' along the same rutted tracks with merely the signposts changed, and instead of the devil and the vices slackness of purpose and instability pointing the downward path.

It had stopped raining. I was being stalked. I looked round and saw nothing, but when I began to write again the rustling that was not due to the wind began also, I stopped and without moving listened. Then I turned my head slowly and caught sight of something dark crawling in the long rushes behind my back. A dog? I waited. No, it was a child, a little girl with black curly hair tossed over her forehead, wearing a dark jersey and having blue print hind-quarters that jutted as she crawled. She got closer, thinking herself unobserved, and after a while she rushed at me, instantly retreating with shyness and then circling round me at a safe distance, frolicking.

Her name was Patsy. She was about four. She lived here at

Talbot Point, 'Hungry Point, Mummy calls it'. She was full of information. 'I have a dog, his name is Jock.' 'Down by the mangoes we saw a little wild cat.' She was rather like a wild-cat kitten herself, fearless and wanting to talk and play. We raced to the mangoes, crossing a stubble field where her bare feet did not falter; we knocked the heads off some toadstools. Her clothing was damp, almost wet through. Hadn't she better go back to her Mummy? Not a bit of it, Mummy didn't mind wet clothes. We came back to the lair under the she-oaks. We romped and she was ticklish. I said I had to write, and without waiting to be asked she trustfully snuggled herself in beside me under the waterproof, a kitten all wet fur and warmth. We shared some biscuits and dates I had with me.

'Who are you writing to?'

'My Daddy.'

'What is he like?'

Ah, here was a sympathetic audience at last. I grabbed for those essentials that four-year-olds most approve. She approved. He was evidently a nice man but could he catch fish? No, he had never caught a fish. Her Mummy's Daddy caught lots of fish. He caught more fish than anyone. He had caught a shark, words failed to indicate its size. She did her best to cheer me up because my Daddy caught no fish but she really did not intend to let me go on writing. After an hour there was nothing to do but to send her home. In a few minutes she came trickling back, supported by Jock, a half-bred Aberdeen. A game was indicated. We played hiding from Jock and then we took him on the mud and watched him bail up a crab. Patsy told how once a crab had clung to his inquisitive nose and he couldn't shake it off. She danced to show the frenzy of the dog-crab constellation.

I took her home. Her mother was not in the least perturbed at her wetness. Patsy was always in the water or the rain and was never ill. They made me sit on the wide veranda at a little table and tried to keep Patsy off. We all talked. I heard the latest gossip from Brisbane, that is what country telephone exchanges are for. We discussed blouse patterns and the *Mother's Mirror*. They were the perfect type of 'Our Readers Outback'. There was another woman there and a grandmother, too. In the kitchen we ate 'griddlers', a sort of scone, and I learnt to make them in a frying pan, an accomplishment that came in handy later on. The women were all very interested in how we cooked on board. At last for shame's sake I went back to the veranda and did a few pages of the article.

At sunset, a sudden flush of pink on the faded cheeks of the grey afternoon, Sven came to take me back. The tide was dead low and the long expanse of mud pitted with crab holes and crawling with life. There were regiments of round-bodied soldier crabs, the kind whose legs do not spread sideways but stand switchbacked like open safety pins holding the body high off the ground. Their bellies were yellowish, the legs mud-coloured, and the backs a vivid blue, the blue of enamelled forget-me-nots. They moved together, a contingent of foragers, packed close, spreading for yards and yards, in a rectangular formation, a flower bed blooming on the mud. Jock turned a machine-gun fire of barking on them and they executed a drilled flank movement with a scuttling flourish of generalship, but they did not retire to their dug-outs. Jock danced round, his claws mud-scattering, putting over a barrage of sound. The army moved in the opposite direction, sideways and backwards, a perfect retreat in good order. They were undaunted. Jock continued to harass them but he had no tactics left in reserve, so, worn out at last, he pretended his throat was sore, lapped ostentatiously at a salt pool, avoided a second and larger army of blue-backs and ran home to his kennel under the house.

We walked on, Patsy capering. Then on a log in the mud we caught sight of a pelican very busy fishing. I had never seen a pelican outside a zoo before. We stopped, hushing Patsy. How grotesque his bill was, his shape made him look like a sour school-master in academic dress, arms in wide sleeves, gown tucked across stomach. He noticed us and with a glance of calm dignity went on fishing. Then he suddenly swooped like a heavy bolt from a cross-bow and came up, the fish gleaming, held crosswise. He gulped and the fish fell featly into the pouch like a letter being posted. He looked at us complacently as much as to say, 'How's that, umpire?' and we could not help laughing. So he flapped away, annoyed, to another fishing site and as he went I longed to give him a more appropriate, more scholarly tail than his own, for surely he needed the rusty, green-black, torn-a-little tail of an old professorial gown.

But the best of the day was yet to come. We stood watching the last flushes of sunset die away. In the east was a false glow, pink almost to the dome of the sky. Against the greyness of evening the she-oaks stood out black, a decorative frieze. Out of the sky came two shapes flying, broad-winged, and rested perched above the mud. By the shout of flame as they folded their wings, by the vermilion of their tall legs, by the grace of their long necks and slender sharp beaks, by a thousand often-ignored pictures we knew them, flamingoes! They sealed in our remembrance this mediocre grey and pink sunset for ever.

For a few minutes they poked in the mud and we wondered at their big and clumsy feet, what they did with them flying. Then something startled them, perhaps it was Patsy, she could not keep still, and they showed us how it was managed: Folding the hanging legs up and back slowly, like part of a machine being wound away, till only the feet protruded, a double, webbed rudder, they flew over us – we thought from the manner of the flight they were tired – two wedges of darkness moving into the composition of flat shore, she-oaks and evening sky.

CHAPTER VIII

TOWARDS THE BARRIER REEF

ON May 31st we left Bribie Island for the Barrier Reef. We had planned visits to a series of island groups, and sailed out by the north-west channel keeping close to the low scrubby eastern side of Bribie Island.

The strange shapes of the Glass House Mountains rose on our lee bow. They were named by Cook who considered them 're-markable on account of their Singulare form of Elivation which much resembles Glass Houses'. A commonplace comparison and one felt inadequate. As we brought them abeam their contours altered, a curious pinnacle of rock projected from one of them – they were swathed in soft blue mist as alluring and mys-terious as their aboriginal names, Beear-burrum, Toomboom-boolla, Coona-warren. They are the cores of old volcanoes and they remain, rounded down by time but still malevolent in out-line, like satiric old ladies with shawls about their humped shoul-ders, hinting of forgotten fierce ardours and bearing a mute testimony of the geological antiquity of the Australian continent.

We had a strong wind behind us and a fair but not heavy swell. The water was green and turbulent from the effects of the storm. Joan and Ruth were sea-sick and remained in that low-pressure bunk-bound existence for a few days. I was robustly well, I enjoyed my long three-hour turn at the tiller during the middle of the day while Sven in the galley below cooked a stew. It was very good.

For the first time I tried out my fishing gear. It took a long time to rig and I had forgotten the knot that ought to have secured the fine green line to the steel trace. I had learnt it laboriously, carefully, just before sailing, and now after a month I had forgotten it. Sven tried a fisherman's bend but I protested that it was not a fisherman's bend. He thought he knew most of the knots that were to be made but none of his was the knot I had learnt and forgotten, for it was a special knot, one of those secrets handed on from one expert to another, a flat-lying, even-pulling, stress-distributed, non-twisting kind of knot that rose to the level of a first-class problem between us. Weeks later a professional fisherman made it for me and said he knew no name for it. It must have been on the index of sailor's knots. I never could be sure of producing it.

In spite of the presence of six months' stores, hanging bunches of bananas, baskets of custard apples, a swinging side of bacon, cheeses, a sack of rice, tins of biscuits and loaves of bread there seemed more room on board. Nobody said anything about it but we were all relieved by the absence of the sixth man. We hardly thought of Cooper again. We were quieter.

Sunset was wild and splendid, wind-streaked, with a few heavy low-moving clouds. One of them was large and dark with open jaws, to my fancy, fishing-excited, like a big schnapper ready to take the golden bait heaven dangled before it. Gradually it moved closer to the setting sun, the two jaws snapped together, the body of the cloud covered the red disc, the sun had been swallowed. Night came quickly, the green stormy waves turned black, there were no wave crests to be seen, blackness obliterated us on the face of the waters, the night had swallowed us too.

It was a night sleepless for me because of the restless night noises, the slapping of the water, the creaking of the timbers, the changing of the watches. Yet I was not unhappy, I was part of it, I had my place.

Next day Ruth was better but not well. She was suffering from seasickness and the results of her vaccination. We had all 'taken' but Ruth and Sven best – or worst. Ruth's arm was dreadful to see and she began to be afflicted with many small boils on her back. I was cook and planned a noble menu, for breakfast her favourite wheat porridge, boiled eggs and coffee. For dinner a fresh soup, boiled bacon with carrots and potatoes and home-made rosella pickle that the baker's wife on Bribie Island had given us, and then the culinary triumph of the day, apple dumplings. I had acquired the recipe in Brisbane as one suitable to boat cookery and the secret of it was not to lift the lid, however sorely tempted, for twenty minutes. Henery, Sven and I were properly appreciative of these dumplings, Joan and Ruth timid, not trusting themselves.

It was warm and pleasant in the sun on deck. We were sailing well. Once past Great Sandy Island and the dangers of Break Sea Spit we followed the steamer route to Bustard Head, whereas Cook with gentle breezes and variable light airs had sailed west following the trend of the land into Hervey Bay. I was beginning to study the route of the great navigator. It was part of the work I had laid down for myself. Ruth made a roster of cook-days and watches. She did it well; she had had practice in time-tables. Cook-day was looked on as an irksome duty that had to be offset by freedom from watches and unbroken rest the night before, so the nautical time-table revolved round cook-day. Ruth numbered us off and as I was cook that day my number was 1.

'Why,' Henery wanted to know, 'Why is Dona 1? Why? and Why?' He slowly rolled a cigarette. The exposition began and continued and was repeated and explained nothing. Was there a talismanic sense about the numeral 1? Could it alone convey the importance of first place? In living have some people to be compensated for like clock pendulums, extra weights added, guarantees of esteem?

'Oh, very well,' snarled Ruth, he was after all the layman when it came to time-tables, and she wrote us down in another way.

When the last plate was washed up that night I got out my letters and read them. They heartened me, they were so gay, so light-hearted, of a different world, unproblematical. I went to bed and did not sleep for a long time. The boat laboured, the wind had come up, the motion was uneasy, straining, with hints of violence. Was Ruth sleeping? I felt she was not. I wished she would speak to me out of the darkness. Perhaps she was asleep – I should not waken her. Sven, sleeping head to head with me, became aware that I was awake and restless. A horny hand came round the wooden partition, groped for a moment or two among my hair on the pillow. I put my hand up in response, it was grasped, held firmly and released, patted again and put down. I enjoyed the confidence of that grasp, the realization that someone cared that I was oppressed and wakeful. The multitude of sounds ceased to distress me. It was as if he had sensed my need evoked by the night and the condition of the sea, that he also was susceptible to these influences, harrowed by the jerking abruptness of the rise and fall. At last I fell to sleep.

It was my watch next day from six till nine a.m. Morning came to us gradually without any blushes on her face. I had a bucket bath. It was cold in the wind. Joan had one after me and it upset her, she was extremely ill. 'Ridiculous,' thought I from the superiority of my wellness, 'this continual sea-sickness, she ought to be used to the motion now . . . I wonder . . .' (Oh heart, had she not said, 'You ought to be hardened off by now,' and had not my heart hardened then and was I not secretly glad that I had hardened while she still could not control her nausea?) 'Yet perhaps . . .' I foresaw all kinds of situations and myself with her in them being very heroic and competent . . . I became bad-tempered with myself, first at my naive glee at her discomfort and then at these musings that were so vainglorious, so adolescent and – if I knew them to be so, why did I find pleasure in fabricating them? Let the hero-worshipping sentiment die quickly, not prolong its unwanted existence.

I took myself and my despondent thoughts up into the spray and the sun in the bows and it felt as if I were bringing musty old clothes out of a dark cupboard and airing them. There was a moderate breeze and we were steering well into it. Ruth was cook to make the roster come right. She had begged for ideas and I had made a suggestion and now I heard bacon sizzling in the pan. Poor Joan.

I read desultorily in *Cook's Journal* of the 'drunken frolic' that occurred when the *Endeavour* was becalmed off Bustard Bay, where we now were. In that escapade Mr. Orton, a clerk, had had not only his clothes cut from his back as he lay in a drunken stupor but part of his ears as well: 'An extraordinary affair to happen in the middle watch,' wrote Cook, who suspected Midshipman Magra and suspended him from duty with the bitter comment that he 'was one of those gentlemen frequently to be found aboard King's ships that can very well be spared'. Cook had the prejudice of those risen by diligence against the frivolous who acquired position by birth. Would we ever be so bored, so antagonistic, that drunken stupors and fisticuffs frolics could occur? Almost.

Among a large crew, such a brawl could be put down as a 'frolic', with a small crew it must be a tragedy. The *Endeavour* men had been bored, ready for mischief. The incident had seriously disturbed the dignified Cook, who kept as by a natural gift the perfect command, the most easy and rightful discipline. He was betrayed by the 'frolic' into one of the few patches of philosophizing that occur in the *Journal*. These pages showed the navigator puzzled, worried by his problem of personal relationships. Strange how Cook leaves on one the impression of an oil painting, warm, living but aloof; as a character a noble work of art, one admires intensely and moves on, awed by the publicness of his progress, the integrity of his conduct and career, the soundness of his instincts.

I iodined Ruth's back. She was a veritable Job. It looked like a sepia landscape when I had finished. Sven had a sore finger. It was rather mysterious. The index finger on the right hand had swelled to about twice its size and was sore and painful with hardly an indication of where a puncture or splinter might exist. He could bend it and do with it all that a finger usually does but it had been hurting for a fortnight. I had suggested hot foments and a probe, Ruth a poultice. Sven had decided on a poultice. I poulticed until there was no more bread and the finger was still the same. Perhaps it needed cold water compresses? Cold water compresses he could manage himself. The finger remained obstinate. Henery at the same time strained his shoulder and though Joan rubbed it a lot, it got no better. She was looking very yellow herself. I was the only flagrantly well one. These petty ills gave us something to think about. There were all the diseases ahead that we had been warned of, malaria, dhobie itch, beri beri.

Next day, June 6th, 1932, we were practically becalmed off Bustard Bay. Morning seeped up out of the sea, which was dark, almost black. We were well in under the headland. The sky above was a dirty grey with rain clouds, to the south and north-west lay a coastline, with serrated hills like superimposed rows of saw teeth, outlined by a band of clear yellow-green behind them and cut off from the rest of the sky by long strata clouds of dark mauve. The mainland was an intense blue. To the north rose a small island, high and bursting in light brown at the top like a freshly-baked cake. On our quarter was a tiny settlement clustered beneath the lighthouse, on the brown hillside it looked like a hurled snowball.

The Brisbane specialist had spoken to me of logging the psychologic effect of the weather on us, he thought that clouds, rain, bad weather brought a depression in the spirits but it seemed that wind on a sailing cruise is more important than sunshine or shadow; given motion there is also freedom, spontaneity, goodwill; with repose comes reflection and subtle insistence on oneself. The absence of wind made me lazy, when I was not on watch I lay curled up on the old jib in the bows reading short stories and eating the last of some chocolate. Sven, despite his sore hand, was making a strop for the squaresail yard. At night I did exercises, skipping a little and then bucketing. The night was perfectly black, the air cold and the water after the first shock by comparison warm. Phosphorescent animalculae made a brave show, sparkling diamond bright as the water slipped over the skin, catching in the hair, frosting the lip of the bucket, falling to the deck in showers like raindrops turned to glass and unexpectedly not tinkling as they broke, then scattering in splintered constellations and pouring over the side into the sea.

I had the 3 a.m. to 5.30 a.m. watch. A wind had sprung up, glorious, the wake was a white fleece rippling. The binnacle light went out. I steered by the stars, occasionally flashing the torch on the compass. Then in attempting to re-light the lamp, I almost put her about and had to call Sven up. I got her back on her course and feared to be reprimanded but the lamp created a diversion; it was empty and had to be refilled. Sven grumbled, it was Henery's turn. 'The kind of thing that's always happening. Then he thinks I fuss . . . but . . .' the nautical possibilities were unrolled for my benefit. I soothed, he went below, made certain calculations and then altered the course.

Another dawn came, grey and as if hesitating. I felt invigorated by the wind and wanted the day to be creative, productive. I went below and began to add to my letter, but there was Ruth's back to be done and then breakfast to be eaten and the cabin to be straightened. At last I got back to my writing. Sven came down from his watch. Joan had been late in relieving him and, what was worse, casual about the lateness. Usually he was generous with the lap-over on the watch, but this morning he had been anxiously waiting to be relieved, besides which the incident of the unfilled binnacle lamp still rankled. His finger hurt more and he thought he would try a hot foment.

I was in charge of the medicines. I put my writing-pad away and decided to get the business over quickly, but quickness and cutter life were more or less incompatible. There was hot water to get and to get it primuses to light, the cook Henery to be disturbed to do so, a needle and the bowl to be sterilized, and an assortment of salves to be found. Sven was very trusting but he howled that the foment was too hot and shook it off. I considered that strong men could be babies and that a hot foment could never be too hot. I put another on. He complained. The water was cooling, the primus out. I could see that finger indefinitely and mysteriously sore and I wanted to get back to the letter. 'Put it in,' I commanded. He whisked the finger in and out of the reserve mug of hot boracic water. 'Oh keep it there, don't be a baby,' and I put my hand over his and held it down firmly while my eye flickered over the last sentence beside me. At this moment Ruth appeared. She had been sharpening a pencil and sweeping up the bits. The Florence Nightingale touch disturbed her.

'Let him hold it in himself,' she burst out in a blaze of passion. We looked up incredulous at the tone and she countered in instant defence, 'The water isn't a bit hot. Look . . .' and she plunged quickly in and out her own distinctly grubby forefinger. Oh, so. It was as if Jehovah had spoken in a lightning flash from his obscure mountain cloud.

'I took a lot of trouble sterilizing that mug of water, you can get some more and finish the job off yourself if you want to. I don't.' There was a convincing ring about this; we so seldom made direct statements. Sven looked a bit bewildered. I turned to the letter beside me. Joan came in from for'ard, stooping to get in and then straightening up. She had a clean yellow linen hat on and under it her eyes were wide and startled. Her expression said, 'Hullo, what's this? *Ruth* breaking out?'

'It's quite clean,' said Ruth, holding up her finger, but the evidence of hand and wrist belied the statement, and the body of public opinion present said nothing.

Sven made a movement to tend himself and fumbled clumsily with the bandages I had got ready. 'I think it's had enough now anyway,' I announced. I could afford to be generous, I was still startled by the suddenness of the outburst, the importance of unimportant things. How intimate we must be, how extraordinarily attuned to feel the same about the little things. I had been feeling ordinary, practical, unemotional, somewhat bored and impatient at the bathing, while Ruth had been seething with annoyance and complicated emotions. She went away, Joan began to roll a cigarette. The incident was over, but not quite. I was looking for the suspected splinter and Sven's free hand crept over my left hand as it rested on his wrist and gave it a prodigious squeeze, an overt schoolboyish squeeze. I looked up, he was staring at the porthole opposite in assumed innocence, as if disclaiming any responsibility for anything his hand might do. I looked at Joan. She must have seen that squeeze. Our eyes met. I grinned. She smiled too, with me, not at me, the first friendly motion for weeks. It was a delicious moment. The whole episode from the beginning was tinged with humour. We both glanced at Sven, he was still staring at the porthole. 'Does it hurt there, Sven?' I asked, and through my heart sang an echo, 'My enemy drew nigh . . . and I . . . should have kissed him if I had not fled.' Joan went to finish her watch, Henery had been minding the tiller for her.

The day was a good one, at peace with me. I wrote a great deal. It seemed to me possible that if Joan and I could still understand the same values in living she must continue to appreciate some of my qualities in the old way, not condemn me utterly. Maybe the row was only a black frost that could blight but not entirely destroy.

At 1 a.m. that night Ruth called me to relieve her. The wind was favourable, the tiller stiff. We chatted for a moment or two, the binnacle had been misbehaving and the watch by which the helmsman told the time had stopped. The light on Bustard Head was visible. Sven was to be called when it came abeam. She handed over the sea coat she had been wearing, for the night was very cold.

Night watch again, still no moon and the light on Bustard Head an eye winking through the darkness.

> 'Oh no, it is an ever fixed beam
> That alters not. . . .'

Long vague thoughts drifted by. How different all this was. When in an ordinary life did a woman get a feeling of isolation, of dead midnight? In sick watches perhaps. Here was I steering a boat, wide awake, a responsible person not a domestic missus with her head on a pillow sleeping easily . . . I recollected our blue satin sheets. Those sheets were a luxury symbol, so cat-sleek, so becoming, so turned-down, smooth as flowing water; waiting to receive one after a late night, glamorous to creep between them and switch off the shaded light. I rubbed my cheek on the collar of the sea coat and ran my hand up and down the coarse canvas. My nails grated on the texture and I took the accompanying shudder gratefully for I preferred the canvas – infinitely. Down with satin sheets! If women kept awake sometimes and went out walking in the night, in the great quiet of night, might it not lift us off our feet just a little, out of the pettiness of day to day living, the ever-present closeness of walls and floors, dishes and pillow-cases? Did nurses and men on night shift coming home from furnaces and printing presses feel occasionally as they walked the great eyelid of the world shutting over them and rolling back. Did it stamp them with a difference from the day creatures, the sleeping ones?

The course was taking us very close to the lighthouse. Perhaps it was too close? Perhaps I had made an error or not listened properly when taking over. There was another light. It progressed steadily, was it a ship coming towards us or another land light? I stood up to have a better look and almost let her gybe. Sven sprang up at the flutter of canvas. We were nearly abeam of the Bustard Head light. The other light was a steamer. It passed very close. We carried no sidelights, possibly we were invisible to them, fellow wayfarers black as assassins in the gloom, a mere periwinkle shell floating. Henery came up. They altered the course. At 3 a.m. I went down, tired. I slept soundly, entered at last on the new routine of living.

CHAPTER IX

FIRST BARRIER REEF ISLANDS

WE were busy, happy, and had nautical aspirations. Sven showed us how to plot our position from three bearings; then I was 'boy' while he 'served', that is he used a serving mallet to wind spun yarn round a wire rope neatly and firmly. It was a strop to go on the squaresail yard and had two eyes at each end and a thimble for the hook to go through in the centre.

I took the 10.30 p.m. to 1.0 a.m. watch that night and only remember how long it seemed and the damperish indigestion I had.

Next came a day chiefly memorable for the hoisting of the squaresail, a curious sail, perfectly square, hoisted on a yard in front of the mast and bellying loose like those in pictures of old Viking ships. It had come with the *Skaga* from Sweden and had worn thin with the long run on the trade winds across the Pacific. It was patterned all over with mildew, and since our acquisition of the boat it had not been used; the heavy yard for it had been lashed along the deck, a prodigious piece of timber for so small a craft. At first the yard was incorrectly adjusted and the sail swayed to and fro like the breasts of a big and slovenly woman, loose and sideways sloppy. They lowered it.

Sven went up by the stays to fix the tackle that raised the yard. He swung to the mast – there were no cradles for the mainsail was down – and tied a rope from stay to stay high up. Then he stood on the rope he had just tied. One must be sure of one's knots to do that in a pitching sea. As I watched from the tiller his body swung in an arc through the reeling sky. It looked dangerous. I was full of admiration. He had the assuredness of years of sea-craft about him. For the first time I realized that his was the typical build of the sailor, short-legged, thick-chested, arms with muscles knotted like cables; the lines of the face, although he was only thirty, already deeply scored by exposure; the eyes blue like the sea on a dull day, puckered in the corners, long-sighted; the hair sandy, straight and coarse, obstinately unmanageable, sticking up like tufts of beach grass, in port horribly oiled down; his hands broad, scarred and calloused from his employment. Generations of seamen had formed him for what he was.

Steering under the new rig seemed awkward at first, uncontrolled, but by adjusting the braces and slewing the yard it was easier and freer than the fore and aft rig; and with a good wind in it the very shape of the sail looked exhilarating.

We passed by Port Curtis, its magnificent harbour sandbanked at the entrance, without wanting to go in. We were making for the Percy Islands.

Another sea day passed. Early the following morning the islands showed up, blue and high. A few miles before making our anchorage I caught my first, and only, big game fish by trolling. I had flung the silver-gilt spinner overboard without thinking that there might be a fish ready to take the bait, and was adjusting the harness designated to hold the butt of the rod when there was a sudden formidable tug and the line whizzing out from the reel with a noise like an aeroplane engine. I made frantic efforts to check it, I did not want the line to overwind, slacken and lose the fish. Foolishly I let the palm of my hand touch the line as it was running out, it raised a blister over a long deep burn. After the first mad rush I began to wind in. Sven at the tiller had brought her up into the wind as much as he could without stopping for there were currents and rocks and he was anxious.

At last I could see the silver gleam of fish, then I had to give it a short run again. The reel, not securely lashed, was wobbling on the rod. Henery came up and finished hauling in the line hand over hand. It was a very fine line and I was frightened of it breaking. We had no gaff so he yanked the fish on board, a thirty-odd pound mackerel. It was the first big edible fish of the cruise.

Ruth's exclamations were sweet to hear. Henery took photographs.

Sven brought us back to the immanent nearness of the Percy Islands. We were sailing in a mile-and-a-half-wide channel between Middle Island, the main island of the group, and two others, on one of which stood a lighthouse. The other was only an islet with two spits of rock running out from it. All the islands were densely wooded and rocky, but the precipitous sides of Middle Island were interrupted by a small white beach in the shelter of a bay, our anchorage. On the north rose the green swell of a cleared hill that looked as if stock had grazed there. We dropped anchor a fair way out and rowed to the beach where there were two sheds of slab and corrugated iron, one with shut doors and the other open. On the left hand the beach ended in rocks and hills that fell sheer to the water. On the right lay the entrance, marked by mangrove swamps, of a lagoon into which a creek of good water ran, cascading down a fantastic porphyritic bed. Behind the swamp rose the green hill. Big mud oysters, large as the palm of one's hand, grew in the lagoon and sandflies teemed there.

With the little islands, the beach, the lighthouse rising from pine trees, it was a water-colour scene, of the sort that is copied on picture-postcards, and the feeling of it, though it was north of Capricorn, was essentially temperate. The wash of watery blue in the sky, the green of the sea, the dark foliage of the pines were temperate too. We saw it in May, before the hot season.

This was probably one of the earliest islands in the Barrier to be settled and in its size, isolation and the use to which it is put by a single patriarchal family it is typical of a number of other large and temperate Barrier Islands that are used as sheep stations. Mr. White, who at present holds a twenty-years' lease of it from the Queensland government and has lived there for the past fourteen years, took it over from a Colonel Armitage who had it for the previous twenty, and an old retired skipper said that when he called in in 1877 a shipwright named Jimmie Ross was living there and had been for a number of years. Ross had had a companion at one time, a man whose grave is on the island, and there is a story of buried treasure not yet located, probably the savings of the shipwright, who could not read or write.

The island is about 4,500 acres with 1,500 sheep on it and many wild goats. The highest point is 816 feet and the house is built on piles and with cool verandas shaded by venerable mango trees at about the 700 feet level. This means a troublesome climb with pack horses up the steep foot-path but living is pleasanter at that height than near the beach. The island would be worth more if it were not for the problem of transport, for instance poultry do well but there is no profit in taking them to the mainland. The freight on a single bale of wool to the nearest port is over £1. No boats call there. Stores and mail come once a month by courtesy of the lighthouse supply service.

The path to the house was up a hill through heavily timbered country with coarse grass knee high and bladed on both edges. We walked through a sea of fallen gum blossom, their fringed heads still fresh and open, wet from a light rain. We had never seen such a profusion of bloom. It was extraordinary, too, that the flower heads had all been broken off in their clusters four or five inches down the main stem. We could not remember a wind so recent as to have wrought this damage, and its regularity and the absence of any big broken branches were puzzling till one noticed the cockatoos, both black and white, that were screeching in flocks overhead making the air dizzy with protest. Sometimes a blossoming twig would fall sharply, but not by watching could we catch them at work, sawing with their beaks at the tough stems to get at the juices, sweet parrot nectar, within. It was hard to say if the heady liquor had had any effect on them, their flight was still steady, though they only essayed short distances – but to a keen ear there seemed a shade more vituperation in their garrulity than usual. They scolded us unceasingly as we walked and clearly they could bear to brook no contradiction.

We crossed a small creek and went up a long steep hillside, the sandy path strewn with she-oak needles, then down a sharp descent and up again on hard ground from which all the soil had been washed leaving brown knobbly boulders. We came at last, after a detour through wild and basaltic country, to the plateau of the island where there were patches of couch grass nibbled short by the sheep. On a ridge near the house grew straight grey-trunked hoop pines, three hundred years old at least and consequently indigenous. Only occasionally in the underbrush was there a clump of vivid green, flag of a vegetative tropical outpost, and the stiff and saluting fingers of pandanus palms strange to us.

Mr. White welcomed us and gave us home-made mango wine, a greenish amber in colour, in texture like a dry sherry a little thin, with an acid tang of fruited fire in it and a distinct but not overpowering flavour of mango.

He had heard of us and the dinghy adventure over the radio, and he was a cheerful host. Once a cattle rancher in Canada and the States he had scores of anecdotes to tell us, of musters and fire-fighting and stampedes. We talked till Harold, the younger of his two sons, came in. The elder brother was on a health trip to the mainland. Harold was excited and pleased by this sudden invasion of visitors, two men and three women in shorts, with rapscallion knapsacks and insatiable curiosities, something new in the history of the island. He was a tall man of powerful physique, a runner, yet his legs looked short for the muscles of his calves were tremendous. The hills and valleys of the island were his playground and his condition was such that the next day he easily outpaced Sven, with a heavier boat over a longer distance, with a short chopping stroke of his own. His expression was unusual, the eyes an extremely light blue, the lines of his face shaping it like the war-mask of a medieval Japanese samurai. His voice was high-pitched, falsettoing through several conversational scales in a sentence, yet I heard him call his dogs with a holloa, deep, controlled, reverberating, a blast furnace of sound.

He led us through a tropical scrub to the cove where the *Skaga* lay. We passed an old coffee plantation, gone wild, relic of a former tenant and now in berry, brilliant clusters of red on the shiny green shrubs. Inside each red skin were two slime-coated seeds. They have to be boiled to get rid of the skin or soaked and rubbed smooth before husking and roasting. On many of the bushes hung nests of leaves drawn together, swarming with big stinging ants, their bodies fat and transparently green. The aboriginals make a drink out of the ants, a drink intoxicating enough to encraze, and no wonder it is potent, for the ants are so many, so large, so bellicose, and the smell of them, the reek of insect sweat in the dusk!

We made a fire on the beach, cooked a wheat damper in the ashes and fried big steaks of the mackerel. Night had fallen. It was cold. Having eaten we reclined close to the fire, tired, comatose, unwilling to leave the warmth, our faces so many painted designs in crimson and black, impersonal, the logs black in the fire-glow, the leaping flames scarlet knives slashing at the sombre fabric of night. Our first camp on a Barrier Island. Attentions wavered, conversation disintegrated, eyelids flickered. To keep awake I had to concentrate on the end of a twiggy log projecting a few feet out of the fire, and it did not seem at all strange that one of the twigs should move and gently undulate up and down. Not strange at all. This day I should remember as one of green wine, of semi-tropical intoxication, of mango wine, ant beer, parrot nectar. I had the warmth of sunburn stroking my skin, the sleep it brings somnambulating in my blood. That moving twig was thick and had legs, lots of legs. A five-inch centipede? Is that a centipede, Ruth? There, Sven, look. Then her shrieks, the sudden irruption of danger. The centipede, disturbed, ran on the sand, scuffled, and was lost.

We sat down again, cautiously, but spells were broken. Into the dinghy we packed, five of us; the water slapping at our backsides, splashing saltily in our faces, the fire a red beacon behind, the lighthouse a white beacon ahead, and our ship rolling, keeping its intense individual life to itself between beacons, waiting for us as a dog waits, as a wife waits, as the grave waits for us all.

We slept the heavy sleep of tired explorers and woke again to my cook-day and the island inviting discovery. We had breakfast ashore and then the others went oystering while I finished my work for the day. It came on to rain, I had a shower bath, washed my hair and swam nude as Ruth and Joan had done earlier. It rained harder. The others returned and we sheltered in the open boat shed. Harold came down riding his horse; a sack of limes, a loaf of bread and a dressed kid slung in bags over his saddle. As he wore only a bathing suit and a pair of heavy boots and carried on his shoulder a pair of sculls he was, to say the least, an unusual equestrian figure.

Henery made a fire in half a kerosene tin; the wood was damp and it smoked us out into the rain but we managed to brew coffee. Mr. White appeared with an invitation to come to the house and stay to dinner that night. We all had a merry lunch, dates and wholemeal biscuits, cheese and ham, chocolate and cigarettes. 'Ages since I had cheese,' said Mr. White, and Harold smoked a cigarette in reverent silence. All the eight dogs gaped hungrily round hoping for ham. The smoke of the fire made us cough and our eyes water. We drank more and more coffee. We told anecdotes of houses on fire. Then the father and son were shown the boat and we went up the hill to the house, taking it in turns to ride the horses, Mr. White's with a Mexican saddle embossed in copper and silver, a big peak in front and square stirrups of wood. What joy it was to gallop over the short grass of the plateau, the odour of the camp-fire smoke thick in one's hair, the black dogs with their brown-set eyes running beside, the air crisp and the pine trees sibilant with drops of water.

We met Mrs. White and her daughter and had more mango wine. A large tumbler had only been a sensation to be analysed the day before but now a smaller glass became an adventure, was warm and stung like a serpent, coiled itself in my stomach and sprang darting fire to my head. I sat still and confused by the veranda rail while talk spouted and a shower of rain beat on the iron roof. No one could recall an occasion when so many women had been together on the island. The talk was a spate, it flowed out torrentially, questions stood out like boulders in it, answers and comments raced on, extended, swirled in explanation, re-united with the main stream again. It was exhausting, all our woman-knowledge, woman quickness. Ruth was exuberant. The wine? No, she had come home, this was afternoon tea-time at her home. Her laughter was the ceaseless high spattering of rain on big leaves, mango leaves.

We had a meal, a meal that women had made in a proper kitchen and served with refinement, poultry, potatoes, bread sauce, incomparable bread sauce, jelly, a paw-paw salad and little mince pies. Civilization breathed fragrantly from the little mince pies.

After dinner I found that Harold was going to milk the goats, a task usually performed by Miss White before sunset but neglected that night because of the duties of hospitality. It was a common-place proceeding to him but to me extraordinarily interesting. There were about seventeen goats in a stable fourteen feet by twelve. I held the stable lamp while he selected his first goat, a pretty black silky one with two brown lines down its face and a black coat marked with white. She had a kid called Jason, it was all black with the brown maternal marks on its face and horns coming like black planted bulbs ready to sprout. She was very gentle and tame. She came to be fondled and liked being milked first. It was an honour she appreciated. Her feelings would have been hurt had Harold not taken her first.

I had been full of an unwarrantable prejudice against goats, there had been Horace's line;

'Sed nimis arta premunt olidae convivia caprae,'

but now, after the banquet, I found that these nannies did not smell unpleasantly, I could like them without being Whitmanish about armpits; their coats were smooth and silky, full of colour, warm fawns and browns, ornamented with cravats and stockings and bodices that might have just come from a first-class laundry. Their eyes were large luminous jewels, gazelle eyes melting with trust, flashing emerald from dark corners, the pupils oblong slits of fire.

They sniffed delicately at me and then accepted me, took me into their confidence, approved my fumbling caresses. Each one yielded from half a big enamel mug to a whole one, about half a pint. The mug was emptied into a round can. It was all very primitive. I was reminded of a shepherd in Ancient Greece milking his goats. Harold called to them and they answered to their names. As he milked he gossiped to me about them as if they had been people; what a pretty kid this one had been and that this other had just had her firstborn, the little black and white one tethered on the lawn, how she was so proud of it that she stayed all day by the railings and had to be driven off to feed. I tried to milk one. The udder was warm and full, the teat small and hairy, I could not get a drop. A number of nannies were dry and had come in by accident or for the sake of the conversation, yet, in that tiny pen, Harold had not a moment's hesitation between the milked, the milkless and the unmilked. The last goat was obstinate. It was long past the usual milking time and she had been kept waiting. She sat down on her hind legs and protested. Harold laughed. She got furious and more sulky. He gave me the big can of milk to hold in case of accidents, held her shoulders between his knees and milked her as she lay, sprawling on her back in undignified obstreperation. I swear the other goats drew their thin lips back and smiled a little haughtily.

There was one goat I had not cared to stroke, one that had been maimed and was disfigured. It kept pushing itself forward for notice and I could not touch it. Harold explained the accident that had hurt it. He was even kinder to it than to the others with a kindness that overcame repugnance. Do not deny any creature, however pitiable, the right to live. So the saints must have walked among the lepers. I was not rebuked by his attitude for no rebuke was administered, but I did not wish willingly to look at those clouded and mattery eyes, that scarred and ugly coat. I had been struck by the extraordinary gentleness of Harold and his sister, their patience and quietness in contract to the animation of their parents. A lonely life for the young, desperately lonely at times.

We let the goats out, they accepted freedom as they had enjoyed company, with reserve, unostentatiously. At the other gate the dogs were waiting impatiently; they made no secret of their friendliness, they were effusive in welcome. What a lord is man! On the way back we stopped to milk an old ewe whose coal-black lamb was also tethered on the lawn. It was the first time I had ever seen a sheep milked. In the kitchen I tasted the goats' milk. It was full and creamy, one could get used to it. The ablative absolute of happiness was on me, that puts a *mirabile dictu* to everything. I enthused about the goat-milking to Ruth and Joan. They were interested but Henery blew a cold wind upon me, didn't I really know that the Eskimos milked their sheep? He hated to see my spirit ballooning and Ruth and Joan impressed. I was not to be forced down. The ablative absolute is a little spiritual construction complete in itself.

It was an evening of talk and more talk, crossword puzzles and a little chess. We went home after eleven. Henery refused guidance and got bushed. It took an hour and forty minutes to get back to the boat, a precipitous dangerous journey with a new moon that gave no light. A rough passage aboard. That inadequate dinghy.

CHAPTER X

MIDDLE ISLAND IN THE PERCY GROUP

An interrupted night. Roll, roll, roll; thirsty; awake, awake, still awake. Sandfly bites itching abominably.

Just after dawn across to the shore with my books and some biscuits, away by myself to a cranny noticed the day before. Sven, the cook, was chained to the camp-fire and breakfast and intent on grilling the short loin chops from the kid Harold had brought us. They were only about an inch long. Poor little thing. I walked away as if I had escaped from a massacre.

Where I sat in a green pocket thick with maidenhair fern on the edge of the precipice was too steep for the sheep baaing on the hillside above to get to. It was so steep a place that if one leant far enough over one could spit directly into the sea, blue on the rocks eighty feet below. The pines were very old. Their needles had been falling for centuries upholstering the bare places under the trees. A white cedar grew on the edge of the slope and a pretty kind of plane or maple beside it. A curious bunchy eucalpytus stood in a tangle of vines and strange shrubs. I read there and smoked and did not think about anything particularly. Seconds forgot to tick, minutes went soundlessly, the hours mooned by.

Having read for a long time of explorers and naturalists, of murders and shipwrecks in the Barrier, I got very hungry and it seemed quite natural for me to wander back to the camp and fall upon the wee chop and the minute kidney that Sven had thoughtfully left on a plate as my share of the breakfast. Presently he appeared from the bush and watched me with a cold eye. It was about three o'clock.

Perhaps I had been a little hoity-toity, over-Shelleyish, about kid chops in those few early morning minutes. Now as I ate the meat I felt meek and apologetic as a maiden lady caught revoking at cards.

Where had I been gallivanting? But how could I say? How can one communicate laziness to the virtuous and Sven was perspiring with virtue. He had served breakfast and lunch too, baked a damper and done his washing as well. It hung dismally about, slung on properly knotted lines and secure should a hurricane blow. He had been seeking me. The others had gone up to the homestead and we were to follow. Where had I been? Impossible to own up that I hadn't been more than a five minutes' stroll from the camp; that I had heard the muffled thunder of my name among the rocks and quite clearly the arrangements of the departing trio. I could only make mysterious allegations of long walks and marvellous vistas. I praised the chop and the care that had saved it for me. The sun shone again.

He made a careful toilet, did his nails and put on a shop-new shirt. We were promised for afternoon tea and dinner again. It seemed Henery was wearing that attractive blue shirt his sister had given him. It went with his eyes. Joan had ironed it that morning and her own pretty orange shorts and Ruth's blue and white set. Had everyone except me been virtuous then? Perhaps he wanted me to put on evening dress? No, he thought if I washed my face and combed my hair I should do. If I hadn't left it so late he would have offered to row across to the boat for powder and a mirror, but as it was I should just have to do. A pity I hadn't brought over a *clean* sweater and he liked my navy blue slacks best.

To-day seemed no different to me from yesterday, but somehow in my absence we had become involved in a social occasion. Sven had been impressed by the freshness of the others and then I had come strolling along, untidy as a pensioned-off pirate. Even buccaneers must be decorous was his unspoken reservation and so we set off seriously in a let-us-meet-the-vicar-and-take-tea mood that was utterly false to the island, for when we got to the house Miss White set powder and toilet things before me and everyone was much too jolly to care whether a shirt had been ironed or not. Sven had conjured up the social occasion out of the imposed virtue of his cook-day and the general prinking of the family. Cook-day often had a depressingly virtuous effect on the cook.

So we walked slowly over the gum-blossom by a new shorter way to the house, feeling the quietness that comes on warm Sunday afternoons and talking at intervals of the aboriginals and explorers whose murders and discoveries filled my head. I had found out that McGillivray, the botanist, when he called here in 1847, in the *Rattlesnake*, the ship on which the scientist Huxley was, had commented on the huge flocks of parrots and the prodigious clatter they made. It fascinated me that they were still here, still fierce squawking and squabbling, not yet been shot out. The continuity of nature. How many generations of parrots since then? Had McGillivray watched them in gum-blossom time? Was gum-blossom nectar a traditional feast in the cockatoo tribe? Could they have a Spring corroboree about it? Sven did not find it in the least strange. Why should not parrots go on living where they had always lived? Who was McGillivray anyhow? So he told stories of parrots and of captains on sailing ships who had kept parrots.

And what should it matter to me that the first white man to anchor here had been Flinders and that the survey ship *Basilisk* in 1871 had come here to fill their water-barrels from the creek that ran into the swamp after rescuing the few miserable survivors of the Brig *Maria* wrecked on Bramble Reef in Rockingham Bay? That in 1847 three missionaries, Roman Catholics, who were on their way to Port Essington just after it had been discovered by the German Leichhardt, had been drowned in the bay below us? Their cassocks probably. Because I had dug up the facts with difficulty did not make them any more valuable. On that drop-scene South Island just across Broad Sound there had been a particularly treacherous dispatch of four out of the seven white men of the *Vision*, engaged in scientific work on the reef. The white men had been cunningly separated, ambushed, slaughtered, their blood gushing into the fine white sand by the little creek, the remains of supper by the camp fire. The bald words of the old narrative still held their own horror, the words of the man who had escaped by an unreason of chance inconsequent as the killing. He had stepped away into the bush under a call of necessity and come back to the firelight and that other sinister red spilling, and then, when he was able to move, hiding, running, scurrying through the scrub of the island, hare-hunted by his imagination, his foes not to be seen, vanished, the whole episode a five minutes' nightmare, unbelievable except for the bodies, the red spilling. The soil of that drop-scene island could not yet have forgotten the groan of civilization, its downfall under the thrust of primitive malevolence.

He was interested in the murder story but did not find the birds strange, while I found the presence of the birds stranger, more exciting than the incident of the murder. The potency of recorded fact. The supremacy of being over happening. Sven was in the tradition of doing; what he had done all his life were the deeds sailors have performed since Ulysses, the finding of cargoes, passengers, ports, but no mystery about them. On the other hand I had lived by a sort of hocus-pocus of the past, teaching to young Australians the medieval history of a Europe mythical by distance, as a nurse might tell a bedtime story of fairyland.

This insistent emanation of the past into the present worried me. I sneered at it as a corpse-odour joy, a delight Joan would regard with disbelief as a sentimentalism, not a precision of living with the shapes of things clear-cut and themselves. To coat places with an icing of historical association was to falsify them, to make a romanticism out of lands not seen before. If a strange island could whisper so tantalizingly of the unimportant past why had familiar places, saturated with the historically more important, not been grandiloquent? But had they not? Had there not been long ago when the flow of life was quickened by love, in a prosaic suburb of Sydney, streets down which it had been an adventure to walk and doorways susceptible to magic?

If the earth of itself has influences, so strong that a childhood
scene can never be shaken off, and if an event has a field of force
about it, a magnetism of the occurrence only gradually to fade
out with time, perhaps the savage earth, its receptivity not dulled
by the beating about of many passions, not asphalted over by
events, keeps its earth memory fresh, still haunted by actions that
would have died away in a civilized place long before. So that
when a listener arrives the ancient tale is capable of being heard,
faintly, is in fact forced on unwilling ears.

It did not add any merit to the pine trees on the island to know
that Captain King in 1819 had cut top-gallant masts from them and
declared that they were 'as tough as any stay he ever saw', and
yet I had an elation of satisfaction about finding Harold and Mr.
White making a launch for themselves out of the timbers of the
island. The powdery whiteness of the pit where they had been
working, sawing the cedar into planks, somehow possessed an
intense significance because of the fact. I had to accept it as a
pedantry of emotion, book-knowledge surviving like the unwanted
coccyx, a brand of one's spiritual ascent from the classroom.

Ruth found me boring, suspected assertion, stupid high and
mightiness, whenever I pulled out these plums of information.
As I had been irritated by the uncontrolled excitement, the high-
pitched dogmatism, the quick and choppy nodding of the head,
the sound of her laughter, continuous, preceding and punctuating
jokes, hard as stones flung on an iron roof, the pawky inherited
mannerisms. Were unpleasant essences of upbringing brought
out by the warmth of sociability, the simple garrulity of kind
meeting kind? Hateful that parents pattern our movements as
well as our faces. Social feeling can only be real when there has
been separation. Separation is the valley to the hill, the shadow
to the light, the failure to the achievement – the unspeakable
relief. Let us crawl into a den and live alone before we dare meet
the prolonged amiability of our friends.

And in the warm afternoon Sven and I walked slowly, talking
of sea captains who kept parrots – and miles apart. It was plea-

sant, striped sandshoes treading on the gum blossom, walking up-hill, going to meet the vicar and take tea. Mary had given me those sandshoes, they were bright and strong, well-made, 'You will always be walking about in rainbows,' Kim had said of them, and looked with an affectation of self-pity at his own brown brogues destined to wear themselves out on city pavements. We had laughed at that, unsubstantial things rainbows.

Sven wanted to kiss me, and why not? Why bring the crow ghosts of school-teachers who were dead and deserved to be forgotten, to croak and frighten away the parrots on a semi-tropical island?

That night there were many stories. We were not the only ones, who in isolation had failed to live amicably at close quarters. Once the Whites had gone to pay a formal afternoon call on a lighthouse-keeper newly-installed in the island opposite, and during the call a storm sprang up of such intensity that they were compelled to stay on the island for eight days, at the end of which time the keeper's wife could barely be civil. No other call was ever exchanged, though they were neighbours for years. When the elements leave visiting cards no one else need apply. The keeper at the time of our visit was a bachelor, an old man and a misanthrope who sent little notes across to Miss White informing her of the occasions when she did not wear stockings. This at a distance of three and a half miles! He must have had a rare focus, declared Sven. One may go without stockings and a lot more on the beaches and streets of Europe but alone on one's own tropical island a squinting lighthouse-keeper's propriety demands stockings! So morality zigzags round the world.

Lighthouse-keepers are by profession the most inquisitive people in the world. At Cape Hawke during those three miserable rain-swept days Ruth and I had done some exercises on deck, thinking not a person save Pluvius around. It had only taken a few minutes but the light-keeper there had telephoned to our home papers, 'Crew in fine spirits, storm-tossed but happy. Girls doing exercises. All very merry.' Which was a strange story to read when we limped into Brisbane ten days later with the row behind us. Once when in Singapore the boat was anchored in a basin off the Yacht Club I remained alone on board for several days. I read a great deal and seldom ventured beyond the shade of the awning. I thought nobody in the world was interested in me till at the end of the second day a launch arrived with a large bundle of magazines and old nautical calendars and a short note from the Pilot Station complimenting me on the way I had kept my 'lone watch' and suggesting that the literature might 'ameliorate it a little'.

After our performance of the morning on what we had imagined was a secluded beach we three women warned our hostess that an ultimatum might be forthcoming on the morrow.

I discovered Mr. White had a passion for navigators and history. His bookshelves were packed with accounts of adventurous voyages and he enjoyed hearing about King and McGillivray. On the strength of our common interest he gave me a copy of Washington Irving's *Life of Columbus*, but even our voyage was not long enough to read it. I never got beyond the Miltonic syntax of the opening sentences, they reminded me too forcibly of Intermediate Passages for analysis and parsing.

Miss White wanted us to relieve them of some religious tracts in gaudy covers, yellow, mauve, green, and red. She told us how they had come into the house. Of one Richardson, father of a milkman about whom no more was known than that he had been fined for watering the milk. This elderly man, clad in black alpaca, came up the path one midday, exhausted from carrying a heavy bag up the hill and introducing himself as an agent.

He examined the bookshelves closely. 'I see you are students', he observed. They agreed, modestly. 'I bring you the light,' he announced importantly. As it sounded like the beginning of a long sales talk his listener assured him that they were already well supplied with reading lamps, thank you. But she was mistaken. It was *The Light* he brought, a new revelation at two shillings a copy, but he was giving it away, illuminating the outermost islands with the truth, literally, according to the Word. The books in his bag had cost him £20 wholesale and he was distributing them personally. The Whites had had difficulty in limiting their share of illumination to twelve copies. 'And what black thing had that man on his conscience?' Mrs. White wanted to know. Nobody could tell her; a son who watered the milk did not seem an altogether adequate explanation. The light of self-righteousness hides its own darkness.

We were later than ever that night. Tired. It was long past time for going, the final good nights had been said and the five women and Sven waited in the doorway, the lit lantern swinging impatiently. Still Henery talks. It is a new topic just introduced. Boats, of all things boats. Plans of the launch that is to be built are brought out. When boats are to be spoken of one should dedicate a whole evening to it. At this hour boats! The group in the doorway shuffles, changes postures. Fifteen minutes. A mutiny is brewing, our silence is dark and thick. Now Joan insists. Insists again. Good for Joan. He is drawn into the net of our going, he is enmeshed, we are moving down the steps out into the night. It is cold and we shiver. If ever there was a moon it has been sensible and gone to bed long before.

He takes the lamp from Sven and we move in single file over the narrow crazy path. Joan steps forward to be next him. Her brown legs move regularly like short blunt scissors clipping the ground. She wears a bandage round one ankle, it is to protect a sandfly bite. She has not enough calcium in her blood and a fester takes a long time to get better. Never does she quite put down her right heel. The light only shows our legs. Ruth stumbles. Joan moves ahead so that Ruth coming after Henery will have the benefit of the light. The lamp makes the obscurity of the night greater, its iron base casts a pool of shadow in which Henery's feet paddle. He is talking, something has excited him to-night, he is more garrulous than usual. Joan ahead of him grunts a sound of interest from time to time. Ruth draws in her breath, hissing over the sharpness of the stones; Sven comes last of all, out of the light. He mutters at the rough going.

We have lost the way. There are rocks that we know to be red and long sharp grass. Henery will take the lamp ahead and find the path; Sven scouts round too. Ruth and I crouch in the long grass. We are tired but not unalive. We note the wildness, the effect of the lamp shadows. She has a word for it, a French word, *cliquetis*. Yes it is a good word, it has the right sound. Doesn't she think if a lighthouse put to sea and bobbed up and down in a storm the lamp would make similar swathes of shadow? Harold had embarrassed her, giving her that big shell he had taken so much trouble to polish the instant she had admired it, and again, the second gift, her admiration of that had been simple and unthinking. She would be frightened to admire anything lest he believe she wanted it and hand it over. But it is more blessed to give than to receive and don't snub him too much Ruth. Oh, yes, you did. Don't you feel the impelling loneliness of this situation? There can't be too much friendliness when the pain of isolation is so acute. Joan comes up to us and rests. Conversation dies. Henery calls. Here is a path.

We bustle into our five sets of legs walking centipede, a creature not visible above our waists, the night drapes itself over our shoulders as the painted cloth of a scaly dragon is hooped over the coolies who bear the monster in symbolic procession. We are linked by the burden of night, we are a crew again. Those of us who carry the tail are quite blind except for the ground under our feet, only the man ahead can see; hurry, do not get left behind, he carries the Light, two shillings a copy. The dragon breathes fire and is garrulous. Now we come to pandanus palms that are perfectly dry, the dragon is in anecdotage. He speaks of the Western plains and lights the pandanus palm. The flame hesitates, then leaps, firing the darkness; from every finger-tip of the palm explode rockets, they hurl themselves into the night. The uproar is enormous, it is a salvo of fireworks suddenly apt for a dragon reverie; the heat scorches us back, the whole tree is ablaze. Is it dangerous? Will it set the other scrub on fire? Dreadful, after hospitality, to fire the island. No, it is too wet he says, but we are not at ease; the sparks shower around, we stamp on those that lie like lit cigarette butts in the grass beside us. This tree burns electrically, with flashing and noise; it is not Burning Bush in the wilderness glowing away sedately in a pious fervour of faith. Approach thou not near me. That is Joan. Now the fire is over, it is too dark to see what has happened to the stump. We murmur admiration of the spectacle and move on. Henery seeks another tree. He strikes match after match and at last finds one. There are the petty explosions of more matches, for this palm hesitates, will not commit suicide. Then it gains courage and yields itself to the oily fury of self-destruction. This second burning is not as the first; we are cold, it is late, a miracle ceases to be miraculous when it happens too often. Ruth, Sven and I edge off towards the track over the creek. Ruth mentions Prometheus. No, a dragon not Prometheus. The glare has shown up another pandanus waiting to be set off. Prometheus thinks it is fun but the rabble can see a slow progress, lighting a chain of tree torches all the way home. We do not bother to agree that it is pretty, we are after all not Chinese coolies with the need to light crackers scaring symbolical dragons. We go ahead lanternless.

If it were not so tiring to talk Ruth and I might gossip about the Burning Bush and comfortably share some botanical half-knowledge about it. She and I can scrap and hate each other and then be done with it. We can hurt each other and understand each other but we do not ultimately matter to each other. When we have argued we fall back on the old mattress of affection. We can discuss business without emotion.

Now we are off the path, let us return to the creek where we were most certainly on it. Away behind us is another blazing bush. Ruth shouts crossly into the night, 'Come on, hurry up with the lamp.' So simple a thing. Yet I should not have been able to do it.

CHAPTER XI

SHAW ISLAND–MOLLE ISLAND– BOWEN

ANOTHER day in the Percy Islands with talk of turtle hunting and then the departure at dusk, the exchange of mementoes, the reverberation of pistol shots round the silent bay in token of fare-well and then the settling down to the routine of night at sea, the lapping noises on the sides, the slight snoring of the keel cutting the water, the living vibration of the mast where it passed into the cabin just by my head. To put a hand out and touch it in the night was to feel the pulse of the journey.

The next day, Friday, May 10th, was fine with a fair wind blowing. We were using the squaresail well slewed, Sven wanted to add the reefed mainsail but he proposed it instead of mentioning it, and Henery said that it would not work and if it did it might be uncomfortable steering. It was the unorthodoxy of the thing that appalled his yachtsman's soul trying to be born. Sven maintained that it would work and that we could do seven knots with it on that wind. It was not tried; he gave in. When a disagreement on nautical matters arose the women were all tacitly dumb.

Shaw Island was the next island, barren, scrubby, with rocky hills and twisted gum-trees, a typically Australian island; it looked tough and inhospitable and positively challenged the visitor: 'Come on, you won't get anything out of me.' But we did. There were coco-nuts growing in a grove behind a white beach with a creek flowing in at one end of it. Most of the colour in this other-wise drab island came from the earth itself, the brown round faces of some of the cliffs were splashed with patches of grey, with white or green lichens. Near one summit was a large cup-shaped hollow of yellow limestone, the nest of a roc with the surrounding lichens as the realistic droppings of that gigantic wild-fowl. We three women and Sven rowed home through an indigo and gold sunset, singing, the bows of the dinghy filled with brown, golden and half-green coco-nuts. We bailed out, to the rhythm of the songs, the water that plopped in over stern and sides. It was a long, heavy, strenuous row against the wind; a happy effort. It was pleasant to feel one's own strength, though the end left us tired. We stayed there that night, a night of quiet rest in a smooth anchorage.

Next day we were in the Whitsunday Passage, sailing past Pentecost Island, queer, abrupt, razor-backed; past Whitsunday Island, rugged, wooded, with the strength and reticence of an honest man's face about it. These islands are of the mainland and not the tropical type of coral island. They are summits that have not been drowned.

We were having a contented domestic morning, Ruth making a wheatmeal damper, Sven helping Joan husk coco-nuts, Henery at the tiller and myself fishing with *Cook's Voyages* open on my lap. It was the silent doing what one pleased that grew more common with us, the only conversation was connected with cooking or sailing. Sven's finger that had seemed to get better was bad again, so I antiphlogestined it and split a peg to make a splint so that he should not be tempted to use it too much. He had been intimidated before over the hot foments and now he only mentioned feebly that the plaster was very hot, so he got a large-sized blister out of my ministrations, and when in the course of time the blister healed it took the mysterious malady with it.

We made Molle Island, twenty-seven miles from Shaw Island, by midday. We were coming in north-west from the Percy Islands, approaching the mainland again. Major Murray's yacht, the *Day Dream*, was in the bay, and he and Mr. Lammond, owner of Molle Island, came aboard as soon as we had anchored. In talking to them about the wind and the Whitsunday Passage we were lured into using the word 'beautiful' more than once. 'Mustn't do that,' announced Mr. Lammond, and we remembered that we were in the presence of the Author, the literary stylist.

Mr. Lammond runs about 400 sheep on the 3000 acres of the island – much of the land is as yet uncleared, or pest-ridden, and we gathered that most of the family income depended on royalties and journalism. Bill, the youngest of the three children, a stocky, freckled youngster of ten, lent me, not without misgivings, his own copy of his father's book, *Horns and Hooves*, which describes handling stock in the out-back of Australia. Offered a choice of birthday presents, Bill had chosen that to everyone's surprise, for he was not a bookish boy. 'My most favourable reviewer,' Mr. Lammond called him. Bill had been known to refuse visiting ladies a loan of the precious copy so I was made to feel honoured, but confess here that the grounds of my acceptance were honour-less. In the first few minutes of our acquaintance I had owned up to being decidedly scared of the pet bull that came nuzzling round my shirt pocket for tit-bits, in fact I had hastily climbed a tree, while Bill, very superior, had acted the knight errant and given him a contemptuous push away. Secondly I had not blinked an eyelid at the possibility of taming an oyster, I had even offered to go on the reef and tickle his beard with some oatmeal while Bill called 'Open Sesame', Sesame to be the conveniently sexless name of the oyster.

One felt that family life on this island was fun. As well as Bill, there were Harold close on sixteen and a half and Amy about fifteen. They received instruction in formal subjects from the Correspondence School for isolated children established by the government of Queensland and the elder children were well on in High School subjects. Their neat school books with the sympa-thetic corrections impressed me. They had the advantage of organized courses without the penalties and tempers of the class-room and they had the inestimable advantage of island life. What a fascinating playground for children. This was how we should educate our city children, buy a temperate and well-watered island and turn them loose on it like colts. The possibility of such a scheme is still attractive to me, but one would have to have a perfect house-mother like Mrs. Lammond to help things along.

She told us the only drawback to the children's environment was that Amy had no girl companions of her own age. We gossiped in the kitchen while Amy baked the family loaves of bread, a task she had taken on at the age of ten because the flour gave her mother hay-fever. There were no servants on Molle Island, and work as well as pleasures were shared. Every month there was a strict household budgetting with all the family present, store accounts were gone into and checked. If it were more than £10 a month there was a 'Court of Inquiry'. Most things they could raise for themselves on the island, or grew there already. Sugar was the heaviest expense, this although there was a crushing mill only twenty miles away. They bought a seventy-five-pound bag for about twenty-eight shillings, almost fivepence a pound, yet the same sugar after freight and handling charges have been paid is only twopence on the English breakfast table. The general election had taken place in Queensland a few days before and the island was still waiting news of the results, so the current of talk ran politically, on the sugar bounty, the seasonal nature of cane-cutting, the Moratorium Act. But we were a month away from a daily newspaper and election results were only something that people made bets on.

We were at Molle Island for four long sunlit days. What remains of them now? A kaleidoscope of events and views; the getting up at dawn to find the world breathless, not a ripple on the water, not a movement in the air, two boats, one green and ducklike, the other white and elegant as a swan, lying above their reflections that never wavered; the quiet hills mirrored there holding an inaudible converse with the sea, the islands far away hanging like motionless clouds above the horizon, the coastline of Queensland a misty smear, and round the still bay a scimitar of creamy sand narrowing at the point of the blade and curving to the brown reef for a handle, holding by an immutable law the silenced sea from the resting land. Then the sun thrust silver swords from the east, the stricken clouds fell into the sea and became islands again, Elysian blue but material islands; the water trembled with the new vibration of light and the reflections of the hill-tops shivered, while the boats rocked slowly as if an invisible hand had passed to and fro over them. One travelling ripple broke on the beach. As if it had been a signal from the trees suddenly hurtled thousands of pieces of white paper fluttering, flung upward by a common impulse, making a clamour loud as the printed word, a cockatoo newspaper shrieking out, not to be gainsaid. They wheeled on the silent air, attacking it as if it were a battlefield, the sound of their wings flapping was like the unfolding of large pages. From another dip in the island came a rival flock, squalling in gossip columns, ready to contest the events of the day. It was such a morning as Aphrodite might have chosen for a Southern hemisphere reincarnation, ascending in a parrot-drawn chariot, first having struck the birds mercifully dumb.

Then at midday on a ledge of rock high up on the ridge of Spion Kopje, the sun blazing down on one's back, lying flat, sprawled out and still as a lizard, with only the mind working fast like a lizard's flickering tongue, all around the chipped matrices and discarded imperfect chert implements of an aboriginal armament factory centuries old – the weapon and the tool so inseparable – the virulent flavour of crushed lantana in the air; looking down into an unsuspected basin in the hills, a cup-like hollow with a line of trees at the bottom and patterned with the verdigris of newly-grown grass sprung up after the burning off at the end of the wet season.

Or sitting at night in deck chairs on the vine-shaded veranda, listening to fishing and stock-raising stories, Mr. Lammond acting with the pantomime of the raconteur, prancing nervously near an imaginary shark, twisting out of the way of a charging steer, letting go a poisonous fish inadvertently caught at night, his motions incredibly amusing, inevitably convincing, a rough gusto of the enjoyment of life in every action. Or Major Murry, one of Australia's well-known airmen, chanting in a voice as resonant as his own personality, 'Why was I born so beautiful?' and capping Mr. Lammond's yarns with the exciting gossip of the air, the how and why of events that had recently stirred Australia profoundly. And through the long evenings a dribble of information, of new facts and new points of view that make travelling stimulating. When people who are vital and doing unusual things meet in unexpected places with nothing to gain from each other but enjoyment and knowledge, life sparkles into an unforgettable brilliance, a jollity that warms even the memories of such encounters.

Then there were family parties on the reef, gathering oysters. I had the thrill of actually spearing a stone fish, the most venomous fish that lives, its poison produces death after agony. Mrs. Lammond saw it first, it was hard to detect as it lurked beneath a seaweeded rock, its dorsal and side fins spotted and waving like clumps of seaweed. It was not more than five inches long, a slaty-brown in colour with transverse markings, broken bars of dark brown, the mouth small compared with that of the rock cod whose young it rather resembled, the head ugly with bulges above the eyes and feathered antennae. When it was speared it barked, a hoarse, hollow sound, and when Mr. Lammond stroked it along the side with a stick it exuded its venom that resembled condensed milk.

Our politely-mouthed manners were mocked by a Rabelaisian directness here. 'Hey, don't bring the dinghy too close, you'll knock a dint in the island.' 'Here is an orange, not much good but I'm keeping the best for myself.' 'Bet you you can't get your knife into the shark in one go. Right into the belly mind you and no making a mess.' The Fastidious Female that used to be oneself accepting the challenge, winning it, watching interestedly the dissection of a six-foot grey nurse shark, its enormous liver, its unhatched brood of young, its softest skin coarser than sandpaper, tougher than parchment.

There was no feeling of loneliness and isolation on Molle Island as there had been on the Percy Islands; there was a perpetual busyness about it and a sense of company. If one went for a walk with Amy, the daughter, five motherless lambs not a month old skipped with her, insisted on coming to the top of the Balancing Rock perched high on the skyline. Had she not adopted them as pets they would have been left to die after the rounding up. Also a launch with mail and supplies called once a week and fishermen and occasional visitors like ourselves came, too, but the number of pets extended the family circle; the jokes we laughed at were simple things, family jokes, a cat swigging from the teat of the lamb's bottle, bright eyes fixed on the bleating owner, at the fat sow waddling to her supper with three fowls perched on her broad back, at the bull developing a taste for apples and gazing aloft. Laughter and work were both prerogatives of Molle Island.

There was a northerly wind blowing that kept the *Skaga* and the *Day Dream* from making north. 'If it doesn't last for three days it will for seven,' announced the islanders cheerfully. On the fourth day we decided to risk it and left for Grassy Island where we knew bananas grew wild. Ruth was very keen on pirating a few big bunches of bananas. But though the tide helped us out the wind was dead against us and a choppy swell pushed us back, so we gave up the idea of Grassy Island and determined to anchor for the night off a little unnamed island.

Henery was at the lead, Sven at the tiller. *Skaga* ran from eight fathoms to less than five feet six inches in one step and instantly we were on the reef with a dull thud and a horrible scrunching as of sugar spilled underfoot. We drew five feet six. Sven ran along with a pole, pushed us off and held us there. We dropped the mainsail, pulled the staysail to windward, which helped bring the bow off the reef, and in a few moments the rising tide completed the job. Then we hoisted the mainsail and found that there was no perceptible leak. It was a great relief. There was no personal danger, we could all have swum ashore, but the boat might have gone. Joan was white with the implications of the crash. I had never seen her so white, so upset before. We said little, we took the deliverance of our possessions very calmly, and finally we made an anchorage at sunset to the lee of West Molle, directly opposite our anchorage at Molle Island, which we could see quite plainly.

Next day the wind was still unfavourable so we spent the time on the reef where the soft corals were very large and amazingly coloured. Pushed my way thirty yards into the matted scrub of this tropically dense and absolutely virgin island. Close to the shore a scrub hen was using a nest. I say using advisedly because it was a large earth mansion of the kind that are let out on lease for ninety-nine seasons. No one fowl could have ever scratched it together, generations had clawed at the task, for it was over ten feet high and many yards in circumference. Tall slender trees had pushed their way up through the rounded sides. A crown of freshly-scratched earth at the top showed that it was still in use; but though I scrambled to the top and saw the crater, no eggs were visible. Lying nearby and writing I heard, after a long time, a discreet rustling and looked up to see an insignificant black hen, about as large as a well-grown domestic chicken but with taller, thicker brilliant yellow legs scurrying out of sight on the other side. She was evidently the present owner of this colossal bird property but she looked as timid and unpretentious as the badly-paid caretaker of a big institution.

We were still eating the mackerel that I had caught off the Percy Islands, the remains of which had been salted. Joan and Henery went fishing in the early evening but caught nothing except an enthusiasm for phosphorescent effects. We read until very late by the miserable light and then articles were begun. They were sitting heavily on our consciences. Scratch, scratch, scratch, went the pens of Ruth, Joan, and Dona. The cabin had become an examination room, you remember how worried you felt when the person next you scribbled, scribbled, scribbled away and you could think of nothing and despairingly believed that you had failed already? It was like that. I had read again that night all my letters, the nicest parts were almost worn away. I looked up and there was his portrait opposite me across the narrow table. I suddenly felt I would give anything, everything I had, to be sitting opposite him in my own dining-room. I could have burst into tears with wanting, instead I lit one of my precious cigarettes and went on deck. It was low tide, the muddy reef was quite bare for fifty yards, the water spread to the edge of it without a splash, darkly luminous, steel quiet. We were anchored very close to the edge. The moonlight was so thick, like yellow cheese waiting to be cut. I could not sleep for the moonlight. It threw a coverlet down the open hatch on to my bunk. At two o'clock I went up again and was rewarded. A turtle was swimming against the current with its head just out of the water. I was not certain at first, it looked like a duck in the distance. There were others too. I could hear them blowing and swimming about and catch the dark break of their heads on the water surface. Eerie alone sounds they made in the night. This reef was a good feeding ground for them, undisturbed, and with lush meadows of seaweed pasture. Those soft corals, vegetable roses four feet across, lettuce green tipped with mustard, amythestine spinach, could they eat those?

The following day there was a light SE. wind. We made one of our vacillating badly-managed departures. Sven was leaving it to Henery, because it was a late start and he always resented having to approach the uncommunicative Henery with the query, 'What are we going to do?' Ruth and he and I had laughed at 'Admiral's orders' on a walk up Spion Kopje on Molle Island, Ruth mimicking Henery's inevitable turning from Sven to Joan with, 'Shall we do so-and-so, Joaney?' Now for the first time since leaving Newcastle I heard Sven get openly annoyed. We were preparing to go out, Henery he-hawing giving instructions about this and that. The anchor was up and we were drifting towards the rocks. Finally he said, 'No, wait a moment Joaney, untie the hitching strap.'

Whereupon Sven, with the memory of the reef-episode fresh in his mind, said venomously, 'For goodness sake leave the blessed kicking strap alone.' At this unexpected, disgusted, order instead of Henery's gentlemanly valeting of the sails, Joan dropped the rope as if it were a dangerous cobra and Henery meekly said, 'All right, Sven'. I was glad, and so I think was Ruth, who never hesitated to give her own honest opinions. 'Good for Sven, his being definite and strong for once.' But later we found that he was worrying lest he had been too rude! The problem of command and saying what we really thought we never solved.

The islands were strewn thickly here, prickling the sea with green; especially noteworthy was Double Cone with its connecting reefs between the two high hills and their precipices on the northern sides. On one face a landslide had occurred and blazed a yellow scar down the length of the cliff. The day had its beauty of islands and lisping wind. The episode of the morning over, we slid along without care as if time would always be like this, an endless and gentle slipping away, quiet as the water past our bow.

We made the entrance to Bowen at nine o'clock at night, forty-three miles in twelve hours. It was bright moonlight with not an eddy of wind. We got between wharves and to an anchorage with the help of our famous engine, the *Skaga* two-man-powered dinghy towed us in! By the time we were made fast and I was dressed it was late, but after three weeks without news I was hungry for mail and determined to find the post office and try for letters, whatever the hour. Sven thought it crazy but pleasing and came too.

Bowen seemed to be nothing but a long jetty with railway lines on it, black wooden piles round a small basin, goods sheds and a clump of impossibly tall attenuated palm trees, holding their heads high together and snickering inanely at our enterprise. They were too scraggly, too ancient ever to have borne fruit or been young themselves; I disliked them at sight, there was something stupid about them, as about the remnant of a degenerate aristocracy which has nothing to be proud of but its aloofness. They were arboreal ostriches, each standing on one leg and all of them hiding their heads under meagre ruffs of feathers.

Close to a wilderness of railway points under the shelter of a thick-leaved mango tree was a night watchman with a yellow lantern. He gave us directions for the post office. In a den at the rear of it a surprised-looking youth was reading a detective story and smoking. He obligingly hunted for letters but could find none. I was incredulous, I could hardly believe there were none so I went to the pigeon-holes myself and for all my trouble found only one, from a child who told me as news the questions in the examination paper I had set for them myself in that other life so many feeling-years away. So I decided to 'phone, a decision that roused a number of sleepy operators to the help of the surprised youth who was convinced by the glitter of brass buttons on my jacket that there must be something official about this domineering young woman. Had I only had a red tape down the seam of my slacks he might have lowered the price or extended the time, but as it was he only listened, mouth wide open, to a frightfully irrelevant conversation about cats. The conversation went a roundabout way, 2,000 miles, and I had extensions. When I had paid the bill I had twopence left, but it had been worth it.

Walking back past the ostriches they no longer snickered. I capered and patted Sven on the back. Even the jetty danced a little too. But in the early morning as I lay sleepless and excited a grim thought struck me. It is now possible to ring up from every part of the world, even England, and how expensive that would be. When should I have to suppress my longing and say, 'Enough, no more?'

Next morning we all got mail, lots of it. The postmaster had locked a big packet of it away with the registered post. Home doings; home feelings. We shared items of news as seagulls break up a loaf of bread on the beach, tearing the pieces from each other and gobbling them down. Sven had a nephew and Ruth's father had bought a new car. Dorothy had started a new literary circle and the General was giving three public lectures. My sweet peas were blooming and the cat, driven either by love or loneliness, had left home. Grandfather Maxby's cold was better. There were maid troubles, bridge parties and a geology excursion that had turned into a mushroom hunt. How extraordinarily alike were the handwritings of all our mothers, finely pointed, the ups thin and the downs thick, the letters large and clear and firm, no doubts in their minds of their daughters not being as nice girls as one could wish to meet in a day's march, as they all might have said, none of them being the kind of mother who ever took such an irregular and tiring thing as a day's march.

Joan and I went back to the boat to regurgitate the swallowed news. It seemed to be the occasion for a celebration, news always excited us, we shared the last nip out of the bottle, and Joan for the first time – for how long, how long – spoke to me spontaneously, as if it were not a tearing of the will to do so. We became very warm, confidential, friendly; the mail had already inebriated us. Of course Henery was contra-suggestible, hadn't I known that before? A very grave danger if Sven were to leave us at Cairns.

If we could manage to talk so easily now might we not always agree? About everything? Oh, damn . . .

I went back to the town to make purchases, while Joan waited for Henery. Bowen has a wide main street that looks as if it used to be, and still is, the terminus of a stock route. Dust was ankle deep, there were few shade trees, the houses were wooden iron-roofed structures low on the ground. A thirsty place, every third house was a licensed one. It is the outlet for the Mount Isa tin mines when they work. I was walking along the main street busy on its Saturday morning shopping; I carried five long loaves of bread and was deciding that ninepence a pound was too much to pay for tomatoes when the chief merit of the place, according to the stationmaster, was that in the season it exported 400 tons of tomatoes to the south, when I met Henery. He was 'wandering vag–ue–ly,' as Joan said, with four brilliantly coloured leaves in his hand and the disintegration of artistic rapture about him. His hair and clothing were wild and his movements of the sea, too large and aimless for the restraint of the Saturday morning business crowd in Bowen. People stared. We spoke, for the sake of speaking, as people of the same race do in a foreign port. Did he remember that Joan was waiting for him? The leaves were lovely, where had he found them? On a tree . . . Well! He drifted on. Some current that was not his will sent him down the hill towards the boat.

Then I met Ruth fresh in a dimity frock and with her large leather dilly-bag for purchases. She had been trying to buy narrow black elastic. She had an idea for a completely mosquito-proof anti-malarial garment but it depended entirely on the presence of elastic. There was no narrow black elastic in the town.

What did she think about tomatoes? Emphatically, at nine-pence, no. Hadn't we tinned tomatoes? Besides, Henery was interviewing a tomato grower from the Chamber of Commerce and some bank manager who owned a yacht. Perhaps somebody might *give* us a case of tomatoes . . .

But Henery didn't look as if he had been interviewing bank managers . . . he had four coloured leaves . . . We were blocking the traffic of the footpath, she and I standing still with our bread and bundles of cabbage under the iron veranda of the fruit shop. In the road cars sped by splashing dust. Some gins in flowered print dresses looked bright-eyed at us. They were speaking about our clothes. It was as well, it had been trouble enough putting them on, expanding all frills and sunshine like muslin jack-in-the-boxes out of the little cabin in the *Skaga*. We were fashionables at last – in Bowen for some black gins! Across the street the sunlight on a new tin roof smote the eyeballs like a blow. We were about to separate, as ants who meet, confer, wag antennae, and pass on. Who was this coming tiredly up the street? Joan. She told us that Sven was minding the boat. Had we seen Henery? Had the bank manager or the tomatoes materialized? No, but he had some pretty leaves and he went in that direction. What did we think of Bowen? Let us leave, let us leave as soon as we can. To-morrow morning. Joan will fix it. We will have to take water on board to-night. Bowen had no votes in its favour.

In the afternoon we had a visit from a professional fisherman whose launch was tied up on the other side of the jetty, he got his living by trailing for mackerel. Formerly he had fished for barra-mundi, an edible fish that live near a mud shore. It takes a fine net to catch them and it is dirty work, wading at night up to the waist in mud and washing it off next morning and always mending nets. Now when he was lucky and hit a mackerel spawning spot he could bring in 1300 lbs. of fish a day. He showed me the controversial knot and how to improvise a spinner out of a teaspoon and the best way to bait a hook with a piece of white rag. There were fish stories and tales of cyclones.

That night I walked alone up the main street to the accompaniment of a soft rustle of seductive whistling. I held my book hard and my head high. I should have to get used to walking unescorted in strange cities. It amused me that the scallawag population should note so quickly the presence of a strange female in the town and without exception try her out. I walked into the local School of Arts where the greybeards were brooding over the newspapers, the silence notices were loud enough on the walls to prevent any of the roomful of men from intruding on the intruder. I spread my elbows as if I were a member and wrote vigorously. The Institute closed at ten o'clock.

At a quarter to ten Sven arrived. He had tracked me down. I was sorry to relinquish the independence of taking myself about strange places at night, but Bowen was hardly a good town to start and it was decent of him to worry about me. We looked at the photographs of aboriginal tribes on the walls and at a few fishes and turtle eggs in glass bottles on some shelves. There was a skeleton of a seahorse and some abnormal rodent embryos, but the contents of those bottles would daunt the most ardent tippler – even in so thirsty a town as Bowen.

Sven reported that he had thought of going to the pictures but the proprietor was having trouble with the steam engine that worked the music and sometimes it came in blasts and sometimes not at all; moreover, the fire brigade band were practising in the iron hall next door. There was a whist drive on in the Social Hall of the Church of England and there would be a dance next

Wednesday at the Agricultural Society's showroom. I could see he was a good sailor and had reconnoitred the town well. It was only ten o'clock now and by eleven when the pictures came out there might be some people in the streets. Should we wait and have supper in a glow with the crowd? There was a café open near the picture house which was in a back street. He had marked the café from over the way.

We went around. They specialized in fish and chips and a kind of pork pasty. They would be ready in half an hour. No. No. No, thank you! The main street again. Darkness. By a billiard saloon a bright green doorway, on the other side of the road a dim kerosene light outside a shop. Perhaps we could get an ice-cream? An ice-cream wasn't much to ask of a town of 20,000 inhabitants, north of Capricorn and exporting 400 tons of tomatoes in the season as well as tin and the chief outlet for the Mount Isa mines. But the shopkeeper said it wasn't time for ice-cream yet. When it was *really* hot they got a churn sent by rail three times a week, but it didn't last long. However, he recommended some nice pork sausages wrapped in celophane paper and fresh that night from the refrigerating car. No, no, thank you. The telephone boy had heard me say over the phone, 'What? Oh, Bowen's a hole of a place.' That was why the stationmaster, the postal clerk and the storekeeper had all stopped me and been careful to point out how important and progressive Bowen really was. I saw no reason to change my mind. We bought chocolate and went back in the moonlight past the arboreal ostriches who were laughing brainlessly to themselves in the moonlight by the iron goods shed where the railway met the black wooden piles of the port.

CHAPTER XII

TOWNSVILLE–BRISK ISLAND

GOOD-BYE Bowen. After all you gave us mail and a fair wind to leave by, we drank whisky with you and you had a friendly neighbour, Middle Island, just six miles away where we found tomatoes and paw-paws, bananas, a pineapple and a pumpkin. It was a marauding party. The fisherman had told us about the island. The owner had long been gone, gold-prospecting, someone said. There were left only empty beer bottles, kerosene tins and the framework of what had once been an iron and sacking hut. Our spirits were high as we carried back the booty. I had a big sack of ripe tomatoes on my back and a wet oozing trickled down from them.

There was too much freight for us all to go aboard in the dinghy together, so Ruth and I gathered opportunity by its forelock and swam in the cove. The water was deep close in, emerald green, the bottom white powdered coral, a few feet from the shore we were shoulder deep, washed green as if we were in thick shrubbery with the light pouring through on us; our limbs looked remote and wavering, felt insubstantial like light imprisoned by the sea. We swam inshore up and down, frightened by the thought of sharks, yet joyous with light; cities could go hang themselves in their telegraph wires. The swim was short, already Joan was rowing the dinghy back for us, bringing towels and shouting, 'Hurry up, the wind may change, we don't want to miss it,' as if the wind were an express train just starting. So we went back to the stowing and stacking and the glamour of the paw-paws, tomatoes, bananas, received in bulk, gratis.

We rigged the square sail but the wind dropped. It rose again with the coming of night. During my watch we raced along, not a star to be seen, the moon hidden and giving a diffused grey light that made the sea a polished pearl black shell and the sky a curdled oyster with a beard of black cloud.

Why was it that the helmsman felt responsible for the wind, pleased as if he had blown it along himself when the ship made good time? In the mornings when we compared notes of our night watches we always liked to be able to say that at any rate she sailed well in *our* watch, and we estimated the rate, five knots at least, or four, or six. To Sven's inquiry, '*All* the time?' the answer usually was, 'Well, most of the time.' He always took a discount off our estimated rate of the night watches and said nothing about it.

The wind got weaker and weaker. The coastline was dreary and in Cook's words, 'afforded but a very barren prospect'. The following afternoon when we were only twelve miles off Townsville it dropped to a weak breath. I had the afternoon watch. In a drowsy lacuna of mind I let *Skaga* get off her course and had to box the compass. Everyone was lazy, sleeping and lying about. I kept quiet and hoped that in a few minutes all would be well and my sin undetected, but Sven, who had been lying on his bunk below, ostensibly reading but never turning a page, was presumably orientated even in snoozing, for he came up and took a puzzled look at the sun. He glanced at the compass and then at me. At the moment we were steering the compass course he had laid down, but stern on! 'I hope I haven't made you giddy, Sven?' There was a bolshevism about this politeness. He tried to look as if Neptune and the ancient tradition of the sea would blister me off the deck, but he knew that when he took over women as crew he was already listed on the charge sheet of nautical propriety.

The mackerel, salted, from Percy Islands, was still in the larder, and as Henery added fragments to the tomato soup for the evening meal Sven said reflectively that in Japan raw fish was a national dish and in Sweden raw salt mackerel a favourite hors-d'œuvre. Profoundly and silently we all hoped that our old friend the mackerel, which was fast becoming as hoary as stockfish, would be finished before Sven's cook-day came round again.

Imperceptibly we drew nearer Townsville, arriving off the entrance about two a.m. For long moonlit hours we were becalmed, barely drifting. It was a night of silver and onyx, the sail cutting an empty triangle out of the silver paper of the sky. I felt I wanted to write a poem about paw-paw blossoms. I had seen them on the pirate island off Bowen.

There are two trees, male and female, the male one grows here and there among the female trees. It is branchy with long spikes of small creamy wax blossoms each with a cluster of stamens. The charming efflorescence resembles a wedding bouquet but the bridegroom not the bride carries it. The female flower is very large, three or four or five times as big as the male and the base of the pistil swells to ungainly proportions like a pregnant woman; the female flower is dominant, to me like the maternal instinct triumphant, the male is pretty, effete, like the men under matriarchy. 'A woman is a branchy tree', but not the paw-paw. A romantic fidelity left one free to be oneself and independent of anyone else.

We were all tired, it was a laborious entry, tacking long distances to gain a little headway. The engine would have saved us a lot of trouble but the knowledge that even if it were lifted out of its resting-place under Sven's bunk it would probably not go, kept us silent. Henery who had bought the engine and who was the only one who knew how it was supposed to work, hated it. It was an outboard with a tendency to take the skin off the knuckles of whoever tried to start it. Ruth said it had only once been coaxed to go, on a small boat in Melbourne. Sailing every inch of the way. She was in bed. Joan and I had remained up to help in making the anchorage. In spite of fatigue there was a beauty about this unknown port, the red and yellow lights of the harbour, the dark masses of distant boats and the still gliding in the breathless air over the oily water. We did not share this beauty; Joan had regained her non-committal silence whenever I was near her, only by moving away could I hope to hear the sound of her voice. All four watchers had our silent undercurrents of thoughts. Sven's came to the surface easily; he complained of a tack Henery took, as he thought needlessly, and Henery muttered something and then Sven asked, 'What are you saying?' and Henery answered, 'It's you. You're always grumbling to yourself, why don't you speak out?' To which Sven answered tartly, 'If I want things done properly it is for your own good and the good of the ship.' Joan and I retired, there was a long pow-wow above. Sven, according to Henery, was indecisive, and since indecision was a quality incompatible with command Henery would tell Sven whenever he was indecisive! Sven was beaten but not grateful. The ground had been changed from a matter of tacking to regions of the soul, where an honest sailor admits he needs a pilot. After these 'quiet talks' it was invariably the same, the talker was pleased and satisfied with himself and the other was doubly furious with outrage.

Townsville was a gay town, red, white and black; the buildings were white, the flowers and croton leaves in the public borders flaming red, and a new element in the population, black. One splendid aboriginal, six feet tall, came sauntering along the footpath picking his teeth, flamboyant as an advertisement. Some oil company's representative told us that ninety per cent of the shops are Chinese owned. In the streets were many aboriginals and half-castes. 'Colourful Townsville' as the travel posters said, but in a different sense. The cinema was tropical, too, with its deck-chairs and their clean linen covers on the head rests. The audience, which was mostly half-caste, roared with enjoyment at the sight of the villain being dragged in the dust at the end of a lariat while the hero galloped on – the brutality was revolting but roused their enthusiasm; the Hollywood men knew their mob appeal better than we did.

At sunset we climbed Castle Rock, a goat-tracked pinnacle that thrusts itself up like a giant ant-hill behind the town. It seemed from that eminence that most of the residential districts lay in black swamps, but we were told later that they were not swamps but the shallow basin of what had once been a large salt pan, which, if one were a householder and paid rates, might be a flattering distinction. It is a city of mango trees and the weeping fig, that pretty softly-drooping tree widow that is gentle in ever-green grief. They line the streets and shade most of the houses. The flying foxes love them and when the fruit is ripe hang by the feet, gorged, unable to fly. The children love them, too, in the season their mouths are always mango-yellow.

At Townsville we collected £10 for articles and spent a good deal of it on mosquito nets for all of us. At the time we were very solemn about malaria risks. Photography was running its course as well. Ruth borrowed the lens out of my camera and turned the whole boat into an enlarging apparatus in order to save the ex-pense of having our pictures enlarged. Hatchways were shut and blanketed, the fixed portholes covered inside and out with card-board and black cloth; a carpenter made, to Ruth's design, a sliding box arrangement that opened one eye through the fore porthole and stretched itself along the cabin roof inside. There were yards of black tape and innumerable drawing-pins that in the course of days were retrieved by our bare feet. After two days of effort, just when everything was ready, the sun disobligingly went down. Ruth had left it out of her calculations! The hungry crew thankfully watched it set. After another homeless day, shut out of the cabin below and watched by a staring multitude from the jetty above, there were prints, not successful, but still prints.

We felt Ruth was, literally, sweating for the common good, but it seemed to me a false and uncomfortable economy and we had different attitudes towards it. Joan was definitely encouraging, if she had her doubts of the ultimate value of the efforts she kept them to herself. I was sceptical and I was also concerned for the safety of my lens in that dark and littered cabin. At the same time I applauded and was amazed at the persistency that sought to overcome the obstacles in the way and that toiled on in spite of a meagre chance of success. Sven was merely inconvenienced and uncomfortable. 'Just Ruth,' he said. He was learning to know us. Henery was shut out from collaboration. Ruth, who was keen on photography, was showing him what she could do with the boat-owned camera whose mysteries he had hitherto managed. She had taken a photograph of *Skaga* and the *Day Dream* at Molle Island and it had been sold to a local paper for ten shillings, but it had been Henery's idea of news value so honours were even. They felt that ten shillings was the beginning of a fortune and on the strength of it bought a great many developers, reducers and intensifiers; but, serious omission, no new film, depending on a stock of old cinema film that Henery had 'gibbeted' way back in Sydney. It was destined to cause us great disappointment.

Ruth had also taken a snapshot of me bucketing in the early morning at Molle Island and Henery wanted to send it to an art journal for the sake of the money it might earn. I objected. Besides the exhibition of a large bruise, I had feelings in the matter. They seemed to think I was unreasonable, disobliging, and I had to drag in Kim as a moral bolster to my refusal. To their argument that it did not matter who had posed for the picture I suggested that one of them should, a reply that touched Ruth. Living together. We were bundles of anomalies. She thought it highly objectionable for Sven to see the print, but perfectly in order for Henery to get it enlarged without my knowledge and discuss its merits with several photographers on shore! A more scientific state of mind on his part perhaps. The whole thing might have been simplified by letting it go and collecting in due course the editorial rejection slips, 'Lady with a bruise not wanted.'

Our week in Townsville was fragmentary, dispersed, petty. It was too long to have spent there. My last moments ashore were hurried ones. To get the advantage of the outgoing tide that would float us the whole way down the river without the need of using the engine or getting a tow, it was necessary to slip our moorings at 7.20 in the morning. Late the night before I had left my wrist-watch in the bathroom of a friend who had invited us all up for a bath and supper and who lived on a hill at the back of the town. That was the supreme hospitality in port, a bath. At half-past six I was knocking discreetly at the door of the sleeping porch, at seven I was back in the town, posting letters, getting laundry, buying bread and meat; at twenty-five past I was standing on the wharf watching *Skaga* already slipping round the first bend of the stream. It had been arranged that if I missed the tide I should go to the breakwater at the entrance to the port, but there were two breakwaters, which one should I go to?

Major Murray, doing exercises on his immaculate deck, shouted, 'left,' but the baker who had given me a lift from the bakery in his high light cart said the only road was on the right hand break-water. We went to the left. I should have believed him and gone to the right. He whipped up his horse and away we bowled through streets in which coloured folk were just beginning to wake up and stretch themselves in their doorways; we passed the municipal water-sprinkling cart that was being filled before trundling off on its first round of the day. Housewives called out for bread, but the baker did not stop. Our wheels clattered over the stony road.

When we came to the long breakwater there was neither cart nor foot-track and we could see over the top of it the sail of *Skaga* getting nearer and nearer. We should have to scramble over the great granite slabs to the very end and the parcels were bulky and heavy. The baker obligingly left all the breakfast tables waiting and helped carry the bundles, an act of pure philanthropy, to where Sven backed in with the dinghy and *Skaga* waited impatient to be off.

There was a good breeze. We hoisted the mainsail with three reefs as well as the square sail and made good time. It was a blue warm day, smooth and lazy. The islands were thick as flies on a window pane in summer. They passed by, we steered for others, asked their names and forgot them. They were so many.

The charts were fascinating. It was here that Flinders wrote a warning in his journal to any skipper sailing through the Barrier not to be one who 'throws his ship's head round in a hurry as soon as breakers are announced from aloft. If he do not feel his nerves strong enough to "thread the needle" as it is called amongst the reefs while he directs the steering from the mast-head, I would strongly recommend him not to approach this part of the coast'. He had been glad enough to sail the *Investigator* through Flinders Passage to open water. Now we were 'threading the needle' and the wake was a slowly unrolling strand of white cotton sewing a little seam on the seas.

After sunset we drifted along against a head wind and at ten o'clock on the night of Friday, 24th June, made our objective, Brisk Island, or Culgarool, as the natives called it. There was a mist thick and white over the water as we anchored. In the morning we found that we were about sixty yards off two nasty tooth-shaped rocks, sticking up like black fangs out of the smooth water. The island was really two, two small hills with a mottled garment of light and dark scrub flung over them, connected by a wide reef impassable at high water.

We had heard only a little about the people, Mr. and Mrs. Frings and their son, who lived on the island, but everyone who had mentioned them had done so with great curiosity tinged with scorn, or malice, laughter or outraged convention. Any unusual form of thought or behaviour attracts animosity in the borders of the empire, where survival demands a bitter sinking to the same level.

In all our calls this was perhaps the most unusual we ever made. Yet there was nothing unusual about our leisured breakfast as we floated on the sparkling water, nor about Mr. Frings' quiet approach in his launch, or in his greeting and his invitation to come on shore. Somehow we had been frightened of a rebuff, it demands a certain assurance to sail up to a lonely island and say, 'Here we are. Isn't it a lovely day?' when the islander might have chosen to be lonely, might have decided that visitors were not to be encouraged. The Frings had. He had lived alone on the island for some years testing himself. Then he had gone back to London to settle his affairs and announce to the circle of his friends that 'I had resolved to camp on the beach of a tropic island for the rest of my life'. They had thought him mad; he had known his madness to be wisdom.

About the austerity of that camping there was no doubt. Life there had been reduced to its simplest elements. They grew and produced nothing. This their Barrier neighbours could neither understand nor forgive. When the earth was there to be used, its fertility a source of power, when people were poor and the life of the world meant *earning*, it was madness to refuse to cultivate, to run stock or to make money. But the Frings did not think so, both of them wrote, augmenting a slender income when it needed helping, satisfied with being alive and with happiness.

The dwelling consisted of two iron sheds with concrete floors and shaded by vines, about twenty yards away from each other. One was the kitchen, eating-room and larder, the other the bedrooms and living-room. Though everything was very simple it was not uncomfortable. There was a home-cured goatskin rug, a smoothwood easy chair, a gramophone and records.

They lived meagrely, mostly out of tins, and looked well. He was a man of medium build and about fifty-five, but I am not a good judge of ages, his torso and face were bronzed magnificently, his hair scanty and grey, but his movements active. He was a man of whom it could be said that he was unafraid, there was a fatalism about his courage that would have politely denied its own existence. He was neither a merry man nor a sad, he was happy.

His partner in their adventure of living was olive-skinned, slender, dark-haired, unostentatiously dignified and with a tender beauty in her great luminous dark eyes; about thirty-four I judged her to be, but she might have been younger. There was an intensity about her, controlled and under her will. She attracted and returned one's sympathies by a metabolism of quiet. As she went about the kitchen in her scarlet dress unobtrusively preparing a meal for us and listening intently to the conversation, she seemed to brighten the shadow of the screen-darkened room like a moving flame, to concentrate the vitality of the hot earth-burning island in the light of her red dress.

The baby was a boy about four, formed in the perfection at which nature strives, courageous, joyous, intelligent, physically perfect.

We talked of the quantum theory, Henery and Ruth both knew a little about it. Mr. Frings' chief interests were advanced physics and philosophy; I judged that at one time he might have been a nature mystic. Now he confessed to an ultimate hedonism, a considered reflection after a lifetime of diverse experience that the black fellow's attitude to life was the best one; walk-about, talk-about, sleep-out the ideal existence; the most perfect feeling to ruminate without thought after eating. To make this statement in a drawing-room for the sake of the effect it produces is one thing, but to deliberately model one's life on it is another. To obtain this exquisiteness of simple sensation demands, for the civilized man, a series of rigid exclusions. The exclusions had been made. Few new possessions ever came to the island, the wash of current literature scraped on other shores, there only arrived a few carefully chosen books to supplement old friends on the big bookshelves.

The logic of Mr. Frings' attitude was complete. No doubt garden produce would be pleasant to eat, but making a garden would mean building a fence to keep the wild goats out, and digging a well, and then the effort of drawing up buckets of water would demand a windlass, and a bigger garden demand in its turn further water storage, an underground tank. Love of comfort was an insidious enemy, men gave themselves endless labour in order to save themselves trouble. He said all this with a twinkle in his blue eyes, yet beneath the jocularity lay an intense seriousness.

He admitted backsliding, even at the moment George, an aboriginal from the nearby Palm Island settlement, was sinking posts for a fence to keep the house paddock free from goats who came down in the night and took a fancy to the washing or the stores.

Leisure, Mrs. Frings said, was the supremely valuable thing. Leisure for what? To think, to write, to experience slowly. Lonely? No. In order to be relieved of some of the housework and to have someone to mind the baby they had employed George's wife – a black gin who had run into the scrub on our appearance and who afterwards crept back, smoking her pipe to give herself confidence – but she had proved sulky, unamenable, would not play with the little boy and seldom spoke. Then, too, she had dirty habits – Missus had come upon her blowing her nose on the tea towel – so when the fence was built George was to take her back to the settlement.

We walked about the island that was too small to be pastorally valuable and too poor for intense cultivation, though there were pockets of dense scrub on it. It was not the kind of island to spur a land-ambitious person, it was no more than a little place set apart by distance from the rest of the world. We walked quickly to the highest point and then came down, back to *Skaga* for tea and music. As we walked Mrs. Frings spoke to me of London. 'You will like it,' she said, 'with the lights down Piccadilly, the buses, the great shops and the trees in the parks in springtime,' but there was no homesickness in her voice. London was there, but life was here. We spoke quietly as women do, of clothes, prices and knitting patterns, of the cyclone that had once wrecked the island and demolished the first hut, of the blacks who had escaped from Palm Island, stolen the Frings' boat and gone in it to the mainland where they sold it for a pea rifle, and how after a lot of trouble Mr. Frings had got a new boat out of the Home Secretary's department and how now they kept the new boat heavily padlocked to a half-ton mooring.

At sunset Ruth and Sven and I swam on a sandy spit on the northern end of the island. It grew cold quickly and we went for a run on the stony eastern, the windward, side of the island where the land dropped steeply into the sea without a coral shelf. The contradictions of the day teased me. Longing for movement, wanderlust, was the reason for the existence of our group; the enjoyment of infinite repose, of a static mode, theirs. Was it the difference between youth unfulfilled and age achieved? After one had done what one had set out to do was there anything better than this, to camp on a tropical beach for the rest of one's life? No, there was nothing better, but – Fear – did not Fear camp there too? In the shouted warnings against sharks, in the brooding madonna look in the luminous great eyes? Yet fear was everywhere, not confined to a tropical beach.

Over on Great Palm Island was a circle of native fires, three big ones in the centre and a dozen small ones making a jewelled and perfect hoop on the sombre hillside behind which burned the last embers of a tropical sunset, a sunset red with anger, barred against it a black woolly cloud like a curly-haired ram charging the forces of night and desolation. I went to bed haunted by the dread of endless separation.

CHAPTER XIII

GREAT PALM ISLAND

NEXT morning I was still bemused and during my bucketing dropped overboard the tin dish I was washing in. It twirled slowly downwards through the blue clear water like a silver coin spinning and I could not make up my mind to dive after it until it was too late. How far away was I from the time when Ruth's dropped buckets could annoy me. Now I had dropped one myself and it didn't matter in the least.

We sailed to Great Palm Island which is an aboriginal settlement under state control. Wandering remnants of tribes and difficult, delinquent or sick individuals are sent there and some, so the matron boasted, come of their own will to holiday or to receive the rations with work that are supplied.

Our approach to the island was typical of my final impression of it. The tide was out and we rowed in from the anchorage as far as we could, bumping on coral rocks and scraping the bottom of the dinghy over them till it was impossible to go further. Then we plodded the dreary distance to the shore through a wide stretch of shallow water underneath which lay a thin crust of mud, and beneath that inches of greasy slime from which every footstep disinterred sinister odours. We felt unknown infections, fish-bones and animal corpses awaited our naked ankles.

Some blacks, old men and boys, were sitting under the shade of the palm trees on the shore watching us. They were motionless, they did not even spit. They were so black in the shadow that when they shut their eyes their faces disappeared. They were so incurious that they did not turn their heads when we passed. They wore torn football jerseys and smoked a bitter green-smelling tobacco that scratched at the nostrils. The salt-caked ribs of an old whale boat lay rotting on the beach.

The atmosphere of the island was depressing, how out of old injustices could a new life be built? Something more than justice? Not even the clergymen, optimists by profession, seemed sanguine. On Great Palm there were thirteen whites and about eleven hundred blacks from the islands and the north and west of Queensland. Indirectly we discovered that there were also about thirteen different social grades on the island, perhaps less, it depended on who was counting.

We visited the farm, the saw mill, the new tobacco plantation that if it were successful would save the government £800 per annum, the hospital, the school and the two churches. We made many inquiries and tried to get at the facts behind the lives of the blacks and the attitude to them of the people who administered the settlement. The lust for statistics seizes all serious visitors the doctor said. He had not been there more than a few months then and was hoping to do some research on the racial mixtures in the island, it was a unique opportunity. He had been taking index figures and learning family histories, some of the natives could go back four generations by oral tradition but the value of the statements verged at times on the mythological and there was not much time to devote to it. His routine work took up most of his day; the blacks were not healthy, they were subject to continual colds and took pneumonia easily. Across the water, at Fantome Island, was a lock hospital with, at the time of our visit, one hundred and twenty-six cases.

Every project was held up for lack of funds. Australia does not treat her black population generously; their shanties were far worse than the kerosene-tin and sacking hovels the unemployed build on waste ground outside some of our towns. The miserable mia-mias haunted one, housing plans were going on slowly, oh so slowly; there was a shortage of timber fit to be used and in the meantime there were administrative buildings and staff bungalows to be built.

The school had an average daily attendance of 147. There was only one white master with several young half-caste girls to help him. The children sat on long forms in a big room and wrote on slates. They folded their arms tightly and looked up with faces of varying hues and bone formation, white mixed with aboriginal, aboriginal with Chinese, white with aboriginal and Chinese, Torres Strait island and aboriginal, inland tribes and coastal tribes. Some of them still looked bright and eager, but white education and the circumstances of their lives had stamped on most of them a look of resentful bewilderment, of fear, of inferiority, and a determination not to learn more than they could help. If they were well-dressed, the boys wore cut down football jerseys, the girls had tightly-plaited little pigtails tied with string; all of them had runny noses. The eldest girls of fourteen and fifteen were terribly shy. They were writing compositions, a letter to an imaginary friend on the mainland: 'I hope you are well. We are well here. We like playing games and are getting on well at school. We hope you will come and see us soon.' That was all, the writing was as neat as a copy-book model, but one didn't quite see what good it was doing them.

There was a lot of talking and chatter because school was so much time to be filled in. Every now and then the big stick of the little master whanged down on the front desk and shouted with its wooden and self-contradictory clatter, 'Be quiet, can't you!' But what could the man do? One against 147 and a pretentious syllabus to carry out. The children liked the doctor and his wife. They showed them how to weave neat little fans of pandanus grass and after the Chant of the Multiplication Tables sang another song, 'Come to Dinner, Come to Dinner, Bacon and potatoes, Bacon and potatoes . . .' Had they tasted bacon? It wasn't on the ration list: Flour, tea, sugar, some tobacco, salt meat twice a week. Every morning the sick, aged or ailing got an extra ration of rice, sugar and condensed milk.

Most of the girls and boys are taken from the parents and live in quarters, we heard them singing their prayers at sunset. At maturity and before marriage they are put in other dormitories in the white settlement and locked up each night. Yet in spite of that the girls manage to 'fall', even the nice ones who have been trained in white homes. This shocked the lady in charge of the girls' morals. She was hampered in her endeavours to put the sex life of the aboriginals on the standard pattern of married monogomy by a regulation that forbade marriage before the age of twenty-one though the young people were mature much earlier. If the parties were suitable she approved of marriages at an early age. She was, on the subject of aboriginal behaviour, kindly, jolly, and with lots of practical good sense. To continue to live happily in this atmosphere of race tragedy one would have to see humour in rather grim situations. There was the story that was told us twice, of the girl who had 'fallen' and who, to keep 'safe' because she had persisted in her offence and climbed out of the dormitory windows, had been locked in the jail, a small hut built of heavy split sleepers, the bark still on them, with a barred window high up and very narrow. However the amorous lover was not to be defeated. He continued to visit his beloved nightly, no one knew how, it was by wriggling through the tiny trap-door of the lavatory. When you have laughed, and if the story is told with gusto you do laugh, the authority behind the incident is most repellent.

The Matron held a kind of court matrimonial to straighten out domestic problems and through her marriages were arranged. She liked, when there was a birthday, to marry off a bunch together. Cakes, veils, church and the paraphernalia of a white wedding brought the corroboree up to date. George Tomahawk, who had money in the bank and good intentions, came to her and said, 'I bin brought up properly, Matron. I want nice half-caste girl, not dirty gin round my house.' Then, diffidently, stubbing his toe in the dust, 'You know that fat Maudie? Well, she bin after me. Yes, she after me alright. She send me a message. She send Billy 'Possum, Sunday afternoon.'

'You want me to speak for you?'

But Maudie, half-caste and superior to money in the bank and a steady, if all-black husband, only showed intense scorn and

144

indignation. 'What, that fella? I no send him message. I no want that fella. Pooh – him!'

One aboriginal had been sent here because he had murdered his wife. He wanted to marry again.

'I couldn't let you marry Flora. Remember what you did to your last wife. (He had bashed her head in.)

'Oh, I wouldn't do that to Flora, Matron. Oh no. She different. Other wife wouldn't cook, wouldn't make damper. All time walk about. What I do? I no do that to Flora.' It had been an awkward problem for the Matron, but disease came to her assistance. George had to go to Fantome Island.

The hunting is not always on the men's side. One old hag came sidling up and smirking: 'Me want new petticoat, Matron'.

'You don't want a petticoat. What is the use of a petticoat?' (They love them.)

'Me no got petticoat. Got to wear dress.' Indeed she had on her entire wardrobe, five dresses, the newest and cleanest on top and the rest . . . But Bella insisted on her trousseau. She said, as if it settled the petticoat business: 'Tommy Butler want me, Matron.'

'What?'

'He want me.' Twitching the dress sideways.

'How do you know?'

'I know.' Mysteriously.

Later Tommy Butler approached Matron. She said: 'What is this I hear? You are after Bella?'

'Don't you believe that, Matron.' Stoutly: 'Her 'lations won't allow that.'

'Why not?' The taboos of the tribe still reign in Great Palm Island.

'They won't 'low that.' Further explanation had to be dragged out of him: 'They won't 'low that. I'm one of the 'lations.'

Everyone who can has to work three and a half days a week, sweeping the paths in the settlement, scrubbing, getting timber, planting out tobacco, hunting for trochus. In their leisure they sit or go spearing fish or have rows with their wives or play soccer, and at evening there floats over the water the smell of hundreds of greasy cooking-pots simmering over hundreds of little grass fires with a bubbling of unsavoury black tit-bits, goannas, grubs, salt pork, fish heads, an odour that brings with it the image of an old and corrupt male crocodile sitting on a muddy bank and laughing after committing unspeakable lecheries. An over-refined fastidiousness does not say this. To smell the land breeze of Great Palm Island at sunset was to know the concentrated domestic essence of the Dark Continent before Godliness had time to bring cleanliness with it. One learns to smell and ignore the scents of the Fragrant East, one can get used to many and like some but never since have I sniffed, as on a shelf of slowly moving warm air, the incontestable taste of black, an invisible slime coating the atmosphere with an odour that was centuries old before Noah went sailing. Not acrid nor fetid nor rancid could describe its penetrating whisper, those are ugly but honest savours and they were streaked on the substance of this island breath almost pleasingly like the colours that oil makes on water.

The great diversion of island life are the corroborees, often held because they are a safety valve. Permission to hold one at night for our benefit was given, but the whites present assured us that it was not as fine a corroboree as some that had been held. It began tardily in a cold wind, without much enthusiasm to start with; the enthusiasm came later. It was so cold the doctor kept mentioning pneumonia. A number of dimly-burning lamps burnt round a dusty, hard-trodden circle of earth. One stuttering acetylene light beat white on the blackness of the band, for there was a brass band that could play 'Blue Danube', 'Swanee River', 'Old Black Joe' and 'God Save Victoria, Long to Reign Overa, Happy and Gloria'. For the sake of the rhyme Palm Island was a little out of date in its patriotism. The aged people, mothers, grand-mothers and old men were sitting muffled in rugs and sacking behind the lamps. We had not noticed how many piccaninnies there were till a dog-fight disturbed fifty or so and sent them scattering. The performers in the corroboree were all men; between dances they stayed in the circle and argued about what they were to do next.

A corroboree at night and bitter, bitter cold.
We sit on benches and watch the corruptly-civilized blacks,
the old ones like the corroboree dances
but the young ones
wait for the jazz at the end
and the brass band is anxious to blow its own trumpet.

It is all confused; painted stripes of whitewash on black bodies
yet khaki knickers round the genitals –
the Superintendent, sitting beside me,
Gives them leave to be circumspectly savage.

Only the old myall with the boomerangs
beating, beating time, all the time beating,
likes it.
And the two gins, clap-clapping with hollowed hands on hollowed
thighs,

like it.

'Talla bindi, talla bindi, talla bindi yacamadoo.
Talla bindi, talla bindi, talla bindi yacamadoo.'

Till a fellow in a red sulu
shakes himself rigid
from the toes
through the bent knees
to the thighs
over and over and over again.

It is a superb piece of exhibitionism;
everyone bursts into frantic applause.
Boys in puberty rush into the ring
and try to do it also.

On the boat we gave a late supper. We had mixed the thirteen social classes and they sat on the deckhouse and gunwales talking of this prison for the sick and the dispossessed. The younger people looked on living there as an exile, the older ones had different ideas, they cherished thoughts of service. Some of them wanted gratitude.

'The blacks will always let you down,' said the Matron. There were fallen girl anecdotes and tales of an averted rising the year before after a melancholic white had gone berserk and done some shooting. Gratitude and ingratitude. The clergyman would not hear of it. He was tall, spare, about sixty-five, with a purpose that kept his spirit and constitution iron-hard and rustless. His eyes glowed sombrely, he had spent a lifetime among the blacks of the Northern Territory and Queensland and he knew them, they were his friends. Why should they be grateful to their natural enemies who had taken their land and who called their customs crimes? When the government rested a too-heavy hand on them he, a respected clergyman, was not afraid to be agin the government. It had not made him a popular figure. He had fought many fights and written fiercely, for a newer, freer, more liberal Black Australia Policy. He burned against injustice.

Opinions differed about the effect of a tourist steamer that had begun to make weekly visits. Did it 'spoil 'the blacks? Tales were told of their tricks. They had set up as vendors of curiosities, coral that was not properly boiled and that stank in a few days, boomerangs made falsely to adorn mantelshelves, dogs' teeth exhumed from middens, nullas daubed with ochre and given a murderous history in pidgin English, of corroborees where dance steps seen on the cinema were being introduced.

How could they be spoiled when they were what they were, not self-sufficing in a primitive community nor comfortably civilized, but poor, sick, herded together, either apathetic or criminal and, according to doctor and parson, a dying race? Any symptom that showed they could still be stirred must be good. Soccer, making a business of a corroboree, tricking tourists. The steamer's visits were a new movement, an eddy in the stagnation of dying, perhaps a hope for the future; transitions come in strange ways. The Matron was teaching the girls to embroider doilies to sell. The argument fell again into anecdote. I should not like to give my life trying to help on Great Palm, it demands too much. I brought out an eight-pound tin of sweets that on somebody's advice had been encumbering my locker since Brisbane waiting for such a contingency. The Matron was pleased, ration allowances did not run to bribery for piccaninnies. To me it felt like putting threepence in the plate when one has a very bad conscience. Great Palm Island is something most Australians do not know about, or, if they know, they do not like to think about.

CHAPTER XIV

NORTH PALM ISLAND AND CAIRNS

WE sailed on a smart breeze to North Palm Island where we hoped to shoot a goat. Fresh meat and fish had been unprocurable at Great Palm. Vegetables were scarce too, and even the coco-nuts on the trees in the groves had the eye of God on them as if they had all been counted and not one ever fell to the ground but was missed and a black hue and cry set up for it.

North Palm was only a couple of hours away, a pretty, high-rising island clothed in dense scrub at the base. Ruth stayed on board washing clothes and Joan wrote on the beach while Henery, Sven and I with the shot gun and the revolver looked for goat.

We scrambled and panted through a tropical profusion of foliage. Vines bearing large red flowers curtained the trees, and in the more open parts blue convolvuli laughed with wide-open faces back at the sky they mirrored. The saw-edged grass cut our hands and wrists as we pulled ourselves up over the rocks. I had been wise, warned by a previous experience on Molle Island I had worn long slacks through which the barbs could not penetrate. The sun blazed down, I could feel my avoirdupois melting away and I rejoiced. When I had left home I had weighed eight stone – oh that incomparable figure! – now I was eight stone twelve and disgusted about it.

Over the hot grass, around huge boulders, not a goat save ourselves to be seen. Climbing upwards in the tropics is heavy work, we wished we were out of the prickles and back on the cool shore. Suddenly we smelt goat, the stink of goat on the hot grass, immediately I knew that goat-herds in Arcady looked on goat-keeping as a business proposition as well as an idyll by Theocritus. Suddenly Henery in front held up a warning hand, his face was transfigured with excitement; he gave us an injunction to creep. We crept. We crept on. We peered over the tall grass, they were quite close, I caught a glimpse of horns, attentive eyes and a couple of venerable beards.

Henery fired. Twice. In the hot blue stillness the sounds pierced the universe; there was a scrambling of hooves over rock as the herd of about twenty got away. Henery turned round, a boyish look on his face. He held up one finger. One. We went round the rocks to the goat. 'An old stinker,' he said; 'I made a mistake, I fired for the brown nanny next him'. The goat lay shot in the neck, the blood oozing out, the eyes glazing and appealing, the sides heaving. 'I shan't eat any of you,' I thought. All round us was a circle of trampled long grass, reeking of goat; they had been resting there a long time in the open sunlight. I gave up my sheath knife for the skinning and took the revolver. 'He'll be good enough to eat,' said Henery, examining the teeth. 'About two and a half, not so old after all. You try and get another one, that brown nanny, and I'll finish this one up, I've often had to do it with cows on the station.' He had spent some time on a cattle station in Western Queensland.

Glad to be excused Sven and I went off; flies had already begun to gather. Knowing that the alarmed goats had all the advantages we worked our way higher over boulders and between widely-spaced spotted gums, and at last got a good sight of the whole herd including the brown nanny we wanted. They were standing still but suspicious, the leader looking back in our direction. 'Shoot, Sven!' But Sven crawled round another rock to get a better view and the movement of his big straw hat frightened the patriarch who upped wi' his hindquarters in a magnificent leap and after him the startled herd, over the rocks and away.

We climbed to the very top of the island without much hope of catching up with them again. I thought that though I could justly claim the privilege of sex and absent myself from the butchering Sven ought to return or else keep on hunting. I was virtuous on his behalf. Besides I wanted to get rid of him. I had a diary to write up and an apple in my pocket that had been hoarded since, was it Townsville? I had purchased those vitamins dearly and carried them a long way. The rest had been shared but I did not want to share this last one. It wouldn't go very far between hungry Sven and me, it was small. I wanted to enjoy the island by myself. What had I climbed all this way for if I couldn't enjoy being alone? I tried to arouse his enthusiasm for hunting but he had other ideas. The thought of butchering upset him; he wasn't a butcher. Henery was used to it, hadn't he said so? Shooting was no good either; he hadn't a hope of seeing those goats again. One goat would be all the meat we could eat, and, in any case and conclusively, his legs were scratched quite badly enough. He would like to sit down and rest too. Why we hadn't been alone together since Percy Island! Wasn't I ever going to give him any of my precious company?

No, I wanted to be alone; I wanted to write. (I wanted to eat that apple too.)

'You're always writing. You wrote all day on West Molle.'

'That wasn't writing, that was an article.'

'You can write on the boat.'

'No, I can't. It is always too rough or too unpleasant or the light bad or something else to do. Go on, you help Henery.' (Perhaps if you shared the apple he might go. You are selfish you know, wanting to be alone, it isn't much of a life for him.) But I kept obstinate.

Sven was obstinate too, but over-conscientious, the good boy in him could always be counted on, he knew his duty. Not for nothing had he been a choir-boy and stuck out icy watches on rainy nights in uneventful seas. The dead goat and the unattractive task called with the voice of duty and off he went. As he went he looked so miserable I almost called him back, but it had been a ten-minute battle too hardly-won to be given up easily. The right to privacy was one prolonged and formidable fight. He looked so dejected that any goat might have stalked him through the grass, leering at him with satyr eyes and holding a cloven hoof to its nose and he would have taken no notice. When he went his disgruntled feelings took with them some of the pleasure of being alone, sitting on top of a hill with the strangely contorted Hinchinbrook Passage before me like a twisted blue pin gathering up the spangled scarf of islands that clothed the sea.

At last I had a wild and uninhabited island to myself. There was no trace of black in the air, no shame of humanity to distress the empty world, there was time to grow and to think. The wind had uprooted a gum tree whose knuckly roots had not let go the crumbling boulders they still clutched and held uneasily balanced in the air. In the grass beside me grew a minute pink flower, an insignificant little thing, commonplace in colour, simple in form, with a radius of white round its dotted yellow eye; it was domestic, attached to this island, flowering and seeding in fixed design; the gum tree against which I leaned spread its branches over its entire world as the consolation of religion laps a simple soul. Staying at home. Kitty with her family about her was like this fragile blossom, strong enough to survive when bigger things went down.

The goats Harold milked on Percy Island had hardly smelt at all, yet here, in savagery, the wild goats stank as if the hot sun had drawn the virility out of them, a potent goatish aphrodisiac for the humble nannies.

I ate the apple, the little pink flower shamed me; I did not enjoy it, neither did I attempt to write. Quite soon I went, I would not coo-ee to the others, I would find my own way down. I passed from the open grass of the hill-top into the scrub and came upon Sven, Henery and the goat, skinned and slung between them on a pole. In this tangled undergrowth it was an awkward burden. It kept jolting forward against Henery's shoulders and Sven did not seem to care if the carcass or Henery got bruised or not. He seemed to have a spite on that goat and Henery loved it, he had shot it. It grew younger, two years old now, in a week it was eighteen months. The branches as the trio passed through whipped back and cut Sven in the face. Might they quarrel? Make Sven laugh. Henery was cheerful enough, he was bringing home the goat. Home is the hunter home from the hill and the sailor home from the sea.

In the afternoon we were at sea again with a good breeze and the squaresail up. Our stay of three days at Great Palm Island had interrupted the roster of duties so I had the 1 a.m. to 3 a.m. watch again and enlarged my experience of the sea. The course was north by a half west and ahead of us was a solitary rock about one and a half miles off a point on the coast. The night was black and cloudy, there was a strong swell, and so that we could get our distance from the shore and our margin of safety from the rock, I had to take the time when a shore light bore north-west by west and again when it came abeam. Sven explained this to me and went below. He explained it officially for I was not yet taken back to the fold of his regard. I was apprehensive about that rock; I could feel it irresistibly attracting us, toothing a siren song out of the night, and I grew dizzy with the effort of continually watching for the right bearing and the right moment. When at last we came abeam I called Sven and he worked the problem out, we had three miles to spare. The comfort of my relief told me how worried I had been. I confessed to the apple. Sven laughed, he too was relieved; his officialdom broke and he engulfed me in a hug that almost broke my ribs.

Presently he asked: 'What would you do if you had a lot of money?'

'Buy a boat like this and sail it all over the world.'

'All over?'

'Wherever there was wind; into all the big harbours and the little creeks and the ancient ports that nobody has visited since the Portuguese and where an old Chinaman sits counting on an abacus hoping to do a trade with his Elixir of Life in exchange for the True Faith. He'd have English sovereigns instead of buttons on his coat and he'd say . . . You're a polar bear. Stop hurting my ribs.'

'No, seriously, what would you do? Buy a boat like this?'

'It's a good boat.'

'It's a grand boat. One man could manage her easily if he had someone to help with the watches. I don't know about a woman handling it alone though.'

'I'd get a winch for the anchor and a decent oil engine.'

'You'd want an ice-chest then.'

'If it didn't make a noise when it was running like the one on the *Day Dream*. I can't stand fussy intermittently noisy little machines. They remind me of trying to keep children quiet. I'd be wanting to say "Shut up" to it.'

'You'd have to take a man along to stand all the worst watches and to navigate. Then you'd have all the time you wanted to write in.'

'I could learn to navigate and if I couldn't I'd smell my way about. Snuff the breeze the way . . .'

'But hauling up the mainsail in a hurry?'

'Um. That would be difficult. He's strong but he's not a sailor.'

'That's a pity. You'd better take a sailor.'

'I think it's a good job I haven't a lot of money.'

The wind held till the following day, sweeping us along, the water broken and green, slopping over the bows, the sky cluttered with skipping white clouds. We were making for Green Island, just off the entrance to Cairns. Vance and Nettie Palmer, two Australian authors, were camping there for the winter, writing and enjoying the simple life. We were all looking forward to meeting them.

On the chart the island was a mere spot with a wide saucer of reef about it and an anchorage marked a long way out. As we approached we took the squaresail down and used the staysail only. Even then we were wet to the skin and flying along. It was mid-tide. We tried to get in by the long jetty that stood up on black stork legs high above the water; niggerheads of coral showed their brown tusks in a grin above the water with a smother of evil white foam among the green seas. We could not get anywhere near the jetty for them. We sailed past and came in a little on the windward side and then beat back again. It was obviously dangerous. No look-out could hope to detect in time an upthrusting piece of reef under that scurry of wind and wave and water. We passed over an ominous patch of dark brown that was reef, over light green that was shallow water above a sandy bottom, over a patch of pale blue that was deeper water, and once more over the sinister brown that was almost black. The corals and weed on the bottom swam up to our alarmed vision, we could see fronds moving, we were travelling fast and there were two nigger-heads quite close. 'We can't do it,' shouted Sven and put her about. *Skaga* spun round and away from the reef. I had never seen her move so smartly. In a few minutes we were clear. It had been the most exciting fifteen minutes' sailing on the trip, we were all drenched and stimulated by the excitement of it. Just at this juncture our trolling line with the goatskin bait caught us a fish, a big trevalli with worms like thin bent wires in the peritoneal lining, but we had been forewarned of them and hailed the fish with joy.

Under the staysail and reefed mainsail we made Cairns and anchored in the stream. It was evening but by hurrying we might be in time to telegraph and collect mail. The dinghy was leaking worse than ever, like a sieve. I bailed while Sven pulled against wind and current to the only available landing, the piles of the back veranda of a swimming club. A dance was just about to commence and there was no way out save over the dance floor, so abashed and barefooted we crossed the polished desert, sat down outside in the gutter and put on shoes and socks that I had kept dry in a sack on my lap. The post-office was shut but a back-door application got the mail. We went to the biggest hotel and ordered drinks; sitting in immense leather armchairs that yawned easefully we read and exchanged letters.

This was large-sized comfort. Nowhere on *Skaga* could one of those chairs have possibly rested. They were leviathans of upholstery, capitalist barons of the furniture world robbing one of any desire to move away. How long was it since we had sat in such chairs? Oh, Brisbane at least. Sven straightened his tie, he was wearing one, and smoothed his hair. A few people in conventional evening dress came in the lounge to play cards. Presently, the letters in the sack, we went casually through the dance hall and then hung by the feet, heads downward getting the dinghy that rested waterlogged six feet below empty enough to row home in. Next day we tied up beside a launch at a jetty where we could walk ashore.

The *Manunda*, a tourist ship from Sydney, was moored there too, and Sven discovered old friends among the officers and only looked in on *Skaga* after dinner at night, bathed, fed, very happy and on the way to a party. He brought with him an invitation to hot baths and a supper. Ruth had decided to spend the next day enlarging on board, so with vivid recollections of Townsville behind us Sven made up an excursion to Barron Falls. The others assumed Barron Falls to be a stupidity nature had committed for the benefit of the Tourist Bureau. Nevertheless we went. We climbed up and up by a narrow-gauge railway through cataclysmic gorges past ribbons of water that continually fell. The little puffing engine stopped at some of the cascades on the way so that we could get out and listen to the roar and feel the spray damp on our hair. The waters swirled away under the line. The great falls at the end of the journey were worthy of more than the superlatives with which the guide-books described them. They were Wordsworthian, cataracting their trumpets from the steep. They drenched the air with sound, the white vapour of their descent lit up the sombre floor of that ancient and sunless valley, a valley of tree-ferns, black rocks and water that rushed irresistibly down, down, down.

It was a day of butterflies and tropical blossoms. On the paths there were tourists with cameras and feeble jokes. Sven was buoyant with confidence, telling me about the party the night before. There had been songs and a good supper but the girls, oh slyboots, the girls were not pretty. He said that the nicest thing a sailor can have is an hospitable family pleased to welcome him in each port, that where there are ships there are always friends. He told me on which voyages and for how long he had been shipmates with Roberts of the *Manunda*, how the shipping slump had caught him and what the other chaps had thought of *Skaga* as a ship and how curious they had been about us all. He spoke of his first command, a string of lighters from Balipapan to somewhere else. He had met his friends and he was gay, lifted out of *Skaga*-given inferiority by their simple assumption that he shared with them the security of the commanding officer class. He was himself again, to Captain Tucker of the *Manunda* the master of the *Skaga*, a little ship but one to be navigated, a joke and a reality too.

We walked up for tea under trees with flowers like pink silk lampshades hung with fringe. Sven wished to buy it at the hot, gravelled railway station, a temporary structure left like a for-gotten wagon on the top of the plateau, but I had touristy notions and wanted to sit high up on the veranda of the pretty, and expensive-looking, hotel and pour tea from a shiny silver pot into thin china cups and have cakes, cumquot jam and a view. Words-worth and waterfalls had lifted me beyond the *Skaga* adventuring station in life. So we had two teas, his where the cups were thick, the tea cold and the cakes mediocre and chunky, and mine with the view, a waiter, lots of polished silver and hot tea but the cakes stale and no cumquot jam.

Then we slid down through the mountains past the biblical stern rocks and the voice of tumbling water, through wind-waving green cane fields that were almost ready for cutting, to the narrow strip of fertile coastal plain and the flat roadstead that was Cairns harbour. We had enjoyed the day.

At the boat everything was flat and the same. Ruth had not enlarged after all; nothing had happened, she could not be persuaded that she had missed anything by not coming; even the mountains collapsed and went flat. We ate a miserable meal. Economies had been gone into during our absence and neither bread nor vegetables, fruit nor meat were to be afforded here. Moreover there was a doubt that the fish we were eating might not have kept well in the heat. 'Eat it at your own risk,' said Ruth, the cook, 'there's nothing else, and Joan thinks it tastes funny but I've eaten some.' In retrospect our double extravagance, two afternoon teas, seemed criminal.

Joan's father was coming to Cairns to bid her another farewell. The day of his arrival was uncertain, we were a couple of days waiting for a telegram and when it came it said he would be with us in another week, on July 8th. Joan and Henery explained what we could do while waiting, go to Green Island and see the Palmers, but there was no need to give reasons, I did not mind waiting. Fathers were fathers and the General was a Very Important Person.

It was another hot and humid day. Ill at ease living aboard in port. Ruth prepared for enlarging and in the afternoon the rest of us went aboard the *Manunda* for a hot bath, but for me the water would not come hot; accidentally I locked myself out of the officer friend's cabin and was nothing but dripping wet hair and worry. Ridiculous petty misadventures. I felt ill. Acquaintances of a relation of Henery's had come in two cars and were waiting to drive us out to their home. The house was charming, on a hill with large grounds and a sunken swimming pool, but they gave us no tea and we must have been too many to invite to the evening meal, so, without knowing why we had gone except to admire their swimming-pool, we drove back to town.

I felt worse. It was seven o'clock. By the accident of distribution I was in the same car with Joan and Henery. It so rarely, it never happened. Would they have a drink with me? We were very thirsty and tea-less. Perhaps we could become warm and friendly with each other as Joan and I had at Bowen. Perhaps I could let Joan know that I didn't in the least mind waiting, that I had always liked her father and looked forward to his coming, that nothing, no plans or pretentions mattered as long as we felt friendly and could be honest and easy with each other.

We did not get friendly. They would not get over feeling invited. We had to make conversation, and could not flow together. I could not lift myself over the obstacles, my backbone had gradually changed to jelly; if I stayed longer in this chair the cushions would absorb me as they had already absorbed my vitality. It was my cook-day and Ruth and Sven would be wondering what had happened to us. We walked the short distance to the boat in silence. How horrible stockings and tight afternoon clothes were. Heat. Fatigue. Failure.

On board Sven was filling the primuses. Everyone was hungry, it was late and my cook-day. We had all wasted the day, Ruth's prints were failures, the bath hadn't been hot, nothing had succeeded and there was still work to be done.

I peeled off my clothes in one skin and flung them on the bunk in disorder. Ruth was lying down on her bunk in her petticoat wriggling her bare feet; Henery and Joan were undressing on the hatch, Sven's coat and collar and tie were laid neatly on his bunk, he was trying not to drip kerosene on his best trousers as he filled the lamps. To cook in I put on the purple shirt I disliked, it hung down outside like a tunic, I was too tired to tuck it in properly. Soon there was a hot meal. I was glad I could cook quickly. The two primuses droned and buzzed like fast-moving circular saws set at different frequencies and running hot. They were sawing the top of my head off, cutting a neat slice through the bone. The pain in my middle was getting worse but no need to mention it. The lamp hanging from the roof jiggled from the backwash of passing launches and spilled shadows over the frying pans on the primuses. I was not hungry any more. Spaghetti, onions, cheese, tomatoes and some bully beef. Quite savoury. At last the kettle had boiled and there was tea. The tea would be good for the pain. Now that everyone was served I could turn out the primuses singing their out of tune sawing and straighten my back bent double cooking over them. There. It was all quiet, everything was done.

Henery stirred some sugar in his tall beaker of tea. Ruth and

Within the ramparts Babi Mandi (a small fort
on Lonthoir Island)

(*top*) Charting Cook's course (Great Barrier)
(*bottom*) 'Up she rises' – On the anchor

[by courtesy Kodak, Townsville, N.S.W.

Piccaninnies (Great Palm Island)

Sugar bag dance by lugger boys

Dressed for the pig feast

Within the ramparts Babi Mandi (a small fort
on Lonthoir Island)

(*top*) Charting Cook's course (Great Barrier)
(*bottom*) 'Up she rises' – On the anchor

[by courtesy Kodak, Townsville, N.S.W.

Piccaninnies (Great Palm Island)

Dressed for the pig feast

Sugar bag dance by lugger boys

Within the ramparts Babi Mandi (a small fort
on Lonthoir Island)

(*top*) Charting Cook's course (Great Barrier)
(*bottom*) 'Up she rises' – On the anchor

[by courtesy Kodak, Townsville, N.S.W.

Piccaninnies (Great Palm Island)

Dressed for the pig feast

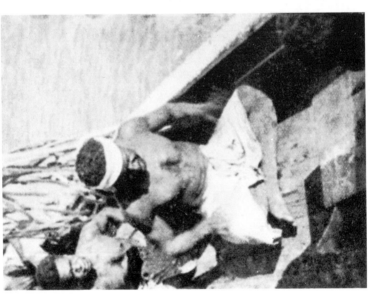

Sugar bag dance by lugger boys

Joan were sitting together at the table by the other lamp in the cabin. They were feeling better already and had begun to talk. Sven, wedged in opposite them, was staring at me. Then they were laying me out on the hatch above in the cool dark night and there was a hot comet of tea spilled down my purple shirt and turning cold. They were wrapping me up in my rug and giving me a hot-water bottle. Sven scolded me, then went below to wash up while the water was warm. Ruth dried the dishes for him. They were doing my work. Bless Sven, bless Ruth.

The water boat came alongside in the dark and Henery got very busy. The nozzles of the water-supply hoses were too big for the small opening in our watertanks, even at their lowest pressure the water came too fast and gushed out over the cabin floor. There were shouts and explanations, the deck and the cabin were running with fresh water. The girls too were wet with it and I could tell from their voices how tired they were. At ten o'clock Sven was still throwing buckets of water overboard and wringing out cloths, the water-boat had gone away, everyone was going to bed. I could hear people walking hollowly on the long wharf that went above and beyond us. Then from the excursion boat to which we were tied came raucous shouts and two boys banging away on the battered piano, 'Nelly Bly, Nelly Bly'. It was all they could do and they did it again and again. The pain that had been trickling away came back sharply. Other people from the wharf complained to the boys. There was an angry altercation and the noise began defiantly, hesitated, and then, still defiantly, stopped.

Sven came up and put his hand on my forehead. Hadn't I better go below? When I was ready, I wasn't ready yet. I shouldn't sleep. Yes the pain was quite better. Good night.

A wretched day, honeycombed with misadventures, not happy like yesterday. No one could imagine this actuality of living. At midnight I was cramped and cold and went below. Everyone was asleep, the snores made a morse code of sound, the longs and the shorts alternating irregularly. My pillow and the top of the mattress were soaked from the flood, the opening of the water tank was directly below my head. This was what people ashore meant without realizing it when they spoke of hardship. 'Brave young women.' Put a medal on your chest. Good night.

CHAPTER XV

GREEN ISLAND AND BACK IN CAIRNS

EARLY next morning, with one of the piano-vamping boys from the launch for a pilot, we crossed to Green Island, taking with us Mr. and Mrs. Palmer, who had been over on the mainland at a sugar-mill for a few days.

Vance Palmer was quiet and bronzed. For a tall man he moved restrainedly and neatly, as if, should he need to, he could fold up his long arms and legs and put them away tidily like the blades of a clasp knife. His disposition was like that too, retiring and yet sharp. One felt that he audited his statements before uttering them and stamped them with unassuming tabs for his own information, 'Thought over and found correct'. Consequently they sank into the stream of conversation with the weight of plumb-bobs. A man difficult to anger or annoy because he kept detached from events and inaccessible for the same reason, as if he had built a fortress for his soul to dwell in and only his wife, like an army of occupation, could move freely in and out. Yet he was cheery and pleasant, he would have come out of his fortress had he been able, and, since he could not, was determined to use it peacefully as an observation tower.

He was interested in doing perhaps more than in being. It would have been a subtle pleasure to have introduced him to Mr. Frings, to have watched the passive serenity of his accepted life of action meeting the intensely mental activity of Mr. Frings' philosophy of passivity. I admired him, I respected his poise, and I was somewhat awed; a reserved person with the weight of considered judgment about him has always that effect on a babbling shallow creature.

Nettie Palmer was very different. She was small, in the middle forties, with sad-looking clothes that she did not worry about and a dull complexion from which open-air living had abstracted the colour without burnishing. An inconspicuous woman till she spoke and then forceful, animated, intuitive, talking quickly, well, and a great deal. There was something inquisitive and bird-like about her; she hopped from subject to subject and was penetratingly curious and friendly. She could not help being friendly. She liked people, she found out whatever was worthy of appreciation in them and encouraged them with a small personal song of praise. She took pains with me; I was surprised and pleased, but wary at first, for she was Joan's friend and Joan admired the Palmers, and since Joan had found no merit in me they might not either. I did not want to give myself and be found wanting. So I was merely polite, but I wanted to respond to her gentleness and I liked her inquiring mind, her honesty and – her housekeeping. We met on common grounds of practicality.

The second afternoon of our stay we went out reefing together at low tide, collecting small cowrie shells under rocks in the shallow water and just where the ripple of the tide curled over on the beach of brown desiccated coral. We found a lot of shells and became enthusiastic, noting the changes in the pattern of the markings, according to their resting-places; they were to make presents, sleeve-links and buttons on a dress for the younger daughter. We found cat's eyes too, the cat's eye that is the operculum the Turbo Petholatus shuts when it is not at home to visitors. A long way out on the reef we got spider shells, big ones, larger than one's two closed fists together, those creamy brown-backed shells with four spiky fingers and a shorter thumb stretching out from the lip and inside, when the fish is evicted, a porcelain-hard glaze, cream-rosy, bride-blushing. It was fun to catch them as they moved pantechnicon slow over some sandy submarine cross-roads, to put them out of the water on their backs and then watch the yellow brown foot of the fish gradually protrude, feel in the sand like a blind man fumbling with strange fastenings, scuttle a little, make one or two false efforts, and then by digging the spikes in, turn over, come to rest and take up again the burden of their progress.

She spoke of their life on the island and how the lugger boys visited them sometimes and sat round the camp fire and sang. How Old Charlie Sailor, King of Malay Town near Cairns, had found a giant clam, brought it to Green Island and anchored it there by the jetty for the tourists to see when they came over on Sundays. How he sang as he rowed in, lifted it up, and dropped the cumbersome alive thing overboard.

Her mind played with associations, she saw similitudes everywhere; a shell an inch high, the colour of old ivory and stained with brown, was to her immediately a Burmese pagoda; the gemmed orifice of a clam an old medieval tapestry, while a sea-weeded rock had the colour and patina of old Chinese porcelain. These were not strained similitudes, they arose spontaneously as she spoke, but nothing in itself was. This was poetry thinking. It was how my mind liked to work, in images and not in argument, but my images were not so finished, so literary. I wondered what it would be like to know the clam simply, unrelated to a universe of artificial experience, as a native might think clam and be aware of clam only, of the clammishness of clam, these sea-creatures who shut their beautiful mouths so quickly at the least shadow, the least strange trembling of the waters, who draw their tender velvet lips back and purse them up crossly into insensitive folds of ugly sea-flesh and then close the two shells tightly together so that the four or five scollops of the teeth interlock and there is no prying them open. They are barricaded against communication by a muscular will and from the hidden inner colours one is shut out. Till one has to go away. Like Joan. Now *her* thought did not work quickly in images, it built up slowly a line of argument, it wanted to square every bit of experience into something rational, making a brick of it to build into living. A political rather than poetical or mathematical thinking; it led to a parliamentary expediency of behaviour, to brooding meditation and delayed action.

The natives can wait hours, absolutely motionless, infinitely patient, and when the clam is deceived by the stillness and opens ever so little, they take a great knife and with one slash sever the strong muscle. Should they miss and the clam be a big one it is dangerous.

When we were a very long way out where the crest of this gigantic reef sloped slowly down to the sea it came on to rain, blowing in fierce cold gusts. We sheltered by a niggerhead, waist high against the hummoch of coral, the little island obscured by the driving rain. It was as if it had been stolen away; at this distance it was so small that the wind could easily have put a hollowed paw over it and moved it over the sea as a cat pushes a leaf down a path. The others were obliterated along with the island; I had seen Ruth running shoreward before the rain shut down and two of the men farther away to the south-east. The rain was cold and drenched us, then as suddenly as it had begun it stopped, the sun came out, and the island was back in its place as if it had just stopped running, panting a little, its breath steaming, the trees winking in the new and steady brilliance of light.

We spoke of husbands and children. There were anecdotes of dear ones, hers and mine; old jokes lightly told. She said that the time came when the only thing the fondest, friendliest, most comradely parent could do was to leave her children absolutely alone. It was a blow to parental pride but it had to be faced. And this early marriage, this impetuous running into love of the very young and growing up together, did it work, ten years after? From complacency to run away. Did the young of this generation think like that then? Having missed the war must they seek suffering? Separation was suffering. One needed to be brave and have strength. Travelling was exciting. (But to oneself, how dreary, unshared.) Our relationships on board were unmentioned yet with her quick intuition she must have been aware of the strain even if Joan had not told her, but loyalty must never open the tiniest chink through which the spear of criticism could penetrate.

We spent four happy, occupied days on the island. It was wild in a civilized way. At the end of the jetty there was a tea house looked after by a caretaker, and behind the tea house a small museum of corals, sea-woods and the ant-eaten skin of a giant sea hawk. Former campers had left sleeping tents with home-made stretchers of sacking in them, a dining tent with tables and forms and a fireplace with a length of railway line across it for the pots to stand on. We used them all without scruple. It was an island freed from any litter by the caretaker and perpetually swept clean by the wind. The undergrowth was luxuriant without being dense and a surprising variety of trees grew there. Over the ground spread wild passion fruit vines. The flowers have three furry green sepals to the calyx and are perfectly formed miniature passion flowers with a faint tinge of purple in the frilly white petticoat. The sepals turn brown, brittle and sticky when the fruit is ripe. The wild passion fruit is smaller than a walnut, green in colour, soft-skinned. The way to eat them is to bite off an end, hold it to the lips, pop, and the contents shoot into one's mouth. They taste more exotic, sweeter than the cultivated passion fruit; our lips smarted from the bitter fire of their skins, our hands got bird-limed with stickiness from the sepals.

The island was full of little singing birds, fruit-eating and insec-tivorous, only on the reef did the big fishing birds come. I threw the skin of a paw-paw in a thicket and in a few minutes there were a dozen or more silver-eyes, yellowy-green and perky, pecking and chattering over it. Sven put a cake of soap on a stump and they feasted on it, as if anything green must of necessity be good to eat. They were acquiring new tastes. They found and liked some butter left with a wet linen cloth over the basin to keep it cool; their beaks were stilettos and sieved the cloth with innumer-able neat round punctures. They were companionable, gossiping little busybodies, they chirruped all the time like kindergartners at play.

During the mornings the Palmers wrote, in the afternoons we went reefing or fishing with them and at night we had suppers

167

together. They had two small tents tucked away under an arch of trees in a secluded grove just off the leeward side of the island. They cooked and wrote out of doors, Vance sitting on an upturned box and typing. He was as brown as a coffee berry.

On the second night we played the Bach records we had with us and sat by the fire talking of books and authors. Lying on my back under the big leaves of a giant beach hibiscus I could see the stars through a jagged rent where the branches of a sea cedar met the hibiscus. The smoke of the fire drifted bluely up to the gap to be lost between the velvet paws of night. Near us the high tide rose; lap, lap, lap; swish, swish, swish, about ten or fifteen feet away. Overhead the wind went pouring, a river of air, washing the palm trees, beating out their tattered fronds in a surf of motion. We underneath were calm, the leaves near us hardly moved, we were in a green cave, a green tent of leaves with the wind flowing above us. Every moment I expected it to cascade through, to break with a rush into our frail shelter, built too slightly to keep out that sweeping torrent of air. But never did it break through. The wind went on and the waves went on and the swish and roll of the sea went on and we were still secure in our green-leafed tent.

The next night after a goat-stew supper – the goat was the *Skaga* contribution to the board, he was still with us, sun-dried and rather tough with keeping – Mr. Palmer read us a short story from Tchekov, a simple story of a father telling his son not to smoke and using death and images of desolation in his explanation, and then being bewildered, knowing that honour and morality and property ideas have no place in the world of the child. As he read in a smooth calm voice it seemed that there were more important considerations to remember than oneself and that always the way out of things was by writing them down and being able to forget them.

The wind was not so noisy, it sighed high up, the tide at our elbows lapping a muted accompaniment to the words. We were all remote, blessedly remote and selfish. Green Island was a small island, in ten minutes one could run round it barefooted on a leaf-soft path through the jungle, but we could get away from each other.

Ruth was satisfied, it was the kind of coral island she had long imagined and been plaguing to be shown, but though it was a jewel of an island, it was not my idea of a perfect and typical coral island. It was too civilized, too close to the mainland. Once I had been on a fishing expedition to North-West Island in the Capricorn group and knew an intenser green foliage, all the same, of the same sort of trees, white sand shining like mica, riddled with the burrows of mutton birds, and a reef that dropped on the edge into dark blue water many fathoms deep and had clear pools where fish fluttered like rainbows and where if one dived and stayed down long enough, eyes open, they would come out of their hiding-places and sing at one, little mouths open.

At sunset I watched an old native fisherman and a boy casting a circular net of fine mesh off the jetty for bait. After a successful throw he caught six sardines and ten ugly fragments of coral that were hard to disentangle from the net without tearing it. The boy had to dive down from the high jetty into water that was so clear that it looked dangerously shallow and loosen the strands from under coral ledges. A fast current kept blowing the net into crevices. When it was freed they put the sardines into a bottle of water and the old man cast again, using an open circular sweep with the skill of a retiarius in some ancient arena. The net came up full, like a purse of shining water, but not a fish in it. So St. Peter must have fished for the small shining souls of men, using unlimited patience for so scanty a reward.

Sven too had been fishing all the afternoon. He caught only a few, the best one a big blue parrot fish striped with orange, its scales large and coarse, its mouth exactly like a parrot's beak. We wrapped it up in wet newspaper and cooked it in the hot ashes; it was delicious. A family tea that night. Ruth and I helped Mrs. Palmer lay the long plank table and stir the custard, Joan was somewhere else, Sven and Mr. Palmer were talking about fishing, Henery was scraping the ashes over a damper he had made, the sparks flew out and were extinguished in the wind.

After the meal I walked alone on the narrow strip of beach, the wind was still blowing, this ceaseless south-east trade wind that made the nerves jangle like harp strings, fretful and tense, and then that by sheer insistence set up a kind of long rhythm, an isolated fundamental, a prolonged single note of melancholy, without bitterness and not unsweet for all its ceaseless plaint. The fan-shaped leaves of the coco-nut palms moved continually up and down, turning like the vanes of a windmill, looking black like windmills against the starry sky. Presently the new moon rose out of the water, a thin yellow crescent elongated by some trick of atmospherics into a taut bow of light. A triangular black cloud, the shape of a spear-head, came down on the centre of the bow and bisected it, leaving nothing but a pair of golden cow's horns mooing in the sky. The cloud descended till the horns dwindled to points and then they too were banished, leaving the sky luminous with starshine. The palm fronds whirred round drily and the rising tide swished on the sand.

It was enough, the loneliness that could come suddenly, sharp and unwanted as an attack of indigestion, was over. Round the fire we sat close, for the wind was cold and the noise of the leaves colder. That day I had begun a story and written a poem, a birthday poem for Kim. It was not a good poem, but I had started, I had felt poetically, I had been creative and out of myself; Mrs. Palmer had made me want to. When a handful of sand is flung into deep water it takes a long time to settle, each grain, indivisible by itself, sinking but making at last a smooth fine layer on the bottom.

We had hot coffee and Mr. Palmer read again. I heard the beginning but not the end of the story. Sounds did not bring ideas with them; it was a saga in contest with the sighing of the wind, and the wind and tiredness won. I was asleep.

7th July. Back in Cairns. Joan's father had arrived. I organized my locker for the fifth time. Being a coffin it had some skeletons inside it. That black georgette. The Best Dress. It was certainly smart, in fact a model, but it took a whole box to itself and I had borne it a grudge since I fell in the water in Brisbane wearing it. So I took it with some other things to a shop-lady who said she could certainly sell it, it was as good as new, and where had it been made? She would send the cheque home for me. I was very pleased with myself; I thought I had done good business, but it was only folly. 'Where is your guarantee that she will send the money?' asked Henery, and he was quite right, she never did. In his turn he tried to be clever. Coming from Green Island we had caught two big game fish, more than we could eat, so he took one to the editor of a paper, who accepted the fish but none of the photographs Henery hoped to sell him! The *Manunda* had sailed away, Sven's friends on it, and none of Ruth's enlarge-ments were any good, so we were all, except Joan, rather unful-filled.

At night we had dinner at an hotel with the General. He was looking ill and worried. It was a difficult meal, a travesty of the gay and similar occasion in Newcastle when enterprise was hot and expectation fluttered from the masthead. However he had a joke for me. 'If a girl gains twelve pounds in two months, what will be her weight in troy measure at the end of the trip?'

Ruth foundered early in the conversation, she wouldn't take wine and was socially waterlogged; Sven steered under bare poles in the heavy seas and made a little gallant headway, a remark at a time; Joan could be pardoned her inauspicious silence for there must have been emotional currents and secret whirlpools we were not aware of, and Henery had suddenly become that strange barque, a son-in-law expected to trim his sails the right way and wondering where on the compass the matrimonial breeze would be coming from. So he turned about and tried to run down the modest sloop of my dinner-table endeavour, but nobody applauded and all he earned was my animosity. I should have liked to have given a broadside and scuttled him there and then.

Instead I cast anchor in the safe harbour of silence and held a court over my pudding plate.

'Look here, begging your pardon, Excellency, you're a wise man and you see how it is. Couldn't you make the chief witnesses talk, get it out of their systems, end the dispute and wipe the case off the lists?'

'Not by talking is it to be done. A silent witness says most.'

'Nonsense, that is only your love of the dramatic that says that. You like play-going. That Silent Witness stuff was in old-style melodrama, wasn't it? This isn't a play, it's serious – and yet at the same time it's such a silly thing, such a trifle. I don't know what it is, but it would be a little thing, a little stone the size of a pea in the gall bladder, a nuisance that a clever man like you could get rid of – but, if it's left, dangerous.'

'A little thing to you may bulk large as a mountain to someone else. It depends on the point of view.'

'I know, if you'll excuse me, that you're strong on the point of view, but some people squint, others look cross-eyed or shut their eyes altogether, or get so close they can see nothing else, and the rest get a telescope and glance from omniscience afar off. You can multiply instances yourself. But you, you're in a unique position, in this matter you've got eyes all round, you know all the witnesses, and their pasts, though there may be some circumstances of the case that have been distorted and need clearing up. If you don't help us, who can?'

'You forget. In this matter I can't be impartial. No judge can try a case in which he has so strong an interest as I have in this.'

'What is impartiality? Seeing through spectacles that are uniformly tinted? We don't need an impartial man, we need a sensible man and we don't need a judge. There has been too much judgment in this already. Judging is punishing. We need an arbitrator, someone who'll put the pudding on the right end of the see-saw and set us all off balanced again, jigging up and down in this toy of a boat and happy about it. You ought to know something about arbitrating now, or what is the point of view worth at the end of a life-time?'

'I'm afraid I can't help you. As far as I can understand . . .'

'Why don't you go on? That is just where you can help. I don't understand at all what all this underhand understanding is about. There is Ruth bewildered, crossing from side to side on the see-saw and not heavy enough to influence it, and Sven and I flung together in defence, up in the air and not able to get our feet on the ground. . . .'

'You exaggerate.'

'Come with us as far as Cooktown and live with us. It would only take two days with a good wind.'

'I have to get back. Besides, it's too uncomfortable. I'd be sick, and anyway I couldn't stand it. I'll take your word. Joan is difficult, I've known her difficult myself and she used to adore me. She's the most difficult of all the children and they're not easy – but there's a lot in the child, she's a strong character. She's as strong and inflexible in flight as a mating eagle. More of me in her than in any of the others.'

'Strong character. Admittedly, but we all don't have to live in a novel because of that, do we? You may be mistaken. Silence, this perpetual silence, isn't strength, it is an inability to face facts.'

'I seem to have heard that phrase before.'

'. . . a fundamental weakness, spiritual blindness, equivocation about motives. . . .'

'That is quite enough.'

'All right, I apologize, but if the point of view is the thing, doesn't mine count?'

'You emphasize your sufferings, perhaps she suffers too.'

'No, not in the same way, not to the same extent. Rancour can never be sensitive, if it were it couldn't be kept up over a long stretch of time.'

'I'm uncomfortable; I'm getting indigestion with all this heaviness, this talk. I felt gloomy enough before. I wish you wouldn't distress me. Silence is strength, silence is admirable.'

'Then we are back at the beginning? The Silent Witness?'

'Yes.'

'Reticence is a good quality, General, but the other thing is damnable. The unforgiving insolence of the not noticing. You know the *Borg*, don't you?'

'Yes, I admire the play.'

'Then you know how when the Borg comes up out of the water and spreads out like a clammy cold mist and its invisible fingers don't clutch the outside of your throat and squeeze the life out of you and have done with it, but poke down the inside and hold your tongue when you want to speak and twist the very words crooked as they come springing up straight and uncorrupted from the heart and wring the natural feelings dry and pitiless, then there isn't any compass that can give you the true direction and let you escape when you've got to go on – when you've got to go on – when you've got. . . .'

'Don't get hysterical.'

'No, of course not. I'm not in the least emotional to-night, I'm only emphatic.'

'Perhaps the Borg will lift. I remember in the play it went away quite suddenly.

'Perhaps it will.'

'Sorry I can't help you – but you see where I stand?'

'Yes. That's quite all right. It was only an idea. By the way, you weren't impressed by that superiority talk and snubbing at the table, were you?'

'Oh no, that doesn't mean anything to me, that's only just his way.'

'He's a bit old for that now, isn't he?'

'Don't you want me to get any peace to-night? You're a bad child. How are the others?'

'She's doing well. She's improving, and he, you must have noticed, he's a decent sort.'

'They're both dumb with me. Well, this is enough. Glad to have had the little talk. . . . I've got to say good-bye to her, good-bye on this mad adventure. It is the third good-bye, and they get worse. I don't know what I'll tell her mother when I get back. Good-bye, and I may never see her again.'

'Good-bye. Thanks for lending us the £10. We could have raised it in several places, but we all trust you. That holds, doesn't it? Good-bye, no hard feelings?'

'No, no hard feelings.'

Nobody heard the conversation, it had been inaudible, only the pudding wondered why it had been mangled, and the answer was easy, it had met the Borg and been wrestled with.

No thanks, no more wine, and if you'll excuse me from the cinema. . . .

Oh, you must come to the movies. (It is the last night, we're all so horribly gloomy, he's saying good-bye and we must celebrate, the film is a poor one, a prison story, but we're all jail-birds.)

I'll come. (But what I want is to think a poem, a poem about a beautiful island and two happy people. Did you know that islands have personalities? That every island is different from every other island and tells new strange different things and beckons inscrutably over the horizon to be sought for and found out? Even if they are reticent they like to be found out. Silence is a thing that doesn't exist. Only not-hearing exists. I am going to find out the secret of every island we come to, that will be something to do. Every island. And I shall continue to plot the course of that old ship, the *Endeavour Bark*, and nothing shall disturb me any more.

What a boaster you are!

Well, here is the first island. I give it to you, and I know it is true, for I have lain on its leafy paths and held my ear to the soil, and if one listens attentively enough one can hear the island talking.

This island seen from the sea at low tide
is nothing but a commonplace helping of spinach
on the brown plate of the reef.
But at noon in its jungly paths
it sighs and moves mysteriously,
for the wind is always busy here
tossing and shaking the green bannerettes of the trees
and snatching at the soft creeper curtains;
it flakes the sea to a moving madness of sun-speckled water;
it pours over the island, a cataract of air,
one fears to stand upright lest one be drenched in the waterfall
    of the wind.

At night the coco-nut palms are its cymbal.
The wind charges at their Don Quixote vanes
perpetually turning them to and fro.
Impossible to stop them,
they drip romance thick and sweet as nutmegged milk.

The moon is new, slim as a golden girl,
ecstatically she giggles through the coco-nut palms,
high and dry above the plumaged wind.

The whole island dances with her laughter,
it is not fixed like other islands;
it is only moored by a moonbeam and may drift like Laputa
magnetized by the moon and holding up palm-leaf sails
against the onrush of the wind.

CHAPTER XVI

SNAPPER ISLAND

THE launch against which we were moored was on schedule to leave at seven o'clock, so perforce we were, for the first time, away early. The reefs were so numerous as to make night sailing dangerous, and from now on till Thursday Island we anchored each night. We were to try to make Snapper Island before sundown, for we had been told of a deserted plantation there and we were in need of fruit and vegetables. Sven, who loved punctuality and an objective, and hated wait, wait, waiting around, roused me with a roll of drums in the voice, 'Dona, we've got to make an early start'. Bunks were for laggards and lovers. Grand to feel that there was a whole new day, begun well, fresh and white like a new page waiting to be written on.

He and I were beginning a new arrangement, a tentative agreement to share cook-days; he had difficulty in selecting menus, the problem of our likes and dislikes worried him, cooking was to him a fiddling business and he took it too seriously; as for me, frankly I didn't like washing greasy pots and pans soot-blackened from smoking primuses. And vegetables! Potatoes, of the earth earthy, stored in soil; and always onions to be peeled, strong brown onions; and some pumpkins we had bought because they were cheap – they were armoured in steel plate, not skin, and full of 'bone'. Two months' silent disciplining the soul by wiping pots and scrubbing floors had not thrust sainthood upon me. I was not going to thirst after sainthood any longer. Sven always did the pots and the floor better than anyone else; he believed in being 'thorough' about everything, and we had all come to count on him doing them, with disastrous cumulative effects. I had a conscience about the pots I had left and I rather liked cooking, so he and I had struck the bargain. I was to plan, cook, serve and wipe up for two days, while he did the nasty work. The joint plan was not to interfere with watches.

It was a pleasant, warm, easy day's sailing. We spread the charts out on the deckhouse and continued plotting Cook's route on our Admiralty charts, using the *Journal* as our authority. It was something I had been doing since Bribie Island, but the detailed nature of the bearings and courses had often puzzled me, and from being at hand with nautical whys and why nots Sven had now got involved with me in the text. There were discrepancies between the correct latitudes and longitudes and Cook's. The errors in longitude could be ascribed to the deficiencies in the chronometers and nautical tables of the eighteenth century. Flinders, thirty years after Cook, had suffered from similar inaccuracies and had had to re-check all his own positions owing to errors in the Greenwich tables which he used on his voyage of circumnavigation. He had re-identified the features of the eastern coast and had found that a reduction of twelve minutes in some parts of Cook's charts obtained a correction in the longitude of twenty and a half minutes west of Cape Gloucester, and that consequently his longitudes were at times as much as twenty and a half minutes greater than those of Cook.

Sven at first, because of these inaccuracies, was inclined to the attitude, 'Is that the best your great navigator could do?' but gradually the magnitude of Cook's accomplishment stimulated him and he came to agree with the French navigators, Marion and Duclesmeur. The account of their voyage, though published in a war year between the two countries, yet pays this magnificent tribute to Cook's map: 'Je l'ai trouvée d'une exactitude & d'un détail qui m'a étonné au-delà de toute expression. Je doute que les cartes de nos côtes de France soient dressées avec plus de précision.'

We got absorbed in it during those weeks, changing Cook's West of Greenwich to our East of Greenwich, laying down forgotten courses, taking bearings, feeling changes in winds that had blown one hundred and sixty years before, experiencing the blankness, the reef-prickled dangers that had lain in the unknown seas ahead of him, wondering why he did this and guessing how he came to miss something else. Once we had him sailing on dry land; often we went wrong, then we would go back to the tightly-packed text, a sailorly text meant to be read by sailors and misinterpreted by landlubberly grammarians, as if a navigator, writing concisely, could be expected to have the long-winded inexact kind of precision lawyers achieve. Sven would h'm over the chart and then lay down a line to reconcile all the facts. Sometimes when we had shuffled through the brief strict phrases of those tantalizing sentences heaped like a pack of cards in sequence we found ourselves in doubt about time, for Cook's day began officially at noon, not midnight, a puzzling thing, two dates covering the same hours of daylight.

Interpreting charts was new to me, a fascinating work. Currents, shoals, the places of old wrecks – Maria, 1871, that had been a crew of adventurers on the way to New Guinea gold prospecting; the survivors had all been eaten when they had struggled to the mainland – anchorages, 'foul ground', 'the beacons are liable to be washed away', the dotted lines of famous voyages, and beyond them white spaces, unsounded waters. What a lot remained to be filled in! Some of the detail still depended on no more recent a survey than that of Flinders himself.

After all, sailors were a hurrying road-conscious crowd following the furrow-beaten track, this broad red-ink highway that some senior officer had laid down on the Company's charts and steamed over a dozen times or so, for our charts were not new. Henery had collected them from various sources, but we were new voyagers and the shortest distance between two points was not our method of travelling; fortunately the broad red line, even in glass chart-rooms on the Company's bridge, had been only an imaginative progress; by the very characteristic of sea the highway remained unruled, to be travelled afresh and strangely every time.

In the afternoon, content with the morning's work and with the onus of two cook-days upon me, I resolved to make pastry.

Pastry, nothing less would satisfy me. Why of all dishes pastry above a hissing primus at sea when there was surely no need to take trouble? Oh reason, not the need. The urge that tried to make a lyric poem one day turned to pastry the next with perhaps more success. When everyone had settled down to the afternoon coma of still going along and no change in the breeze, I scrubbed the top of the water tank and floured it. There were difficulties in the way of the project; to begin with I had never made pastry before, not real stock-in-trade pastry with flour and water and butter, only an easy imitation called rough puff with an egg. A succession of helps had all been, conveniently, expert pastry makers. It took cool hands M——, best of them, used to say. Well, cool hands in the tropics, the same hands that tended the primuses and the oven, would have to be dispensed with, that was all. So would butter, for we had none, but there was goat fat carefully melted down and saved. No flour dredger, no rolling pin, no recipe. Did one put baking powder in pastry? But there was no baking powder, so that problem was solved. Not a smooth bottle on board! All the bottles were printed in relief with the names of the manufacturers of their contents, 'This bottle remains the property of . . .' The printing made a pattern on the pastry. One could at least eat the imprint of a threatening gentleman's inalienable right to a bottle; would he send divers down if one threw it overboard? Lastly the oven. I was fond of that oven though I had dratted it frequently. Had I not discovered it, a neglected and despised child on board, and coaxed it into pro-ducing the first damper? Like most delinquent children it was not really naughty, it only needed to be encouraged and under-stood.

There is a lot in the psychology of inanimate things. The fish lines for instance, they hadn't caught a fish until Ruth dyed them brown, and then they had responded to colour treatment like the lady in the advertisement for hair wash, 'no admirers before, three caught already'. Actually the oven was home-made, of galvanized iron, the size and shape of a biscuit tin, with a hole cut in the underside and meant to fit over the flame of the primus. There was a shelf one-third of the height of the oven above the hole. That was all, no packing, no flue, no browning shelf, just a thin metal box with a door that did not shut properly and a shelf that stood on two wobbling bands of metal. The whole oven too large to fit on the inner ring of the gimbal so that with every roll of the boat the oven and the pastry inside the oven rolled and pitched and tossed as well. Presumably the exercise made it lose weight, for it was unmistakably light. The material result of my effort was a jam tart, put aside and hidden till next day, a turnover and some Johnny slices with sugar and currants in them; but the satis-faction of the effort was much more, it lay in the achievement of making the oven bring forth pastry, of circumventing and overcoming its will to resistance, of climbing to a culinary civiliza-tion after days of low and monotonous living on onions and bully-beef and potatoes, hackneyed and faithful friends of the sea but stolid; beside them pastry was positively ethereal, an Ode to a Skylark in flour.

That day Joan had come upon the tin of dried pears, unseen since the day of their stowing in Brisbane. They were fine pears and had unexpectedly borne a harvest of fat succulent white grubs, big fellows that floated to the top of the bowl as the pears were washed before being spread out to dry in the sun and put back into the tin for future use. 'Shall I save the grubs?' asked Ruth, emptying the bowl overboard. 'You could make meat pies. . . .' I never made pastry again, this remained the culinary peak of the adventure, a gastronomic record best not re-attempted.

About four o'clock we came to Snapper Island, a large high island, densely wooded, with a rock-bound shore. It promised all sorts of things. We anchored in deep water close in, opposite the only strip of sand we could see, a length of twenty or thirty yards held between rocky arms that ran out and made a little lap of quiet water behind which the green bosom of the island rose steeply. To find the hidden paps of plenty we separated; if there were to be spoils we wanted to get them on board the same evening.

I chose the rocks to the north and clambered over them and along a windswept shore whose shelly surface was held together by trails of wild passion vines and another coarse binding vine, a 'likely-looking herbage', that I thought resembled the seakale Cook frequently used in anti-scorbutic brews for his crew. I gathered a small quantity. A reef ran out on this side of the island, shallow and even more desolate in appearance than nature had made it because the stumps of what had once been a low jetty stood abandoned and decaying at its farther end.

The jetty had led to the plantation. I know these deserted plantations sound too good to be true and that possibly the reader like a sceptical mother when her son brings home 'found' apples will query the 'deserted', but deserted it assuredly was, unless the monstrous and gaily-coloured spiders that mounted guard over it and the battalions of big cockroaches that lurked under every piece of timber or iron could be said to own the plantation they infested.

As I came struggling through a crop of what had once been a legitimate, aristocratic and imported turnip family Joan came, a stumpy diminutive figure, through the wall of scrub on the south-eastern side of the hill. We met by some paw-paw trees in fruit. There was no need for words, a delectable specimen fell at the first shake of the tree and split open on the ground. We each took a large half and – what is a good word for the indrawn sucking, the guzzling that a melting, neither liquid nor solid paw-paw demands in order to be appreciated at its proper worth? Paw-paws are not fruit that carry and if picked when green they ripen unhappily, their dispositions not entirely soured but thwarted, not mellowed into the brave happiness congealed sunshine ought to have, for they are congealed sunshine, or rather sunshine that is just on the point of being frozen solid without turning cold in the process. There is a just time for the eating of paw-paw, it comes at the moment when the fruit tumbles off the tree because it can hang on no longer and the eaters stand beneath, hot, thirsty, empty-stomached and with the fulfilment of finding on them. If you add to this the circumstance that the paw-paw was a mammoth of its kind, had cost us nothing to procure and had evidently been waiting for us to arrive, you get what might be known as the orgasm of paw-paw eating, the apogee of the delight of tasting. We stood in the shade, the fruit a segment of light slung from ear to ear, a sunlit brightness that turned Joan's olive skin to the brass of an old and laughing idol and my redness to vermilion. We glistened with paw-paw juice, it dripped round us. Sven came along and then Henery; we all ate on but none was so good as the first.

With pieces of galvanized iron we dug up turnips and sweet potatoes, grubbing at the rich red earth and tearing at the vines that rioted on the ground, hacking down bunches of bananas and collecting as many paw-paws as we could, green ones to use as boiled vegetable, as well as those turning yellow. I had never seen such a choking profusion of growth; the tall walls of the jungle were advancing on the clearing with slow and menacing steps; the plants civilization had brought to the island were turning savage in their fight against the springing upthrust of native grasses and weeds and were developing strange habits, losing the thick roots for which they had originally been cultivated, growing to heights unforeseen in their domesticated lives in the effort to spread and spread and by extension to shut out every other striving form of life from the too-fertile, the rankly-suckling earth. On this island battle-front, rainy season after dry season, green blood was being shed, the soil was liquid with it and the air was liquid with the taint of it; our legs were stained with green, with yellow and purple splotches from unknown vegetable essences.

The man who had begun the battle, planting his forces against the established dominion of nature, had given up the struggle and left. His kitchen, separate from the hut, was in ruins, but the hut remained for a little longer, its walls neatly made of bundles of blady grass dried and wired together over a framework of wire netting; within it a bunk, a book on engineering, a paper-backed novel, *Henry of Navarre*, the fragments of a smashed violin, and some but not a disproportionate number of empty bottles. Things brought to the island for a purpose but not worth while taking away. What evidences of personality could one get from a book on engineering, an historical novel and an aspiration after music? Had he deliberately trampled on the violin? It looked like it. From the debris of one's own possessions what conclusions would chance inheritors draw? Might they suppose more knowledge and skill than one had, credit one with a wider range of interests than one actually possessed? Make one not so human as one had been, so full of failings? The contents of the hut told nothing, the Man Who Had Gone Away remained an enigma.

At dusk we carried back to the anchorage the surplus booty that we could not pile in the dinghy. Sandflies bit our legs on the way, there was no shooing them off, the only protection would be to grow a pelt like the men whose hairy legs baffled them. English people loathe the Australian mosquitoes that pimple the smooth terrain of their complexions with huge and unsightly swellings and Australians have a tendency to be amused at it, but even we never got used to the sandflies that wielded a deadlier proboscis. They waged bitter war on us till the end of the trip. The insidious thing about them was that the stings did not begin to hurt till twenty-four hours afterwards. Till then one did not know how badly one had been bitten.

The sunset was lavish in colour, spectacular with reds, yellows and black, over-exuberant with splendour as the whole island was over-vital and struggling under its superabundant fertility like an unreproductive and unoccupied woman.

After supper and the stowing of the produce from the plantation I lay on the deckhouse to enjoy the late and feeble moonrise that turned Snapper Island into the humped outline of a camel resting; the still and coal-black surface of the sea reflected the diffused moonlight and filled the air with grey shapes that filched consciousness stealthily from me. I fell asleep in my clothes and was only roused when Ruth, who had been reading late and then leisurely preparing for bed, cried out in fright. As she had rolled up the canvas blind she had distinctly seen the rat in the pot shelf, a little place at the after end of the galley under the steering cockpit. Caught by the sudden illumination it had looked at her for an instant before hurdling the primuses and getting away into the food stowage space under the bilge bunk. A *big* rat. Ruth was impressive. We must have taken it on at Cairns. That morning we had found some gnawed pumpkin, now we were certain and the knowledge was not pleasant, even if the rat's arrival was an omen of good luck.

Wind again, at first light airs and then the south-east trade wind freshening. We had the squaresail up and that left all the deck house free for charts and books. Sven and I worked for three hours on the stretch between Sandy Cape and Cape Cleveland. He showed me how to use the sextant, but I got lost in a wilderness of tables in calculating my own observation and never found the correct answer. Instead of working it out I told them about grandfather's museum-pieces, a quadrant, too sacred for us ever to be allowed to touch, and an old-fashioned sextant with a double set of prisms and reflecting mirrors, a cumbersome thing of ebony wood, with chips of ivory inlaid to mark the degrees. He used to take it out on the veranda for the grandchildren's benefit and 'shoot the sun from the quarter-deck'.

A real old Sindbad he was: Welsh, religious, with a beard and a past so romantic as to be legendary; his father had 'drunk away three ships, a clipper, a coaler and a barquentine' – for a long time I believed he swallowed them, masts and all – and so grandfather's mother had made him promise never, never to touch strong drink, and he never had, not once in ninety years. At the age of twelve, the ships being drunk and the drinker dead from the effects, grandfather was apprenticed to a friendly captain and shipped on an outward voyage round the Horn, but at Rio de Janeiro he had fallen down one of the hatches, broken a leg and been left behind in a Spanish Roman Catholic hospital where a German 'sawbones' wanted to take the leg off but an American doctor saved it. 'He's only a boy and doesn't want to take a peg-leg home to Wales.' Nearly eighty years afterwards the 'boy's' voice still trembled with gratitude to the American doctor. Five months he was in hospital and it was three years before he saw his mother again.

The yarns he used to tell us. How he was once on a ship carrying coal across the Indian Ocean and for three weeks they were on fire, and only managed to save the boat by beaching her on the coast of Java. How with three companions he had deserted a merchantman at Calcutta and taking the ship's boat had stolen away to join the Queen's forces and help against the Mutiny. They had got twenty-seven miles up the main stream and were caught, brought back and clapped in irons and then let off, ostensibly owing to the skipper's 'sensibility of their patriotism' but actually because half his crew had already deserted and he had to have them to work the ship. How they had carried a cargo of cattle for the use of the troops in China and how a disease smote the cattle and they all swelled up, and though the skipper looked up a medical book and it said . . . there used to be gruesome and realistic details here . . . no one on board could find the right spot and they only saved six out of one hundred and fifty. How in the opium war the Chinese threw stink-pots on board . . . and what a wild place Hobart Town had been in the 'sixties. His milkman had been a 'lag' sent over for rioting in the Liverpool troubles. How grannie had come over in the first free emigrant ship, and how he had met her and taken a coasting job and finally left the sea. A settled-down Sindbad of a Grandfather.

He used to take me down to the sailing ships that had Welsh captains and that were tied up at the Stockton wharves waiting their turns to go under the cranes and load coal for South America. In those days Newcastle harbour was so busy sailing ships had to wait three weeks for a berth in the Inner Basin. He had given me a bos'n's whistle with a thick yellow cord to put round my neck and I had a sailor collar with three lines of braid on it. In these interviews he used to get excited in Welsh and when I got bored and fidgeted he would tell me to go and look at

Captain Davis' (or Williams' or Evans') pig, or chickens, and not to climb higher than the cross-trees. At one time his home was a regular port of call for Welsh sailor boys who came up to Sunday dinner and tea and had to pay for it afterwards by going to a service, a long Welsh service, and probably a lot of good advice on the way. A pious old Sindbad.

Saturday, July 9th. Joan's cook-day. She surprised and cheered us with a new dish, fried scones, fatty things dripping with golden syrup, sweet, delectable, very satisfying after a morning spent in the south-easter. They were not so much an answer to the famous pastry as a sudden stimulation of her imagination by it. When had we had the same dish before? Because we had had it together and it had been new to me. Oh yes, years ago, when we were camping at Gerringong, Mildred had made them then. 'Puff-de-loonies' she had called them, and we had all sung 'Au clair de la lune' over and over again and she couldn't cook quickly enough to satisfy us. Joan would have forgotten those puff-de-loonies, and if they were recalled to her she would think it sentimental, or gluttonous. Only a glutton would remember such a long-ago meal. In any case I was sentimental and I had eaten far too many fried scones.

It was my watch in the afternoon. We were now near Endeavour Reef where Cook had been wrecked, and I had read and re-read the vivid account of those unhappy twenty-three hours when every man aboard had worked feverishly to lighten the ship and get her off. Now the reefs were beaconed and buoyed, but then the situation had been desperate, the nearest settlement in the Dutch East Indies, thousands of miles from help. The guns had gone overboard first, most properly, they could best be spared from a scientific expedition. But the other things that could so ill be spared? How to choose? Then when the ship was lightened the feverish work of pumping, the alarm when a new leadsman took over and swung in the water-filled hold and measured the leak as gaining, the relief when his mistake was noticed, the slow painfully careful work of fothering and warping, the joy when the ship came off and was still floating.

Prayerfully they had steered for Hope Islands. 'I have named them Hope Islands because we were always in hopes of being able to reach those islands.' Hope Islands! We passed close to them, any islands more hopeless I have yet to see. They were low and bare, waterless, shadeless, two sandy freckles on the sea's hot blue face. They looked as if a high tide would cover them. Hope Islands! But a 'Merciful Providence' had sent the *Endeavour* creeping past them to the harbour of refuge the ship's boats had located on the little river where Cooktown now stands. Before they got to it a fresh gale had sprung up that prevented them making the anchorage for another thirty-six hours; the tiring, tireless reiteration of the pumps continued, while, mocking their labour, lay the distant and forbidding stretch of Weary Bay whose sombre blue shoreline we could see, the inhospitable façade of a great continent that held no easily-opened door to European explorers. After that had come the exact, the deliberate running-aground of the 'cat-built' barque in the safety of Endeavour River.

CHAPTER XVII

COOKTOWN AND LIZARD ISLAND

BECAUSE of these studies Cooktown had become one of my objectives. We reached it at night, coming close in under a headland that clipped off the wind so suddenly that the sails flapped, *Skaga* paused, and for a few minutes drifted astern with the ebb tide. In the blackness we dropped anchor, but a stentorian bellow from the darkness of the cliff over our heads warned us out of the way of traffic. Traffic? Was there traffic then in Cooktown? We moved, the harbour-master was satisfied. Cooktown. In eleven hours we had done fifty-five miles; the very light airs of the first few hours had been compensated for by the favourable northward set of the current.

Late as it was, Ruth, Sven and I, to stretch our legs, went for a walk. It was a straggling one-streeted town with heavily foliaged trees growing on the side open to the waterfront. Near the wharf where we had landed was an old wooden public-house with a square-glassed ancient lantern flickering outside it; it looked as though at any moment a gold-coach, escorted by mounted police, might dash up and shatter the sleeping silence.

The town smelt of the mainland, it smelt Australian; it had an odour of the bush, of honey, of eucalyptus and wattle, a fragrance that was sticky and warm and clean, a land breath with thousands of square miles of dry poor earth behind it yawning emptily and openly; quite a different breath from the island scent, the lush wet tropical odour of leaf-mould and flagrant vegetative growth that is almost animal with fatness, with the heaviness of generative potency.

In the morning Cooktown looked almost as deserted as it had felt at night. It was a town manifestly with a past, a town of ghosts, a moribund old town taking an unconscionable long time about

dying. When we were there it was still a town, the smallest
municipality in Australia, but arrangements were in progress to
disfranchise it and turn it over to the shire. We are a very young
country and our towns grow and wither like mushrooms; the land
is one of outposts, one has but to travel north to find it out.
Between Cooktown and Cairns there is no railway, only a small
vessel that calls once, sometimes twice a week. In the 'eighties of
last century the Palmer goldfields were in full swing and in three
years, from 1880 to 1884, fifteen thousand white men and twenty
thousand Chinese landed at Cooktown on their way to the diggings.
Now there are deserted houses everywhere, the last of the fossickers
has gone, wallabies hop down the main street at night, and the
little local railway still goes no farther than it did in 1888, to
Laura, where three families live.

What did the present population of Cooktown do for a living?
There was peanut growing, stockraising and a lot of unemploy-
ment. But everyone who could had left, except the old people,
they stayed on and drew the pension; one-fifth of the population
lived on pensions said the Town Clerk. The place was healthy
and they lived to a good old age. Schemes to develop the territory
were being floated; land grants for tobacco farming were being
taken up and if the new Batavia goldfield farther north on the
western side of Cape York Peninsula were successful – with the
introduction of capital and good machinery it might be, for they
had come upon alluvial gold at a depth of eighty feet, the buried
bed of an old river – and if . . . if a road were built . . . Cooktown might again flourish. Let us hope it will, but *Post cineres
gloria venit*, said the monument to Cook. Was it Cooktown's
epitaph as well?

As I photographed the monument with a herd of straying goats
cropping the grass at its base a man in his shirtsleeves, collarless,
out of breath and urgent, dashed up and asked if I were one of the
party going to England. I was, but I wasn't hurrying there, it
would be a long time. . . . Please would I call on his sister at the
end of the Ramsdown Pier, she kept a bar there, the name was

F——. He had spoken to the other young lady about it (Ruth), she had promised to call but had forgotten to take the name, the name was F——. He was so excited and insistent, it was strange. Didn't anybody ever leave Cooktown for England? Or for any place at all? England was of course a mythical country that older people call 'Home' and realize a little sadly they would never see again. 'When my ship comes in I'll take a trip home', is the Australian word of promise. Letters would not travel fast either between Cooktown and Ramsdown, it would take years between deliveries and the delay would not be due to the postal service; we, strangers, but Australian, could carry verbally the love that couldn't be trusted to paper and perhaps, when we delivered the message, we should get a free half-pint.

Perhaps it was thinking of beer that made me count, at any rate I did count, twenty-seven hotels, nine of them permanently closed and the rest still licensed to assuage the thirst of so few inhabitants! Most of the shops were shuttered for good and not merely for Sunday. There was only one stone building, that of the Queensland National Bank, designed in creamy sandstone and pleasingly proportioned. The main street continued out through the township and I walked on top of my spot of shadow down a long rocky road. The fences were of corrugated iron, six foot high, stripped from the roofs of deserted shanties and ugly as unimaginative sin but necessary to protect gardens from hot drying winds and goats. When goat-racing was a popular sport down south, in Sydney, before legislation stopped it, hadn't the winning goats and the boys who drove them always come from Cooktown? And these weedy, low-lying enclosures had been market gardens abandoned by the last enterprising people to leave, the Chinese.

From the dry thinly-timbered landscape still poured the peculiar sweet odour of wattle and heath, of wild lavender and a low-growing thyme; pungent, in the heat a little sickly. Why should I think of death chambers? I had only been in one once, in childhood. Why not think of other hot aromatic dusty walks?

That walk near Loftus when we picked armloads of pink boronia, days of young love and early springtime? Thoughts of death refused to be driven away. *Post cineres gloria venit.* Cook was dead and Cooktown moribund.

When, unexpectedly, a couple of miles out of the town I came to the cemetery I leant against its respectable paling fence and laughed. So this was what had been calling to me across the noonday heat, dragging as I walked unwillingly. I had asperged Cooktown, called it dead, and the dead that lived in eternity had resented it, challenged me, summoned me out to witness the testimony of 'They live for evermore'; 'The dead yet speaketh'; 'Asleep in the Lord'; and 'Gone before' cut in Gothic letters on white marble and grey polished granite. How appropriate of Cooktown to have shown me this! What a lot of Irish rested here; how boldly and confidently they claimed immortality. Perhaps the resurrection of the spirit they were so sure of was here in this honey smell of wattle, this intangible dry-season exhalation of the earth? With Mount Cook in the background I took a picture of a tombstone beginning to totter and over which spread the bare arms of a leafless frangipanni breaking at the tips into waxen heavy-scented blossom, the flower of life everlasting springing from the true wood and independent of any foliage of flesh. That photograph would be the fitting symbol of Cooktown, sleeping alive and proudly dead.

I went back by another way, through the town and to the top of the boulder-littered Grassy Hill. Young Wallabies, joeys, hopped in the long grass, this was where white men had caught their first kangaroo. It was hot, the same time of the year when Mr. Banks, Dr. Solander and Captain Cook had made the ascent of Grassy Hill. What clothes did they wear? The knee breeches of the period? Then the prickles must have stuck into their legs as they did into mine. Grass fires were burning on top of the hill and on the seaward side was a telegraph and signal station; below, beyond the township, winding away into mangrove swamps, was the Endeavour River, right branch and left, two

'Hard Labour' at Merauke

The fore and aft rig (up the Merauke River)

Skaga on the reef at Pulo Babi

'Coco-nut Tree coverlet' (Dobo)

(*top*) Helmets found on Lonthoir
(*bottom*) Ramparts (Fort Belgicae – Banda)

(*top*) Early morning on the way to market (Macassar)
(*bottom*) Mace drying in a kampong (Spice Islands)

(*top*) Malay wharf labourer, Proa Harbour
(*bottom*) Sampans

(*top*) Rescued
(*bottom*) Buying our first fresh food

Singapore — End of the Journey

loosely coiled brown snakes pinned between oyster stakes. On the northern shore, where we had heard a lonely Lutheran mission stood in the centre of a large aboriginal reserve, rose bare hills with steep valleys between them, land of no value; to the west more mangrove swamps and open flats, the honey-coloured brown of poor pasture.

I went downhill. It was an important Sunday for the town; the crew of the *Wandana*, the passenger, mail and cargo steamer that had come into port that morning and was the 'traffic' the harbour-master had been expecting, were playing the townsmen cricket. On one side of the pitch there were two cars, a lorry, benches and a few groups of spectators, most of the town. Several aboriginals were playing with the local team and their women had come down to watch. Clean and fresh in bright clothes they stood aloof from the whites, giggling nervously and not sure of themselves. Sven was watching the cricket. He had been with Henery and Ruth searching for limes, they had managed to get a sackful from an orchard. With our *Skaga* good fortune it was now afternoon tea-time. At an up-country cricket match there is tea for all. Tea, sandwiches, cake and ham. We were strangers and nobody had spoken to us but they brought us tea as a matter of course.

On the way back we passed the public school on whose veranda lay a charred log of wood about four feet long and one foot through, bearing an inscription on a brass plate: 'This tree was used to moor the *Endeavour* by Capt. Cook, June, 1770'. Whether local tradition in a country of white ants is to be relied on is another matter. An old gentleman I met later on in Thursday Island got excessively heated, apart from the weather, explaining to me that vandals had deliberately burnt the log. He lamented that Australians, with so few historical relics to boast of, had so little sense of their interest that they could burn them. Indeed I had occasion to regret that the old custom-house records of Cook-town, packed with the facts of the great goldrush, had been burned through official shortsightedness shortly before and that the cairn of stones erected by Cook on Possession Island when he claimed for England all the coastline he had discovered, had been demolished by larrikins. It didn't mollify the old gentleman to suggest that perhaps a grown-up schoolboy, tired of the name of the town and so much school-talk of the famous navigator, had, after leaving school, begun adulthood by revolution and gone secretly back at night and fired the one historical record the town was proud of possessing.

The night was overcast, the air sullen with the apprehension of thunder, only the red harbour light showing the channel lit the darkness. Occasionally came the plop, plop of a fish jumping, a curlew wailed miserably, a long thin wailing like a young baby crying. We were restless too, writing letters and copying articles that had to be dispatched by the *Wandana* early next morning. The lateness of the hour, fatigue, the sandfly bites that itched exasperatingly – Joan's had blistered and she had them swathed in bandages like the wrappings on a mummy – all these boded danger; yet under tribulation the heavy shutter of animosity, the barrier, was withdrawn; the oil of politeness on the hinge and the groove made things run smoothly between us. In difficulties we could count on each other. It was puzzling, but when there was anything real to be done it was the same. At two-thirty in the morning we went to bed but not to sleep. From time to time we got up, alternately, to swab our respective bites. Then Ruth, sleeping on deck, felt cold, came down for a coat and knocked the oven over with a clatter; and when everything was at last still the rat began to gnaw. Gnaw, gnaw, gnaw. Curse his tusks, would he have so little sense as to gnaw a hole right through and sink us all? Why hadn't we thought to buy a rat-trap? Sunday. No shops open. Throw a boot at Sunday.

On Monday, July 11th, we went off under a light land breeze followed by calms, then the wind came from two points aft of the beam and we added the mainsail reefed down to the squaresail and ran out the jib and . . . they all drew! A comical rig, like a towel horse. It led Sven to enumerate all the sails a ship could carry and the ships he had been on that carried which, and when they had been used – a great parade of canvas and a long sea-going gossip. He recalled the occasion when, under orders, he had had to wash a naked lady at sea – the figurehead of the *Beatrice*. The hills north of Cooktown harbour resembled brown plush shot with green and lying in a heavy heap, the folds of the earth rich and soft in colour, impermanent, as if they might easily be rearranged should the designer who had carelessly dropped the cloth feel displeased with the shifting blue shadows the clouds cast on the texture.

Cook had stood to the north-east when he left the Endeavour River, and we had wondered for what reason, because that course brought him close to several reefs while to the north and inshore there was a clear pasage. The sailing directions gave us the clue, they announced that the water inshore frequently had a muddy appearance, it was clear enough now for us but then it must have been muddy and spoken a warning of shoals. Between Cooktown and Cape Flattery (it had flattered Cook into the false belief that a passage lay to the north-west) the line of low hills continued, grassed in parts but in others showing large patches of white sand glistening like snow waiting to be melted away by the tropical sun.

Just another day at sea, curled up in the bows between the stowed staysail and a sack of sweet potatoes, the water swishing by slowly, evenly, soothingly, so that it seemed it was passing us, flowing away behind us while we remained stationary, the big sail bellying out above one's head, the wind cold on one's skin, the comforting sound of someone else preparing food below. And what was the date please? We had different opinions. Sven produced the date out of the log book. We believed it for want of better evidence, but we accepted it with reservations, like taking a stranger on trust, for all dates were foreign to us. If that were the date then it was a birthday date, an anniversary; well I hoped he had received the 'pome' – a poem, particularly a not-so-good poem, was a poor gift to get for one's birthday – inexpensive however.

It was late and another dark night when we made our anchorage, much too far out and dark to see anything of the island, but we could glimpse the outline of another boat closer inshore, a lugger carrying no riding light but with the glow of a fire on deck. They felt like pirates. Half in fun we got the idea of being boarded and our throats cut by the lightless ones. Joan and Henery rowed closer to investigate – and took the small revolver with them. They came back excited – an adventure is 'something that happens when one goes out by oneself' – and with the report that the lugger boys were a mixed crew, aborigines, Torres Strait islanders and a Chinese with a yellow rag twisted round his head, a villainous and picturesque group.

We were to leave Lizard Island early in the morning to make the next day's run to Bewick Island, fifty-three miles ahead. Ruth and Sven had been persuaded to get up at 5 a.m. to climb the 1200 feet peak of the island by sunrise, as Cook had done, in order to spy a way out through the innumerable reefs and shoals that barricaded the coast.

Five o'clock came in pitch blackness; we rowed to the shore, it was farther than we had thought, almost a mile. Against the starry sky bulked the bald dome of the hill with a long ridge sloping up to it. We decided to get on to the ridge and walk along it. Using the torch we stumbled through a belt of mangroves and began to climb, we wanted to race the sunrise to the top. Gradually it got lighter, but the ascent was steep for three people hurrying. We were playing a game of Captain Cook, Mr. Banks and Dr. Solander. Dr. Solander fell behind, Mr. Banks pushed ahead. Lying around on decks was not good training for hill climbing and nine stone was much more inconvenient to take up a hill than eight stone. The meanness of it, as if Captain Cook oughtn't to get there first! 'You might let me get to the top first,' raged Captain Cook. 'What difference does it make?' retorted Mr. Banks, but he was not indifferent. Climbing hills is an act of assertion, it develops pugnacity, it becomes a contest. Mr. Banks hurried more. Someone Else would have teased, saying: 'What!

If you can't win by fair means you'll try foul!' – and – waited, saying, 'Poor old Captain Cook, we must give you a leg up'.

We got to the top. The sun had not risen though the horizon was golden with light. There was a large cairn of stones and some smaller heaps, used by bêche-de-mer or trochus fishing luggers to take bearings from possibly or perhaps erected by the crew of some survey ship, there was no way of telling. Ruth came panting up and at that moment the sun began to rise, a big red surprised-looking globe above the rim of the sea. Two black clouds daubed his face like angry warts. He winked them away and shut one eye. 'Hullo, whom have we here?' he inquired, with some irony, 'Mr. Banks, Captain Cook and Dr. Solander? How interesting!' Then quickly he climbed higher, lost his ruddy rising-out-of-bed look, turned professional and shaven, a pale and burning gold, and went about his heavenly business.

We stared eastward. When Cook had looked he had seen plainly the breakers white on the outer edge of the Barrier, where the great Continental shelf encrusted with reefs drops suddenly into deep ocean. The channels, Cook's Passage through which he went and two smaller ones, had been gaps in the foaming surf piled up by strong south-east winds for many days before he took his observations. Now in the clear air we could make out, when long-sighted Sven had shown us exactly where to look, the patches of deep blue water dark against the lighter blue that covered the reef, but when the sun rose higher and cast down thousands of sparkling images of himself on the glittering surface, they were gone, snatched away in a universal shimmer.

On the landward side the view was remarkable. We could see Cape Flattery and a wide shallow bay that stretched northwards, then a low sandy shore ending in a headland and beyond a misty smear of mainland. But the true glory of the view was beneath us, in the colours that showed every gradation of depth and changing bottom of the sea. Eagle Island was closest, a tiny islet held like a drop of ink on a tremendous translucent pale green palette. Em reef – the reefs were doing their second progression through the alphabet – was brown and opaque; the muddle of reefs to the south of Lizard Island yellow sand pencilled with crayoned veinings of rock; immediately beneath we could see the anchorage where we lay and the channel up which the lugger had crept so much nearer the shore than we had dared. The flooring of the sea had revealed itself to us – 'and the waters covered the earth' – just so, from the peak of Lizard Island it was demonstrated to us, the sea bottom was submerged earth, earth frescoed with new growths, for we could see dark forests down there, fields of seaweed mustard and gleaming rivers of shining white sand running between blue pastures in that submarine landscape, but it was earth, not sea at all but a new earth that we looked at through a transparent window-glass of water and that even as we looked withdrew itself a little, was misted by a wind, a light air that came with full daylight and did not break up the surface so much as ripple it languidly, distort it, falsify it by slipping another thicker, more refractive sheet of glass over the picture of that sunken land.

A light air, the wind would soon be coming, it was time to be off. Captain Cook owned up to Dr. Solander and Mr. Banks that she had been crabby at being beaten to the top by the Dr. which was certainly not in the tradition of equanimity always preserved by the great navigator, and that the sun in rising had remarked on the fact and politely suggested to her that the roles in our play-acting had been wrongly cast, a confession that amused and enlivened the actors so much that they dared slide down the steep side of the peak directly in front of them instead of traversing the ridge again. 'Sheer madness,' quoth Dr. Solander half-way down, 'I can't go back and if I go forward down this blasted precipice I'll break either myself or my spectacles and I can't afford to do either.' Sven and I were more goat-nimble, we had had practice on North Palm.

In the mouth of the one valley of Lizard Island where the long silvery grass was bent one way, stroked into a sideways acquiescence by the prevailing wind, there stood the crumbling walls of a stone hut and piled in the corner a heap of roofing iron with the command: 'Do not touch, Property of the Cape Bedford Mission' painted in tarry letters on it. Why? Had the black souls refused to be converted and the white souls retaliated with an eighth and essentially practical addition to the Mosaic prohibitions? No 'Please'. The will of God.

There was a tragic story about this island, perhaps about this hut. Mrs. Watson, a pioneer's wife, was left here with her infant child and two Chinese servants while her husband went to the mainland. In his absence blacks came and murdered one Chinese but the other, with Mrs. Watson and the child, managed to escape and float away in an old water tank. They had no means of steering and drifted a long way; the tank came to Orpheus Island eventually. For five days they drifted, without water. On the sixth day Mrs. Watson made the last entry in her diary: 'Near dead with thirst'. There is a monument to her fortitude at Cooktown, in the main street, not far from the Cook memorial.

Rowing back past the lugger we heard an orchestration of snoring. The lugger boys were taking things easily. At the sound of our oars a frizzy-haired islander in a crumpled red and white check lap-lap pulled himself up from the hatch where he had been sleeping and stared at us, his eyeballs rolling white, sleep dripping from him stupidly. He had bleached his hair with lime and sea water; it had gone a vivid orange, and his two front teeth were filed. Unattractive, but exciting, our first Barrier encounter.

CHAPTER XVIII

THE SEVEN BLIGHTED SISTERS

A DAY of wind and on the sea a short sharp swell; the *Skaga* was buoyant, positively skittish. She frisked through these petty billows, turning her nose up over them, playing with them, rolling with them from side to side merrily and then flattening them out under her duck-tail stern, the keel cutting a bubbling, deep-foaming wake, the sails gulping at the air, swallowing it in a con-tinuous draught, their fat canvas cheeks always bulging, the leech opposite the throat rippling ever so slightly, spilling the wind out again after its passage over the full sheet.

The girls weren't seasick. They sang. Everybody sang. We sat in a row along the deckhouse and holloaed in the wind. Ruth tied herself to the sail by the reef points so that she would not slip off when it rolled. We all sat tightly packed together and sang all the songs we knew or remembered or had forgotten, nursery songs, ballads, concert programme lyrics, 'wobbly' songs, hymns, a muddle of five repertoires. Henery and I were strong on hymns, the same church had nourished our musical beginnings. It was as if nobody had ever been unhappy or could be unhappy again.

A big fish, a trevalli, was hooked, there was always more chance of catching a fish when we were travelling fast. Bewick Island in the early afternoon. A flat island, the shore edged with a fringe of mangroves, the rest of it bare with sandy soil, coarse grass and a few trees scrubby in character. 'Crabs in abundance', reported the pilot book but instead we only found sandflies. The others lit a fire on shore, it glowed ruddily through the dusk, I watched it from the boat, it was my turn to mount guard and distance lent enchantment when there were sandflies about.

Bewick Island was a disagreeable kind of island to me, it had a sour breath of seaweed and fish remains washed up by a storm and not yet turned aseptic by time. It was the first of the seven blighted sisters in this week of seven shining days, seven glistening beads strung together on the strong thread of the south-east wind; seven anchorages; seven journeys of exploration on seven islands, no six, for Escape River was not itself an island though it had Turtlehead like a flat doorstep before the entrance. Six islands and a half-sister, the seven blighted princesses in a fairy-story, beautiful unmarried princesses, for princes in the guise of men had not come with axes and spades to lead them into settled lives of production and bearing. They still had the charm of the first creation on them and were living under a spell that a malignant destiny had put on them such a remote time ago that enduring it had become no hardship but a thing of wont, and from their sleeping unawareness no number of casual visitors like ourselves could draw them for lack of the talisman, the necessary word, that had been forgotten from the beginning of Australia and cast down, a magic key, into the waters of the Great Barrier where the coral polyps had found it and worked upon it, gemming it with a crown of reefs and disguising it from the knowledge of men. Perhaps one day an aboriginal diver with more breath in his lungs than usual will come upon it and give it a tug and unlock a new industry in the north and open the doors of the palace of the Seven Blighted Sisters to the princes and the children of princes in a new generation of men.

All good fairy stories have a basis of fact and the facts in this one are the names of the Seven Blighted Sisters, the islands themselves, if you go looking for them they are probably still there: Bewick Island that was cursed with a foul breath; Stanley Island in the Flinders Group that had some points of beauty but had been cursed with leanness, with a barren and spiky malevolence; Morris Island, unutterably desolate, rat-ridden and bearing a memorial to two hundred and fifty-three souls drowned in a cyclone thereabouts; an Unnamed Island in the Lloyd group, a pimple of land slighted at birth and never given an Admiralty christening; Gore Island in the Palumna Passage where witchcraft was practised and where lugger boys with black fire and not blood in their veins danced through a night of wind; Bushy Islet where we met a Gibbet and his ghost – a Gibbet is one who always gets and never gives – this Gibbet complained of a gin sling, 'I can taste the lemon' and appropriated the rest of the alcohol on board with a lean and fever-smitten hand; Escape River where the mangroves draw back their black lips and grimace over hot mud flats; and beyond them, round the northernmost cape of our continent there was Peak Point, which presented us with sandbanks, fleas and an inhospitable anti-climax to the eerie septarchy of the Blighted Seven.

If there were the space I could make your flesh creep coming to these islands at nightfall, but there is not, so you shall go un-harrowed, except for one or two minor conundrums, like the rats. Morris Island was infested with them, its sparse soil honeycombed with their tunnellings. Yet there was no sign of fresh water, per-haps it existed, filtered by the sand, at the depth of a few feet and they had reached it. On the other hand there were the birds, thousands of them, tiny ones the size of swallows with a fluttering, a very quick flight; gulls, the rosy-beaked and red-legged kind; big solemn gannets fishing; a flock of about eight pelicans and many beautiful narrow-winged birds, flying elegantly, blessed with the grace of effortless motion, terns possibly. They wheeled swiftly about us, squawking and swooping, making haloes of flight round us as we ran below them. 'Impossible to trap or catch', Laperouse had reported of them. Now there were both rat corpses and suspicious tufts of feathers. The problem was, did the rats live on the birds or did the birds attack the rats as a change from sea-diet? Perhaps it was neither but what Nature calls striking a balance.

It was brilliant moonlight that night. Henery lit a fire of sandal-wood, jetsam that we had found; he piled it in a pyramid, fisher-man fashion, out of the wind in a hollow we dug in the sand. It burnt pungently, with a blue flame, and as long as we stayed there the birds refused to settle anywhere on the island but remained in the air, a feathered and fluttering cloud uttering harsh occasional cries.

At 5 a.m. the next morning all hands hauled at the anchor. 'Heave-ho, now then, yo-ho,' grunted Sven encouraging us, and then came the last effort, 'Up she rises,' and the anchor came up like an iron fish and rattled on the chain. The chain gang Joan called us; comradely to be called that, one of a gang. There was a sunrise like the golden fleece hung out to dry, the water very blue and clear, turquoise blue but not opaque, limpid with clarity, and in the air the breath of fallen dew. A whale, longer than *Skaga*, basked near us on the surface and blew languidly from time to time. The fisherman at Bowen had said that sometimes they came so far north – to rub against the coral and scrape the barnacles off! There was a damper of Henery's so hard that Ruth had to use a marline-spike on it and I broke a tooth trying to bite it. Joan decided importantly on this day of dazzling sunshine and shadow to sieve the barley for weevils. She found lots, black ones like beetles, and got a headache out of it and was grumpy. Amusing to see her getting cross and banging things down. Before sunset we had come to the unnamed island, a steep round little hill with rocks and mangroves on three sides and on the fourth, the north-west, off which we were anchored, a shelf of coarse sand, grass-covered. We swam, we ran about, we shouted and threw stones at a white ant's nest fifteen feet high. We knocked the top off it, and pelted it with stones, the south-east wind was in our blood. At nightfall Joan and I set fire to the long dry grass, liberating our own explosiveness. Our fires blazed magnificently, spurting forwards as if fed with petrol, racing up the hill with the wind behind them, hers in a golden circle, mine in a hissing red half S, the two fire forms drawing nearer until only a thin bank of grass divided them, then coalescing with a roar, a fiery surf in which a fresh wave meets the backwash from a previous one and the two leap high in the air until the bigger one has the mastery and passes on, triumphant but diminished.

Another day. 15th July. Ruth inherited an unholy mess in the galley and cleared it up with a stoicism so thick that it could be felt. We passed Cape Direction where Bligh took his first Australian bearings. Bligh, the autocrat, the blunt-tongued, the seaman, put by the mutineers of the *Bounty* into an open boat twenty-three feet long with seventeen other men, and making his way three thousand six hundred miles to Timor in storms, cold, rain and in the end baking heat. The ration per man twice a day had been one-twenty-fifth of a pound of bread and a quarter of a pint of water with occasionally a precious teaspoonful of rum. The incredible endurance of men, the toughness of their souls that had held the bony framework of their bodies together. Living skeletons they had become by the time they reached Timor, so that on-lookers wept to behold them. The iron discipline of Bligh, a discipline of necessity and terror only justified by the event, their salvation. He had only the recollection of Cook's charts to aid him in navigating the most dangerous waters in the world and they had feared to land because on the shore there were threatening natives and they had once already escaped the cannibal pots by running. As we passed along the coast backed by the Macrossan Range the whole appearance of the country was unspeakably barren, the bare rocks scattered like clinker on the burnt grassless slopes; a hopeless, desolate country, a Job's comforter to an explorer, Nature in a sackcloth and ashes garb of repentance; the supreme merit of such a land and of the men who first went through it and rowed past it, endurance.

One-twenty-fifth of a pound of bread, weighed out scrupulously in a pan against a pathetically small heap of roundshot. That was something to think about. As for us, we were all getting fat and no wonder, this was a typical menu I had served on one day that week:

Breakfast: Fresh paw-paw. Steamed fish and potatoes. (They had eaten mandarins after that.)

Morning Tea, and a sweet biscuit with it. (My weakness, I had had three or it might have been four biscuits.)

Midday: Fish soup. (Henery had compared it more than favourably with that of a famous hostelry). Readymeal with bully-beef, spiced barley and turnips. A steamed raisin pudding, and coffee.

Supper: Savoury rice, cheese, damper and syrup.

Then I read Bligh and was ashamed. We were eating too much, we should have to ration. Ruth thought so, too, especially since we were getting so little exercise. But we were always so hungry! And in the middle of the day dinner was an adventure to be looked forward to. Though in the days ahead we were almost to starve, it never happened that we rationed ourselves when we had plenty of food. All I ever did was to make private resolutions against gluttony, resolutions that were made, that lapsed and were renewed after the manner of such resolutions.

The reefs were getting closer, on each was a beacon. I had always thought of a beacon as a light, as a friendly beckoning harbourwards, but these were black unlighted triangles of wood and they did not beckon, they said, 'Keep away, reefs'.

The sky and the sea were definitely out of harmony that morning, the only time on the trip that I recall that their moods clashed and their hues were so discordant as to be ugly. The sky was a pale blue, the blue of a washed-out last summer's dress, dirty-white clouds were piled like stale and sedentary buns on the western horizon, while the sea was vivid, sparkling, alive, a jade full of energy and decked out with white handkerchiefs, all smiles and laughter, like a jolly girl mated with a disillusioned, pasty old man.

By afternoon we had done more than our scheduled run and continued north through Palumna Passage, a half-mile wide channel between Gore Island and Cape Grenville on the west and on the east Hicks Island and some reefs. There was a coco-nut and banana plantation on Hicks Island that the eager Ruth had hopes of despoiling, but when we got near it the water was too deep for us to anchor in, so we followed a native lugger which was making for an anchorage off Gore Island. They ran straight for the shore; when almost upon it they flung the anchor over-board, threw the helm round, ran down and made fast the sails with a swiftness that was beautiful to see. If only we could do that. Because it was so deep we tied up behind them. We became friendly with them.

That night they began to dance among themselves and continued to dance for us. They had a bundle of burra-burra bean pods that they shook and rattled like castanets as they danced on the afterdeck, their bare feet pad-padding on the planking. One of them, called Comedy, who saw a joke in everything and was for ever giggling, caught in the snare of some subtle joke of his own, sat drumming on a kerosene tin. He got music out of it, soft and melancholy, then loud and fierce. Sometimes the rolling of the ship in the swell put the boys out of step, broke up the rhythm of the dance.

Miro, the lugger master, hung from the shrouds, a dusky spider in an old panama hat, and I could not help thinking of the Emperor Jones. He cheered them on, urging them to begin again, not to mind the swaying of the dance floor, to show the ladies what they could do. His way of encouraging them was to shout, 'Hoo . . . Hoo . . . Hoo-oo,' a fierce sound that a man would make to a dog in the chase. He laughed more wildly than any of them and flourished his hat about in the starlight. A hurricane lamp swung from the rigging at his feet. When they got worked up by his cries, by the insistent throbbing of the drum and the skirl of the bean pods, they shouted back, an ugly, forceful sound, a grunt, 'Ugh – Ugh – Ugh', the reply of the hunting warrior to the medicine man, a volcano of primitive power behind it. This was no corroboree but something real, something in the blood that had to be spilled out; such a sound might have preceded the hurling of a spear, the pulling back of a wommera, the bringing down of a waddy on a thin white skull. When that dance was over they were unwilling to dance again, they had to be coaxed, but at last one or two of them danced the Sugar Bag, a dance which represents hunters going out after a wild bees' nest and getting stung, something funny to amuse the ladies and Comedy who was drumming away on his kerosene tin drum. But the 'Ugh' of the previous dance still echoed in the rigging, was carried away over long distances by the wind, dying slowly, a dirge to an old-time madness. Politely, subserviently, a little slyly, they helped us home.

The next night, 17th July, we met the Gibbet and his off-sider the Ghost at Bushy Islet, 11° 15′ S. There are several Bushy Islands, this one a 'Small spott of land with some trees upon it' and surrounded by a very large reef. The Gibbet and the Ghost were going south in a launch. They cursed the southerly wind that had helped us along. Their hands trembled. They had yarns to tell, hair-raising yarns. They also brought us news of the outside world, a three years' moratorium of war debts agreed to at Lausanne, a boycott of Irish goods by England that they reckoned would do Australian trade 'a world of good', and finally, what was most important to them, the Dublin Horse Show had been a failure as there were no English entries. After hearing the news the world seemed a dull place to us; we went on the reef looking for oysters and turtle.

The wind increased, gale force Sven estimated. A lugger with a Japanese master came running in for shelter and anchored beside us. He had two live turtles aboard, a hawk-bill and a smaller green-back. Gibbet and the Ghost stayed to dinner. They were apprehensive of drifting and gallantly Henery offered to let them tie up to us, though it would mean putting down Moses, the big anchor, and how we should ever get it up again from that depth without a winch was another matter. But the 'boy' who pulled their dinghy saved us, 'That no good, Boss', said he, hearing the plan, 'Then we all drift'. A corroboration of Sven's refusal to second Henery's invitation that made even the Gibbet decline something.

When he and the Ghost rose to go, the Gibbet very red and post-prandial, the Ghost pale and lank, the wraith of a man, the launch was not to be seen save as a dark smear on the far horizon. I should not have liked to have gone looking for it with them, the two boys pulling like black devils after the shadow, the wind piercingly cold, and the swearing, like the sea, very heavy. It was full moon and high tide. About a mile of tossing water separated us from the 'small spott of land' that was giving us all such a narrow margin of shelter. Uncomfortable to drift on a night like this. Draggle-skirted clouds flurried across the moon. From time to time Sven or Henery went up to make sure that we were holding. It was a sleepless night of rolling, banging, rattling and wind. Wind. *Wind*. WIND. Wind blowing louder, trumpeting its way along, the sound writhing over the sea, shouting down a megaphone of movement, 'North, North, North.' But *Skaga* held. We did not drift. The ships hung out the night, close together, and on either side the currents sucked by, away from us.

Next day I was up early and waiting in uncertainty, anxious to explore Escape River, to follow the exact directions and perhaps come upon the place of Kennedy's burial that had never yet been found, not knowing if Henery were willing, he had said neither yea nor nay when asked the day before. The pin-pricks of being kept waiting.

He rose late and then the Gibbet appeared. The Gibbet was in no hurry to go south. He had found his launch and weathered the night. He could have talked all day, so could Henery. Two men who meet on the track outback and sit down for a day or two to talk things over could not have been more deliberate, slower between sentences. The good wind that had been blowing steadily for hours drooped, revived, drooped again and finally dropped to a light air. On deck Sven sat watching it die, chief mourner at the obsequies and yabbering to the Gibbet's dinghy boy about 'up-river'. This boy had not been to any mission school and knew nothing about white chief explorer dead long time. Neither did he know much about up-river. 'Why-for go there, Boss? Only crocodile him live there.'

The Ghost was laid low this morning with fever. Fever?

Fever . . .? A euphemism? Or would they like to have some of our quinine? Fever. The word reminded Ruth of her anti-malaria outfit, begun but not finished. It consisted of two long-sleeved jackets and two long-legged pairs of trousers and two sets of braces that were to be the mainstays of a complicated system of buttons, in a case of emergency there were to be no less than six-teen unbuttonings. There were ventilators of doubled net puffing out at the ankles and wrists and drawn tight with elastic. A pale blue, entirely mosquito-proof garment as ungraceful as she hoped it would be efficacious. Her joy in making it had languished since Townsville, but as the conversation with the Gibbet looked like being a long session, obviously a time for task work, out came this piece of sewing. She was silent. The day before on the reef she had found a black pearl in an edible oyster, it might be valuable (it wasn't), and she didn't really trust the Gibbet.

The Cook was silent too. She was the frustrated explorer and she blew at the primuses and concocted publicly oyster soup, macaroni cheese and dampers. It was lunch time but lunch was not served. The Gibbet *must* go. At last Joan appeared, looking refreshed. Like us she had not slept during the night but she had made up for it in the morning. What a shame training had made her such a good listener and that she came fresh to the listening post. The Gibbet talked airily of a little motor boat he had that might be available at Escape River, his headquarters. A good Gibbet, after all? His motor boat? No, his company's. Lunch was served. Cookie smiled. If there was a motor boat the freedom of the river might be hers. A fine soup, the Gibbet was not un-gracious. Permission granted to use the boat *if it were there*.

It wasn't. When after exasperating light airs we arrived at Escape River in the late afternoon there were a lot of mudbanks, dull, strong-flowing muddy water, a heat haze, mosquitoes, one iron dwelling, some sorry-looking coco-nut palms and a hut with a high peaked native roof made of bundles of grass. From the black overseer Sven found that a motor boat, a new one, was expected. When? Next week. Which to an aborigine just means a long time ahead. So Sven and I laboured in the dinghy across a tide rip in the estuary and landed on some sandbanks upstream. The dinghy leaked. The happy days when its timbers would take up enough water to close the cracks in it seemed further off than ever. We had the Spare Part, the service revolver, with us because 'crocodile him live there' and both of us had a hankering to try a shot with it. We fired one shot each into the mangroves that lined the shore and made landing anywhere impossible. The gun kicked a good deal. Back on *Skaga* they heard the shots. When we got back they asked us, 'Did you get a crocodile?' and then, 'We've only fifty cartridges.' (Extravagance to fire those shots if it wasn't *at* anything.) So it had to be a crocodile, we couldn't improvize a kangaroo, not in mangroves. Sven added circumstantial detail, a thrashing tail vividly described. I had not known he had it in him. But why, oh why, to oneself afterwards, why be so weak as to fib, there didn't have to be a reason for trying out a gun, one's own gun, surely?

As for Escape River nobody wanted to stay. It was the kind of place one glimpsed and left quickly, if one didn't one would be turned into a Gibbet or a Ghost. This half-sister was the most unattractive of the Blighted Seven. She had all the elements of sordid tragedy about her, of tragedy unmitigated by comic relief, never rising into rapid or lyrical action but gathering in its forbidding drabness the potential, the dark intensity of a featureless and selfish existence that cumulates suddenly in madness. We remained overnight for the sake of the anchorage. In the morning we sailed through Albany Passage and called in at Somerset, the administrative headquarters of Northern Queensland from 1863 till 1877 when the settlement was moved to Thursday Island where it now is.

Somerset was the home of the Jardine family, the pioneers of Cape York peninsula. It was a place of vanished splendour, scene of a patriarchal autocracy, the benevolent despotism of a Scots explorer and wanderer become magistrate, ruling it over a small red-coated garrison, pearlers, shipwrecked crews, black trackers, naked savages, and missionaries. Now the slow-growing scrub had obliterated all traces of occupation save what remained of the old homestead where the coco-nut plantation was being kept in order and a little copra cured. The depression and the moving of the settlement had killed all other enterprise. The jetty had fallen to pieces, no boats were at anchor. Somerset had about it the mainland perfume, the odour of wild lavender, of honey-sweet shrubs and gum trees drying out in the heat. In countries of variegated greens, of pastures dappled and rain-brimming, whenever I think of Australia, grey-green, sunburnt Australia, I like to recall the memory of that perfume, the last taste of homeland, its first greeting to returning prodigals. Only once since Cape York have I smelt that fragrance, in the public gardens in Madrid, when it pulled me up suddenly like an invisible rein, eucalypts and honeysuckle growing together, and then – oh the nostalgia for Austria-del-Sud, the original Southern Continent of the Hapsburgs, that can be so grim and so magnificent.

CHAPTER XIX

THURSDAY ISLAND

THURSDAY ISLAND, the last Australian outpost in the north, a town that spoke of 'the good old days' before the pearling fleets moved westward, when copra was still worth growing, when piracy flourished, in a business form certainly, and when men were men and missionaries got eaten.

The Chief Pearler claimed that missionaries – he had an hereditary feud with them – either corrupted the natives by giving them religion instead of liquor, or hoodwinked the government into passing legislation that brought an honest industry to ruin. A resolute fellow that pearler, he had stood up to his neck in water on a sandbank for twelve hours during a cyclone and seen some of his companions drowned and more picked off by sharks, he had been in five shipwrecks, he had helped find a sunken Spanish galleon, he had made two fortunes, lost one and now the other was being white-anted away by taxation.

On the other hand the Chief Missionary was even more entertaining and possibly more accurate. The anecdotes he knew of Barrier and Torres Strait tribal customs were as explicit as those in Havelock Ellis or the records of the Cambridge Anthropological Society and more mythological than Jung. I was ready to believe anything by the time I heard the full symbolism of the coco-nut and the rites that accompany the ceremonial spearing of turtle. He was an ally in the historical field, a mine of information, a generous host and his wife was charming. I should have liked to have been a simple savage so that I could have had the privilege of being converted by him.

When pearlers wish to decry missionary efforts they tell Bible stories in pidgin English like this one, 'Big phella all-same pussy-cat, he come to Daniel and he say, "Look see Boss, me no want'em eat you. Me all-same lie down alonga Daniel. Me eat'em you. God send this phella big-time belly-ache".'

There is no way to understand Thursday Island unless one meets people who have settled there. They are of all the types that wander through current romantic fiction. Many of them have done odd pieces of work in incongruous places. Strange human craft pull into this port and finally drift out on an ebb, nobody knows where they go but after they have gone a flotsam of anecdote marks their passage, and the queer things that do happen in Thursday Island make any yarn seem credible. We had letters of introduction, chance acquaintances and interests that brought us into contact with some of the most interesting people on the Island, but perhaps that is an aspersion on Thursday Islanders and perhaps all the people who live there have that background of romantic endeavour or even more romantic failure that makes characters in real life fascinating.

To happen to live on Thursday Island was itself a strange phenomenon, for it was no ordinary Australian town. Indeed it was hardly Australian at all, so many of its inhabitants were Chinese or Japanese, aboriginals, New Guinea boys, or gay human fish from the net of the Polynesian islands, the offspring of curious mixings of race. It had essentially an eastern and tropical outlook on life.

Trade was bad, nor was shipping as numerous as it had been; and as Thursday Island depended on trade and shipping, when there was none it slept, which was a lot of the time. So many towns in Australia sleep. On the way north we met three sleeping beauties; Bowen that had been busily walking in its sleep, pretending to be a very progressive important town; Cooktown that had slept the tranquil sleep of the dying whose senses have blissfully left the body, which is still alive but in a coma; and Somerset that had slept the never-to-be-wakened sleep of death. But Thursday Island slept with its eyes open, in back rooms, behind shaded verandas, taking a siesta and planning what might turn out to be a forbidden, a sinister action, quick as the flash of a knife on a hot dark night.

Why badge Thursday Island with 'sinister'?

It might have been the hambone. I got to know that hambone quite well. It stood alone in a shop window, the small window of a small-goods shop in the main street, a hambone already well-carved but still with sufficient meat on it for a pound or two to be cut off. I noticed it for the first time a few days after we arrived and thereafter every day, several times a day, till we left, when it was just the same, a trifle browner maybe, for no slice to my knowledge had been taken off since we arrived. It fascinated me, it was no plaster and paint model of a hambone, but built of genuine bone, fat and sinew, and how, in the heat, without ice, it kept in that paralysed condition just before decomposition should set in, puzzled me.

Or the sinister impression may have arisen quite simply out of ordinary things, the downhill dusty main street with its low wooden buildings and their wide awnings of iron; the sharpness of the light and the blackness of the shadows cast by the mango trees, to walk out of the sunshine under their shade was to revive for an instant as if one had stepped into a cool bath; the infinitely high hazy light blue sky; the questionable back alleys down which an occasional girl, loudly painted and gaily dressed, slunk; at night the wooden sound of Chinese clogs, the shuffling of geta; the sight in mid-afternoon of a Japanese shop-keeper in pink-striped silk pyjamas sitting playing with his two yellow children on the foot-path near the fire brigade station and behind him a shop empty of goods. What did he sell? Nothing that I ever found out. It was a large shop, too, with scales, show-cases, counters, a couple of tables with austrian chairs set to them, two coloured paper scrolls on the walls and nothing besides; nothing, not a cake, not a suspender, not a handkerchief nor a barbering utensil, not a billiard table, nothing.

Or it might have been the blue velvet cushion of the pearl sellers, in a tiny office, heavily barred, with a great safe at one side and under the low and powerful electric light the flawless lustre of a single pearl, mocking and complete in itself, like the smile on the face of the Great Buddha at Kamakura, the hands that placed it there flickering in swift motion, detached by the artificial cone of brilliance from the body to which they belonged.

Or perhaps it came from sudden encounters that happened with the clear and isolated ringing of a single note. Walking across an unfenced allotment to save going round a corner and meeting an old aborigine, very black, very decent, with a grey moustache and a broad expansively-nostrilled nose, an honest nose. He greeted me 'Good day'. That was all, but from his manner and tone it was as if he knew all about me, as if he were a very old friend, as if he had been a trusty coachman to my family for years and had watched me grow up.

Or perhaps that exciting hint of something unusual and gruesome that might happen when Thursday Island stirred itself after sleeping came from the two wooden statues stored in the little iron-roofed museum at the back of the Council Chambers. They were from Torres Strait islands not far away, both deeply, strongly carved in reddish wood, flat figures of men, one narrow and tall, nine feet high and six inches wide, the other wider and about half as high. Together they insisted on the penis, primitively, clamorously shrieked Creation, LIFE! LIFE! LIFE! In face of them I felt humbled, over-civilized, shocked, not out of a previous ignorance but rather into a fuller knowledge; life and life and life, a feeble echo, was all I could answer to their challenge. When their red flannel coverings were tied round their waists again I felt more secure, yet I was glad to have seen them, they made me know a little better the lugger boys who had danced for us, the easy-going black old men who fished from the end of the big jetty, the glimpses of huts and hovels with their shuttered windows and open doors, tucked away behind bushes, under redir trees in odd corners of the more haphazard parts of the island; I was aware of the arrogant and at the same time furtive look in the eyes of the youths we passed in the street. The urge that had fashioned the statues, cruel, generative, impassive, still lived in the blood, the mixed blood, of these islanders, and the Chief Missionary knew it, understood it and accepted it: Man had made God in his own image.

I should like to go back to Thursday Island despite the fact that, except for the jewelled seas about it and the sensationalism of palm trees poster-printed against sunsets, the island has no intrinsic beauties, is badly laid out, the buildings cheaply erected, the climate trying. I should like to return because about it is the sense of currents of people as well as of ocean streams meeting. Its chief attraction is not that individuals or races stay there but that they move on. Despite the trade stagnation it had the eddies of a flowing life in it, the quickening life that the passing of people through gives to towns, the same heightening of vitality that we assume animated the industrial and fair centres on the trade routes of medieval Europe. Above all, the silence of Thursday Island was no silence, but the reticence of the East, discreet, mysterious, polite.

Perhaps I shall go back, for the old doctor there gave me quandong to eat, little woody blue-black fruit with big stones, like loquat stones, in them, and he said that those who have eaten of the quandong always return.

For me our stay at Thursday Island marked a period of furious activity in my life, seldom have I lived at such pressure and never experienced such a complexity of emotions, such a devastating negation of happiness, such a sense of bitterness and failure muddled with the registered delights, the intense interests that sprang from an absorbingly new scene, extraordinarily friendly and informative acquaintances, and a surface activity of unremitting hard work.

It was hard work, for all of us. We lived aboard, always a trial in ports; we burnt and scraped off the old paint on the hull and repainted it; we cleaned up inside, scouring white paintwork that had shown up every dirty fingermark. Ruth took the dinghy in hand, went over every crack in it with a patent preparation and painted it, making a good job of it. She also spent a great deal of time on the camera, prints and enlargements. I had a series of six historical articles to do and three or four others as well. They worried me. I also wanted to use the opportunity to look over old records and make notes on them, the Chief Missionary had given me access to a lot of material unavailable elsewhere. As well we had a number of invitations that brought us pleasant meetings and a wealth of information about life in Barrier waters. For me appointments and work fitted together like the pieces of a jigsaw puzzle.

I had my broken tooth filled, not by the local dentist, a clever young man of indeterminate race who was also bandmaster, pearl expert, optician, sporting coach, jeweller, shop-keeper and general mechanical expert, but by a visiting dentist who had called in on the island for three weeks and set up a chair in a local hotel, working under difficulties, turning a drill by foot pressure and having for his surgery fittings a tea tray, a jug of water, a glass and a large brass funereal urn in which as one spat one could not help but see the globular efforts of one's predecessors floating. Nevertheless I felt lucky to have come upon the island during a period when it had been serviced by a qualified dentist.

Towards the end of my stay I tried to have some shoes mended, but the shoemaker was away pig-shooting. It was Monday, and probably he would not get back till Thursday. Though at intervals I haunted his doorstep till Saturday he did not come back in time to do the shoes. I did not blame him, there is leisure enough on Thursday Island for everything and shooting wild pig a more entertaining way of passing a week than waiting drearily in a shop for a casual half-sole to walk in and ask to be mended.

I could not have managed at all had it not been for the civic hospitality of Thursday Island that gave me a cool room to work in. This was due to a letter of introduction from the mayor of my home town which I had presented diffidently, for Henery and Joan had found something irresistibly comic, astoundingly provincial, about civic authorities and being connected with aldermanic traditions. How was it that his laughter went *at* things, made their owners weaponless? For instance, at the pole Ruth and Sven had cut and carried down from Somerset and that had vindicated its existence that night off the telegraph station, at the 'corpse cover', at the green umbrella I had brought on board and that ultimately became a good friend to all of us. The thing possessed, when possessions are limited, becomes an extension of the self, a sneer at one strikes both, otherwise how should three of us resent this kind of laughter, this foolishness so little worthy of notice? It could not be due entirely to thin-skinned sensitiveness, legacy of teasing in childhood, that aroused this unrighteous, utterly ridiculous, indignation of the ridiculed. And what of this desire to tease, this inability to tease without malice? Why was it that after the smooth emotional waters of Barrier sailing, windruffled waters not entirely without friction, but roughly hearty, filled with enjoyment as well as the laborious building-up of the fortifications of our going-on together, why after these happy weeks should I suffer this relapse, be hurled again into the morass of conflict of Brisbane days? For I was and the others were, profoundly, and the matter of it trifles.

Not money, this time. We only had £8 boat money on which to get to Singapore. Economy, an unwise economy, denied ourselves fresh provisions and led us to eat of the stores on board so that when we were not invited out we lived on sago, sago, sago (Ruth had discovered it), rice, rice, rice, rice, and bully beef in about those proportions. Even bread we hardly bought. We were writing articles to make more money, and when the owner of the *Orion*, a luxury yacht on a world cruise, said pityingly to us, of another world adventurer, 'Poor chap, he had no money and had to write articles to get himself along', Joan and I could look across the wealth-breathing cabin and over our iced beer, their beer, smile at each other – oh rare rainbow moment! – and say nothing. No, not money.

Not Sven either. I had been over-scrupulous about that,

offending him rather than risk a harsh opinion from them, perversely trying to win their approval on a matter in which they could have, ultimately, no interest. Though I did not believe in the validity of their judgment or any reasons they might have for it, yet for practical considerations and motives, as well as on grounds of deep feeling, behaving coldly, not daring to enjoy the comfort I craved of the tenderness, the benediction of a casual caress, trying to become the paragon of untouchable unawareness that they had wished me to be. And in spite of this pathetic striving no sign of recognition of the attempt, no encouragement by friendliness, no lessening of the perpetual antagonism. Sven was still friendly though thwarted, still patient with me, often burning under his own resentments against Henery, at a loss for the reasons that had led me voluntarily to elect Joan to the judgeship upon me and amazed at my rejection of this little outing, or that small pleasure that he loved to suggest for us. Ruth, by the exceptional circumstances of her outlook and inexperience was incapable of understanding fully or of making any gesture of sympathy because she too was caught up by the spell of Joan's aloofness and under the compulsion of acting as she did.

Not work. I had done my share of painting and scrubbing, of linseed-oiling and holding the blow-lamp in the wind, arms aching, fingers burning, eyes smarting, while Sven scraped the paint off. Joan had done the same for Henery's scraping.

Not Henery. I had grown accustomed to the slow process of letting him make up his mind, used to the idea of being a passive partner and not a co-director in the adventure, resigned to the knowledge that to him Ruth and I at any rate should never get beyond being able-bodied deckhands, fellow-travellers, almost pieces of luggage, incurable amateurs in sailing, not the idea I had set out with, but it had grown a workable one. I had learnt to listen to him patiently, even to enjoy the repetition of his anecdotes, to get at last a feeling of assurance that somehow, in unnecessary discomfort, after delay, he, and we, should blunder through. I had begun to wait for suggestions to fall down like manna and to realize myself as soon leaving and of little things not mattering.

Yet it was precisely those little things that upset me most. Joan, uninvited, taking my place at the desk, the best light, moving my papers, shutting the piles of reference books, insensitive to the fact that I had gone to a lot of trouble and spent a whole morning arranging to get out of her way for a few days, and that if she appropriated the privilege of having her higher centres perpetually jarred by me, I for my part might want to get away sometimes, might not feel free to work within the cold circle of her continuous disapproval; that my writing, if she were by, was blighted. And how when I suggested that she work in the outer office she gathered up her things and never came back, leaving a red weal across our life on Thursday Island. I was made to suffer guilt for that. Then Ruth who had promised to go for a walk with me when I had washed up the supper things going off with them without saying anything while I was still doing the pots; the acute disappointment at it, so that, lonely, I went round to see the old doctor whom I liked and who had been enthusiastic about my poems. How, standing at the gate, I saw inside the lighted room the three, and how I could not go within but stood outside and went away without being seen, feeling more keenly than ever the symbolism of that bright room and the outer darkness.

At this distance one knows it was probably bad food, over-work, strain and worry, a dozen things that brought me low, but then it felt like one of those betrayals that are no less harrowing for being in a minor key.

Into this composition of morbidity came the Chinese Lady who had a face like a sunflower, a disposition turned towards cheerfulness and hospitality, an epicurean taste in food, and a low husky voice that broke into a shower of high light laughter whenever she thought of something funny, which was often. From her lips flowed a torrent of gossip, witty, good-humoured, shrewd. Her understanding after a calamitous and extraordinary life was rich in the knowledge of the intricacies of human nature. Weather-beaten, a quarter of her race inheritance Scotch, more or less poverty-stricken, the odds hopelessly against her, she was a fighter, getting and giving with an unconquerable zest for living.

Meeting her turned out later to be due to an error, she was, because of the colour question, on the wrong side of some family escutcheon: the right side, to which it was intended I should have made myself known, heard of our meeting and held aloof — which under the circumstances I count my good fortune, for the Chinese Lady was a great piece of luck. She was vastly entertaining. We had seen only the decorous or the colourful sides of Thursday Island life hitherto, but she presented us with its under-surface. Listening to her it became a different kind of island, a place of laughter and tears, of social anomalies and economic struggles to the death. Had she been born in an older civilization she would have been a professional teller of stories, she had a knack of making far-off events and unknown people dance into reality.

Out of her store of great wisdom I give the reader one small but valuable fragment, the recipe for genuine Chinese bêche-de-mer soup, a glutinous soup not at all fishy in taste she had ordered to be made for me. Soak the bêche-de-mer, the prickly green kind is really the best but the brown will do, for a day and a night. It will swell. (It has already been dried and smoke cured.) Scrape it well. Boil a chicken in the water that the soup is to be made with, take out the fowl, cook the bêche-de-mer gently a long time, many hours. Add garlic and ginger. Chop half the fowl, the best parts, into dice and last of all add a *whole cup of whisky or brandy*. I especially remember this recipe because of the night that came after hearing it, the night of Black Wednesday.

Black Wednesday, a bad day for me, one that I don't like to go back and think about. It began badly, the rat's nest fell into my hands as I fumbled among the tinned stores in the bilge-bunk locker. We were in despair about that rat, he, or as we now knew it to be, she, refused to leave and could not be caught with a variety of baits. Joan and Ruth had seen her plainly. She was a brute with a body about a foot long, and at night the sound of her teeth gnawing! It was a miracle that she had managed to keep out of sight so well, there wasn't much spare room in which to hide aboard the *Skaga*. Only on the last day of our stay did Sven get her with a toasted pumpkin seed tied to the trap.

The tide at Thursday Island behaves erratically, sometimes it is dead low for days on end with a new shore line a quarter of a mile out and all the fishing boats high and dry, then for another indefinite period it will be more or less full with little variation in the ebb and flow. Black Wednesday came at the end of a set of low tides during which we had been able to burn off the old paint, but a high wind had made it an irksome job. Then Henery found the opening of what looked like a teredos hole in the rudder; teredos is the dreaded ship worm that infests warm seas and the *Skaga* was not copper-bottomed against it. A minute examination of the lower part of the hull and along the water-line revealed a few chinky places, old screw holes and depressions that would offer attractive lodgement to the borers. These abrasions we plugged or puttied up.

Wednesday evening found me with a broken blister the size of a shilling in the palm of my right hand from some tool I had been using and tired, dispirited, sago-glum, wandering up to the hotel to pay a small bill. The proprietress was a companionable, motherly kind of woman, and she and I were sitting in her private little parlour off the bar when Sven, the pilot and the pilot's friend entered.

The Torres Straits pilots must have an unblemished record of twenty years' service before they get their positions, which are supposed to be good ones, exciting, exacting, with plenty of leisure, and lucrative. Except in special circumstances every liner and steamer threading the Barrier has to take a pilot on board to navigate the passage from Thursday Island to Cairns or Cooktown. The pilot may have an easy trip or a hard one, he may not sleep for two nights but he knows the channels like the face of an old friend – and the fee is, or was, as much as £50 or £60 a trip.

The pilot's friend was in the shell business – and a good humour.

He produced a small black pearl or two. Please keep one, no value I assure you, see, one side is flawed.

Drinks. Be sociable. Another cocktail. You've been working without any time off for three or four days, you've worked yourself out, the stuff you're writing now isn't good. You might as well have gone to the dance with Sven last night instead of sticking to those dryasdust records and sending him off by himself. No wonder he's miserable. You, you're a cross-patch shutting yourself off from pleasure the way someone else shuts you off from happiness. The pilot wants to make a good impression. That was interesting about the Japanese chief officer. No, I don't like whisky, not even if it is a blend you can't buy in Australia.

It isn't sold, if it was it couldn't be because of the duty . . . It's the best whisky in the world. You don't drink whisky? You can't get a headache out of this whisky, it's like cream. I drink such a lot of whisky it has to be good whisky when I have to get a ship through, due in at five a.m. Yes I'll take mail for you, not a regular mail boat though.

Tall stories, heavens how they must drink in these places, if half what he is telling me is true. Does he think I am Desdemona? Shall we go, Sven?

Just another one. You won't get any work done to-night, it's after nine already. You can't work up there by yourself at this hour.

I won't get any work done to-night. No I won't get any work done to-night. Thursday Island must be a tough place. The sun must get into their bones and bleach white men outwards, always being thirsty like that. One fire drives out one fire, one thought another. A man who didn't drink in the tropics would turn to dust and ashes. The fire of the liquor holds the bones together like an electric current flowing through the skeleton. Reticulated. Electrically reticulated is the phrase. Lovely phrase. Electrically gesticulating reticulated bones. The Chief Missionary doesn't drink. No, and look at him, yellow, fever-thin. Falling apart, not reticulated, fever-thin. The febrile intoxication of the fire-

223

fluttering moth. I wish I could make it flutter a little more. Soft as the fluttering fall of a flute divine, Columbine, Columbine, that's how a good line ought to flutter. This is what Joan meant when she defended whisky. Conventional feeling bright. That brilliant conversation she remembers having with Alex, it occurs to me now, she never could remember afterwards what they talked about.

Sandwiches. I should like some sandwiches please. Only sago below hatches. Better have something to eat. What happens when whisky meets sago? Does it go leathery like little oysters and kill you? Sven had sago too, more sago than I. He's stronger. It would take more whisky to kill him. The Specialist in Brisbane who said he always chewed cereals grain by grain and Ruth said quickly, 'What about sago?' and I said, 'A chameleon on tartan.' That was a good lunch. We'll have coffee too. What, coffee? Insist coffee. I wish she hadn't put so much mustard on the sandwiches.

Good story, the feud between the Gilbert Islanders and the Thursday Island boys and the moonlit corpses – falling over one under the mango tree with his throat cut, that corroborates what the Chinese Lady said. Corroborates, stupid word, an historical records word. You won't get any work done to-night. I won't get any work done to-night. Why do people put in the corroborative detail that makes everything horrible instead of factual? Because that man saw it, he didn't know at first if it were the shadow of a branch or not across the throat – and the shadow was wet. He felt it to make sure. That's what he can't forget. He forgets why the boys had to fight, fifty odd a side, but he can't forget the shadow that was wet and didn't move.

I'm glad she took me out and showed me her curios. Tactful. Tactful. She's a lady. She has taste but no fixed interest in her collecting. I think she likes people for what they give her, she says who gave her this and how much everything is worth. No purpose in it. Not like the Bishop's historical collection. These are very wonderful but owning things is silly, people get like that inside themselves too, storehouses of memories, repositories of recollections, like furniture. Sven isn't a drinking man. How many has he had? It's terrible, the pilot always drinks doubles. She is a nice woman, she stands out rounds with me without making it obvious. She serves the drinks that's why.

I've got serious. I'm not enjoying the others any more. Sven is listening far too hard, his speech is always metic – meticulous, that's because he comes from Adelaide. He looks as if listening took as much effort as hoisting the mainsail – more. Reticulous – rediculous – rediculated. There, separated them. Words get drunk too.

Now I know the hollow feeling, the duality of being oneself. Conviviality that isn't fun. It doesn't matter how many I had I wouldn't feel any different. It's macabre. It's so busily impotent in the head, like those ants, no, caterpillars. It was caterpillars Fabre saw that went walking round and round the top of the flower-pot head to tail, head to tail till they died. The head might be clear but the legs mightn't walk. If you had six legs or eight legs. It goes in waves. The hollow men, the stuffed men. This was how Sol felt before he committed suicide – calmly to contemplate a gas oven, to boast dying, Hail Horrors, Hail infernal world! Best not think about it – ages ago. Well I feel how that poet Rollan used to look as if he felt, staring in front of him and red rims round his eyes. Fair, a white rabbit. They say he drank an awful lot. I never got to know any more of him than that, just his staring.

I knew this man would tell us his troubles. I knew he had troubles. I don't blame the woman if he drank like this, these strong men of the sea are invariably sentimentalists. Sentimentalism is repressed brutalism – I mean brutality. The tails of words like to slither away. Repressed brutalism. Who said that? It sounds as if it ought to be queried, as if – it sounds cleverer than it is.

Impossible to be so miserable, deplorable to have fallen to the bottom of a well like this. That's what scorn does, pushes one off into black water; not despair, too futile for despair. To self-esteem a husband is a buttress . . . betteraword bolster, more bedtime. Should you worry? Letters and presents. The enlarging camera, the face cream and powder – mother thought of that – the books he sent. He wants to turn me into a sea-dog all those sea books he sent. The Flinders edition must have been expensive. The lap-laps Ve sent. The enlarging camera was no good to Ruth. The lap-laps Henery thought the wrong kind too. Probably are.

Quite coherent. I knew I was quite coherent. The last yarns weren't as good as the first or was I fresher then? It's a strain listening. I ought to make the effort and get back . . . home. Home. Home. We must go home. No dirty stories. Not to her, not to me. She has quiet eyes, like mother. If she weren't a lady in a hotel and if I'd met her more than twice I'd kiss her. I wonder how much of it is business and how much real liking? Sven is worried about me. I mixed my drinks, badly. Half seas over, got a cargo aboard, drowning one's cares. All nautical. Amusing, isn't it? All nautical? I'm nautical too. Half-past eleven, very late for here. Oh the pilot goes our way does he? His hotel just opposite our jetty? That jetty, notice up, go along it at your own risk, a single plank with gaps in it and the cross timbers rotten, a twenty-foot drop. A cyclone knocked it down. Wind still high. Good night. Good ni . . . The wind blew her word away. Puff. Wiped the good night off her lips.

Quite all right. Quite all right, really. Quite pleasant and exhilarating in the wind, not hollow, meaning empty like the room, being in a cage. One of them on each side holding my arm tight. What is he talking about now? Spanish coins and a wreck he found. Every one in this town keeps talking de Vega's Memorial to me. The doctor read a paper on it at the historical society, a strong historical society, that is why everybody knows about the Memorial. An aston – ishing town. Remember to photograph those Spanish coins. You might say the stars hiccup when they twinkle at you, that the wind makes them drunk, drinking a draught of air. That cloud a celestial bar-parlour inlaid with

226

pattins of bright gold. Table-topped instead. With a black pearl.
You've spoilt the idea, it was a pretty idea, the stars getting drunk,
no drunken – Be Drunken is Baudelaire. Or did Zarathustra say
it? How clearly I think, I can tell when I'm wrong. Can't I Sven?
He wouldn't know if I was right or wrong. He doesn't know
poetry.

The Blessed Damozel leaned out – On such a night as this. The
gold bar of heaven. It snapped didn't it? Somebody said it
snapped. That was the General's Wife Refuses.

No. No, thank you. We mustn't have another. Not for our
road. It's a plank. Yes we are going to walk out. You couldn't
get a dinghy anywhere at this time – unless you stole it. You'd
have to raise the town to get a motor-boat. Couldn't stay ashore.
No. No. Couldn't possibly. To-morrow morning, or the afternoon, will do for the coins. You'll be gone? That's a pity but the
proprietor will show me them. As a matter of fact someone else
mentioned to me that he had them. Don't come out on the jetty.
Dangerous. Very dangerous. It's dark but we can see the plank.
Thank you for the nice evening and the stories. Sorry we wouldn't
make it a party?

You go in front Sven. What does he call a party? Yes I'm
all right. If you stay on the sand and hold your hand up I can just
reach it to balance me over this bit of railway girder. Only the
bare iron rail left. Eight steps before the plank begins. A foot-
wide plank across eternity. You can climb the pile can't you?
Never mind the oyster shells. We're both on the plank. I'll stay
ahead. It's all right, you couldn't pass me anyway. If I keep my
eyes on the board I can tell when we come to the gaps by the
water underneath. I know you don't want to swim. What's that
you say? It's not falling it's cracking your skull as you fall.
You needn't worry. You won't have to dive in after me. I can
swim better than you anyway. The tide's in, she must be floating.
I can't see her. You moved her farther out didn't you? It seems
a long way. You can pass me here, there's a cross piece. There she
is. I can see her now. She's straining away from the wharf. You'll

have to lie down on the cross timber and heave at the mooring.
I'll hold your feet down. You'll never be able to bring the nose
close with that current against you. I'll jump for the stays when
she swings nearer and get down to the deck that way. I *can*
manage it. You don't think I can? Wait a moment now, we don't
want to wake Henery. I wish it wasn't rocking as well as a good
jump. That's the wind. The wind's been a nuisance all day.
Take off these shoes? Well they are my best shoes, don't drop
them between the beams. And my purse. When I get down I'll
hold out my dress and you can toss them down.

On deck. Are you all right?

The rope hurt my instep. No, not much. Good night . . .
What are you so fierce about? My fault? Didn't I say 'Let's go'
before nine o'clock and you said, 'Let's have another'?

Because it was my turn to pay. What would they have thought
of us if I'd gone just when it came to my turn to pay? I'm not
like. . . .

S'sh. Don't talk so loud. Sorry. I wasn't noticing who paid
but I thought he said that whisky was his own whisky. He brought
it. He smuggled it in off a Dutch skipper and there was only the
soda water to pay for.

You do know a lot. I suppose you believed everything he told
us?

Well, some of it was true wasn't it? And if it wasn't true it was
good enough to be true, it had the authentic note.

That's all you care about, the authentic note and those blasted
books. You don't care a straw for. . . .

Did I ever say or pretend I did? Haven't I always been
perfectly honest? And you, you might be polite, at least I'm
always polite to everybody. The nurse said when I came out of
anaesthetic I was fiendishly polite.

You can't change the subject this time. That's always your
trick to make me laugh. Anaesthetic! and that's what you feel
like is it? You're a disgrace!

I'm not.

You are. An anaesthetic. You actually said you felt like an anaesthetic. I had to watch you. You wanted to see those Spanish coins, you would have gone and got us into a worse mess.

Oh, I did not. I refused first, before ever you did. I was interested but I hadn't the faintest intention of going. I refused first and politely.

You wouldn't have minded going all the same.

You're just being ridiculous; you're jealous and telling lies.

I wanted you to come home earlier.

Well why didn't you say so? I only stayed because I thought you wanted to stay. Anyway I'm going below, it's madness standing up here and whispering. We'll wake Ruth.

You do nothing else but think of Ruth, Ruth, Ruth. And when it isn't Ruth it's Joan. I get sick of hearing the name.

You've no right to call me a disgrace. After all I haven't thrown up or anything and I did walk along that plank, even the bit of railway line at the beginning and nothing else beneath it. That ought to be a good enough test for anyone. It's bad enough in daytime. I'm sick too, I'm sick of being criticized. The whole thing's an impossible situation.

All right. I'll go. They'd take me on the *Orion* to-morrow. He dropped a hint yesterday. They've got more gear than we have and only three to stand the watches. It's hard work for them.

Sober truth. Sober. So that was the matter. The *Orion* and a settled position. No psychology.

Don't you want to finish the trip with us?

Yes I do. I've never started anything that I haven't finished.

He held me by both forearms steadying me. A long long silence. The boat pitching in a tumult no less chaotic than our emotions, the wind blowing the stars about and rattling at the rigging.

I said, We can't go on like this. Either you stay or you don't. We'll have to begin all over again, as if we'd just met. Everything is so impossible.

That is impossible too, isn't it? Pretending we've just met. It

is hard enough on me as it is. Don't be too hard. I've never met
. . . I . . . Pleading.

If you stay you'll have to promise. We can't argue all night.
I'm tired. Let me go. I want to go to bed. *Let me go.*

I said you were a disgrace.

You're the disgrace if you go on repeating yourself. It's a sure
sign.

Who's polite now?

I won't stay. Good night.

No good night from him. His chin thrust up against the starry
sky.

Unable to sleep. The tide going out again. Bump, bump,
bump on the bottom. She would settle soon and the bumping
would stop. A sandy bottom, couldn't hurt. After she settled if
the tide fell any more she'd heel right over on one side. It would
be the side away from the wharf, unless she fell that way and the
ropes kept her up. In that case no need to get the things out of
the locker, they wouldn't get wet as they had last time. Ruth was
awake. I'd done for myself now with her over this. Put myself
in the wrong all along the line after all this damned trying to please
them. These sheets smell. I wish I had some clean sheets from a
proper laundry. Frightfully thirsty. Sven up getting a drink. He
must be thirsty too. Thoughtful, he never pumps at night to
wake us all up. He got a cockroach right in his mouth the other
night syphoning in the dark. Give me a drink please Sven.

Sven, we mustn't get angry with each other. We can't afford to.
So silly of us. But we'll have to start all over again. Yes, that
holds. S'sh. S'sh. Ruth. Ruth. Joan. Oh go to bed. I'll see you
in the morning.

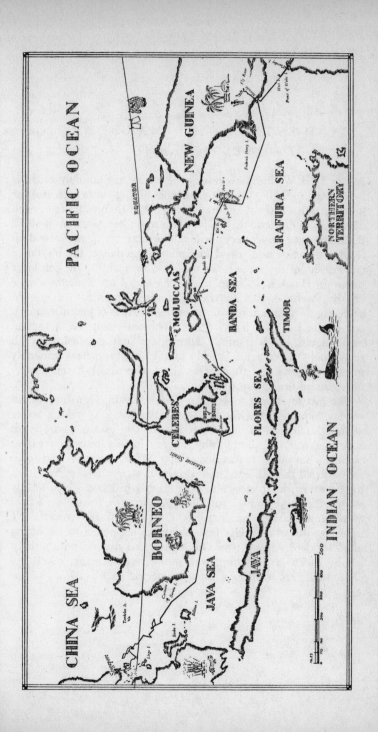

CHAPTER XX

PIG-HUNTING, AND MAROONED ON WEST ISLAND

AFTER Black Wednesday came the headache, the hot light burning behind the eyeballs, the torture of the shining sun-scaled sea, the ignorance that did not know anything better than water to quench an unslakable thirst; the dusty white street hot as an oven shelf; the shame; the Missionary's wife talking about education, modern women novelists and why I had missed the dance; the ink-faded calligraphy of the records too spiderish to read, the smooth large pages of Hawkes' edition of the *Voyage of the Rattlesnake* cool on the forehead, the illustrated Flinders, the voice of my old professor rising sonorously with the mannerisms of his enthusiasms out of the book he had written. They all said, 'Never again, never again, never again.' Three days that crawled by each repeating, 'Never again'. Sven and I calm and flat, resolutely meeting for the first time. The grind of getting all the articles finished and neatly copied out.

The last afternoon and night of our stay in Thursday Island we lay alongside but far below the steamer jetty taking water aboard. The top of our mast did not rise above wharf level. Beside us was a sardine fishing lugger come in from the treating works for supplies. It was bigger than *Skaga*, our ropes had to go round it, all the cable we had was out mooring us stem and stern to the wharf, its fenders and ours sandwiched both ships tightly so that they rose and fell together. At night we floated on a pool of ink in an aura of dazzling light flung downwards from the arc lights on the wharf high, high above. I happened to be sitting alone on deck when a New Guinea boy, very black, with a dirty sarong tucked round him, was suddenly beside me, much too close beside me, rattling a brown paper package.

Advice before we left Brisbane, 'Never let them put a foot on your deck without being invited. Rap their knuckles when they put their hands on the gunwale to try'.

But this one was already on board! He was rattling his paper bag at me and uttering incomprehensible talk out of which I ultimately picked the words, 'You buy 'em bead?'

'Let me see.'

He took a long time to undo his package and when he did so out fell long strings of red beads dripping through his dirty fingers like dark drops of blood. 'All same white girl buy 'em, coloured girl like 'em, everybody wear 'em.' Pregnant pidgin English, 'like, buy, wear'. 'One t'chillun.' One t'chillun, the aboriginal formula of price. We had met it before on Great Palm Island.

I took the beads into the softer lamp-light of the cabin and their colour won my heart. The giddi-gid is an oval shiny seed, about the size of a caper, hard and brilliantly red. It wears on one end a small black cap. These giddi-gids had been perforated through the black ends and strung so that there was a black serpent worming its way through an irregular jungle of flame.

At last, after a fortnight's stay we left Thursday Island and anchored in the lee of Prince of Wales Island a few miles off. Next morning, Joan and Ruth wrote last letters and printed last snapshots to be mailed by Miro, the Emperor Jones with the panama hat, master of the lugger boys who had danced for us at Gore Island. We had met him again on our way out from Thursday Island and he had anchored near us. I had no snapshots and I would not write another word, not even a last word. I had written enough and Black Wednesday still burnt. Instead of writing I went pig-hunting with Henery and Sven.

The tide was at half-ebb. We rowed to the shore, stuck an oar up in the ooze as a mooring for the dinghy and made for the mangroves. The mud was a grey-cream in colour, from a distance deceptively like sand but the true globergerina ooze for all that. At each step we sank above the knees and black water welled up in little geysers from all manner of tiny holes within a radius of several feet. I tried to ski quickly over the gluey stuff but it was quite impossible, it would have needed snow shoes.

If one stopped still one would go on sinking, down and down and down till the top of one's head was sucked under. I thought of stock caught in swamps and helplessly lowing at the sky for help that did not come. It was like that. Under the thickness of the mud a black crab struggled up my bare leg and made me consider other creatures that might be lurking in that soft stew of sea-soil and water. A stone fish? A stingaree? The snout of a mud-wallowing croc? I had on broken sand shoes and drill slacks rolled up to my thighs, no protection against unseen horrors. Some unhealed cuts were filled with this uncooked pudding of earth. We had three hundred yards to cross and in the centre a depression where the water came to one's waist and the mud below was more leg-clogging than ever. At length we got to the mangroves where the creamy globergerina turned to black mud, hot, bad, fetid mud. We tried to get across it by pushing our way over the mangrove roots that reclaim and clutch a hold on the seaward-slipping shore. Their bent stiff fingers strike at the mud like the strong claws of emus toe-dancing. The big roots were tough as old habits and bore us easily, but the young rootlets that had not struck the mud were smooth and pliant. The tips broke easily and were milky. After twenty or thirty minutes of bobbing, jumping and slipping over the mangroves we came to the true beach, a narrow strip of coarse white sand.

Prince of Wales Island is quite large, about twenty miles long, covered with light timber and poor grassland. We all separated, the better to scout for pig. 'I want to be alone, Sven.' No demur now, not like North Palm Island; meeting for the first time.

I had a stout rope to bind the feet of any hog we might capture but the only big game I saw was an old grey horse almost blind. Presently I went back and up the far bank of a creek, a golden brown stream, sun-speckled with dark shadows and golden bells of light ringing below, an effect of round ripe apricots and gulping dwarfs opening black mouths at them. Along the creek the trees were thick and varied. There were many kinds of gum trees, she-oaks, paper barks and one new to me, narrow leafed with open yellow blossoms that flopped like pats of butter on the amber water. Hundreds of small butterflies, blue, black and white, flying flowers, moved through the air.

By following the creek we all met again. None of us had seen any pigs though we had noticed tracks. The usual way to hunt wild pig in these parts is to use horses and dogs which catch the pigs by the ears, they are too agile to come up with on foot. At this distance from the sea the water in the creek was brackish, almost fresh. Probably there were crocodiles, the muddy shore of the island would appeal to them. Nevertheless we took the risk and swam, the men in a deep pool and I in shallower water round a bend. It would have been pleasant to have swum altogether not alone fearing crocodiles, but we were not emancipated enough for that. As I swam the feeling of mud came off my body and Black Wednesday went too, got washed away without notice in the speckledy water. We could not stay very long, we had to consider our mission, pig, and a rising tide.

On the way back we found wild ginger, ant-hills big as red cement skyscrapers that must have taken many years to build, and cabbage palms. These, like those Cook found, 'Yielded little or no cabbage'. I tried boiling some afterwards but it was terrible stuff. Henery was affable, out of port he was always nicer, his nautical hat stowed away. Crossing the mud flat was worse than coming over it had been, I was tired and the mud for all its slimy lethargy was unwearied, tenacious, gripping greasily, loath to part with either weary limb that plopped and glugged on its glutinous way. Only pride, outcome of meeting for the first time made me struggle unassisted back. Wherever the sun touched a flake of mud it dried into grey putty.

Ruth, Henery and I rowed over to Miro's lugger to take photographs. The dinghy was at last water-tight, it floated well and we did not have to bail, Ruth had made a good job of it. We found that one of the recruits to Miro's crew was of the type of New

Guinea boy who is descended from the lost tribe of Israel. The oddness of the hooked nose, the brilliant dark eyes, the woolly head and the full lips with their ingratiating smile, the semetic manner carried out in ebony above a yellow lap-lap were startling at first. Miro, as usual, was merry. Henery, taking a portrait of him, asked him for the sake of the contrast, to stand against the sail. 'You want make me white phella, eh?' he said and chuckled. For a group photograph the boys were sitting, proud and somewhat shy, opposite us on the gunwale. Miro from a position of vantage pointed first to the sun and then to my legs, often burned but still, by comparison, snow-white. 'Sun make you all same black like me. By'm'by, by'm'by. Wait plenty.' That crew had no cares, they all joined in the joke.

Miro was very obliging. That afternoon he took the others in his motor dinghy to Friday Island just opposite in order to hunt wild pig after which we still lusted. Cape York Peninsula, reputed by friends and journalists in the south to be the lair of wild pig, ferocious blacks and alligators, had shown us, apart from the denizens of Great Palm, only amiable black gins, friendly lugger boys and a very sensitive, highly-skilled half-caste. No alligators and no wild pig. Its savagery had been over-written by those who conceived adventure in terms of black and white headline events and found no journalistic glamour in subtle ordinary things. We credit that alligators and pigs do live there, but as we went north the porkers seemed to emigrate too, and when we thought we had them penned in Peak Point at the very tip of Australia the man who had been described to us as the best hunter and most pig-providing person in the territory had leaned out of his window and talked for hours about the 'bloody Bolsheviks' so that we left Australia pigless. Then, in Thursday Island, the right side of the Chinese Lady's escutcheon was to have taken us pig-hunting but unwittingly we had fouled their cables or smirched their blazonings or something, so *that* hadn't come off. In its turn Prince of Wales Island had been a blank as far as pig-getting went, so Friday Island was our last hope. Indeed the hunters got pig there, ran down three little brown and black spotted suckers, not much bigger than guinea pigs, the mother's milk still wet on their snouts. I did not go hunting with them, the mud of the morning expedition had left me blasé to pig-hunting, I minded the boat and fished. Tranquillity and a few flathead attended me.

Next day, August 4th, we made for West Island twenty miles away where the Chief Pearler had told us orchids carpeted the ground at this season. It was a day of good sailing. Luggers crossed our course skimming like birds, their hulls black, the sails slanting white. The sea was the light green of shallow water and the peculiar creamy globergerina bottom gave it an underlay as of milk beneath the transparency. A vivacious day, the breeze tempering the heat and the waves slapping *Skaga's* stout sides in play. A day when just to be alive and on the sea was an intoxication of the spirit.

'The dragon-green, the luminous, the dark, the serpent-haunted sea,
The snow-besprinkled wine of earth, the white and blue flower-foaming sea.'

On board Henery, the cook, was making elaborate preparation for roast pork, we were actually to eat the biggest of the little pigs. Miro had saved the others still alive, he intended to let them grow up. By noon we made our anchorage off the south-west of West Island, in seven fathoms with fifteen fathoms of cable out, not a particularly safe anchorage should the wind get round to the west. Then we dawdled over the pig. Ruth and I had each a back leg, riddled with shot, Sven and Joan miniature fore-quarters and the cook what remained of that pittance of a skeleton. We were all content and glad to be having a decent meal again, happy to be out of port and adventure-bound towards New Guinea. Sven was to stay aboard in case the anchor dragged, he was a little anxious and not particularly keen on orchids.

The headland which we were destined to know very closely was a hillock of black rock separated from the main island by a wide reef over which the tide ran; a common enough island formation, but this hillock and the reef were unusual in their geologic structure. The hillock looked like the peak of a drowned volcano. The rock composing it was iron hard, metallic sounding, with smooth, curved surfaces, dark in colour, almost green, obsidian. The reef was a blue clinker with little coral and that on the outer edge only. Round the base of the hillock were small fine oysters, for flavour the best we ever met, but on the reef itself there was an almost total absence of shells, sea-creatures, sea-litter or seaweed. Except for the poisonous kind of oyster that has red and green stripes on the edge of the mantle it was practically bare of life.

We wandered off separately. I leisurely collected a few oysters, and investigated the reef on which I disturbed a young alligator that was basking in the sun, a real alligator this time, a little adventure that was swallowed up in the greater calamity that came upon us. Then I scrambled through the thickets on the main island hunting orchids and at length found some, puce ones modelled like sweet peas in a cluster on a stem and rarer, prettier hooded ones, yellow with dark brown veinings. I sat under a shady tree and they lulled me into day-dreams of London, oysters, orchid shoulder sprays, evening dress and iced drinks. Iced drinks. I was very thirsty. It would be too much trouble to go and get the dinghy and row to the boat for a drink. I dozed on. Then I heard shots and saw Sven signalling from the *Skaga*. I thought she must be drifting, but it was not so. It was the dinghy. Sven had noticed it first floating then banging against the rocks and then drifting outwards and he had been trying to draw our attention to it. By the time I crossed the reef and got to the place where we had left the dinghy he had swum to bring it back, but the current and the wind had turned it and were sweeping it away round the point of the hillock and out to sea, away from *Skaga* and faster than he could swim. At one time he almost got it, was within yards of it. Then he realized that it was gaining on him and that he was getting tired so he turned back towards the island. The current was dead against him. He just managed to get back. Just. He thought he was done for. It had been a long swim and he said he would have never have made the last dreadful twenty yards if Ruth hadn't got there in time to give him a hand in. When Henery, Joan and I arrived he was lying exhausted on a rock a couple of yards from the shore which dipped straight from the cliff into several fathoms. I pumped the water from his lungs and it came up red and frothy.

Henery ran to the main island with the idea of making a smoke signal to a lugger that Ruth had seen pass by shortly before. He did not come back that night. We could do nothing but remain where we were till morning. By this time it was sunset and turning cold. We gathered all the scanty stock of wood the hillock near us afforded. We were perched on a shelf of its precipitous side where a split-off fragment of the cliff made a cave of sorts, beneath us was stark rock, below that the sea, above the sheer cliff face and out at sea the black mast-top rolling in a circle against the darkening sky. Joan and Ruth each gave a garment to Sven who had none and was shivering. Between us we had nothing warm, our wearing apparel in the daytime was always a minimum.

It was a night of great discomfort. We suffered from cold, thirst, sandflies, a bitter wind and the rough surface on which we lay. We worried too lest Henery attempt to cross the reef in the dark and get swept off by the rising tide. But out chief fear was lest *Skaga* drift and leave us to die, which we assuredly would have done on this waterless island. A mere carelessness, a trifle of a lost dinghy and the thread of life depending on it.

Soon we could not see even the mast-top rolling, tracing its erratic black circle against the darkening sky. It was blotted out altogether. When I could see that distant shadow no longer I knew that *Skaga*, stout sea horse, was our hope. I knew then the depth of the confidence I had always had in her, felt as a child might feel, losing its mother in a crowd. Our *Skaga* rocking by herself, alone and in danger as we were.

To keep warm we lay together feet towards the fire, our legs roasting and swelling as they roasted, the rest of our persons miserably cold. The supply of firewood threatened to go out, so we kept the fire small, it smoked and the smoke made us thirstier than ever. Flurries of wind struck down from the rock wall like a black cat's paw trying to dab out of existence our poor mouse of a fire. When morning came at last *Skaga* was still there, rocking grandmotherly, squat and unromantic, the anchor still holding.

We made a raft of five logs, three big ones and two smaller ones. It took us till well after midday because there was little driftwood on West Island and the vines that we bound the contrivance with kept breaking. We launched it at the most favourable spot so that the current and the tide on its last gasp of the ebb would bear us close to the *Skaga*. There was a doubt if the raft would carry us all. It did, but barely. When we all sat on it the water rose above it to our waists. We managed to drift, paddle, steer near the boat, over a half mile of water, plunge in, swim the last short distance, climb up her low green sides, fall over the broad white ledge of the gunwale, drink – blessed, divine water – eat a little, lie down and try to rest. The adventure was over.

Our first coral island, press-story kind of adventure, with subheadings: WATERLESS ISLAND. Search for Orchids. *Dinghy Adrift*. NAVIGATOR'S EFFORT. *The Raft Floats*. LET'S HAVE TEA.

And what conclusions after the event, in this calm after action, vainly trying to sleep?

First the poor body. On the face and arms scratches, happy scratches, got in the orchid hunt, sandfly bites, forty-three of them, mostly on the legs and back, swollen and itchy, on the feet and ankles coral cuts, two deep ones that might fester and take a long time to heal after the manner of coral cuts, for there is a slime on coral that is a dangerous irritant; worst of all there was a Sahara of sunburn on abdomen, arms, shoulders and back. I had given up my cretonne jacket to be torn in strips to help bind the raft together. Body why did your skin still burn while theirs went brown? The crude coco-nut oil that was the only dressing we had would grow a pelt long, hairy and goatish on you.

But for all that you were still fit and strong, and though you came out of it red and lumpy, unutterably weary, you were still fastened on to the Me, not left behind stretched empty; why not even a toe of you was missing, taken off by a shark. You were a lucky body.

And the mind? Tranquil. When it had come to a big difficulty we had pulled it off. There had been no leadership or heroics. As a group we had behaved well; no moaning, not a reference to the thirst that had tortured us, no recriminations, just working feverishly to make the raft in time.

And heart? You had been low enough and unhappy enough before and now why were you high and a little proud? Because something, it might be what people call courage, had come cool and assured, pushing the raft out with the men, till the water came chin-high, not minding the coral underfoot, amused even at the moment when, the water only knee-deep, he had said, 'Jump on Joan', not 'Jump on girls'. And she had jumped, too promptly, and Ruth had hesitated waiting to be spoken to and then scrambled on too.

Without the need of speech I knew that Joan had not had during the escape that serenity approaching indifference that, though aware of fear, can calculate chances and then take them, almost laughingly. Perhaps to let life taste bitter brought this small reward. Perhaps the poise I had always admired so was a mirrored thing, the reflection of an idealized vision of the self that always saw itself acting. The strength of the attitude of deliberation was that, as with an actor, it seldom made a false gesture but its weaknesses were those of a slowered perception, and the omission of a right action when a situation arose out of the book of the play. This poise, the ponderous walking of a heavier than air spirit on the thin edge of existence, something nevertheless of greater value than a pose made permanent, could false step, while a calm that resembled courage could elate the undeliberate, the skirmishing, ragamuffin sort of people who make mistakes out of an impetuosity of feeling.

To the rejected a realization of this nature is a victory, as if a scallawag army desultorily attacking an impregnable fortress, garrisoned and held according to the accepted, orthodox and best military tradition, saw suddenly the delusion of ramparts when disease or treason lives within the walls. That is, I think, why Heart felt lighter, the Me for the first time less diffidently inferior.

Each of us must have searched himself after the episode. Sven suffered most. He kept telling himself, and me, what he might have done; improvised a buoy, buoyed the anchor, got the sails up and followed the dinghy in *Skaga* in the hope of picking it up. He blamed himself unnecessarily, seeing that it was entirely our carelessness that had lost us the dinghy. How many times when we went ashore had I smiled at what I thought his exaggerated precautions in mooring the dinghy and keeping the tides always in the back of his mind? It was his observation that had noticed the dinghy floating and then moving off and he had swum where the rest of us would not dare, yet now he fretted and worried and waited in vain for the reassuring word that did not come. The shadow of unspoken blame was a wet-blanket on his horizon, for nobody mentioned openly the events leading to the loss of the dinghy, that was our particular *Skaga* curse. From the sins of omission and not speaking please God deliver us. As for the women, we bore our guilt easily, it was the advantage of not feeling really responsible for anything important except steering. The dinghy was lost, we could not afford to buy another one, we were lucky to be alive and that was all there was to it. We did not have the command or the blame problem rankling between us.

Two uneventful days at sea passed, reading thrillers and doctoring ailments; flat days, reaction days, the sea a muddy green.

At midnight on August 7th after a run of a hundred and fifty miles we dropped anchor in open sea; though the nearest land was twenty miles away the depth was only seven fathoms. A short choppy swell, all the worse because the tide was running against the wind, made everything on board roll and rattle. Nobody slept much. Sven sprang up to fix things about fifte times; thrice the lamp descended on me and everything left on the table or in the recess at the head of it found its way to my bunk, books, Ruth's Kepeg, a patent preparation for preserving eggs, we had used it on almost everything except dampers, the uncorked ink, my calamine lotion, the cigarette lighter and our clam-shell ash tray full of Joan and Henery's butts, a tin of cough lozenges, an empty iodine bottle and over everything kerosene. Only at dawn could I remove my unwelcome bed-fellows.

A new day. Sven was cook. Our cook-day co-operation had lapsed since our new regime of meeting for the first time. During my midday watch he lit the primus with a blast of fire and smoke that scorched up out of the steering cock-pit. As I drew my legs up hastily his voice rumbled aloft in apology, the voice of Vulcan toiling subterraneanly. Presently he put his head out of the hatch and behold, his eyelashes had been singed off! Soon the odour of frying fish surged through the cockpit steeping me in a flow of warm larva from toes to waist. We were at sea again, taking for granted the old familiar discomforts and enjoying them. When one is hungry fried fish smells good.

Now we were at the lead continually, feeling our way in, for here two fathoms was deep. As the water got shallower it changed in colour and became a murky yellow puddled with grey and it grew so stiff with mud that it looked semi-solid. Ajax may have objected to it as a flushing medium for he chose this as the only time on which he ever went seriously wrong and none of us, all become specialists in his humours, could make him work. A predicament with our first foreign port ahead and our gunwales nicely painted to impress the Dutch! However Henery rose to the occasion and achieved the only engineering triumph of the trip. It made us all very cheery and when we stuck on a sandbank, at least a mudbank, apparently in the middle of a wide ocean, we became hilarious. Though we pushed and shoved and grunted with all our might nothing happened. We pushed so hard and the bottom was so sticky that we could hardly get the poles out of the water again. They came up coated to a depth of six feet with thick grey mud. So we waited for a few hours for the tide to turn and lift us off.

Rumour had told us that a Thursday Island skipper had cruised up and down the low monotonous coastline of New Guinea for a whole day and had then returned without finding Merauke, for the entrance to the Merauke River is narrow and the river itself enters the sea slantwise, twisted behind a tongue of land. In spite of a mirage that turned black-fellows fishing on a mud flat into tall beacons marking a non-existent passage that we amateurs would have liked to have tried, Sven brought us to the true harbour without difficulty. We were all in a good mood for Merauke, hopeful, and expectant of strange wonders. Merauke did not disappoint us.

CHAPTER XXI

MERAUKE

'OUT-POST of Empire' sums up Merauke for me. It reverberated with the muffled drums of dominion over palm and pine and the despotism of empire-building in its initial stages. There must be few places still left on the world's surface that parallel Merauke for isolation and, in this mechanical age, the survival of stone-age conditions within coo-ee of a mail boat port of call. A small mail-boat but a mail boat.

The whole of Merauke resembles a stage set for a tropical life problem play, not a glamorous life-in-the-East sort of play with bazaar crowds and thrumming instruments, but a play of essentials and a small cast. It is an epitome of colonial expansion, with the neat small jetty, the clusters of coco-nut palms, their long spindly stems crooked by the prevailing wind, the two frail towers of the wireless station set above the jungle green like Meccano sets, the few small bungalows among the trees, the pink and white administrative buildings that achieved a quaint mixture of Dutch and Moorish influences, and the street of native shops filled with strange and suspect edibles. The settlement is arranged round an open square with one narrow sandy lane leading inland past the Roman Catholic mission and convent. Its boundaries are formed by the river, a swamp, the beach and some small sago plantations. One could not get lost, not even for a few minutes, in Merauke, it is not nearly large enough. One could not even disappear from it or get mislaid, Dutch-efficiency would prevent it.

The Dutch Administrator boarded us as soon as the anchor was down. He welcomed us and took us ashore, down one side of the hollow square, past two bungalows, small and tree-shaded, past the sizzling open compound of the gaol, past another bungalow to the next which was the government rest-house, dignified by the name of 'club'. We drank warm orange pop, at least that was what the women drank, and explained ourselves. No doubt we needed explaining. Our host was courteous, shrewd, genial and possessed of a sharp and tolerant sense of humour. A continental type we thought, but then four of us had never been abroad. At the club were a Dane and a German, mechanics, who had arrived from Darwin the week before in a cockleshell of a boat with a little rice, some sugar, three shillings and no papers. Previous visitors in a small boat had been two Australians, fugitives from justice, who had stolen the boat they came in and made across the Straits with it. No wonder the administrator wanted to have us explained. But our papers were in order, the *Skaga* our own, we were young and – politeness would not say mad – but unusual, and being labelled *unusual* explained us sufficiently for official purposes. What to do with the Dane and the German? Would Australia pay for them? International problems bristled suddenly, an odd feeling for Australians who, in the wateriness of the Southern hemisphere swing about their own affairs like a bob on the end of a pendulum, the creaking clockwork of European relations so remote from our daily lives.

But Merauke was more to us than a colonial outpost. It was an adventure in civilization. The stone age met us at the wharf. These New Guinea natives were stark naked except for a small shell attached to a cord round the waist, a shell just sufficient to hold the important member of the sexual trinity against the abdomen. We had been warned that shells were the *comme il faut* mode for the male creature in Merauke, but Ruth and I had vaguely imagined large-sized shells, say a bailer or half a big clam. However we were forced to admit that the cowrie style, if small, looked quite comfortable, and, carried out in white, even natty, as well as being durable and easily renewable, while the black ones gave the impression of permanent virility.

Within the barbed wire of the gaol compound walked a tall proud native clad in a shell and a friendly smile. He greeted the

Dutch Administrator very cheerily. The Australian equivalent of that greeting would have been, 'Hello, Boss!'

Why is *he* in there?

He murdered a Chinese and ate him.

The Dutchman was plump and looked tender. Did the cannibal think so too?

Has he been here long?

Five or six months.

How long is his sentence?

Four years. Cannibalism, not murder, was the more serious offence; the administration was gradually putting it down.

The other official was busy explaining to Joan, 'They like to go to gaol. Plenty of tucker, nothing to do. Ask to be put inside. They only want meat and their wives for it to be heaven.' Which might have been true, but on one of our walks we met a group of four prisoners carrying logs and they did not seem pleased with their heaven. They had seven armed Malay troopers to guard them. The numbers were not disproportionate, for these New Guinea savages were twice the size of the slender Malays who were burdened with thick uniforms, putties and accoutrement and looked hot and bad-tempered, or maybe only anxious, while the prisoners, even though they sweated, were shell-proofed and cool. They were powerfully built men and magnificently ugly and one of them was vain, at least to consider him vain made him more human than appearances would otherwise warrant. As we approached he slipped through his nose the celebrated tusk ornament of New Guinea, a curved scimitar of ivory about four inches across from tip to tip. The operation of putting it in was done in a flash, more dexterously than a woman powders her nose, but where in his scanty attire he had carried the tusks was beyond my intuition.

We were walking to a native village called Buti about four miles distant. Part of the way was along a beach, the tide was out and there were acres and acres of brown mud striped with blue channels of water, and over everything a general dazzle of light as if the air were made of thin stretched metal wires reflecting in all directions every ray of sunlight that struck them. On either hand was a mirage; a false sea glistened ahead behind the palm trees and on the horizon there were two mud shores, the real one duplicated in the sky. We trod on a glistening parquet of tiny delicate white shells and so fine and glittering were they that until I picked some up I thought they were flakes of salt dried out of the sea water by the strength of the sun.

We passed three or four canoes, big tree trunks about thirty-five feet long with a duck-tailed stern. They were each cut from a single trunk and were very smooth inside and extremely heavy, though the wood was not exceptionally hard. At the top the curve-over of the trunk had been preserved, a necessary precaution with these keelless craft that would roll and capsize easily. An elementary boat. I had seen one that morning in the harbour, a native paddling at the nose, motionless figures like a set of cardboard cut-outs between him and a man steering with a paddle at the stern.

Near the village under the shade of some trees was a group of about eight women, a few children, an immense sow and an elderly man. The old man was still young enough to be a dandy. His hair was in tiny twirls ornamented with long strings of coco-nut fibre, the ends red-tipped, so many twirls and plaited coco-nut strips that they made an Egyptian bang round the head. He wore the trappings of a primitive hunter that hitherto I had only seen in museums, a plaited cane cuff on the left arm carried his arrows, his six-foot bow lay beside him. A horn on his head held a tuft of feathers and the lobes of the ears hung down a couple of inches freighted with a garish cargo of pearl shell. The top of his nose was slit and two solid rings of bamboo the size of pennies inserted in them so that they stood on end, upright; a horrible effect.

An old, very old, lady was holding a court in the shade. She was withered, curious and intelligent. Her frizzled hair was grey and short, her mouth betel-stained, her necklace of large pieces of pearl shell splashed with red saliva and beside her was a polished gourd containing a mixture of betel and lime into which she dug

from time to time with a palmwood spatula. She motioned me to
sit beside her on her mat, but, fearing germs of an extremely
unpleasant nature from the many bare bottoms that must have
already sat there, I preferred to remain standing. Presently she
tentatively put a finger out and shyly, very slyly, with a touch
light as a pussy's paw, touched my grey silk stockings. It was our
first morning ashore and we were dressed for the Administrator –
with care. She had never encountered stockings before. 'White
face and grey legs,' I could see her thinking, 'I wonder what the
flesh feels like.' She looked up at me, full of inquisitive wonder
and yet polite. Then she pretended to be looking at something
else. I kept quite still. Surreptitiously she looked and touched
again. I could tell that she was dying to raise the fluttering hem
of my blue dress and peer beneath and up! She resisted the impulse, I had a look in my eye that said, 'No'. After all civilization
must keep its own secrets.

Along the village street stood neat houses walled with plaited
palm matting and roofed with atap thatch, the flooring was of
split bamboo. The huts stood four or five feet above the ground.
The heat was terrific, the glare overpowering. It was siesta hour
and under such conditions an hour can last all day. Within the
dark doorway of a house I saw a man asleep, wrapped in his big
grass mat and on the veranda a woman listlessly pounding something in a mortar. A collection of old crones were standing in a
patch of shadow, so dark and still that at first I did not notice
them. Asked by signs to come out so that I should have a figure
in the foreground of a photograph one advanced, understanding
me, to the edge of the shadow. She paused, put out a bare foot
on the hot sand, withdrew it hastily and returned to the shade.
Much too hot. Under the shade of the coco-nut trees behind the
village were the bucks, recumbent and gossiping. The only one
not lying down was either the barber or the physician of the
village. He was engaged in de-lousing the fuzzy topknots of his
friends or clients. He seemed to be having excellent hunting.
Farther away was a group of women – the Younger Set of this

society – young matrons and girls. One of them was nursing a young pig at one breast and her baby at the other.

It was cool under the coco-nuts, cathedral cool and high. Sven ordered green coco-nuts through the native policeman, who accompanied us, and whose bare feet, pierced nose and dangling ear lobes accorded but ill with the splendour of his khaki and red uniform. The coco-nuts came, nicely husked, the top cut off with a big kris, and a strip of the green husk turned down and left to form a handle. The drink was delicious and absolutely germ proof. Such a lot in one! We swigged lustily. Mother's milk was never so sweet or welcome as this slightly fizzy green ginger beer, still cool from its perch in the tree top. But green coco-nut milk makes heavy walking. We staggered boatwards, barrel-blown. 'Eat a couple of sago cakes' – we had seen them in native shops like pinky dog biscuits – 'drink some k'lapa muda and die,' said a planter to us later. Without sampling the sago biscuits, staple native diet, I believe him.

That night I developed films, and Henery tinkered with the boat camera that had gone wrong. We were busy and all of us intensely enthusiastic.

Henery had come into his own. He fixed up the papers, explained us to the Administrator and kept on talking. The four of us waggled after him like a tail, a starched tail in white suits and cotton dresses, and heavens the ironing of them! There was a joke about those white suits. The beginning of it we noticed ourselves, amused, maliciously, and the end of it Henery told us. The General had given his son-in-law some tropical suits for which he had no more use. Now the General was large, rotund, bearish, and Henery tall, thin, giraffe-like. The suits had to be well-reefed to even approximate to a fit. Some had been altered by a tailor, others not. Henery, unsupervised by Joan, had donned one of those that had not been altered, and until we got on shore and in tail formation we had not noticed it. When we did we could not mention it lest it affect his aplomb, for he was going to an interview on the success of which depended a lot, and Joan had a furrow in her forehead that made her not laughter-wise. The slack of the suit bellied and crackled starchily. The end of the tail wagged merrily. 'Carrying too much canvas,' whispered Sven. The end of the story came weeks later, in the laundering of that suit. 'Ah tuan,' said the Chinese laundryman, bulk is a sign of health as well as wealth in the orient, 'Ah tuan you bin sick man, velly sick man. Me solly for you, velly solly'. He sighed condolingly as he folded up the General's linen and ran his eye over Henery's meagre carcass.

Unconsciously we were diplomatic in Merauke. At the beginning of our stay we spent money. That fact and our papers, news of which had been noised abroad, made us important people, or shall we say potentially important people, for we had little money and spent carefully. But in the first few hours we had dispatched a parcel, sent a cable, and bought stamps, tooth paste, vegetables, coco-nuts, trade tobacco, betel and a topee. Sven bought the topee. We, and as much of the population as could see through the window or squeeze into the shop, assisted him. He got so embarrassed he could hardly look in the mirror and to a state when all the topees felt the wrong size. Ruth almost bought a hat too, a large coarse brown straw, with a sailor brim, a leather chin strap and a curious stud let in one side, but she subsequently rejoiced over the narrowness of her escape. The hat she had chosen proved to be the regulation all-year uniform of the native police and the favourite and coveted headgear of every Malay boat boy and of every native plutocrat returning villageward from a spell of prison or labour in the metropolis of Merauke.

Our money prestige gradually died away. We ordered 'Loaves of bread' at the 'roti' or baker's shop, at a cost to us of ninepence a loaf, but the size of the loaf had been indicated to us by a fisherman's gesture, and when those ninepenny loaves arrived we found them to be the size of small buns and sickly sweet. No more bread. It had never been the staff of life here and there was a heavy duty on flour, Australian flour. Fowls? Henery was buying a small one at a price to us about two shillings and threepence, and the Manillaman who sold it to us was aghast. Ostentatiously he counted us up, one, two, three, one, two – five, five large-sized and hungry people. Then he demonstrated the carving into portions of the pullet, very thin for all its feathers, that was even then kicking between his hands. Basely Joan and I fled. We had in some things the same touchable points.

Henery's aplomb was successful and the Dutch Administrator extremely courteous, unless he had private reasons for keeping a set of apparent lunatics – mad Australians – under observation. He invited us to accompany him on the tour of inspection he made every two months up country in the border between British and Dutch New Guinea, a hundred and sixty-five miles up the meandering Merauke River. We were to take our own bedding and food. So feverishly we packed – rugs, cushions, biscuits, prunes, peanut butter, sago, rice, potatoes, kumali – a native sweet potato that the chief missionary's wife had given us – limes, bananas, shorts – no more starched suits or dresses – pyjamas and the chronometer, which had to be wound daily and which Sven would not trust to anyone ashore. We were ready.

The government launch on which we went carried some curious passengers, other than ourselves. In the bow was a Japanese butcher who was going to kill wild cattle that the Administrator hoped to salt, a very dignified person that butcher. What happened to him? I don't recollect him on the homeward trip and there certainly were no wild cattle, not one. Perhaps the Japanese was only a spectre who arose for me out of an inadequate understanding of our host's English. Perhaps the launch put him off by stealth and he was to come back on the next trip, two months later with the carcasses. Perhaps – perhaps (confess it) in the kaleidoscopic impressions of that first marvellous jungle day you confused him with Sakota, the Malay chief of staff, who aspired to learn English and was writing a book on Primitive Ceremonies and Magic for which he had been gathering material for fourteen years and would finish in another ten years' time. There was also the Pastor, a young Roman Catholic German priest, who spoke eight languages and had recently come to this remote missionary field pledged to a stay of ten years. Ten years here! (If one were also pledged to celibacy perhaps ten years anywhere wouldn't matter.) He had a taste in wine, a soft voice, a D. H. Lawrence beard and carried his luggage in a big basket made of split and coloured bamboo intricately patterned with shells. Then there was a cluster of Kai-kai (Kai-kai literally means eaters of men, and is the Malay name for the native) who were being returned to their kampongs and carried their wages or their rewards in coloured handkerchief bundles. There was a group of native police, these clothed in trousers with dignity to match, and the staff – cooks, attendants, the Malay boat boys and the engineer.

I liked these Malay boys very much. They were not pure Malay. Their hair waved in various degrees of curliness and their faces showed traces of New Guinea, Chinese and other racial characteristics, but they were smart and attractive in their matelot blue uniforms with red collars. They were very clean, bathed often, used tooth paste, scented toilet soap, and were gentlemen. That is, they knew how to achieve and spend a lot of leisure time, how to loaf gracefully, sing, play cards, be merry or good-humoured all day, to delight in conversation, quips and mechanical gadgets and leave really hard work to the white men and coolies.

A strong current made going upstream slow work, but we could make some use of the tide, for fifty miles the river was tidal. Gradually the banks closed in. There was a 'young' jungle growth along the margin and prairie country beyond. The banks were lined with yellow foliaged trees, with low river palms, feathery fluttering bamboos and sago palms. Sago palms do not grow as high as the elegant coco-nuts, the fronds are bigger, the trunks rougher and thicker. Our passage disturbed many brown water birds of the moorhen variety, bronze-winged pigeons, and blue fishing birds of the kingfisher family. Overhead flew flocks of white egrets.

I was anxious to notice and remember everything on this first day of a new adventure but the heat, the attentive listening to polite and foreign conversation, the drowsiness and the strange loud mechanical pulsing of the engine heart that throbbed through the decks and out through the water to ripple in pulsations of the reeds growing by the banks and die shudderingly away long after we had passed, lulled me to such a sleepiness that I only remember a sliding by of unbroken green walls and the one irrelevant fact that Joan smoked a cigar, a whole, strong, Dutch cigar, and said, insisted, that it tasted fine!

At 3 p.m. we anchored for the night off a little native village in the jungle. Most of the population was at the jetty, a handful of twenty or thirty. An outbreak of influenza some years before had killed many of the inhabitants and the remainder had left their old houses standing and moved inland a little way off. The Administrator distributed largesse, pads of tobacco to an old woman to be divded among the women, a larger quantity to the headman for the men, and boiled sweets for the children.

The children. They were so unlaughing, their toys weapons of the chase, small bows and arrows. A three-year-old meeting us on a path howled with fright at our hideous white faces, his father had to pick him up and comfort him. The men and women carried grass purses or dilly bags in which they carried their immediate stock of betel or their most cherished small possessions. The smallest children had their dilly bags, too, in that of a four-year-old whose hair started like black lamb's wool from the scalp, were an ancient chocolate tin, a green tobacco leaf, and an assortment of coloured stones and feathers. A baby lay in his carrying basket, it was the shape and size of a carpenter's tool bag and – oh Chief Missionary, how wise you were – it was protected against evil by two white cowrie shells, symbol of the female, the protecting mother.

Next day on again, up-river. Now it was so narrow that it seemed impossible for the sixty-five foot launch to negotiate the turns, for the river ran in the most original way, the way a child likes to draw a river, all loops and snakes and ladders. We chugged round one curve that almost joined itself in a ring. The inner banks where the current flowed were steep and thick with jungle, on the outer curves the mud banks shelved, mirrors of mud indescribably greasy. Crocodiles basked in sunny stretches. The Malay boys shot at many. One beauty, about twelve or fourteen feet long, was shiny black, polished like harness leather, and the brown mud on which he sprawled squeezed out in furrows as he lashed round and slithered into the water.

Some of the trees in the ramparts of green were entirely curtained over with creepers and the original shapes remaining below made strange arboreal figures, jungle jokes in tree effects. We had not seen green, deep forest green, for so long, not since Cairns. Occasionally vivid clusters of red berries, lillipillies perhaps, lit up the green darkness. The reflections of the trees turned the muddy water to bronze, the bronze of an ancient Celtic mirror. Beyond the immediate convulsion of our wake these reflections wavered like green candles lighted beneath the surface, like columns of smoky-green fire, and the reeds in which the reflections were bedded undulated with our motion till it seemed that the very banks rocked and trembled into the flickering of the bamboos.

Those bamboos. Their infinite tenderness as they softly caressed every puff of air wafted through them, for they moved more gently than the quietest rocking of a cradle, they bent over the water, looking at their own pretty stems reflected there; miles and miles of bamboo thickets, all of whose leafy conversation was in whispers. I wanted my mind to burn to a pin-point of dry light; by an unwinking observation to give sharply-defined images ready for immediate transference to paper, my eyes to be nothing but the finest of ground lenses, eliminating presonal refraction, but the drowsy heat, the thick undulation of mud along the river-bank, the onomatopoeia of the engine, deceived me. Then the bamboos fluttered their green wings over my eyelids, I awoke feather-brained, my mind a photographic blur.

The Administrator left us on the afternoon of the second day to ascend a small tributary stream and make a survey of the border. His gear, that included a bicycle, went on two rafts each made with a platform of bamboos between two canoes. Poling one raft was a New Guinea dwarf, perfectly formed but just over four feet high. He was decked with an immense and elaborate head-dress of bird of paradise plumes, bracelets of boar tusks, necklaces of dog or crocodile teeth, and a great many earrings the size of small bangles. Two small ivory tusks were inlaid on the sides of his spacious nose, a girdle of white shells supported a small black codpiece, woven grass armlets, arrow cuff, ornamental bowyangs and anklets completed his costume. There was also one of the vilest black cross-eyed fellows it has ever been my lot to behold. So ugly, so indirect was his gaze that instinctively I crossed my fingers to avert the curse.

A few miles higher up the river was a jetty beyond which the launch could not go further because of snags and mud-banks. We stayed here for five days using the boat as our headquarters and making excursions from it along narrow paths cut through the jungle, a foot wide pad in the centre with border of softer earth scraped bare of undergrowth on either side. These pads are very good in dry weather. The Administrator could ride his bicycle on them. About the jetty and landing the land was cleared for some distance and resembled an Australian landscape with gum trees and light timber. Through the trees the sunset was ethereal, tender mauves and blue unlike the tropic blaze of red and yellow we had grown used to. The foliage was delicate, the horizon indeterminate. They had been burning off, the blue smoke cast an impalpable haze like tissue veils in the air. Everything was subdued, homeward going. We passed hunters returning to the village. Their pronged fish spears and stock of bow and arrows, sharp ones for hunting pig, blunt-ended ones for birds, some feather-tipped, others not, were carried loosely in their right hands. One hunter was nursing a young pup that had tired in the chase, another had a baby, invisible save for its feet, slung in a basket on his back. His wife trudged after him carrying the heavier load, a collection of baskets filled with roots, ubi kaiou, pisang leaves, scorched black wallaby roasts and several fire-blackened birds that had been caught in the burning off, all of them suspended from bands round her forehead. In her hands were more full dilly bags. They were both tired, silent and late. In the dusk near the huts a few small fires burnt smokily, a few shadowy naked figures moved slowly out of the darkness or sat waiting a little before sleeping, waiting as primitive hunting man has waited longer than memory. As we passed through the last kampong, a neat street of huts ruled straight beside the path, every dog began to wail. There must have been hundreds of them for every hunter has about ten. They were miserable, skulking, skinny, flea-bitten, sharp-nosed, mean-featured dogs, only half-tamed, and they never barked. Like their better-bred wild cousins, the dingoes of Australia, they could only whine in a long-drawn-out canine weeping, a hideous cast-iron crying that filled the air with howling echoes, a melancholy and savage brute-singing that spoke of fear and hate and that gave the for ever isolated challenge of the pack against the rest of creation. It was a universal wail that did not cease till we were within sight of the boat, well out of listening range.

CHAPTER XXII

STILL UP RIVER

THE five days we spent moored against the jetty waiting for the Administrator to come back were crammed with interest, so much was strange and it was all so primitive that everything that happened was exciting. The Ambonese boys on board found us as novel and amusing as we found them. I did not know how closely they watched us until as I was about to undress one night something went wrong with the switch of the electric light in our cabin and instantly as my fingers left the knob dusky ones descended on it to correct the fault. Then I remembered the skylights on the hatch above that were open wide to admit air and after that we always took precautions against observation at awkward moments. Though inquisitive they were always polite and they chattered continually learning 'Ingris'. From their vantage point above they would rush down the stairs to kill a scorpion or an invading dragonfly large as a cicada, or to mop up a blot of ink. Once as I was writing such a commotion arose that I glanced up to find three dark heads pushed far through the skylight counting. I wrote again and the counting continued, excited counting. They were calculating the number of words I wrote! Following the movements of my pen and possibly betting on the number of lifts to a line.

In the village we acquired a native guide who spoke a little Malay. He was a person of some consequence because not only did he have pyjama pants on and a shirt but also a pair of much older and dirtier underpants and an undershirt. This we discovered when he climbed a coco-nut tree, carefully stripping to do so. He was a cadger, too, demanding 'the makings' at frequent intervals. He would stop suddenly in his tracks like a mule and mutter 'rocco' and Henery with a grin would dole out from the knapsack the cadger carried on his back a little of our tobacco that looked like the horsehair of an ancient mattress and reeked strongly of the stable. I have carried that knapsack since in the Tyrol and in the freshness of snow and mountain air recalled how it nestled on the scaly back of the cadger in hot New Guinea.

Many of the Kai-kai had a skin disease that covered them in small grey circles and left the skin loose and flaky. A minor complaint, the Administrator assured us, compared with some that they had. I shall never forget the vision of the human body, its beauty, ugliness and decrepitude as it was revealed to me on the Upper Merauke, a vision that in civilized communities is reserved for the medical man; the sight of pregnant women swollen to great size, the shrunken breasts of the very old, the immense udders of the fat milking mothers. With hard work and child-bearing the women age quickly, beside them how taken care of, how kept perfect, was the white woman-body. Some of the younger women walked very well, the burdens they carried by a band round the forehead kept them straight at first but speedily bowed them. Formerly the old were given a good meal and then buried alive in a pit in the earth that left the head above the surface, the practice was being put down, along with cannibalism, and now they shuffled along dragging one withered leg after the other, their skin wrinkled, diseased, slack and the ugly grey of a zoo-dirty elephant.

A pleasant contrast were the children, happily naked. We once met a group of seven a long way from their home, boys and girls between the ages of five and ten. They walked spryly with long swinging steps, their eyes bright as young birds, their bodies thin and sinewy and the skin free from disease. As we passed them a bird of paradise flew overhead and they gave a sudden shout of interest to draw our attention and pointed upwards. But they hesitated about eating our food. A little fellow of four who had come with his elder sister to the boat was tempted by a date or a preserved fruit and nibbled at it but the bigger child sharply bade him not to eat and carried her own biscuits gingerly as if even touching them might poison her. Her fingers gripped tightly a film tin that had been given her. Tins and containers were valuable treasure trove. They were used for holding lime and betel.

The nearest village was kept very clean, women bushed at the red earth with witches' brooms of gorse, perhaps because it was inspection time. I admired their dress, it was the best craft work of the primitive community. As an alternative to the long flounces of bark hanging from knees to feet suspended by a network of strings from the waist, these village belles had adopted what Sven called the 'fore and aft' rig, a thick long horsetail of grass in front and behind. As well some wore a tight band of woven grass round the bust but the most unusual and interesting part of the native costume was the hoods that fitted over the head and hung down at the back in a long wide tail, ending in a fringe at the ankles. The garments resembled the sacks coal-heavers wear in wet weather or that butchers use when they carry a carcass, and were a protection against rain and sun. They were made of woven grass finely plaited in intricate patterns like those in clever parquet flooring.

I hankered for one of those hoods and got out my trade lap-laps. They were straight strips of material about one and a half yards long ornamented with coloured bands and braid and edged with a row of deep red points, they had been guaranteed as, literally, the peak of fashion in British New Guinea but here they were obviously far in advance of the sartorial ideas of the simple Kai-kai. Still I took several, figured and peaked, to the village where a group of women were sitting under a house. One of them was the local dressmaker. She had a string of plaited grass round her big toe and with both hands was busy on a modish – and *new* grass skirt. With grunts, and much display of the best lap-lap, a wide strip of prettily coloured artificial silk, a bargain was struck, the skirt should be mine in two days' time. I could not approach the hood question, however, it was too complicated and I did not want to confuse the negotiations.

As the launch had been moved downstream for loading the taxes when the evening of the promised day came I had to go upstream to collect the trophy. There was no dinghy or escort available, and with a grand flourish one of the boat boys hailed a big canoe that was passing and entrusted me, not without secret misgivings on my part, to the care of six or seven Kai-kai who seemed a little dubious about having me with them and owned between them exactly one leg of a pair of short pants. I had realized by this that covered *legs* were what the Kai-kai aspired to, not loose lap-laps that they had not seen before, but manly legs in trousers like the boat boys. So I carried with me for traffic my spare pyjamas, very feminine, old and of a deplorable cut. I was squatting on my heels in the canoe, my knees on a level with the top of its sides, a difficult position to hold for any length of time. Did I ease my weight ever so slightly there was an ominous roll from what was, after all, only a hollowed-out log. I put my hands lightly on the edges to get a little relief but there was such a unanimous growl of disapproval that I took them off quickly enough. I had no more desire than the Kai-kai to form part of a crocodile menu, we had passed a little one on the bank. I don't know which of us was the more alarmed, they or I, but I do know that when I got out of the canoe there was a mutual relief to be rid of each other. As I handed over some tobacco for the lift I felt a curious closeness behind me and turning sharply found the head of a Kai-kai, nostrils distended, eyes wide and cunning coming slowly up my back. He had been smelling me! I was the unknown quantity, the white man's woman, not seen – or smelt – before. I had at the moment an overpowering sense that he was tasting the odour of me. Fortunately western toilet products are standardized to imitate flowers, a savour of roast pork would have been fatal just then.

In the Kampong I sought out the Malay teacher to help me. The skirt was ready and I handed over the lap-lap. The dressmaker did not keep it herself but gave it at once to the woman for whom the skirt had been intended. Own materials made up presumably. I indicated my desire. A hood. Nobody stirred. Then a woman ran across the track and came back with the dirtiest oldest specimen I had seen. 'Tidah Bike?' queried the school-master of me.

'Tidah bike,' I agreed. No good. Then I produced the pyjamas and flourished them, and the dressmaker, who of all the women there was most clothes conscious, produced a fair specimen of a hood. She still seemed a little dubious however. Hoods took a long time to weave and milanese was new to the jungle. She stretched at the elastic in the waist of my pyjamas, and did not like it. String that did not behave as string ought to behave must be regarded as inferior. She held up the silk to the light, it was transparent, not much good. Then how to wear two pieces? She held the top upside down and looked at the armholes rue-fully. One's legs would go through, but what a poor fit! Hastily I brought out the peaked lap-lap intending to display it à la mannequin but there was no opportunity. The red and the peaks made an instantaneous appeal. She was captivated by them and clutched them from me. I took the hood carefully. It would have to be disinfected. Then I added the pyjamas to her side of the bargain. Next day I saw a brave wearing the lower half; after all pants were pants and why should a man scorn lace and a frill or two at the ankle? Especially so masculine a tusk-wearer as this.

I had begun to see the appeal in tusks. Aesthetics are after all only a matter of geography and custom. Horror can have a certain attraction particularly in a society where the cardinal virtue is a display of courage. Eventually I came to think that on a dark face a pair of ivory tusks passing through the nose and ending their upward sweep at the outer and lower edge of the eye, the points pressing against the cheek-bones, gave a fierce and at the same time a noble air. They were not ludicrous, they had been evolved as an essentially masculine adornment in emulation of the boar. Another effective way of adding horror to a dark face was to put a straight line of red ochre down the nose and rim the eyes with red. It was fearsome met suddenly on a jungle path. Then a big breast-plate of mother-of-pearl, how it shone on a sooty dark bosom; and under a head-dress of paradise plumes a proud man became regal. Undoubtedly they were comic effects too, one man we met out sauntering, was irresistibly funny, his eyes were complacently ringed with mud and a single white feather was stuck upright in his curly hair that fitted on his head like a cap of black astrakan. He had been marked as a buffoon from birth, nothing could give him dignity. It was a diversion of ours to go out and sit beside the jungle pad that joined the kampongs of this thinly-populated country as a knotted string holds beads apart and yet strung together. The pad was sliced out between the coachwoods, turpentine, black-wood and eucalypts that towered high in jungle, and crushed out of the upper air the aspiring undergrowth.

The Administrator had given permission for a pig feast at Jawa a village four miles from the jetty. Formerly these periodic feasts were associated with blood-lust and head-hunting expeditions, but now except for an occasional falling from grace human flesh is absent from the menu though the preparations for the pig drive and the dance take a long time. We attended on the morning of the first day. Elaborate toilets were in progress among the men. A usual mode lay in the lengthening the hair by plaits of grass to each one of which were attached thin cylinders of bamboo separated by trade beads and adorned with many feathers at the ends. One man with the help of a bamboo needle and a grass thread sewed a woven band round his friend's collection of twisted grass plaits. The drums were brought out, double trum-peted wooden drums from three feet to four feet six inches long with the ends covered with stretched pigskin.

The men began to move backwards and forwards in a shuffling dance, singing an endless high chanting. 'Now we come, now we go,' translated Sakota, the expert in magic. That was all, 'Now we come, now we go,' again and again. In the hot sunlight tension mounted slowly. Plenty of time, thought the Kai-kai. There were to be three days of dancing and at night the women, according to custom, would wail for the souls of the slain pigs. The Administrator said that usually the women had been the provocateurs of head-hunting forays, the instigators of trouble. 'Much better we stay on board to-night,' he said, 'To-morrow we go.' It would not do to stay too long at a feast. There was no tourist business about this dance. We were definitely not wanted. The women who were doing nothing but chew betel in the shade did not require our presence, gift tobacco or no tobacco. After the slaughtering of the first pig we left, the dogs had run in to lap up the blood, the drums were beating more regularly, the midday sun poured down without a flicker.

PIG FEAST

It is the beginning of a three-day feast
among savages born in the Stone-age.
The men are excited, vain,
they wear Bird of Paradise head-dresses,
boar's tusks through the nose,
armlets of pigs' scrotum,
and stripes of paint like red marks on a black orchid.
A small shell is their only garment.

From huts like mushrooms under the coco-nuts
they bring out the war drums,
the dance drums, the death drums;
every man has a big drum
and carries it
beating . . . beating, singing . . . and dancing.
It is great fun.

Proudly they pace the dance,
the feast is only begun.
The hunters are bringing in the pigs
Oh, oh, oh, ah, ayee, ayee, ah.
Oh ah ahee ah ah ahee ah.
It is the slaughtering of the pigs,
Oh ah ahee ah ayee ee ee.

The women sit by
plastered with yellow clay,
inscrutable hating faces under the woven grass hoods.
They sit in the shade and mutter together,
their betel-red mouths scarlet fungi on a black log.
'Who are these foreign women, if they are women?
What are they doing at our feast?'
Hate is the significant red and yellow blossom
of the Bird of Paradise tree;
it blossoms like a red lily in the air
of this jungle kampong.
Proudly prance the men,
excitedly,
stimulating themselves,
quite indifferent to the clicking of cameras;
but the women sit by,
hooded, watching everything,
the shadow of antipathy over them.
Till an old crone croaks,
a black witch with a dog's skull for a pendant.

'Trouble not,
to-night they will be gone,
gone from our kampong.
The night is ours,
The men are ours,
the pigs are ours,
We wail the pigs to-night.
To-night and to-morrow night and the third night
they are ours, all ours,
The night is always ours.
The men are ours,
the pigs are ours,
it is our feast.'

We were going away, back to the sea, chugging down the narrow stretches of the river where the evergreens of the jungle dipped straight into the water without any border of mud. Above the noise of the engine came the din of distant cockatoos. It was a day of alternate rain and sunshine when the air was first drenched and misty, mountain-cool, and then bathed in showers of brilliant sunshine that gave to every tree, every branch, every twig and leaf of the matted foliage a separate individuality, a presentiment of growth, and made each living part distinct and vital, urged upwards, rimmed with water and light.

Only a few incidents broke the long and monotonous journey downstream. A shout of laughter arose when the Chief of Staff shot at a crocodile that under the impact rolled over and revealed itself as a log. Five hunters who were paddling by, carrying, of all incongruous things, an Austrian cane chair in their dug-out canoe, caught our backwash. Though our boys had shouted to them to beware they had not understood and the bewilderment on their faces was comic to see. They flung about wildly just saving themselves from capsize. The Administrator was puzzled by their cargo. An Austrian chair. Now where . . .? And why?

The Malay boys were doing their washing in the hot water that came from the exhaust of the small motor-boat under its own power but lashed alongside us because there was no longer any room on deck for it. The decks of the big launch were crowded with a motley collection of objects, two young striped cassowaries in a big wooden cage that the Administrator was taking home as pets; ropes, kettles, sun helmets, miscellaneous plaited bundles, sago in palm-leaf containers; baskets filled with large sweet potatoes and ubi kaiou from which tapioca comes; a gaudy parrot feathered in red, blue, crimson and green. He had a maroon back and a sharp long orange beak and he was fastened with a chain of linked safety pins to a bamboo perch.

I was not the only one that had done a little trading, every boy had struck bargains, there were bundles of native spears, bows, arrows, drums and piglets all going to the Chinese storekeepers in

Merauke. As well we were carrying home the taxes, many big beams of squared timber. Each beam represented the annual poll tax on one Kai-kai. These logs should have had an end measurement of fifteen inches by nine inches, but because large logs were harder to come by the Kai-kai had produced logs only measuring fifteen inches by six inches in section. So a difficult sum in proportion had arisen. It had taken many hours to explain the deficiency to the head man and to reckon the tally for his next instalment of the village income tax. The Kai-kai could count to five and recognize numbers to twenty, the number of the fingers and toes. Sometimes, since the taxes were also paid in coco-nuts, larger numbers were required so knots were tied in a rope and each knot represented twenty. In the school the Malay teacher was using chips of bamboo to familiarize his scholars with counting and monetary ideas. The three R's were progressing slowly in the jungle; it was a painstaking difficult work.

Then, when we were nearly at the mouth of the river we got stuck on a mud-bank, and had to wait a few hours before we floated off.

What are travellers' impressions worth? The things that my memory recapitulates with most pleasure were at the time so inconsequential. The sight of the Administrator and the Pastor tramping back tired after their survey and followed by a rabble of carriers and small children, the strumming on the foredeck at night of a guitar played badly, the plangent cry of a night bird, the bassoon note of a bell frog suspended like a musical bubble out of the water; the crying of the jagga's baby. The jagga was caretaker of the government rest-bungalow and the baby always cried, but a ten months' old child might have the right to protest after a breakfast of banana dipped in scraped coco-nut and fried in cassowary oil. Then the recollection of the morning when the boys shot a cassowary and cut it up; when it was cooked the red flesh tasted like an inferior cut of beef, and the feathers, like black goat's hair, blew in tufts about the wharf. That night we saw the great green eyes of a large crocodile burning like two fiery tennis balls out of the darkness by the opposite bank. The boys hung the cassowary legs with meat and feathers still adhering to them over the stern, but the crocodile could not be enticed nearer and all we got was a faint and musky whiff on the cool and scent-carrying night air. Or the sight one evening as we rowed home of the two honey-coloured sons of the teacher at Merambu bathing with their maid. She was kneeling by the river edge washing garments in a blue enamel bowl, her red sarong tucked round her. The two boys were on the bank lathering each other. They had a small companion with them, a little black boy whose wet skin glistened like chocolate. He was absurd, a replica of the chocolate babies that one sees in shops at Christmas. He was lathering too. Civilization that brought soap, vaccine and arithmetic, was not altogether impotent I decided. Or that other side of jungle life, outside the school at Tourai on Sunday morning, a handful of the 'better element' gathered, that is those whose conversion had advantaged them to the extent of a pair of knickers. Or the river fish that I caught and had to cook. It had long poisonous blue whiskers and tasted as unpleasant as it looked. Or the group of old women beating out the central pith of a felled sago palm with heavy wooden cudgels and pouring water down the hollowed trunk to wash away the woody impurities. Or the eyes of a warrior who saw his first match struck, the myth of fire-bringing come true with a white-helmeted tuan and a box of wax vestas in the leading role. Henery had been Prometheus in earnest that time.

Back in Merauke we spent a couple of days waiting for a Malay vocabulary for Henery, shopping, developing film and having the washing done. Sven, Ruth and I went to an early morning market held under a big tree from six to seven a.m. Nothing in Merauke was ever rolled up. Sven, who had gallantly offered to carry the parcels, took a string of onions, some vegetables in a native basket, and some coco-nuts without demur; he even said nothing when we handed him some raw meat with a few big bones held by a grass loop twisted round them, but we got excited taking pictures and came back much later to find him still sitting on the parapet of a drain keeping a few hungry dogs at bay, his only weapon a ferocious scowl, while close by sat a Kai-kai warrior, nude save for a bow and arrow, minding the Kai-kai baby while the Kai-kai wife did the shopping. Get a picture, Ruth, of the two of them! But Sven wouldn't have it.

On the last morning the Chuchu or laundryman brought the clothes back in our out-size laundry bag, a mattresss cover. The top articles were clean and smooth but as we got lower! They might have been dragged through the water, indeed that could be proved against them for they were still damp, but they were dirtier and more stained than when they went. Henery might have struck too hard a bargain or the water of the hot sulphur spring in which they had been washed been at fault. When Joan discovered a surprising mortality among the number of her shorts Henery rowed across to protest. I went with him. The Chuchu was on the wharf to watch our departure, so was most of Merauke. Henery explained haltingly. The Chuchu let forth a volume of language fast as a river in flood. From time to time Henery nodded wisely, 'He must,' I thought, 'be a marvel to understand that!' The upshot of all the talk seemed to be that if a wretched Kai-kai had taken a fancy to a pair of orange breeks what was he, a mere Malay, to do about it? Certainly nothing. We understood at last that our washing had been sublet, so pretending comprehension and wisdom and accepting the inevitable we left the Chuchu still talking and came back without the garments. Ruth was to miss more during the next few days, it seemed the Kai-kai had been partial to blue, her favourite colour.

CHAPTER XXIII

STORM-TOSSED. MERAUKE TO DOBO

On the morning of our departure from Merauke I had determined to get thin by fasting, so I had no breakfast and a dose of salts. However, after we got outside the weather became rough, the wind whistled cheerlessly, and it was cold and rainy. Smashing steep seas began to come up. We reefed the mainsail and I decided that it might be a good thing to postpone a fasting experiment till normal times. So I hastily mixed and drank some powdered milk and ate a large piece of indigestible currant bun. By the time for the midday meal it was very rough. The two girls were tucked in their bunks. A fortnight ashore had ruined their sea stomachs. Before we had left the harbour Ruth had thrown all manner of left-overs together into a large stew. Unfortunately it was awash with tinned tomatoes which in a juicy state I disliked, and the violent motion of the boat slopped the variegated stew out of the saucepan all over the tank top. My portion included a large weevil that ordinarily I might have disregarded, but now it was in the nature of the last straw. However, attracted by the warmth and in spite of my disapproval of the contents, I tried some and – was ignominiously sick.

So I laid low for awhile. The wind and the waves rose higher and Sven was ill! Sven, the sailor! Sven, who was never ill! Henery too confessed to qualms but he said his stomach refused to throw up. Sven and I blamed the stew, we had to blame something. That afternoon I had the five to eight p.m. watch and reflected gloomily that if I hadn't been so foolish as to change cookdays for Ruth's benefit the day before I might be snugly below instead of on deck in a racket of wind and rain.

Sunset was nothing but a smear of pale light between a green and foam-tossed sea and a cloud-covered sky. It was a dreadful watch. Our tiller was a large wooden handle, a heavy piece of timber without a block or tackle to get any mechanical advantage over the strain. All the weight of sea and wind coming against the keel was thrown directly against the steersman's strength. It was one continuous fight to keep her on her course. Sometimes the combing of the steering cockpit gave a little help. One could push the tiller over and then hold it jammed down against the combing for a few moments, not for long, because the worst blows came in shifting bursts, the wind had not steadied to a fixed direction or force. It leapt, violent and uncertain, at us. The waves too had their menace. They were steep and threatened to break on our deck and poop us. I remember being sick once or twice over the stern and holding on desperately to the kicking tiller, hoping nothing would happen during the crisis. Sven and Henery were making the gear tight for the night, consulting charts, filling lamps and coming up from time to time with anxious faces. The noise of the storm was a prolonged heavy sighing through the rigging. It did not seem loud until one had to shout against it to be heard.

Inside my right hand was a row of blisters. Even the calloused pads, result of long hours of steering, rose into blisters. The spray stung my eyes and dried out saltily on my face. The ends of my hair were little sodden flails whipping my cheeks. I could not push them back, both hands were gripped round the thick clumsy tiller under the sail-cloth cover we wore in bad weather. It made a tent over the steersman through which the water trickled. This was the worst time we had had since that first storm on the day of my leaving home. My arms and shoulders ached. I knew they would have to keep on aching, that nothing could be done about it. I hoped they would last out. The muscles of my back ached. I had to stand up and lean my weight shoving at that obstinate tiller to keep her over. There was no exultation in this storm, it was just a sea-sick misery. Fortunately the wind was favourable.

I recall plenty of heeling-over, water aboard, wind and obscurity but, outside the effort of my job, I cannot remember any detail of wave or wind in that watch. I do know that every moment of that interminable three hours crawled by and, when the end came, and there was still something Henery and Sven had to do and Sven asked, 'Can you hang out a bit longer?' the bit longer felt an age, an unendurable extension of time. When at last he took over he had a flying gybe. The binnacle had not been lashed down and had fallen over in the welter, leaving him in complete darkness, and the course only allowed a narrow margin against jibing.

In my next watch, the dawn watch, the wind had settled. A sooty petrel, storm-caught, made a number of landings on the deck and finally lost its fear and settled below me in the galley, on top of the swinging gimbal, the nearest thing to a tree on board and the position of most stable equilibrium. At the time this odd occurrence roused no excitement in me. The bird and I after the first reconnoitring took no further interest in each other, we were fellow passengers brought together by necessity. A shrewd bird. He deserved to weather the storm. He only left about ten o'clock the next morning and he left in a hurry as a passenger leaves a train, without gratitude. In our first twenty-four hours out from Merauke we had done one hundred and thirty-seven miles, our best daily average for the trip.

There followed another stormy day of steady wind and heavy but not terrible steering. The crew was picking up and three of us eating well. Our main endeavour was to keep warm and dry.

On the third day it was still wet and windy and I woke with tonsils the size of pigeon's eggs. Between watches I slept and dozed, dreamt, and slept again in a mazed and invalidish confusion about time. My uneasy sleep was filled with unpleasant dreams, incoherent dreams of home and childhood so that I rose with joy to take the dog-watch, as we had named the 1 a.m. to 3 a.m. watch. Ruth, whom I relieved said, 'Sit this side, keep the boom end in the track of the moon and she steers easily'. So I sat staring at the moon which was a boat whose sail was invisible, continually passing ours in the opposite direction and never arriving. The sea was its usual midnight blue, a blue that was almost black. Big walls of water rose astern, *Skaga* would tilt up, lift high, shiver, and under us they passed. But I did not have to steady her down each separate slope as on that first agonizing night out.

Dog watch on the Arafura sea. It is strange how night, the moon and silence turn one's thoughts out. I had been thinking of childhood fantasies and of the mystery of birth. Watching it, as we rocked over its heaving waters, the sea became for me the All-Mother, the watery womb that produced the first life, the moon, the eternal female. 'Green-eyed women of the moon.' A Mother Carey's chicken or a petrel kept flying round and round in circles over my head and over the wake stretched like a galloping mare's tail behind the boat. The bird was so black against the moon. I thought that had my dream desires been fulfilled, I had read them as motherhood longings, it might be a disembodied spirit trying to get a lodgment within me. That conviction grew as the bird kept on weaving the rings of its flight about me. Finally it perched near the end of the boom not a yard from me. Its tail folded looked like a pair of scissors half-open. It made no sound, its beak pointing as if it would pierce my breast. Fascinated I let the ship get off the course a little and was aware of a wave bigger than any that night, immediately astern, coming sideways with a hissing indrawn breath and a curl of white on its forehead. So I had to nurse the boat over that and over two more big ones and when I looked again the bird had gone.

To beware of being moon-fey a second time I sat on the other side and steered by the compass and by Capella that shone bright in the sky. We were far from any boat track and it was easy to imagine anything at night and alone on the sea. Our boat was so tiny, such a duckling of a craft, shaped childishly like the moon above or like a pre-historic drawing of the boat in which the sun-myth hero makes his sea journey, that it became impossible not to think anthropomorphically. I had convinced myself that our journey to the west, like the sun's, was symbolical, that the moon had evil desires on me and that if I stared at her boat much longer mooncraft would prevail and I would be infecundated according to some magical ritual which unconsciously I was following and into whose circle I had stepped when we sailed into that name of magic, the Arafura Sea. The Arafura Sea ringed about with savage lands, one of the most primitive of which we had just left.

So I practised an exorcism of my own, repeating to myself such fragments of poetry about the moon as swam into my head. Presently I became tired; my back ached; my head, bedazzled by moon and the light of the binnacle lamp on the jigging compass card, ached too. I looked at the time. I had forty minutes to go. How wearily they dragged. One could always tell when the steersman was getting tired. He would ask the time or keep bending to look at the watch that hung in the galley.

When at last it was time to wake Sven I was glad. He came up sleepy and I noticed that he had on his bathing suit. Ready for the worst in case he had to swim? No. Had the Chuchu at Merauke stolen his pyjamas? No. It was merely that in rough weather he rarely undressed because he was called up so frequently and the woollen bathing suit was the only warm clothing he had left that was dry.

We had our cycle of awakenings. Henery woke Ruth and was wakened by Joan. He slept heavily and an ordinary call would not rouse him, the cycle was arranged so that Joan should suffer if he didn't come up. She managed to wake him quietly. In her turn she was wakened by Sven, whom I woke, while Ruth woke me. The cook for the next day always dropped out the night watch before his cookday and the awakening process stepped on one. The arrangement worked.

On the fourth morning out I still had a sore throat. I fed myself on hot milk and soup made from a set of powders with different labels but all exactly the same, looking, tasting, and smelling like liquorice powder. Their main virtue was that they were hot and slimy. The sea was a deep bottle-green. Joan was the only one still sea-sick. On our dead reckoning we were due to sight the south-eastern extremity of the Aru group round which we had to shape our course, but there was no sign of land and an overcast sky still prevented Sven from taking a sight.

Next morning, August 25th, land appeared. We had rounded the point of the Arus and completed the run of five hundred miles in four days. We had come to Dobo. We had lost nothing except our starboard name-plate; it had come off in the battering.

CHAPTER XXIV

DOBO. IN THE ARU ISLANDS

WITH *Skaga* good fortune we had arrived at Dobo, capital of the Aru group and headquarters of the pearling industry in the East Indies, at the most exciting time of its yearly round. It was the week of the Dutch Queen's Birthday and a big rami-rami, or celebration, lasting two days, was being held. Preparations had been going on for weeks. Water and land sports, distribution of prizes, canoe races, drill displays and dances by the school children had all been arranged. As well the schooner *Ariel*, 'mother ship' of the fleet of pearling luggers owned by the Celebes Trading Company, came to port, something that had only happened three times in the previous six years and was a great occasion in the life of the settlement.

We were part of the show too. We landed when one of the luggers was taking the divers and their paraphernalia, luggage, kettles, rice-pots, matting, and stores aboard. Some of the divers were very drunk and merry; they were being carried down, shoulder-high, heroes, to the lugger. They had spent the last four months ashore while the water was too muddy for pearling and the next eight months they would spend on the field. This was their farewell binge. The population of Dobo was on the jetty to see them off, and a more varied crowd I have never seen; Chinese, Japanese, Malays and Aruese, these last had come in from their small agricultural holdings for the festivities. Europe had contributed some of the accessories to all the costumes but for the most part they held to their national costumes and habits with a stubbornness behind which lay strong racial feeling.

The densely-populated village stood on a narrow sandspit washed by the sea on both sides and connected to the main island by a black swampy isthmus. Ramshackle, squeezed-together two-story houses lined the narrow streets. Most of the lower stories were used as booths or small shops selling the same kind of wares, small red and green chilis, taro, fried taro, small tomatoes, dried peas and beans of many sizes and hues, pomegranates, dark chunks of a mystery that resembled chocolate mould, sweetmeats of scraped coco-nut dipped in burnt sugar and fried in coco-nut oil; red rice, brown rice, natural rice and white rice, sago powder, sago biscuits, sago flakes and all kinds of curried oddments. Because of the rami-rami many gambling establishments had been set up where one could win anything from a pair of fowls to a European brass bedstead.

In the centre of the settlement was an extremely old coco-nut grove. At sunset the fantastically tall trunks were black columns supporting a roof over the village. The evening sky was pale, remotely far beyond, lifted infinitely high for a few moments at the cessation of tropical day. Below the leafy roof dusk had already come, stolen in under the canopy of foliage that kept Dobo cool by day and warm by night.

'I wish I had a rug big enough to cover the whole city,' says an old Chinese poem of a town in winter and in humid Dobo the wish has come true, a lifted coverlet of leaves hid from the high heavens this scabrous village growth. The coco-nut grove redeemed many things, it and a quiet cemetery were the only beautiful things in Dobo. Man was unessential to either, he lived without thinking under the one and was received without notice into the other.

The white population of Dobo at the time of our visit consisted of one Australian family, a handful of Dutch officials and five Australian bachelors, officers of the pearling company. During the ten days of our stay we went the social round; Mrs. Sheldon, daughter of the pioneer of Somerset and Cape York, was a very gracious hostess to us. There were tennis and pahit parties – a pahit is a gin with bitters taken at the cocktail hour – dances, suppers, lunch, a day on the schooner watching the water sports, official receptions, a Dutch dinner on board the mail boat that calls once a month, teas and a billiard tournament. We had a hectic time, and we drank Dobo out of soda water; our party had almost doubled the soda water population of Dobo. Incidentally, the soda water tasted queer, rather salty, very warm and it fizzed in a tired way. Except when the steamer was in there was no ice in Dobo.

It was a vicious circle, a perpetual round of drinks, and it gave us a new view of the East. Merauke had not been large enough to be social, it was a comparatively new settlement, a far out-post, the overwhelming emphasis in its daily life the ever-present contrast between western civilization and pre-history; two habits of human development that passed through each other as two lines intersect, sharply, without a blur. It was a place where *a* always equalled *a* and nothing else and where *b* was undeveloped and incompatible with *a* and yet meeting *a* could no longer remain itself. Out of this spiritual geometry a new social theorem would have to be worked.

On the other hand Dobo had an older history than Merauke and a more mixed tradition. It had been the very end of the old world of the Spice Island days. It had been defended. Fourteen miles up the coast, on a little sungei, were the remains of an old Portuguese fort and there was a sixteenth-century tombstone to a Portuguese captain adventurer with the inscription still decipher-able. The Arus had been the extreme tip of the boomerang of the old Portuguese sea empire, a boomerang of power that was flung out and never returned but was snatched by Spain and then picked up almost casually by the Dutch.

Economic depression had caught Dobo, and of the twenty thousand men formerly employed on the pearling fleets only a small percentage were retained and there were many parasites waiting to sponge a living out of them. Depression had brought demoralization to Dobo as well as to other parts of the world, and, because effort was no longer rewarded, life dropped back into the easy ebb and flow of light and darkness under the coco-nut tree coverlet. Everything was slightly unreal. The tortuous complications of Eastern intrigue were there but they left the end little different from the beginning. Somehow, no one quite knew how, the population managed to exist, and existence became something that happened and did not matter particularly. There were fierce feelings but few changes. If a boom came in the pearling industry Dobo might bustle about, but its anomalies would remain for ever pipe dreams.

One came ashore to dream in Dobo; at sea one did not dream, or dreamt only in spasms. In the channel the fishing boys, short, sturdy, deep-chested and almost naked in the sun, were active and unthinking as fish. Their outrigger canoes had great sails like the wings of big water butterflies. Their boys were splendid sailors and dared to fish, miles off the coast in open water, single-handed for the giant mackerel. Their hollowed-out canoes or koeli-koelis were paddled by a single occupant and were thin light craft, fifteen inches across. If they capsized the boys trod water and lifted them bodily out of the sea. They were passionately active and swam as by second nature. Three of them had piloted us in. An old man and his two sons, he had asked to come all the way to London with us.

Even to the wharf came the vital impulse of the sea. Supervisors urged on the loading of the luggers, coolies trotted about under burdens for an hour or two and then everyone relapsed, limp after the effort. While work was in progress most of Dobo looked on with bored eyes and then wandered back under its coco-nut tree coverlet to dream.

Our friends too had gone beyond feigning interest in most things and they had exhausted the possibilities of their small society of exiles long before we arrived. Individually they were attractive personalities, but as a social group they had ceased to stimulate each other and had dropped into the stagnation that attends hard work and long-deferred hopes. They had not been able to escape altogether the opium dream of unreality that spun in a mist of rose and grey under the palm trees, the rose of the magical descent of evening and the grey of the wind that always sped whispering in from the sea. They had not surrendered to the pipe dream but it had given them all a taste of the futility of things.

We, inhibited, jealous, too close to each other, emotion-torn and despairing as we were at times, were, compared with them, free, energetic and gay. Laughter got tired out in Dobo. When one doubts if anything is worth while doing, nothing is, and so some of the festivities we attended were about as cheerful as riding in a hearse. Even the frolicsome satire of the Funeral March of a Marionette was beyond us, when, to make the comparison quite apt, we had drunk plenty of pahits and attended a church service in Dutch and High Malay.

There was hardly any boat money to spend either. Port affairs fell to Joan and Henery's lot to manage. The social round of drinks began to be a nightmare. It was the chits that remained unsigned that worried some of us. The 'tail' spent a couple of domestic mornings aboard. Sven sewed at a sailcloth curtain to roll up and down at the head of my bunk and shield me from the light in the cabin. He mended three small leather suitcases and overhauled his wardrobe; he was to spend a couple of nights ashore with the bachelors. Ruth let out seams in clothes. With the constant exercise of heaving up sails and hauling at the anchor and handling the tiller our shoulders were broadening and so unfortunately was the rest of our persons. We had insufficient exercise to keep us slim and trim as in former times. I washed and ironed clothes, inspected the medicines, reorganized my locker for the sixth tedious time and settled down to a sorting out of the cowrie shells that I had gathered with Mrs. Palmer on Green Island. They had been buried in a tin of sand stowed well up in the bows. By this time the fishes had kindly expired leaving no trace save a black deposit at the bottom of the tin. I had great satisfaction after the mental gymnastics of article-writing in arranging the shells according to their colours and sizes in matched strings on the deck. I felt childishly happy over this with the infantile pleasure that collectors of stamps, teapots and spoons have, the pleasure of counting, sorting and gloating.

One of the most beautiful dawns I ever knew, and we watched up many dawns, came at Dobo. We had been at a dinner and dance on board the mail boat till almost two in the morning and at six they blew the whistle to tell us of their departure. I went on deck to watch the steamer turning carefully, ponderously, in the narrow Dobo channel. She was the only solid thing in a world of floating mist that hid the shore diaphanously and spread over the water, leaving barely discernible the native boats that had come in from all parts of the Aru Islands to take part in the water sports of the day's rami-rami and that had anchored overnight in the shallow bay beside us. There were all manner of craft strange to us, proas with bamboo shelters like houses built up high on them that would have made them top-heavy had the structure not been so light. In spite of their apparent top-heaviness they sailed well, the passengers balancing like a racing crew. Quite near in a narrow canoe, only wide enough to sit in and probably leaking, were five or six figures sitting bolt upright with woven grass mats round their shoulders. The sight impressed me, to lean on the sides meant a capsize and the sides were only a couple of inches from their bodies; yet they had been sitting like that all night.

As I watched, the mists, warmed by the sun, gradually curled and rose, leaving first the tops of the coco-nuts free and then the water about us. Next the thatched brown cottages, built on piles at the water's edge, appeared. Then the shrouded figures on the flotilla of canoes and proas shifted in their blankets, and smoke began to rise in narrow blue ribbons from hundreds of cooking fires on the shore and in the boats. Everything was still, there was not a ripple on the water, the last mists from the base of the plantation disappeared reluctantly. The sun rose in gold. Day had come. A blue day that would be hot. I had not known such a blue still dawn since Middle Molle, morning of white cockatoos. Here in this perfect half hour before heat, fish came. First the tiniest fish I ever saw. Like the innumerable black pencil marks that build up a shadow in a drawing they made an under-water cloud that moved towards us, under us, away from us as a cloud passes in the sky. They were thin, sharp and black, newly-hatched. They had gold eyes or gold scales near the eyes and they moved with silly, excited, ecstatic little wrigglings, tripping along through the sea on their tails. They were very young and innocent, and after them came fish about four inches long, silver scaled, broad-sided, swimming purposefully like swords, heavy fish, hungry fish, in single layer formation a shining shield below the water.

I felt sorry for the little black fish, poor babies pursued by schoolboy bullies, until the next shoal came, blue fish, eight or nine inches long, not so many of them but in more extended order, for their swimming took more room. They were pretty fish, glinting in gold and blue. They were merry, they broke the water and played leap-frog as they travelled, and they travelled the same way as the black cloud and the silver shield. It was a piscine procession that only took a few minutes to pass by. I was breathless, wondering what would come next. Something had to come.

It did, a school of porpoises, eight-foot fellows, very leisurely strolling by, taking a few lazy somersaults as they went, moving with careless deliberation as if they were not noticing which way they were going – but taking the up-channel path all the same.

I thought there could be nothing after them, no further climax, that Neptune could not be expected to give a better exposition of the struggle for existence, but I had forgotten Fear. The little fish might be frightened, but I had not been. There is a hedonism and *camaraderie* about porpoises, even surfing far out. But an alligator! To vaunt his power and make the lesson complete Neptune brought me an alligator swimming in the sea. Something I had not seen before, a big alligator like a rough-barked brown log swimming just under water, his ugly snout tilted up, his feet not visible but paddling, his motion sly and quiet, not demonstrative and uncaring as the porpoises. I saw him first close beside the boat. Though I had been watching the water I had not seen him come. He was just there, beside me, and I could see the crooked line of his mouth moved dimly for half a minute and then was gone. Ugh. *No swimming here.*

Neptune had had the last word in the display and Neptune was grinning. He lifted up his trident and with one blow smashed the still surface into shimmering particles of vibrating water. He bellowed at the sun and the sun roared back, white hot with defiance. It was full day, all the blankets of the Malay watchers were pulled aside; the boys in the bailers, great war canoes beaked at both ends and needing a crew of thirty-five to fifty to handle them, began to practise for their race, the biggest event of the day. A man perched high on the beak of each bow beat out on a drum the pace desired. The paddles were short, broad-bladed and newly-painted. They flashed blue and silver in the sun and paused decidedly at the top of the stroke, held a definite instant before the next swift dip. We spent the day on the schooner watching the races.

That night just before sunset I went for the consolation of loneliness to the Chinese cemetery beyond the town. Some incident of the day had disturbed me. I wanted exercise and to be alone, letting the cold steel of evening press on my forehead. Under the coco-nut palms a car full of men and women gaudily dressed kept passing, turning and repassing me on the narrow road – there was one road in Dobo and five cars. I did not like being an object of interest to the people in this car, I walked as respectably as if I had an umbrella with me. Another car, coming from the opposite direction, pulled up and the Malay driver called out, 'No more houses that way, only coloured people, much better you come back.' I thanked him off-handedly for the information and went on. Only the tomb would satisfy me.

It was enamelled in the loveliest of blues and rose, embossed with many flowers in frosted and gilt magnificence, cheerful gods gave the salamat at the entrance and the whole of the three-sided little temple was intricately carved and statuetted with the symbolism of Chinese death ideas. In broad daytime it was spoilt by an ugly iron roof. Other tombs, more humble, nestled in close to the hillside that overlooked the sea. Under the palms ferns and soft grass grew right up to the plain rain-worn stones, bare of inscriptions.

A remembrance suddenly occurred to me of the desolate cemetery at Thursday Island with its high sharp white fence and the padlock on the gates, as if that would daunt the dead should they want or be able to go walking. It had had at the entrance two over-large notice boards with all the rules and by-laws set out in big black letters and the scale of prices for graves and funeral services spread out broadly – an *à la carte* menu card of the after-death costs from which the survivors could select an exorbitantly priced and unattractive last resting-place for the departed. It was not cheap to be buried in Thursday Island, and no one living could look without horror on that schedule of single or double graves, rights for one year, for ten years, for a big mausoleum, and prohibitions against overcrowding. There were slums in Thursday Island but the authorities had apparently decided that if the living existed in slums the dead at least should never lie more than two to a grave. In this Chinese cemetery at Dobo there were no horrible rectangular plots, the meanest and most orderly space that Europeans can pack their dead into as they do their tinned meat. Here a curving low stone ridge generously, tenderly enfolded the corpse, spread protecting arms that met at a low stone altar in front. The earth was the last good shepherd holding the dead. The designs were pleasing, simple; each tomb so snugly set in the hillside that the occupant, should he ever have the chance to peep out, could not but admire the view over the sea on one side and the grassy glade on the other.

I brooded about my desire for solitude that had sent me out alone. I was becoming more self-sufficient in my aloneness. Poetry-writing was an antidote to loneliness, it cured homeopathically. It didn't matter that Joan had said drily of one poem, 'Very accurate', two words hard as mathematics, and Ruth of another, petulantly, 'A work of genius'. That was that and they were not interested, but I should go on writing poetry all the same. He would have liked me to have got over things writing poetry. I liked the little poem about the moon on the way from Merauke to Dobo. Li-Peh, very drunk, had written a poem about the moon as he floated a wine-cup down a stream. That was how the ancient aesthetic Chinese had passed a moonlit evening, in a poetry contest. The advantage of writing poetry was that it epitomized feelings, it gave the finest amenity to existence.

It was getting much darker. I went homewards thinking that four months living with her had disciplined me for my own strength, that liking to be liked was a weakness. I thought we were all managing fairly well, Joan mollified in spite of her aloofness; the raft episode, the jungle and the storm had kept us busy since Thursday Island. Sven and Henery had come to another 'understanding'. They were to share, alternately, the chief nautical honour, that of entering a port.

Since Thursday Island I had been depressed, reading a great deal, writing a great deal, taking the 'meeting for the first time' attitude further to the 'let us be friends' stage with Sven, who was prepared to argue about it and who at the same time respected the situation and the emptiness of emotion that had come after Black Wednesday.

He was intensely grateful to Ruth for the rescue at West Island and at the same time he was violently annoyed by some of her absurdities. It was at this time, inspired by the sooty petrel that had spent the night of the storm on the gimbal, that she patented the idea of an anti-seasick chair supported on a triple system of gimbals and lashed to the mast! And she made a swimming bath, trailing astern, so that we could swim unafraid of sharks. It was a good idea except for the problem of stowage space, and the fact that the materials available, bamboo poles, a couple of floats and the storm jacket, were unsuitable so all that happened was that the bath collapsed at its first use and Ruth lost a sheet in the collapse. No propaganda could unite Ruth and Sven, they always had a critical eye for each other.

As for Joan and Henery they pursued the even tenor of their joint way, in the splendid isolation of matrimony, an insular method on a thirty-four-foot cutter. Nothing is ever simple in real life. Had we been in a book the author could have built up our characters into consistent wholes and given us only the circumstances that suited the parts we ought to have played, but in the day to day muddle of living a self-coherent person rarely exists, and character, the sterling and gold standard variety, goes down before the flow of personality over events. Character is a concept of moralists and is supposed to remain stable or march towards good or ill, whereas personality is fluid, and real. Perhaps before the trip I had given to Joan the stability of a work of art and when she did not live up to that idealistic perfection the relationship, but not she, was shattered. Perhaps in the same way she had expected too much of me. I still felt enormously flattered when she asked me for a quotation to embellish an article or praised a piece of my work. Both of these things happened in Dobo. But the splendour of a policy of isolation meant that it tried to stamp the *status quo* with perpetuity and in the flux of living the feeling it produced was that *bellum* might be expected at any moment. It was hypocritical.

At this stage it looked as if we might be able to get to the relationship that is called 'free and easy' for the crust of politeness that constrained us was punctured several times. Once when Henery – an unexpectedly prompt Henery – was ready for an early morning appointment first and nagging, Ruth lost her temper and then I did worse, I told him to go to hell and we were not a happy family at all. The silence after this statement made that piece of temerity an incident in the march to war. Once Sven at the end of a long and tiring day by accident spoilt some coffee to which we had been looking forward, sitting in a steam of anticipation round the galley. For some moments he stood, profile against the hatchway, saying nothing eloquently, and we three women could not but feel the masculine rebellion in him. At the end of a cook-day, particularly in port, the strongest nerves were apt to shred on the calico of the morning's good intentions. In ten minutes we were joking about it.

Our scraps began to have a leaven of amusement in them. Ruth printed some contacts. Her standards were extremely high and she was always disappointed in whatever results there were. We liked the photographs and many that we thought would 'do' she rejected with the contempt of the expert, 'Not enough definition in them'. Sven felt sore about photographs. He had been told that photographs of luggers under sail were wanted and on his camera he had taken a number of lugger photographs, from the nautical point of view all different and highly interesting but to the photographic vision all distressingly the same. We were admiring a portrait of Miro, lugger master, that was very good. 'Yes,' admitted Ruth, 'Not bad,' and then after contemplation, 'Pretty good. I can even see the wrinkles in his thumb.'

'What you'd be satisfied with,' shot out Sven, 'would be to see the dirt in his thumb-nail.' Silence. Ruth took the tiny print and a magnifying glass up through the hatch into the sunlight.

Presently there came a shout of triumph, 'I *can* see the dirt in his thumb-nail.' Everyone rejoiced, Henery, who had taken the picture, was vindicated. For months we had been listening to elaborations of the camera's shortcomings, its mismanagement.

Chewing over these reflections I arrived back at the boat to find Joan, Henery and Sven in war paint going ashore to a party and a billiard tournament. It was our last night in Dobo. Ruth was not interested in billiards, loathed stimulants and at the best of times disliked parties. She and I refused to go. While I developed a film she baked wheat in the oven to kill weevils. We retired full of virtue. Later we were wakened by a series of bumps and found *Skaga* on top of the *Nautilus*, a pearling lugger anchored nearby. Our cable had been let out and the wind against the tide when it turned had brought us round before the larger boat turned. We pushed her off and shouted till we wakened a sleepy lugger boy, who came up and gave us a hand. We swung round and clear of the *Nautilus* but the anchors must have fouled then.

About 1.30 a.m. we were again aroused by the revellers shouting from the shore for a dinghy. As we now had no dinghy we had been dependent on the loan of a dinghy from the lugger. We got the lugger boy up a second time and he rowed across unwillingly. It took a long time. When at last they got aboard Sven was exuberant and wanted to talk. It seemed that the Dobo people had come to life playing billiards and everyone had had a good time. Ruth and I were ostentatiously silent, we were sober, tired and virtuous. I, quite unnecessarily, changed my pillow end, Sven's bunk and mine were, to use his phrase, 'on the same longitude but not in the same latitude'. He protested I had wrong ideas and dragged his mattress on deck to sleep the sleep of the misunderstood while Henery to show that eight beers, Sven claimed eight beers, had had no effect on *him*, talked on and on from the sanctity of the connubial bunk in a very loud and over careful voice of the conjugation of Malay verbs and the technical equipment of a diving suit. An odd conversation for the hour and place.

Ruth, Sven and I had arranged to go with Pamela, Mrs. Sheldon's fifteen-year-old daughter, for a cycle ride at six the next morning, and in spite of beer, a late night and misunderstandings we were all up at five and ashore with the bicycles at six, our morning dispositions as fine as the day.

Except for a few attempts years before round the home block I had never ridden a bicycle. I was dangerous to ride beside, I could only go fast, I steered erratically, wavered at corners and only managed to dismount by falling off.

We pedalled out under the palm trees, past the Mohammedan and Chinese cemeteries, over a couple of covered narrow bridges, and through more coco-nut groves whose shadows feathered the earth with light. The heat had as yet only the texture of chiffon in the air. By a cluster of native houses a few Malays moved slowly as if sleep still held them prisoners and had loaded their limbs with heavy chains. A woman with a brown and red striped garment hooded over her face and draped round her body drew water from a well with a wooden bucket and poured it easily into an earthenware pitcher beside her. Thin silver bracelets tinkled on her wrists and round her ankles were embroidered bands hung with little bells. She lifted her great dark eyes to see us pass and ruddy fair Sven held her regard. From the doorway of her house a dark elderly man dressed in spotless white watched us with contempt. 'Fools,' he thought, 'who pedal so furiously to no purpose and who do not let existence take its course. To be is better than to do.' He kept his eyes on the woman drawing water.

The road had now become a rocky track tumbling over small hills and presently becoming impassable for the bicycles, but it had led us to a long hard beach of clean fine white sand on which we could ride. We raced along it and then, as we were, without changing, we plunged sizzling into a smooth and crystal sea, the bicycle wheels spinning where the machines fell on the sand.

Off the shore was a fairy islet, that might have existed not inappropriately in the land east of the sun and west of the moon, a red knoll rising sheer twenty feet out of the water and shaped like a heart for love. Young casurinas, like our Australian she-oaks, grew on it and its grass soft as green hair was starred with small flowers. A grey crane had its nest there and did not rise at our approach but watched us alertly without a wink of its yellow bright eye. Underwater grew a flower-bed of corals, a sea-garden in full bloom and over it the water breathed softly, not breaking, but rising and falling evenly, touching the red rocks as if to caress them. A honeymoon of a place. Did I say Dobo had but two beautiful things? I had forgotten this, but it was some miles out!

Ruth, who was hiring her bicycle at twenty-five cents the hour, went back determined to have not more than two hours' worth, but I had a mood that was worth more than money and climbed a great tree that hung over the sand and had moon-white blossoms larger than magnolia flowers and filled with rose-tipped stamens and scented with the withdrawn, the negative, essence of night.

The seed-pod too was very large, the shape and size of a cardinal's hat but in colour a vivid green that changed to brown when it was ripe. An old Malay whom I asked called it a name that sounded like 'Ta-hee-tee'. A green frog, almost as big as the seed-pod, squatted on a leaf like an umbrella below me. Alone again and dreaming till it was time to turn back to Dobo, maligned Dobo that had kept this last pure pleasure till the end.

On the way back we drank k'lapa muda offered by the mandoer of one of the groves. He was a pipe-smoker and the opium had left him without flesh on his bones, the sinews prominent, the whole body like a piece of twisted copper wire bent under the weight of a too-heavy turban. My riding so intimidated Pam that she fell and tore the knee out of her pretty pyjamas. Then Sven got a puncture and we left him to it, but the morning had roused my enthusiasm for cycling to the point when I began to plan a tour through the Indies. I never did it, the time never came, or wisdom came instead.

Last good-byes. I went on board with Sven and got the gear ready to go out while the others bought supplies and pitch for using on the boat. We were going to scrape and paint it again and had been told that pitch was as effective as copper paint against borres and much less expensive.

We had taken down the squaresail that we had been using as an awning and cleared up all the port untidiness that had accumulated. Then we made everything in readiness for the departure and began a belated breakfast. It was almost noon and time for the tide, on which we were leaving, to turn. There came a slight bumping, Sven went on deck and I kept on eating. 'Do you want me, Sven?'

There was no answer, and then a loud cry: 'Dona, Dona', and up I sprang to the accompaniment of a terrific crash. Our bowsprit had crumpled like a match as it swung up and came down ramming the bulwark of the *Nautilus*. I seized the fender and raced to where the next impact seemed inevitable. The backstay, lashed to the rigging, broke loose and swung about as we rolled and the shackle caught me on the nose between the eyes; I still carry the mark.

The boats were locked like two rams fighting but the *Nautilus* was the larger and heavier. Every moment it seemed that the *Skaga* would be staved broadside on. We pushed with fenders and deckbrooms holding them apart. Until the very instant before the bowsprit went Sven had been standing on it trying to fend us off.

We worked the *Skaga* round the bow of the *Nautilus* but the choppy waves picked her up and threatened to lift the whole boat in a smashing uppercut against the *Nautilus*' quarter. A couple of the lugger boys had come on their deck to help us. Ruth, Joan and Henery were watching the struggle from the wharf. They got across to us and we all pushed and laboured, averting disaster momently and trying several expedients to get free. In vain. We were badly fouled. Finally we let our anchor go and a launch from the schooner *Ariel* towed us off, then we sailed back and picked up the anchor whose cable had been twisted twice round their chain.

After three-quarters of an hour of fighting and manœuvring we were sailing down the Dobo Channel having chopped away the broken bowsprit and put the smashed bobstay and whiskers aboard.

Everyone was shaken by this misadventure and yet relieved for it had threatened to be a more costly smash. From henceforth *Skaga* was snub-nosed, and looked shorter, more duck-like than ever. What was worse we could no longer use the jib, a loss which in the weeks of light airs and calms that lay ahead was a misfortune as the jib gave us a better balance for light sailing as well as more sail area.

CHAPTER XXV

PULO BABI

PULO BABI is a small island in the Aru group a few hours' sail from
Dobo; Mr. Chum Jardine, planter and retired pearler, owns it.
He had lived in the Arus since 1906. He weighed about twenty-
two stone. His colour, the shape and poise of his bald head, his
bulk, his shell of stiffly starched white linen over the brown
wrinkled skin, reminded me irresistibly of a turtle. He had a soft
low voice that spun a web of anecdote, silky, insinuating, musical.
What he didn't know about the East Indies was hardly worth
knowing and he enjoyed telling a story, no one except the Chinese
Lady among all the raconteurs we had met was his rival and
curiously he and she had several tales in common: the story of the
aboriginal diver who had the whole of his head taken by a shark
and who lived, none the worse except for a necklace of scars, to
tell how he had gouged the shark's eyes with his thumbs till the
brute let go, and the story of the survivors of the *Alice*, a pearling
ship wrecked on the way from the Arus to Broome in Western
Australia. The only ones saved were those who for three days
had clung to the jumper stays and came down to the cross-trees
at low tide. In those parts the tide rises and falls thirty feet and
men who swam to the reef that showed at low tide were 'shark's
meat' when the tide rose, for they could not get back to the wreck,
fierce currents swept them away. There were tales of old revels
and old scandals; stories to shock us. The story of the beautiful
bride on the mail boat who was so distressed when she learned
that her planter husband had kept a Malay girl that she cut off
her 'glorious long red hair that he loved passionately, left it on
the pillow and committed her body to the deep'. Sententious
generalizations. 'No girl ought to marry a man who has lived in
the East. All right for a single chap like me but . . .' He had a

mannerism while telling a story of shutting his eyes as if the light hurt them, opening them and rolling them round in a way that kept his listeners tense for the climax. In spite of having been very ill and of always sounding sleepy Mr. Jardine was the most wideawake man in Dobo.

He was of the race of despots, which was not surprising considering that he was descended from a Scotch laird and a Samoan princess, and he lived in the manner of Robinson Crusoe with about fifteen boys to work the plantation instead of one Man Friday. His island was a Robinson Crusoe island, big billy goats had the run of it. His house was an atap-thatched dwelling with walls of woven palm leaf and it stood in a grove of coco-nut palms overlooking the sea. It was very cool and informal; near it were many coops in which clucky hens were hatching out broods of chickens, guinea fowl and turkeys. One day we saw a hen nestling on the snowy linen of his bed between pillow and turned-down sheet. He would not have her disturbed; she was about to lay!

In his gardens grew bananas, straggling ubi-kaiou that are like Jerusalem artichokes suffering from a purple elephantiasis, sour-sops on shiny dark-leaved trees, paw-paws that hang comically nude of leaves close to the pulpy trunks of the trees, prickly lettuces, red pineapples, low peanut bushes sprawling on the ground and, most fantastic of all, loofahs, bath tub loofahs clad in thick cocoa brown dressing-gowns and full of melon-like seeds.

A herd of red cattle and some agile black and white pigs had a paddock or two to themselves. There were sheds for killing and smoke-rooms for curing the meat. Other storehouses held gathered and dried copra and peanuts and scattered about were various workshops; a Robinson Crusoe prudence watched over the plant, palm trees and poultry. His coco-nuts were the finest we ever saw, cultivated from selected stock, a brilliant orange in colour; each one yielded over a quart of milk.

Had he been born three centuries earlier he might have been a professional buccaneer. He had an insatiable curiosity about practical things and when he laughed it was as if Sleipner had stamped with his six feet, the earth and all his vast body trembled. But he did not often laugh, he preferred to smile, a knowing elusive smile that stretched itself across his thoughts before his face smiled.

We sailed across his reef and beached *Skaga* on a shelf of hard white sand. At the end of the beach was a circular indentation that the sea had scooped out of a red clay headland. It was a wild and picturesque place, a natural quarry sunk into the sea and bastioned with savage crimson, a place that might have been haunted by a woman wailing for her demon lover. At any rate the Aruese had believed an evil spirit inhabited the pool and feared to live on the island. 'So I got it cheap,' said the owner; 'and I've never seen a ghost yet.' He laughed, it would take more than a ghost to frighten him. The pool would have made an ideal bathing place, deep, calm and sheltered, but Ruth and I, having a swim there, were disturbed by what sounded like a rustling in the water, a wind under-water that suggested not shark but alligator. Occasionally in the surf one gets a sudden shark fear, a kind of prickly rash of sensation that spoils the swim. When I feel it I come out. I have a theory that fear stretches elastic cords of communication outwards and that it makes the dreaded horror come catapulting towards one. Ruth got the prickly fear badly that morning and I saw no reason to disbelieve her. We never went again to that attractive pool to swim. It might have been the ghostie or the ghostie might have been an ancient saurian but neither of us felt the urge to investigate mythology closely.

We went native on Pulo Babi, all the port finery was bundled away. Evening dress, lounge pyjamas, muslin afternoon frock, satin slippers; I was glad to see the last of them. Our host no longer wore his turtle shell of white linen. Six collars a day was his average in town clothes, they wilted faster than flowers round his neck. He had a lot to say about the influence of clothing in dealing with a native population. It had seemed to be a major

issue in Dobo between Dutch and Australians. He believed that
prestige was an attribute of the man, a man was a man whatever
he wore. Every twopenny-halfpenny minor official he said did
not dare to take off his kas tutup – a high-collared linen coat –
lest superiority go with it. In his eyes ability to pay a laundry
bill did not give sway over any 'boy'. Certainly it had no connection with Mr. Jardine's undoubted circle of authority. Had
he been washed ashore naked on a cannibal island the flunkey
who ran with the news to the head man would have said: 'Sire, a
chief has come to visit you', and though the population, seeing the
visitor, might have dreamt of roast leviathan, they would have
done nothing about it. In fact in a year's time they might be a
mandated territory paying tribute to King Chum or be under a
trade agreement to sell him all their output of pearl shell or to
buy from this Odysseus an annual thirty gross of first grade duck
eggs preserved in mud. He exported duck eggs to the political
prison camp on the Diegal, in Dutch New Guinea.

Except for Henery and Joan, who were relegated to a
gargantuan *lit-matrimonal* in a room indoors, we all slept on a
wide veranda with the coco-nut palms swishing beside us. It was
good to lie on a bed, not on a hard shelf of horsehair, to wake at
dawn and see the grey light over the sea and the tremendous
jagged patterns, black lightning, that a thick clump of giant bamboo made against the pale morning sky. It was good too to walk
at this hour. We made the circuit of the island, through groves of
slender bamboos and jungle tangled with 'wait-awhile' vines and
here and there the tall kapok trees puffing shrapnel bursts with
every breath of wind. On the far side of the island, the windy
side, the plantations were protected by a break-wind of casurinas,
their green needles combed horizontal by the wind. There was a
breath-taking purity, an innocence about them. Compared with
them palm trees were sombre, black-shadowed, fruitful, a the-
saurus of treasure for the men who used them for food, for fuel,
export, shelter, fibres, baskets, roofing – for innumerable purposes,
while the casurinas were lean; they gave nothing, not even shade,

they rejoiced and were content to be beautiful. They were spinsterish and possibly narrow-minded, but admirable for all that. They dug their roots into the sandy soil netted over by beach vines and said to the persistent tropic wind: 'You can't seduce *us*. We won't yield an inch', and the wind always replied: 'It is not my intention ladies, I respect you too much. Just bow your heads a little lower please, don't be quite so stiff-necked about things'.

We got turtle eggs from that beach. One of the boys had located the nest for us and we dug it up. The turtle, to camouflage her activities, turns up a square about twelve yards in size just above high-water mark and ploughs the soft sand like a tractor. To find the exact spot where the eggs are one prods with a pointed stick and when it comes up wet and yellow the nest is below at a depth of from two to three feet. In the one we dug up there were one hundred and sixty-nine eggs, and the female turtle, in the season, lays every month! The eggs are the shape and size of ping-pong balls and are covered with a soft membrane, not a shell, so that if a dint is made in it the dint remains. When the egg is boiled the yolk goes hard but the white never does, it stays transparent and liquid and a gourmet sucks the contents through a small hole in the membrane as a man swallows oysters.

Skaga had heeled over; we scraped one side and pitched it, heating the pitch in a tin on a fire on the beach and putting it on hot, slapping it on with a big whitewash brush; it was satisfactory to see *Skaga's* fat sides bulge black and shiny at us, puffing negroid cheeks below the water-line. Her under-water curves were beautiful; we always felt proud of her when we saw her undressed thus. 'What do you keep on calling her a boat for?' asked Sven. 'She's a ship,' and he worked another thick dollop of tar round her stern. The next day we gave the same side another coat of pitch. She was lying so far over that we were able to dig a trench under her and Henery removed a rotten covering of galvanized iron that was attached to the false piece on the keel. The day after that we got her lying the other way and scraped and scrubbed the rest of her clean. We plugged and puttied more little holes. Blisters again; if ever I had a daughter she should know how to handle a brace and bit, a spokeshave and a mallet better than I did.

Ruth had been philandering with carpentry; the passion came on her at intervals and she let loose a lot of perverted ingenuity on it. For a couple of days she was missing, working in one of the sheds concocting a tripod for the camera. It was an ambitious scheme. The tripod inherited the framework of the swimming bath, took an age to erect and for its use needed, so she confessed when it was finished, an eye like a crab's swivelled and on a stalk. As no one could develop the necessary eye technique the tripod languished, and to her annoyance silently faded from the deck, piece by piece.

I went fishing with Bottim, a Malay boy. 'A bit stupid but works well enough with a thrashing once a fortnight,' so the Big Chief had said. Bottim's equipment was simple, a kris, a double-pronged fish-spear and a strip of rattan with a stick at the end of it. This was the bag. The strip of rattan was poked through the gills of the catch and the stick at the end kept it secure. I carried a fish-spear too. The method was to poke under crevices as the tide receded until we disturbed a fish which would dart to the cover of another rock. We would follow up hopping among the coral and prodding again, lifting up the rocks and finally, if we were lucky, spearing it or catching it with our hands.

Bottim speared one and could not get it out. The water was stained red but the fish would not budge. Presently he gave it up. 'Tidah', 'no', he said and showed me it was like one we already had, a green one with red stripes and three black raised braids, stinging scars, near the tail, a fish in the uniform of a hussar. We disturbed some big fish but they were so elusive in the light and shade of the shallow water running over the reef that we only got two of them, both parrot fish. Clams were not numerous on this reef, the boy found one and I another and he got very excited about them. His kris performed prodigies of valour and emptied the big shells quickly, adding the great oysterish bodies to our rattan string that now resembled a fishy rainbow. I speared two crayfish, gorgeous creatures, red, black and green and pointed with orange, the feelers deep purple, their armour so brilliant that in milder seas one would have hesitated to eat them, but 'bike maccan' the boy assured me, 'good to eat'. My long boots that I wore against the coral were full of water and heavy, I was tired and my fish-spear broken, but the boy was still eager in the chase. I envied him his eagerness and the quickness of his movements. We were an odd pair as we hunted together, not able to say much to each other, but poking, lifting, running, grunting and trying not to splash. We divided the catch. I took the crayfish, and he kept the rest, we were both content,

A few months before Mr. Jardine had had malaria and in the presence of carrier mosquitoes we began to take quinine again. One night by accident I took a double dose, and in the blackness of the night awoke dizzy, bells ringing in my ears, the plantation of coco-nuts outside swinging round and round, a pulse that fluttered, paused and fluttered again and on me a horrible fear of deafness or dying. I thought eating might mop up the poison inside so when Mr. Jardine returned from some nocturnal expedition I arose and hoarsely whispered to him that I was hungry, whereupon, sympathetically – so unexpected and robust an appetite appealed to him – he led me to a cupboard and in the darkness put bread, jam, and a chunk of cinnamon cake into my hands. Soon the trees left off their confusing antics, the church bells in my ears quietened their tune, my legs felt less quivery and I slept to wake with nothing worse than a headache.

We had been at Pulo Babi from September 3rd to 8th and the work on the boat was done. The moon was almost half-grown and if the neap tides caught us we should not be able to get off the reef for another week, so we loaded water by night, drawing it up from a well, placing the buckets in the koeli koeli and then pulling and pushing it round the point to the boat. The koeli koeli, a shallow dug-out canoe, had been bought in Dobo to replace the dinghy and it had an affinity with it, it leaked like a sieve – and all Ruth's experiments with plastic wood could not make it stop.

At least the others drew water. I made jam out of sugar and dried apricots. We were 'out' of most things, sweet or savoury, and had been living on cereals served with tinned salmon or beef or tomatoes. I did not like jam but I did like sweet biscuits. We still had a large tin of them and I had assisted Joan to seal it up and put it out of my way under the for'ard bunk so that should we ever get engaged in social occasions in future we should still be able to produce something for afternoon tea. With the bowsprit broken, the high price of copper paint and a new dinghy to buy we felt that we should never be able again to afford what most people ate and never by any chance what they seemed to drink, as a matter of course, in the east. So I stood and stirred the jam, over a smoking fire on the beach, by the light of a dim moon and hoped my hand hadn't lost its cunning, that it wouldn't end in a waste of sugar. Jam-making was a philanthropic gesture: Henery liked jam, so did Sven.

From this time on because of our poverty, housekeeping was more important than ever. Mr. Jardine had told us of a new dish, a Malay dish, nasi goring, and we were to live on it for months, it was easy to make, cheap, and suited the climate. Nasi means boiled rice and goring means baked, so nasi goring was rice first boiled and then fried dry in a little peanut or coco-nut oil and mixed with it whatever shredded or grated trimmings were available or suggested themselves to the cook's imagination. We used pigeon, chicken, beef, chillis, raw chopped salad stuff, hard-boiled turtle egg, onion and garlic, grated coco-nut, spices and chutney. But whatever is put in must be kept dry, the mixture must not be messy.

Over the cooking of the rice itself Ruth and I had a long-standing disagreement. To cook a large pot of rice so that every grain comes out separate, dry and yet thoroughly cooked, is an achievement. Much depends on the quality of the rice, if it is poor and floury it will go sticky and blue, but more depends on the amount of water in the pot, too much and the rice remains a morass, too little and the core of the grain is uncooked. Ruth parboiled hers with a lot of stirring and pouring off of water, she quoted as authorities her mother and the legendary Indians who heroically offered to drink the water while the British soldiers had the rice. I quoted the Chinese Lady and steamed mine, not lifting the lid. Now it had always seemed sinister that every day when I took over the pots of office from Ruth, who preceded me, I inherited a gluey mess of rice to be used up. When challenged she had said: 'Of course not, never thought about it,' and the ricy legacy had stopped. We got on well enough with an occasional thunderstorm to clear the air.

She and I were both sorry to leave Pulo Babi, Ruth partly because she hated leaving any place for the open sea and I because it was an island where all adolescent dreams were realized, an island true to Robinson Crusoe pattern and more excitingly situated, a place where one would not wish to stay for ever but where one could lead as healthy a life as one wished, building fish traps, growing vegetables, sitting in the sun and pounding kanari nuts for oil, pounding rhythmically without a thought in one's head.

We left on so light a wind that it was almost a calm. I had the eleven till two watch and sat in the blazing sun, the wind coming in occasional unsteady hot puffs and Henery cooking very leisurely below me, his nose in a book. It was like steering from the summit of Mount Etna. When he sat like that, sucking at his empty cigarette holder, nude save for a pair of shorts, I always saw him as a goat, with his thin face, all nose, his crest of goldy hair that he liked to massage, his long narrow back that a woman could think beautiful, his big ears and knees, his feet and hands that were freckled and whiskered with tufts of hair. Lack of exercise had given him too a little paunch and that was funny because the rest of him was so skinny. When I had hung a bleating goat's bell round his stretched neck with its prominent larynx and under it a large pale blue ribbon bow, the sort little boys were made to wear when they had their photographs taken for albums, I was satisfied. Dressed so, I quite liked him.

The sea and the sky were basking in an incandescence of heat unrimmed by any horizon, Pulo Babi had dropped over the edge of the world. After two hours' hissing of the primus the damper was still damp, the oven, always a makeshift, was getting worse. Ruth was ill again, feeling wretched with small boat motion after a port. She had to give up her watch early and Sven took it, he never minded how long he stood a watch.

I wondered what he and the others thought about when they were on watch. When the wind was like this, gentle and furred with heat, I always dreamed, a lazy-daisy chain of inconsequential imaginings. That night as we strolled along, doing two and a half knots at most, I re-planted my garden, making all kinds of tropical plants and exotic fruit bloom by magic on my rocky sea-bitten plot of ground and adding a room to my house here, a sun-bathing place there and more cupboards everywhere, till a big bird with a tail like a fan and a wing-spread of two or three feet took to flying in our wake, black against the moonlit sky. Then he circled round the boat and made in quick succession three swoops at my head, I had to take off my beret and whirl it round to scare him off. I think my eyes in the moonlight had made him curious and aroused the jackdaw in him, he would not have hesitated to souvenir them.

When at 1.0 a.m. it was time to call Sven he wanted to know if I had seen any light on the high Kei Islands, which he could see looming up six miles away but which I had taken for a cloud bank. When he had looked again in the pilot book to make sure if there was a light or not he took the tiller and settled himself comfortably.

The air was soft and warm, the whole surroundings irresistibly planned for love-making. I sat on the hatch, it was a time for confidences.

'When,' he asked 'do I get my leather medal?'

'The High Command will give us one each, at Singapore.'

'The High Command have a double bunk, and no love-making allowed in the ranks.' We laughed, as we spoke, softly. The sea bird was still flying about, a resentful kind of bird. All alone things must have been resentful that night. 'A spy,' said Sven, referring to the bird. It was black, uttered no cry and kept on eavesdropping. 'I always thought they were frightened of the seagulls telling the world.' The row came vividly into both our minds.

'I wonder if they ever regretted that first attack they made? It did more than nip in the bud, if that was what they wanted, it just about blasted the whole forest.'

'You feel things too much,' said he.

'So do you,' I replied. 'We're both fools.'

'Such a waste of a marvellous night,' he insinuated. 'Meeting for the first time, what rot,' he thought. It was indeed a marvellous night, the air and the sea caressed each other, rising and falling in waves together. 'When does my probation end?'

No answer was necessary, he knew it already. 'You know what I was thinking about before you came up?'

'I can guess . . .' He said it bitterly.

Merewether was a long way away, by the surf. Home, with green shutters and every rose tree named and every plant known – and loved. 'We'd better invent The Little Girl Back Home, hadn't we? Most sailors have one. It would make it easier.'

'Sailors with a Little Girl Back Home and steering for a little Grey Home in the West don't come on this sort of a trip, do they?'

'It's a good trip; getting pleasanter don't you think?'

'Not for me, when I know it won't happen again. Only once in a lifetime.' (Once in a lifetime, for me it was like that too; this wonderful voyage, once in a lifetime.) 'And I could suggest improvements,' he went on.

'Improvements?'

'Why don't you sit over here? Frightened?'

'We might drift backwards . . . instead of going ahead . . . according to plan.'

'We could pull into harbour somewhere. Or we could keep on sailing like this . . . for ever.' (Sailing like this for ever, travelling and never arriving, out of the strife for ever.)

'This side Heaven.'

'Heaven . . .' He began to sing softly in his pleasant flat sailorish kind of way.

It would have been marvellous luck to have been only a little in love, here, now. I was always glad for Joan and Henery when it was a night like this. She would not suspect that. My awkward bunk. Did she appreciate the motive that had made me accept Ruth's change-over as a permanent thing? Moonlight and water, those two ancient allies. One could take a net and go out fishing for the reflection of the moon on such a night as this. If one could move affections as one could pawns on a chess board. Good night.

Another day at sea, a day occupied for me in scraping tar off myself and revising and writing some poems, 'Dog Watch in the Arafura Sea', 'Pulo Babi', 'Storm-tossed'. That said everything, 'Storm-tossed'. At night another bird shared my solitary watch, a different bird, domestic and slightly ridiculous, about the size of a fat duck, with a white chest, strong webbed feet, a wide tail in which the closed feathers lay like multiple toes, and with a pale yellow or white beak and legs to match. It was drizzling and misty, the moon shone dimly and by fits and starts. He perched on the kerosene drum beside me and said nothing. So I stared at him and he stared at me for an hour or more till I was relieved and neither of us knew each other any the better at the end of the time.

The third day out Ruth was better and borrowed an historical atlas to see if there was any way of getting the boat to Europe other than by the way we were going, by the Cape of Good Hope. She found lots of long black rivers in China leading to the borders of Russia whither she wanted to travel, and, by a few porterages, that included the Himalayas, she took us to the Black Sea and the Mediterranean. She was serious in suggesting we try one!

I had never seen Sven look so aghast. After a few jerky sentences from him she was quite willing to give up the scheme but protested it was a shame all the same. She submitted in defence that, allow-ing for three or four days ill after every port of call we made, she would be called upon to endure a solid three months of sea-sickness, and – *was anything worth that*?

She claimed that the only respite she got was when she spread a pad of food on her uneasy stomach and then endured hours of queaziness hoping it wouldn't come up! Joan used to try starvation as a cure. Ruth and I discussed the possibility of hypnotism as a cure for sea-sickness. She assured me that auto-suggestion was not a bit of good and she would have liked to have tried hypnotism, but, fortunately for us all, there was no text book on hypnotic method on board.

On the fourth night out, so that we should not reach Banda entrance in the dark at 1 a.m., we dropped the squaresail, which we had been using with light winds aft since Pulo Babi, and left the staysail only, putting up the mainsail at 5 a.m. In the early morning we sailed gently into the southernmost group of the Moluccas, the fabulous Spice Islands of Renaissance navigators.

CHAPTER XXVI

SPICE ISLANDS

It was a perfect day. Three of the five islands of the Banda group, Run, Lonthoir, and Banda-Neira, rose high and greenly-wooded from a sparkling blue sea. Another, a low level hill that from its name, Pisang, ought to have been planted with bananas, was instead combed regularly in the open light foliage of coco-nut plantations. The last of the five, Gunong Api, was steep, bare, bald of any timber, and with a shallow dip at the top, the crater smiling in an open and loose-lipped grin. Our pilot book, dated 1875, said it was a volcano continuously active and residents affirmed that there was usually a slight tremor every day.

By lunch time we were anchored off Banda-Neira, close to a flat black beach of volcanic ash on which a number of native proas were drawn up and fine fishing nets spread to dry.

Sven and I were eager to explore Banda; it had been a name of interest to me for a long time. We went by a native fruit and vegetable market where all the vendors were old and asleep, lying stretched out by their wares, through a park in which the grass was intensely green and mown. Mown grass! We had not passed through such a park since – yes, Brisbane five months before. A statue to a king! Great trees formed a venerable avenue, tree giants, these hairy with all manner of parasitic fern growths; they made arboreal continents for birds to explore. Opposite them behind smooth gardens, were houses of white plastered stone with decorous Corinthian columns, eighteenth- and nineteenth-century houses with recessed and tiled verandas bearing urns of flowers and fern. The doorways were exquisitely proportioned, fitted with shutters closed in the noon-day heat and painted bright blue, yellow or green. Landing as we had in the native fishing quarter where the houses jostled each other between narrow sandy lanes, a spawn of dwellings close to the best anchorage, I had feared that Banda might be another Dobo, but it was not so. Banda was pre-eminently civilized, clean, washed over with the subtle refinements that come from generations of good taste. Arabs, Dutch and Malays, all highly civilized and luxury-loving peoples, had made their homes here for centuries. The architectural characteristics of all three had been fused together by the heat of the climate; the clean paintwork, the bright tiles sunk here and there into thick white walls, and the heavy stolid masonry were Dutch; over doors and windows, on balustrades and gateways the graceful ironwork was Arabic, so too were several small domes that rose in the air and also a whole house, a bedizened wooden spectre, creaking, over-ornamented, in need of repair, a painfully ancient coquette of a house that we were told some Mohammedan millionaire's whim had transplanted entire from Mecca; while the high roofs that curved downwards and outwards with a generous and sweeping grace, their eaves simple and protecting as the wings of a bird on her nest, they were the building triumph of the Malay race.

In such a park as this a German band might be expected to play *Lohengrin* in the late afternoon. In fact the afternoon promenade had already begun. Young Malay girls in bright dresses, pretty as shoals of coral fish, were walking about, their arms twined round each other. They followed us, watching us closely. Sven waved to them and scored an instantaneous success, they smiled shyly and began to chatter, showing us the way to the steep ridge of the island by tortuous paths.

We went through woods of a fluttering-leafed tree that bore a hard fruit like an almost ripe apricot. It had a hard dark kernel but tasted bitter. Now and then a huge kanari tree towered above the forest, its base buttressed with roots, with immense flanges of wood that would have sheltered many men in a storm. The soil was very rich – dead leaves lay drifted in heaps under the trees, a bronze sea of them. Many faint paths criss-crossed about and we lost our way and came down to the shore to a boat-shed where a

Malay baila was up on rollers. It was capable of seating thirty
men and was very heavy, made of solid planks pegged together
with wooden pins. It had at either end the characteristic high
curved beak like the old Maori war canoes. It was no wonder that
in these fine-lined and yet solid craft, difficult to capsize, the
Polynesians had travelled their long migratory sea-roads.

We came back full of enthusiasm for Banda, *amoenis* Banda.
'No place in the whole world surpasses in beauty the delightful
Baiae', Horace had written, but he had not seen Banda. My
first ancient fort was there, my first introduction to a past that I
had known about from history books for so long and had hitherto
accepted on trust. Australia has no ancient forts and no ancient
churches. It is a land where the arquebus and the crossbow never
came, and where feudalism is a limited, de luxe twentieth-century
edition, which the population does not take seriously. Fort
Nassau was opposite the jetty in Banda. Along its crumbling
façade sprawled the date, 1617. Australia was then still a concealed trade secret, an extension of Java le Grande, or else an
hypothesis of the map-makers, a supposititious counterpoise to the
land mass of Europe and Asia. Had the Portuguese managed to
hide the existence of a continent from the merchant men, the
money explorers, the Dutch? The Professor had thought not, he
believed they had no secret to hide, but the existence of the
Portuguese fort in the Arus so close to Australia had made me
wonder, even Professors might be tricked. Fort Nassau presented
no answer to the problem. Once it had been complete with outworks, moat, baillie, drawbridge and bastions. Now its old black
bones had settled easefully into the earth; grass, soft and smooth,
grew about them; behind the 1617 façade, inside the pretentious
gateway with its absurdly small openings for cannon, were –
tennis lawns!

War had long ceased to trouble Banda. It was so small a place
that the great nations of the earth could forget it, though once in
bitter trade rivalry they had sown these shores with forts like
dragon's teeth, black and snarling against the perpetually blue

skies. Portuguese, Spaniards, Dutch and English had contested these harbours, these green jewels of islands. Banda had been a prize worth fighting for, she represented the spiced wealth of the newest of worlds, her nutmegs the largest, the most fragrant in the world.

Directly above Fort Nassau on the backbone of the island, dominating the channel on both sides, was Fort Belgicae, 1699, still perfectly preserved, complete and impregnable, in the eighteenth-century sense. It was a five-sided fort, the least important of its walls six feet thick: it had dungeons damp and dark out of which bats flew, towers on all five corners, crenellated battlements, sentry boxes, loop-holes, iron bars and, the most interesting relic, left carelessly in a corner, a 'dripping stone', used in the torture chambers of the period, the centre worn down by the continual drip, drip, drip of water on it. It brought Banda into the perspective of Amboyna, that massacre of Amboyna that had antagonized Dutch and English during a century when both were fighting desperately for a Protestant form of religion. Trade had been more important than faith, and English merchants had protested, jealously, of the 'insatiable covetousness of the Hollanders', while the words of the English victims of the Amboyna massacre echoed in their ears: 'We through torment were constrained to speak that which we never meant, nor man imagined. They tortured with that extreme torment of fire and water that flesh and blood could not endure.' All the forts in the East Indies that I saw and photographed were built on the same plan, though modified in size. They were perched on a steep hill or eminence wherever there was one, or close to the safest anchorage. They consisted of thick ramparts enclosing a courtyard, the ramparts hollowed into chambers for garrison, stores, prisoners and officers. The tops of the wide ramparts sloped inwards and leaden pipes carried off the tropical downpour into a well in the centre. They were all sun-traps. No wind nor enemy could scale those high walls, the plush-breeched, Genoa-hatted troops must have grilled inside them. About the town one came upon old brass cannon, muzzle-loaders ornamenting steps or turned into mooring dolphins. Peace comes after war and it seemed that it had come to stay in Banda. We were all at peace too, our animosities sunk fathoms deep in a clear coral sea of contentment, we could look down and see them if we wished to, but we did not wish.

Banda marked a high light in our voyage. The beauty of the islands was such that it impelled an internal harmony on us. Afterwards neither Joan nor I cared to write about Banda. Nothing malevolent, spectacular or exciting happened to us there, the shining perfection of ordinary events was quite enough.

For instance, I remember sitting with Joan in an hotel opposite the park. At least we thought it was an hotel. An old Malay who had noticed us standing a long time in the heat outside the Residency waiting for Henery had led us there, beyond its façade painted a Wedgwood blue and decorated with the usual cream Wedgwood garlands into a cool, dark room, that might have belonged to a rather conventional Dutch nobleman of a past century. There was no advertisement, desk or bar to give any indication of the nature of this house, but though empty it had the air of being prepared for many guests. Tables, furniture, china ornaments and brasses had a rich and formally elaborate beauty and the polished floor of red tiles doubled every dark reflection. The Malay, out of his own feeling of hospitality and without being asked, searched in the neighbourhood for a Dutch lady whom he thought spoke English. She came in for a few moments to play hostess to us but we were not able to converse and could do little more than smile at each other and accept coffee and some of the sweets she offered us, cubes of brownish sugar flavoured with tamarind and decorated as French pats of butter are, with simple flowers raised in relief. After resting a while we went out again. It had all been a little mysterious. It was only one of the small but perfect experiences that Banda gave us.

We fell under the spell of its quiet and dreaming charm on that first evening when Sven and I came back like the spies of Moses to report on the Promised Land. 'Banda is beautiful.' 'Banda is a dream from which you don't want to wake up.' Then Joan had got out the gramophone, always difficult of access, stowed in a for'ard locker and impossible to play unless the water was calm. We had been music-starved for months and we listened as if we were drinking thirstily. The Beethoven Quartet in A minor. It drew out its major theme ineluctably sweet and distant, snow on far-away mountains, and left me serene and touched with sadness. Perhaps that was why that night I dreamt with a startling reality, saw a presence so vivid, such as had not visited me in dreams throughout the voyage. He stepped smiling down the hatch, his small hand moving quickly to his forehead, pushing back his hair, the tip of the tongue ready to slip between the teeth, the eyes to break into that devilish underhand twinkle, that I could never resist. He glanced at me with a sideways look of query as he came down as much as to say: 'Well, what are you all up to now?' All of us, we were all included. He was the sixth man on board – if only I could always feel that. I was sleeping on deck; there was dew on my blanket and a late moonrise had turned the sky to an infinite tenderness, a milky diffusion of beatitude.

Next morning they asked us: 'What about the nutmegs?' We said we hadn't seen a nutmeg.

'But Banda grows nothing else but nutmegs, the biggest in the world, the fragrance floats on the air miles out at sea.'

The air was decidedly balmy and warm but it held no hint of the top of rice puddings in it. Wait. Surely not? Those green apricots we had seen everywhere? Were they nutmegs? They were. 'Muscat' was the Dutch name for them, 'pali' the Malay.

The nutmeg tree was slim, straight, a young-looking tree even when twenty or thirty years old. Its trunk was mottled like a sarsaparilla and it had dark green, shiny leaves like a narrow-leafed fig tree of the Moreton Bay species. The foliage looked light and airy but cast, for all that, a thick shade.

The nutmegs crop continuously all the year round and are picked when the fruit splits. Women and boys go round with 'gai-gais' gathering them. The gai-gai is a little spherical bamboo cage mounted on a long cane, with extensions like a fishing-rod, and it has two crooked bamboo fingers that dislodge the ripe nutmeg and send it into the cage. The picker carries a woven basket or bag on his back as he goes the round of his trees. The fruit is hard and woody, with a spicy tang; it might make a pleasing acid drink; then comes the mace, folding protective cardinal red arms about the dark nutmeg, that glows as if it had been french-polished, a perfect kernel. Before it is cured it is soft and can be bitten through and is speckled inside with tiny brown seagulls just as it is when it comes to the kitchen.

We learnt more about nutmegs and forts when we went on Lonthoir Island for a day excursion and subsequently for a two-day walk. One of the forts on Lonthoir I only reached with the help of a perspiring Coffee Shape just recovering from a bout of – 'fever'. It was a miniature fortress on top of a precipice by the sea directly opposite Forts Nassau and Belgicae. Any ship entering the narrow channel would in the olden times have been caught between a double line of fire but now a casual observer could not have guessed that there had ever been a fort. Rose trees bloomed on the ramparts and turned an old sentry box into a summer-house. Store rooms had been used as living quarters for a Malay family. There were two other forts on Lonthoir, one had a strange name for a fort, 'Concordia'. The seventeenth and twentieth centuries evidently agreed that armaments mean peace.

The kampongs, Spicery, Klein Waling, Groot Waling, Laeontang spoke eloquently of the past. They were all alike and in their way they were forts too. Their thick walls, sometimes topped with broken glass, were defences against earthquakes and the mutinies of forced labour. They enclosed a rectangle of five or six acres. By the great gates that were closed at sunset stood the owner's house, pillared, porticoed, with large, high-ceilinged, marble-floored rooms shaded by deep verandas, the doors and windows closed with brightly-painted shutters, the steeply sloping roofs thatched with sewn palm leaves. Inside round the four walls of the enclosure stood the coolie lines, so many pigeon holes into which the various families on the estate were filed. Detached from them were the cookhouse, the bath-house, the packing and sorting sheds and the smoke-room, two stories high, where the nuts were piled in pens being smoked and turned for two months before they were ready for export. A few trees gave shade and beyond their shadows the sun burnt down on hard red earth. Circular trays of mace were drying in the sun, shallow platters six feet across; sacks which had held nutmegs were spread over bamboo lines to dry and on the verandas women sifted and graded the nuts.

At the corner of the drying sheds usually hung the muster drum, a cylinder of wood six feet long. There was a good deal of white-wash about these Dutch kampongs and the general effect was of immaculate order, cleanliness and restrained industry. The kampong was the centre of life, women washed and ironed clothes; clear water from the hills behind bubbled down through bamboo pipes; old men smoked and made fishing nets out of crochet cotton with a tatting shuttle and girls sat cracking the shells of the kanari nuts, oval brown nuts like smooth hard prunes, the kernels soft and oily, the shape of almonds. Fowls pecked wherever there were kanari nuts.

Outside the kampongs, under the nutmeg trees, were the family tombs. They dated back to the seventeenth and eighteenth centuries, mute records of long generations of planter families.

We stayed over night on one of these kampongs. Somehow Ruth and I had got the idea that we were to camp in an empty 'rumah' or bungalow and take our own food. So we had made our dispositions in like manner carrying with us in the haversack a quantity of food for the party and nothing personal save a pair of pyjamas and a toothbrush. Then instead of a long walk and an empty camp we found ourselves supplied with a proa, boatboys, three carriers (there was little enough in all conscience to carry), our approach heralded by messengers, envoys to meet us and a small banquet waiting to be consumed!

Our host was young, jolly, a bachelor who spoke only Dutch and Malay and who had smart society magazines on his occasional tables. Ruth and I looked at the magazines and at each other.

At dusk he took us all fishing, a romantic excursion in a curved-beaked proa rowed by eight men with two extras steering. A tall ornamented pole like a hat-rack carried the fishing lines looped like stranded liquorice round its pegs.

We rowed close to the shore. The surf of the Banda Sea which broke on the soft rock was not considerable, we were at a distance of a few yards only from a steep high headland reddened by a curious maroon-coloured sea-weed that grew over it. Picturesque pandanus palms swung on the extreme verge and clawed at the air. When the sun had quite gone we let down the net in a small cove. It was a drift net cast from a bamboo platform in the centre of the boat. The wooden floats were kept underwater and the only sign of the net when it was out were two big squares of bamboo at either end. Our anchor was a small piece of coral which dragged. Whenever that happened and it looked as if we would be hurled on the rocks at the base of the cliffs the Malays pulled out, cast the anchor and let us drift in again.

When the net was stretched in a half-circle closing in the little bay and leaving only a narrow exit to the open sea they threw large stones into the opening and then, rowing inside the circle of the net, beat the surface of the water with a plunger on the end of a long pole. It made a sound as if a stone were being thrown in and frightened the fish inside the net into dashing towards the open sea, to be caught in the meshes of the net. We did this twice. The first time we had no luck but the second time we got about sixty fish, seven or eight inches long, dark blue on the backs and flame-coloured beneath. The fish splashed and expired at the bottom of the boat. As we paddled home, the boys sang, high, clear and shrilly: 'Nonyah, manis, sahyah punyah.' Whose is this beautiful lady? She is mine. It was a triumphant home-coming.

The fishing expedition had an unpleasant aftermath for Ruth and me. It left us wet and fishy and with literally nothing to wear except two very disreputable pairs of pyjamas. Not even bathing suits! That had been Joan's idea and dictum. 'Don't cumber yourselves with luggage', and now! A Dutch dinner at nine o'clock is a ceremonial affair. In our circumstances lounge pyjamas were permissible. But our pyjamas! Investigation from the doorway showed us Joan resplendent in orange satin and both men looking brushed-up and clean. Ruth and I were veritable Cinderellas and we hunted round the great stone room that had been allotted to us, one side opening on a lawn and the sea below, and the other on to the immense out-door colonnades of the living-rooms. In vain we searched for draperies that might play the fairy godmother to us, but there was not a cover, not a window curtain, not a doily that might be used. It got later and later. At least her pyjamas, sorry things though they were, were opaque, but mine – had I been in a harem they would have justified the term 'the atrocious Turk'. By themselves they were impossible. 'What about a sheet?' asked Ruth, busy pinning herself together. The bed was eight feet by ten, a monster of a bed, and the sheets Dutch and more generous still – only a Shakespearian ghost could have trailed them. Then in the tucker bag I found the lap-lap wrapped round the damper to keep it fresh. A red-peaked gaudy lap-lap originally intended for the high purpose of trade with the Kai-kai. A couple of half-hitches on one shoulder-strap, our one pooled safety-pin at the waist – 'mustn't breathe hard or eat much' – and the indecent pyjamas were partially obscured. *Skaga* folk lifted eloquent eyebrows when they saw me and I sidled myself under the table as speedily as I might, trying to pretend for my spiritual benefit that I had brought out a new fashion that might blossom in the next issue of one of those smart Dutch magazines.

Owing to the language barrier it was a laboured meal where we watched the moon rise and listened thankfully to Henery stumbling along the stony path of speech. He chose politics and goat-racing in Australia to talk about. On this occasion we made the acquaintance of whisky kring, served in liqueur glasses, a colourless neat spirit that I imagined was a new kind of pahit until

I found it made the whole world different, lifted out of the mood when a peaked lap-lap mattered terribly, lifted to a black ridge over which the moon nodded and the wind blew coolly, while away in a corner of the world the Malay fishermen were singing again the song they had rowed us in with: 'Whose is this beautiful lady? She is mine'. But was it the same song? It was the same tune, I recalled now having heard it before, the conventional pattern tune to which the 'pandans', little personal poems, are sung by Malays. The Specialist in Brisbane had sung one or two for us and told stories of the clever way they sing their wit in company, stroking their compliments with claws, making a chain of insinuations with allusions which only the initiated can follow. Had the boat boys, when they found us so heavy-footed in their language, been singing about us? It was quite possible. It seemed to me now that there had been amusement as well as romance in that song. Whose is the beautiful lady? Three women and two men. Which of us belonged to which? Astute Malays. 'She is mine.' In Banda there was only love-making and living, no problems, no politics, no new-fangled ideas. Men kept their women close beside them. Whisky kring, you were illuminating.

Ruth and I retired early, in backward formation, bowing, to our island of cool linen and starched lace, a glacier of a bed with snow-drifts for pillows; never had I slept in so vast a bed or so cavernous a room. They both belonged to 'old' Banda, the Banda that had been so wealthy that a standing joke was that it sent to the South Pole for its ice.

Next day too, we enjoyed strolling along the cool, winding path of the island, watching the nutmeg pickers like birds in the greenery, and swimming under a screen of trees that spread their branches fifty feet over the water, branches on which grew rock-lilies, hare's foot fern, giant maidenhair and slipper orchids. We had never seen trees to equal these, their limbs were sprawling highways in the air. Little lizards with tails of peacock blue scampered over the paths and dropped their tails when they were frightened. We met an old woman plaiting little baskets from the broad green and silver band of a young split coco-nut leaf. They were diamond shaped and quite closed, for cooking. The 'bras', uncooked rice, was pushed in at one end and the rest of the basket filled with grated coco-nut, then the whole thing plunged in water and cooked in a neat parcel that held one portion.

I had a find. At Celamon in the house of the Guru or head teacher, in a cupboard among the garments used in the annual ceremony of blessing the fishing fleet, I found five ancient Portuguese helmets. Portuguese. Without a doubt. They were of bronze and had crooked peaks at the top and had been found in some litter in one of the rooms of the fort Babi Mandi, a small ruin not far away. I was tempted to purchase them and take them away, but I decided that left there they kept Banda perfect – it needed no souvenir. Besides, where on board the *Skaga* could I stow a few Portuguese helmets?

On one of the estates we visited we saw in captivity some of the rare and celebrated kus-kus, tree kangaroos that have a pouch for the young, ears and claws like a bear's, and a brown and fawn spotted fur. These ate bananas in their hands. The odour was unmistakable too, unimpeachably rare kus-kus and nothing else. On the front portico of this kampong two telescopes were mounted, side by side. The elderly planter and his wife belonged to a world astronomical society and spent their evenings watching the stars and recording their observations to be forwarded as a small contribution to human knowledge. It was a pursuit in keeping with the flow of life on these enchanted islands.

We rowed home from Lonthoir as a harvest moon rose. There was no wind, the water was clear, the boat boys, like us, had had a holiday and were happy. They pulled slowly over sea-growths – cabbage roses six feet or more across, green as emerald, yellow as beaten gold. So that we could see well, they took care not to ruffle the water as they dipped their oars; every fish was parrot gay below us, every feathered sea-weed plain to see. Clear was no word to describe the unimaginable clarity of these waters, purer than air.

At last our evening meal was over, our friends the fisher-boys had gone – our duties were done. Mine had included a damper, for it was my cook-day on the morrow and now we were so far north that it was much too hot to cook except by night. The heat below had been intense, almost unendurable, the oven door had broken off and I knew my temper was tenuous, stretched like a piece of brittle toffee spun out almost to breaking point, like hollow glass tubing in the lab. when one is playing over a bunsen. From an atmosphere of hell I emerged into that of moonlight and mountains, with shadows of indigo and a mist of blue, the water below not water at all but a slightly more liquid air. Air and water interpenetrated but the water was the clearer. The bottom, coral-jewelled, sea-weeded, the garden of Proserpina herself. The solid old *Skaga* rested on a thin sheet of glass, suspended in the air by the frail support of the surface. To see her heavy bulk light on this gossamer glory was to realize that the old Hindoo mythology where the world rested on a pig and the pig on an elephant and the elephant on a tortoise might be feasible after all, or how should our heavy old tub be upheld in the air between moon and sea-garden?

Another merit of this superlative sea was that there were no sharks in it, at least report said there were no sharks, though why there should not be we could not guess, but we took it for truth and swam and dived about the boat, tumbling in whenever we liked. That too was freedom. Ruth spent hours in the koeli enthralled, gloating over the colours and forms below.

Sven and I had designs on Gunong Api, the volcano, but we all contented ourselves with climbing the Popenberg, the highest point on Neira, staggering there on sea-heavy legs and mounting a flagpole that stood on the summit. From that perch we looked over miles of shimmering sea, trembling with heat, burning with barriers of brightness, so that it seemed a host of flashing rapiers, an army of the sun, a mist of swords, denied a distant view.

Back on the boat we watched the sunset. The tide was out. Little Malay girls and old women were catching hermit crabs on the mud flat by the jetty, putting them in baskets to take home as one gathers mushrooms, and laughing and joking about it. The atmosphere was limpid, the sky an ethereal blue, the clouds cherubic pink, the same two colours that meet on Sèvres vases. Banda was a place without haste, even the brief tropical sunset seemed more leisurely here. Till the Dutch came to the Moluccas there was no word in the Malay vocabulary for 'late'. The Malays were never in a hurry and time was only a convenience. To be late meant to be tied to time and how stupid that would be for a civilized man. They measured time by the opening and shutting of flowers, by the heat, by the changes of tide. Early morning, belun terbang lalat, 'before the flies are astir'; later, kering ambun, 'when the dew dries'; noon, 'when the shadows are round'; sunset, 'when the buffaloes go down to the water'; night, jundera burdah, 'when the children have gone to sleep'.

I wish I could convey the limitless bright and lazy vistas of Banda, the irrefragable stillness and quiet of it, the sense of repose that singled it out from other islands. Joan and I were both moved by Banda, I did not know how she felt until, eating supper on deck and watching that miraculous atmosphere, compounded of fire and air, I murmured a reference to Ariel, and it was as if I had turned a key in an old watch, Joan took up the ticking. I had given the intangible between us the right quality and she responded to it by a lift of her heavy sleepy eyelids. A pity that Banda had not happened to us before.

I should like nothing better than to spend a season or two at Lonthoir across from Banda, lying under the nutmeg trees, living in an old kampong, writing in cool rooms and having someone to share it with.

We were at Banda for six days and our last afternoon was amusing. By a concatenation of circumstances Banda, the weather and a rice tafel, played a trick on us. Mrs. Brumsen, a kindly and charming Dutchwoman, hearing that our adventures had not hitherto included a rice tafel, which is supposed to be the gourmands' idea of paradise, had invited us to one at her house. She apologized before we started, saying that as she had only four servants the service might be a little slow, because in an hotel when one orders rice tafel there is a procession of thirty boys, each with a traymobile on which is one dish. We found the four boys more than adequate. We began with two pahits as an *apéritif* Each cover was set with a soup plate and in front of that a dessert plate. First came the rice, we were advised to take a generous helping. When the rice tafel is complete there should be no rice showing, it is all covered with a variety of tiny trimmings that one chooses from the many dishes offered. Titbits that one doesn't want in the general mêlée one places on the spare plate in front. Sven lost count at nineteen different dishes. There were, I suppose, twenty-two. In a big rice tafel there are about twenty-eight. I should not like, uninitiated, to try a big rice tafel.

Each dish was complete with its own sauce. Some of the items were chicken, fried, or done in soup with vegetables and chillis, or in some other fashion. There was wood pigeon too. And fish – several kinds, with garnishes and spices. Curried things. All these titbits were hot and separate. I began to wonder about the size of the stove and the number of cooking pots serving such a meal would mean in an ordinary house. There were small red Macassar fish like anchovies, cucumber with vinegar and chilli – essence of the rice tafel, this, the cool and the violent combined – a chilli paste, fish balls, a strange crushed substance on a stick; lobster, something that looked and tasted as one would expect the flesh of k'lapa muda to taste were it lightly fried, but which was part of a giant prawn found in these waters. The slices were big and light and crisp – something else, was it Bombay duck? Spanish peppers, mushrooms, baked eggs in a sauce . . . I forget the rest. I may have left out something really important – I seem to remember grass clippings that looked cool and tasted more fiery than the chilli.

At first it was delicious and very exciting. We drank beer. Some of the dishes were hotter than I liked. Gradually eating became a labour. I thought I had taken very small portions but

319

the sum total of unconsidered trifles I now found to be alarming and I had to stagger on. I could not leave too much on my plate. Dishes came round again. I motioned them away and began to worry lest I be ill and disgrace good manners. Granny's nasty old childhood rebuke popped into my head, 'One's eyes must never be bigger than . . .' Our hosts were young and considerate. The meal stretched on, the conversation was stimulating. I regretted that in that welter of mixed sapors I could not appreciate each item properly as it ought to have been appreciated. I was very glad when it came to a simple dessert – yes we *did* manage a dessert *after* the rice tafel – Spanish cream with cinnamon on it and some pineapple, then cigarettes, coffee and a liqueur. Even Ruth thawed, she liked maraschino. Lunch ended at five o'clock, but I believe it started late.

Now we had pledged ourselves to leave on the tide that night. It was a group idea. We had to get away.

We went to the boat. The anchor was fouled under coral. All our efforts could not get it up. A Malay boy dived in, feet first, and released us. The 'pome' tells the rest.

RICE TAFEL

We had eaten heavily,
it was our first rice tafel.
We had drunk appropriately,
it had been a farewell luncheon,
and pulling up the anchor at sunset
– for we had to get under weigh –
was an uncomfortable job,
and in the clear Banda air we were all a little tipsy.

So we sailed out with a light wind,
between Pisang and Banda Neira,
old Gunong Api a dunce's cap in the dusk
with a red feather of flame pinned to the side.
It was night and the sky dark-clouded.

But the sea –
Were we really drunk?
Did we imagine it?
The sea was milk-white,
it shone from below with a strange pallor,
as if Neptune were giving a party in an electrically-
    lit palace beneath
And we were flies on his ceiling.

We had an upside-down feeling;
the sky was a solid black pavement
the whole sea a white incandescence.
We were sailing blind in a fog of light.

Shocked into illogicality,
suspicious of fay-bewitched reefs,
Sven got out the lead and tried to sound
In water that drops from four hundred to two thousand
    fathoms.

We were phosphorescent crazy.

Never say
that the sea
has no sense of humour;
and the sky,
the sky
was a conspirator too.

CHAPTER XXVII

TO AMBON AND AWAY

THE day after the rice tafel nobody was very seasick but we all slept a lot. We were on the way to Ambon – Ambonya is the English name – and we had a taste of becalming. At first on a light breeze we travelled at three knots and found our watches boring enough; we each, save the cook for the day, did five and a half hours in the twenty-four at the tiller, sitting frizzling in the sun and thinking brightly for a time, then dully, and then not thinking at all.

On September 17th the wind dropped and the swell kept up. That is the most miserable state of existence in a small sailing boat at sea. What wind there was came in puffs and, as we had to take advantage of every puff, the square sail had to stay up, though in between every breath of wind it wrapped itself round the stays and would have worn itself to pieces quickly if it had not been for the undressed sheepskins we had rolled round them.

At night I heard Ruth whining to have the sail down and bother the puffs of wind, they weren't worth catching, and I heard Sven say that she had to stick it, so until the last minute of the watch I lay on my bunk tensed against the roll and watching the tooth-ached moon seesawing across the opening of the hatch, then I relieved her and in my turn counted my way by five-minute intervals through my spell. I found it long enough though it was the short watch, the dog watch, only two hours long.

We rolled and rolled again on the queasy sea. The moon was a white nutmeg pirouetting on a stalk-like leg under the leafage of the sky. She was a dancer with a chalk-white face and she made a circus-tent of the night. *Skaga* was nothing but a solemn old sea-horse, at the best of times never active, never nimble, never spry, and now she was teetum-toteming him at the end of a long string, pulling him into a sawdust ring, fooling him, and all the stupid beast could do was to wallow with delight, waiting for the smile of her approval and never budging onwards an inch.

Yet, when conditions did not alter, when the sail drew and then did not draw, when the moon kept on her wearisome game of leapfrog, jumping dizzily with every swell, playing this game with Time hardly made it pass and certainly did not make it exist. The clock ticking away was a ridiculous thing, utterly inappropriate and without any extension in reality, for nothing happened except the reeling and rolling of our wretched and moon-bewitched craft.

Next day was the hottest we had had till that time; terribly hot and terribly still; the heavy swell had gone down and left only a slight roll, by comparison blessed. Yet the hatfuls of wind had got us in sight of Ceram and about thirty miles from Ambon. For a long afternoon we watched the blue and tumbled hills of the Ceram coastline. At sunset a wind sprang up and we sailed about in sight of the entrance from 7 p.m. till 3 a.m., not risking the ten miles of an unknown harbour at night. Henery was taking us in.

In the morning we went up Ambon Bay with a light breeze. It was a fine blue day, the shores were attractive, woods and open cleared spaces on the hills, brown-thatched kampongs clinging to the hillsides like colonies of periwinkles on a green rock. Except for the absence of many buildings it was like Sydney Harbour on a blue day. We had heard that in Ambon it always rained. One Dobo resident, just returned from a fortnight there, had said that during his visit the sun had come out once for ten minutes and he had missed even those. Presumably Sol had been thirsty too, and, emerging briefly, had said, 'Have another?' to Ambon and retired to the heavenly bar for a further seven days. But while we were there he had, like us, gone teetotal, and shone gloriously on Ambon.

Had we not been able to tie up inside a jetty it would have been a difficult anchorage for us, fifteen yards off the low water mark the water was sixty fathoms. To keep out the heat we improvised all the awnings we could, the squaresail, the jib, the old spare mainsail, even our holland bunk-covers were utilized.

Ambon was too big to be officially interested in us. It was our biggest Eastern city so far with its crowded native market, narrow streets of tight-fitting shops, native hotels, Chinese chop sueys, shipping agencies, government Residency, Sports' Club, bicycle and sewing machine shops, drapers, perambulating vendors of 'siroops' – a siroop is frozen coloured water or drinks of flaming hues topped by a head of shaved ice – and its Malays playing soccer on the hard mud near the jetty, its crowds of people and a general sense of bustle.

If officially Ambon was not interested, unofficially it was curious. On the jetty, despite a heat that made crossing every road a little expedition over the Sahara and turned shadows that ought to have been black into dusty grey penumbra fenced with a palisade of glare, stood a group, changing its composition, but always a group, of the half or quarter Dutch immaculate in white linen, and of Mohammedan dandies in fezes of red and purple plush, smartly tailored cream coats, sarongs of bright red, green and black checks and heavy brogue shoes. (Ambon had the second highest percentage of lepers in the world, there was no compulsory segration of lepers, contagion is through the feet, so it was necessary to go well-shod.) The group wondered at us, at these people who brought no cargo, who sold nothing, who had women on board though there wasn't much room, who came in such a foreign craft, under a strange flag and who must have been poor for they did their own washing. We let them speculate and crammed what we could into two and a half days in Ambon: tennis, a swim, a fresh-water shower.

The Dutch took the fort from the Portuguese in 1605 and it was disappointing, only the old powder magazines and some of the outworks belonged to the early seventeenth century, and because it was dull it gave me some satisfaction to recall its inglorious military history. However, it contained early tiles and inscriptions collected from smaller ancient forts scattered in the Moluccan isles. We heard here the curious story of the blond, malay-speaking mestizo population of Kysar, descendants of a garrison of Dutch East India Company who remained near an abandoned fort on the little island which is just off the northernmost point of Portuguese Timor.

The old church, the oldest building in Ambon, was dignified and severe. Its lines were all out of plumb and yet it remained standing. It had rocked so much in the 1898 earthquake that its hanging lamps had crashed on the outer walls, the marks still remained. The heavy black carved furniture, underfoot the tombs and their epitaphs, lengthily inscribed, beautifully engraved, the strange pulpit, its weight incongruously upborne in that Dutch interior by one fat cherub, the old silver ewers, salvers and communion cups that the verger was persuaded to show us, the records of the pastors and the memorial tablets to those dead of fever, spoke eloquently of Ambon's pestilential and Puritan past.

I went on a hired bicycle across an isthmus and out to another small fort, my first ride in traffic, native traffic. One yelping dog which didn't know which way to go was the only casualty.

Ambon because of its drainage was a city of smells. The water supply came from a river in the hills, a clean and crystal-bright stream that was deployed in drains from the slopes where the bigger villas were, past the public park to a flat residential quarter, where most of the Malay houses were built. Women sat beside these clear runlets of water and washed the family laundry, urchins stripped naked and splashed in them, refuse collected, the wide drains pleasant as brooks became deep gutters, sewers, one to every street and oh, at the last, where the Chinese professional laundresses sat scrubbing close to the shore the colour of the water and the stench! That was one reason why we did our own washing.

The happiest gift Ambon made us was a long walk into the hills behind the town. At six o'clock one morning Joan, Ruth, Sven and I climbed by the school up a flight of cobbled steps to a bare unshaded path that kept mounting to the uplands along a shoulder of the main ridge of the island. As we toiled up native women were coming down, balancing on their heads enormous round wooden trays piled with produce, bananas, nutmegs, paw-paws, durians, eggs, pyramids of areca leaves, raw sago in cane cases like high explosive shells, bottles of oil, coco-nuts, betel-nut, even firewood in long heavy bundles. One had a stick over her shoulder, at each end of it was a green banana-leaf bucket filled to the very brim with fresh milk, one of the most expensive commodities in the East. They all went down hundreds of steps and an awkward steep gravelly descent without accident, the carriage of these Ambonese women was superb, they performed miracles of transport.

We sat by the path under gum trees, eating mangosteens we had purchased and watching the steady stream of women going to market, the Chinese in stiff and shiny black, the Malays in white coats with gay sarongs. I broke the eucalyptus leaves apart to smell the familiar Australian bush, but they had been too wetly nourished to have the aromatic savour of our trees. Above us rose more heights thickly wooded. Sven and I, lusting after exercise, went on. I hoped that the hill-climbing would do my sluggish nautical liver good and the profuse perspiration bring out my greyhound lines once more. We climbed steadily for an hour or more, the road keeping to the ridge with a steep drop on both sides. No traffic save by foot could come here. Brilliant yellow crotons bordered the path and tidy bright houses sat on terraces cut in the earth of the hillside. A little track led off into the jungle. We went down and discovered two bamboo conduits spouting ice-cold water into a ferny pool. A pretty native girl was bathing, sarong-clad under one of the spouts. Sven retired while I joined her. She was slim and pretty in her wet sarong that came above her breasts, her body the colour of wild honey, her lips the purple of sweet ripe mulberries waiting to be crushed. She was not more than eighteen and wore a wedding ring, but was unspoiled by matrimony. Her black hair had wavy tendrils about the forehead, but was sleek and straight in its prim bun at the back of her head. Her teeth flashed a half-scared smile at me.

I borrowed her soap and splashed, washing my hair too. She washed with the sarong on, lifting it only a little and holding it with one hand on her shoulder while she scoured below decks. Her movements had the inevitability about them of good poetry, they sang for joy under the cold water. So that I should not offend her modesty I had left my undergarment on, an amusingly brief garment that made her laugh. Her feet she rubbed clean on a stone, her mouth she held open under the full force of the rushing water and poking a finger into the moist soil rubbed her teeth with it. Begone to all patent tooth-cleaners! Then she slipped into her dry sarong, as a snake slips out of one skin and is still covered by the new one, so that there could not be any hiatus of flesh. She wrapped a broad band round the waist to keep the sarong up, put on a bodice of the kind that would have been called a camisole and then her white coat, freshly ironed, trimmed with the kind of Swiss embroidery that was fashionable round legs in the Edwardian period and was transformed from a graceful river nymph to a rather shapeless and odd little feminine parcel. She washed out her old sarong and spread it to dry with other sarongs on the bank. I thought it was a triumph on my part to have made so shy and delicately charming a creature confident. She watched me put on my thick linen dress over my transparent wetness and go, steaming, up the hill.

It became steeper and steeper. Now only a few houses clung to the path side, gay flowers before their doors, the clay of the track was baked hard, cut in a series of steps, a slow stairway upwards. There was still a wooded peak above us that looked as if it might give the view over the ocean on both sides that we wanted to see, but we had to abandon it, I had the responsibility of lunch-time and cook-day upon me.

Reluctantly we turned back, but the ferny pool and the spouts of gushing water drew Sven to bathe. I mounted guard for him and then, so irresistible was the lure of unstinted cool fresh water, that, late as we were, I bathed and could not tear myself away from this jungle paradise where water flowed, butterflies fluttered, and a valley led to the sea, and I was meditating playing truant from cook-day when a low coo-ee called me to the roadway. Sven was in difficulties. Three girls coming to bathe were hesitating to pass him. Had there been only one she would have run away, two would have gone back but *three* held their ground and yet were frightened to go forward. Their timid looks and questioning gestures demanded what he was doing there, loitering so near their bathing pool. When I came up, my hair still dripping, the wet garment in my hand, I was a sufficient excuse for him.

We said that the sun was hot and the water cool and they laughed, chattered and examined the garment I held, fingering its fineness and shaking their heads over its shape. I gave it to one of them and she was delighted, but I am sure she would never wear it – them – it would remain for them as my kai-kai hood for me, a trophy, a museum piece, that some strange, barbarous woman had manipulated and worn.

We ran and jumped down the hundreds of steps on the steep path we had so painfully ascended in the blazing heat, passing many of the market women who had been going down when we were coming up. They were resting in the shade or climbing the long steep uphill climb, their baskets and trays bore many small packages, probably little money changed hands at the market but there had been a lot of barter. They brought back gin in the familiar big square bottles, sago in the pink ingot form, trays of tiny fish, bright rolls of cotton goods ready to be made up, a few tin kettles and saucepans, some dressed timber and tobacco. The raw produce of the hills had gone down in the early morning and at noon the manufactured articles and the products of the shore were coming up.

On the third day with a light breeze and a flat sea we sailed out of Ambon.

Ambon had not been a dream, it had a commercial life of its own and been too complex to be set down easily in a phrase or two, but it had been an adventure none the less, a gallant exciting adventure, the pendulum of my happiness was still swinging upwards. There had been one or two friendly people, a German journalist who had gone to no end of trouble over us and the military doctor who had shown me the forts; and there had also been an iced drink that came after cycling as a well greets the traveller in the desert and new fruits and strange marketings.

Ruth and I liked being haus fraus together. She haggled over prices and I stared about me, picked things up and put them down again and was a kind of touchstone for her refusals. I bought a banana for frying that was the size of a young vegetable marrow and she bought kadjong idjou, a small pea that is sprouted into a green vegetable rich in vitamin C, coolies on plantations have it twice a week in their rations as a preventative against beri-beri. When the kadjong idjou were sprouted they resembled young uncooked corn in flavour, we ate them raw mixed with salmon. We could not now afford to buy more tinned vegetables or meat and went back to mashed ubi kaiou, like a purple and coarse sweet potato that felt as if it left an imperial purple stain from aesophagus to bowel as one ate. Our only fresh provisions here were some limes that we used carefully. We knew it was getting late in the season and that because of the late start from Sydney and delays on the way, our original plans to be in Singapore by October might falter through lack of wind. As it was it took us eight days to travel from Ambon in the Moluccas to Macassar in the Celebes. We began to have to endure in earnest heat, long watches, light airs.

The stars were always with us. Formerly I had seen them only with surprise after a late evening out as we were walking home to bed. They would startle me for a few minutes with the sense of their ever-watchful remoteness, then I would forget them. But there was no forgetting the stars when each night one was forced to sit for a few hours with nothing to do but watch them, one's co-watchers of the night. If one took heed of their attributes they had a calming effect; they ironed out the ruffles of the day. They gave poise to the spirit, they lifted one to the grand scale of feeling again. Sometimes they were oppressive and sombre. They bred a kind of melancholy fatalism, the stars and the world were so old, our life was so short, did anything matter? Certainly not lack of money or the holding of a job or the writing of a book, or any effort at all. It was as if the ant struggling with his purposeless load became for an instant aware of the contemptuous ridicule of the watcher above and dropping his burden with the sudden realization that it was of no use to him anyway, and that he had not meant to carry it, was left bewildered on the path. Till he forgot and hurried off after another grain of wheat or barrow-load of gravel. It is no wonder that the Arabs, travellers by night, have a permanent mood of fatalism as a racial characteristic. Just as an air bath refreshes the body so to drench one's soul in that excess of *libido*, with the perfume of star dust in the night, was to be purified. To say that stars wink down at one is a gross misunderstanding of them, for they have no humour, certainly not of the winking order, they are more sombre and remote than the staring stone eyeballs of Greek statues, and no one can look without repugnance on that perpetual blind focusing on infinity.

The northern constellations were in view, the Sickle, the little dim cluster that was the Pleiades, the Scorpion, standing on his tail to the south-west, Orion, shifted so that he was in the opposite quarter of the sky.

So I started off a new diary – my fourth – with a splurge on the stars, it might have been the less exalted topic of getting fat, for the immanence of the stars and of bodily rotundity had been troubling me for days. I had made up a whole philosophy for the fat and now that our food was coarse but plentiful I determined on several things, no more than one helping and no titbits between meals and exercises to be resumed behind the mast even though Joan gave me a silent sneer as I secretively jumped and bent. Perhaps she did not sneer and it was just my imagination; one could do nothing secretly on board and I liked having some things secret, looking in my mirror, and putting on toilet lotions without the guilt of vanity.

It seemed to me that Joan always carried round with her a

spiky circle of antagonism, a *cheval-de-frise* that guarded the inner fortress of a Superior Person. And I felt that the points could shift, like the spines on a sea egg, and grow longer and thicker in my direction! Yet were she to have approved of anything I did or wrote I should have been very happy, as I had been at her praise of the Dobo article. Yet I was perverse and obstinate now in refusing any longer to be a candidate for her praise; I had tried and she had made no sign and now I had begun to want the right to my own feelings. If only I had had someone at hand to protest that my moods and judgments had a validity of their own.

I was hungering for letters. It was two and a half months since any of us had had letters and a last telegram to me at Thursday Island had said, 'Mail at Malacca.' Malacca is a far cry from Macassar and I was in the dark as to whose error it had been, the postal authorities, mine or his. He was not fond of writing letters; I should not expect mail at Macassar.

Jealousy was a strange happening. That she could be jealous when she had everything! I knew what jealousy was, I had spent a long night watch tormenting myself with visions of an old *bête noire* and the beloved having an infant together. Ridiculous. Dragging up spectres to see how they hurt. But this involved jealousy over so intangible a thing as the quality of feelings. Nothing more. It could not be over her husband, there had never been any question of that, the problem could never and had never arisen. Perhaps all this emotional restraint had arisen out of that old hurt, at the time when we were getting ready for the trip, when she had suggested, hesitatingly, that Henery and I . . . and I had flashed out instantly, unthinkingly, the more utterly damaging for its rapid sincerity – 'What, Henery . . .? *He's* not my type.' Just that. It had been enough.

I was, after all, a bit flamboyant and exotic, and there had been that dream of his, after Brisbane, one of his rare dreams, that she, seeing the amusement in my eyes, had stopped the relating of – 'I don't think you'd better tell any more', she had said.

On fundamental things she and I had been scrupulous. There was that question of loverly demonstrativeness. I had brought it up when the preliminaries were being negotiated, saying I knew I should be stupid enough not to be able to stand it, separated as I should be, and she had agreed. We had understood each other then, at least she had wanted to understand me. And she had stuck to her side of the bargain. More or less. Some things she couldn't help, and I didn't mind them, they didn't affect me. I still had enough sympathy in me to cover that. But why had all the sympathy been drained out of her so that a moment of communication such as had happened at Banda became for me an ineffable relief?

All kinds of pettinesses had been sinking away; in this mood of calm, of resignation at being perpetually alone I had seen my first trivial actions as the foothills that stand at the beginning of a mountain range. I had learnt to understand the violence of these months of morbid introspection and the incessant desire for solitude as a necessary corollary following my break-away from all intimate associations.

During these days of hot calm when nothing happened, when the water in the shadow of the ship was so blue, such a thick deep blue, that it was a surprise to put in a foot and find it come out unstained, when the nights were black and oppressive with heat, I had whale fear upon me, fear of a gigantic tail thrashing out of the water and down upon the deck, splitting us in two as had happened to a launch near Cairns. It had sunk within thirty seconds of the blow and a man had been drowned instantly. Schools of whales often came near us, puffing and blowing like old men in the surf. Ruth had had a bad scare at the tiller at night when one had come up close to us and breathed suddenly. Seen in the daytime a quarter of a mile away another had been longer than we were, a lazy cigar-shaped submarine. It seemed to us a long way north for whales to be.

The symbol of the whale had gripped me. On one long still afternoon while I had enlarged in the fore-cabin, Joan's part, in a stifling darkness, when it was so hot the emulsion on the papers blistered in spite of hardeners, I had felt inside the whale dragon, entombed alive in the devouring all-mother; the boat itself become the whale bound up with this long period of blackness, of unwholesome but impelled self-communing out of which I had to get myself. I had begun to think of Kim, in his early worship of Zarathustra, as essentially a sun-hero, and of poetry-writing as best typifying the primitive urges in modern society, for both of us the way of deliverance. Imaginings and theorizings none the less real for being fanciful, much more important than, and having nothing to do with, my old nightmares of claustrophobia that had come on me in thrice reiterated dreams at the end of our Barrier sailing, just before Thursday Island.

Ruth had changed, too, and become less prudish. The familiarity in our relationships was such that I heard Sven say to her as she sat at the tiller, 'I think I'll have a bucketing behind the sail if you don't mind'.

'That's all right', answered Ruth in a matter of fact tone, though such a proposal a few months earlier would have horrified her. She had adopted Fletcherism, a doctrine that demands chewing all food slowly until it becomes a liquid in the mouth, a process that she said, 'induced great digestive tranquillity', but was rather ghastly to watch. She followed the tenets of Fletcher with superb religious rigidity, as she carried out all her schemes.

At this time we took an inventory of the stores aboard and found that we had dried peas and beans, barley, wheat, white flour, tea, seven pounds of prunes, a large tin of ripe olives, the remains of a big tin of sweet biscuits, two tins of salmon, about twelve of bully beef, eight ounce tins these, eight or ten pounds of tinned tomatoes, two tins of peanut butter, one of powdered milk, a packet of patent pudding, some olive oil and a few soup powders. We were out of sugar, baking powder, salt – we had some coarse stuff for salting down the fish we could not catch – pepper, fat, vinegar, sauce or any of the things that make plain fare palatable. Butter we had not bought since Brisbane. Eggs, potatoes, onions, cheese, bacon, bread or plain biscuit were luxuries and we did not have them.

Everything not tinned was weevily. The weevils were like miniature beetles in wheat, rice, and flour. With the onslaught of the great heat they had sprouted wings. Lying on one's back in the bunk or sitting in the cockpit steering one had to be continually trapping the weevils that sauntered out. A leg outstretched was a great weevil trap. They got in our clothes and they taught us bad manners. One was to saunter out a fortnight later on the bosom of my dress as I chatted to a Tuan Bazaar in Macassar, and without thinking I gave it the *coup de grâce*, *Skaga* fashion. And the Tuan Bazaar's eyes when he saw me! Ladies do not wear weevils.

Once I opened the white flour tin and found a concourse of black weevils sitting like politicians at a conference, all happy arguing together. The heat of the day and the force of their own arguments had drawn them to the surface to sunbake. To get rid of weevils from the flour was a tiresome and wasteful job, we used to sieve it through mosquito netting and that raised a cloud of white dust. I thought I should catch these weevils before they got on the hop and burrowing with a pannikin on their blind side I secured a supply of pure flour, only in the last pannikin did a few tumble in. These I plucked forth and, lest any remain, put some spice in the cookies! Trade secrets.

We had trouble with other insects, too. The cockroaches were multiplying visibly, they were still small but they were bolder, they walked about in broad daylight with the assurance of accredited representatives calling for orders. Worse was in store, for Sven. After a sleepless night when we had done nothing but roll and rattle about, lowering the sails when the continual musketry fire of the reef points on the canvas became unbearable and hoisting them again on every hint of wind, Sven came below to take his 8 a.m. observation and found beneath the leather strap on the chronometer case three live bugs and their eggs. Bugs! Detestable vermin. The chronometer was his baby, it slept at the foot of his bunk, padded with socks and pillows against the roll. He had to take up the cheerless task of airing and disinfecting his bedding and all the odds and ends he kept under his mattress, razors, magazines, breast salve – he swore by it for cuts – a screw-driver, letters. He had to take up his bunk boards and scrub and disinfect them and the locker under the galley end of his bunk. Nobody gave him a hand, the company dissociated itself from the proceedings – and bugs. He blamed the launch on which we had gone up the Merauke river for the vermin. He was furious, the possession of bugs is so ignominious, a kind of trade mark of the social pariah, and it had had to happen to him, who was already depressed by the assumption of superiority of the others. However, the bugs gave him no more trouble, his disinfecting was more than adequate.

We all shared another woe. Henery in his recently acquired anxiety over food had saved some tinned tomatoes from Joan's cook-day to his own with the result that we all succumbed to what he called euphemistically – a 'touch of ptomaine' that made night watches an agony and kept us all in a constant state of pilgrimage to Ajax. Also the water we had taken aboard at Bulo Babi had been of poor quality, extremely hard, foul to taste and of doubtful goodness. It had corrupted the water in the three tanks to which it had been added. Any water we drank without boiling had to be syphoned from the tank below Joan's bunk. Yet in spite of heat, coarse food and poor water we all kept superficially well. The dampers were the worst to stomach, they were so often badly made. We wasted a lot of kerosene over them.

One night at 1 a.m. I was startled by the moon rising fierily, a black cloud breaking her form, and I was momentarily sick with dread, positive that it was a steamer on fire, about to call Sven, when the cloud moved and I realized that the ship on fire was only a moon. We had not encountered a steamer at sea for several months, not since the Barrier. We had been off the beaten sea-track.

Somehow with light airs, currents, and freshets of wind to help

335

us we had got to within 193 miles of Macassar notwithstanding hours of calm when even ripples, watermarks that told no date on the blue print of the sea, were erased by the stillness and left only a faint stippling as of dimples under the surface. At last after a harrowing night of becalming and illness, the 'Ptomaine', a stiff breeze sprang up and we went tearing along.

It was perfectly lovely. I never wearied when we had a wind, than I wanted to go on sailing and sailing, just so, for years.

We were racing northward up the second leg of the Celebes to Macassar run after the interminable crossing of the Gulf of Boni. The sea was gently undulating, there were lots of little white tips, the smooth mirror which had been the sea while we were becalmed had shattered into fragments of bright glass without number. The water was green for we were within the shallow coastal reef. The sky was a nondescript grey with a low bank of cloud at the west. But the glory of everything was the clean invigorating quality of the wind. The tiller was fairly hard but steady, the wind blew with a rush and a rustle, a tiger out for play, and the waves made their crunching battering against the bows and fell back on either side. We were cutting a straight furrow in the wind-ploughed field that was the sea. It was so enchanting after days when we had made no perceptible impression on the blue page across which we had listlessly tried to rule a straight line.

I was exhilarated. It was no wonder that wind was the symbol of the Holy Ghost, the breath of life, the creating whisper of divinity. As we allowed ourselves thus to rush with the wind, to fall in with his mood, we became part of the god ourselves, we were of his spirit, there was no impurity or baseness left, hardly even a sense of weight, or the pull of gravity. We almost had wings and should the wind have willed it we could have gone sailing along in the air, so strong was he and so light and buoyed up with freedom were we. His embrace was chaste, his caress cool and pure. From the steaming heat of past days we were delivered.

By nightfall we were coming in to Macassar.

336

CHAPTER XXVIII

WE MAKE MACASSAR

THE wind ended in a calm, eight miles off Macassar. 'Let us drop the anchor and have one good night's sleep,' said Sven. We had not slept properly for eight nights. On deck there was just room for all our mattresses, Joan and Henery for'ard between the mast and the fore hatch, Ruth and I on either side of the deck-house, and Sven aft, wedged in between the compass-box and the main hatch. A blue mist had come down from the uplands beyond the coast. There was no moon, we were floating in a cloud, soft and woolly. The sea had pulled down the sky for a coverlet and was blanketing itself to rest, lying motionless; the world was muffled in slumber; against the sides of the boat the water made no sound. It became chilly and dew fell, I had to rise and get another rug.

Before sunrise I woke. The sky had lifted and was glowing with the anticipation of dawn but the sea remained tranquil, polished, gold upon deep blue, smooth, not breathing as it slept, still dreaming of the night and reflecting unbroken but transitory images of the sky above.

And in that waiting hush we were surrounded by junks; the frail air filled their sails that were like bedroom mats hung out to dry, like rectangular webbed fins of fish, like venetian blinds threaded on slats. They were going out fishing. Though our anchor was now up we were not moving, only drifting sideways a little while they were gliding imperceptibly by, light as ladies on a ballroom floor. The surface of the sea was beginning to be slippery with light. The great sails of patched calicoes, reds, yellows, browns; the bedroom mats of split rattan through which the wind could freely blow, passed by us and spread into a half-circle away on our starboard beam; behind them the shore was still draped with night vapours but the hills beyond stood out prominently, clear and distinct, carved against the sunrise; soon the heat of the day would shroud their unequivocal shapes with haze.

It was ten before a light breeze sufficient to move us sprang up and noon before we were anchored in front of the Macassar Yacht Club – Friday, September 30th. Somehow I had got two days behind in the date. It was my cook-day and I offered to mind *Skaga*. Already a few laundrymen had come touting around. There was no virtue in not going ashore, I could not risk going. Mail. The others knew they were getting mail. They went off excitedly while I with extreme care de-weeviled some barley, opened a tin of tomatoes and concocted a stodge, one of those filling messes that if you are very hungry are good to eat, provided you have not come straight from halls of plenty.

As I sat stirring, pretending it was highly necessary to dissolve every salt crystal and that it was much better to be aboard wearing shorts than tramping in shoes through strange streets, Sven burst in, blew down through the closed hatch like a cool tornado. 'Who thought she wasn't getting any mail? More than any of us. Look at this!' He thrust a pile at me. Newspapers, fat letters, some from mother, some from others and one, two, three, four, four big envelopes from him! Mrs. —— and then *his name*, his whole name like a nameplate on a door, like a key signature in music, a delicious music that sounded above the hissing of the primuses.

'Oh Sven!' I counted again. Four. Four right enough. 'Oh Sven, did you get any?' It was better than Christmas, it was better than a birthday.

'Two,' he grinned, 'Mother and Dona.' It was a joke that he had an aunt Dona and that he was her favourite. 'Full of good advice.'

'Did the others get any?'

'Lots, everyone of us got some.'

The day was quite perfect. 'I'll make you some tea, the kettle's nearly boiling.'

'I can't stay, I've a sampan waiting.' The dear. He had come over specially with my mail and now, just as especially he went away, talking in a rush about somebody they had met on shore. It went over my head. I sat on the galley, sipping tea and reading. Luxuriating, bathed in perspiration and pleasant emotions.

At three o'clock, or was it four? – Ruth and Joan and Sven came back. 'Hot! Good Lord it's hot down here. Hurry up. Come on, pack up. We've been invited to stay for the week-end.' It was a paean, a triumph. Invited to stay the week-end! Baths, meals, a house. A *house*! No wonder her eyes glittered, no wonder her swift brown hands flew like birds into her lockers and brought out clothes, for both of them, putting things into a suit-case.

A week-end? *All* of us?

'Yes,' Ruth said. Joan always took things as if fairies brought them, when one wanted prosaic details one asked Ruth. 'He asked the women first and then he added Henery because – and now we're all going. The car's waiting, Henery's with him. Hurry up.'

I was slow, I was all pins and needles. I had been sitting cramped up and gloating on that narrow, two-legged canvas slide in the galley for more than three hours. 'What kind of a week-end?' (Better put in the best pyjamas, put in the satin slippers, the evening dress and don't forget a nail file.) 'Who is he?'

'He's a Dutchman, he's president of the Yacht Club.'

'Does his wife know there's five of us coming?'

'He's a bachelor. Don't keep him waiting – the car's at the wharf.'

'Who's going to look after the boat?' There must be some snag.

'The yacht club mandoer.' Everything was arranged.

We were ashore, cars and lots of shiny bicycles. Greetings. A drive under trees that made lofty green tunnels; concrete roads. We were there. A villa, white, low, cool as an ice-cream, set on a green lawn, served with a drive entrance and red salvias for cherries. Inside comfort, quietness, carpets, polished furniture, doors that opened and shut, privacy. Oh the joy of spreading oneself on a curtained bed in a peaceful room, with a full length mirror to show how horribly Juno-esque one had got on board, how broad in the shoulders and thick in the arms, as much from constant pounding up and down of the recalcitrant Ajax as from hauling on ropes. What joy to splash in a bathroom white tiled, the usual Eastern bathroom where one dips a bucket into a well and pours water over oneself, a plug would be a meanness, a trickling back of generosity in one's ablutions in the East; to sit at ease, upright and without the dread of being heard at one's devotions in what our host was pleased to call the 'chain locker', to walk back to the tiled veranda hung with ferns and into a bedroom of one's own, to shut the Singapore doors and take a long and uninterrupted gaze at a weather-beaten countenance in the glass over the wash basin – running water, such a plumbing jewel of a wash-basin – to pat one's face into shape, to jump about and prance on the cold floor, to dance and do exercises, to sit at a big desk and write letters with a bowl of flowers before one, to admire the colour scheme of the curtains and chairs and cushions.

Then when one began to feel civilized to go to a table set with finger bowls and spotless linen and to eat meals that one had forgotten all about, spinach and leeks, green peas and puddings – I liked puddings, sweet things, iced custards, and egg and lemon concoctions, and sherry in the trifle – to have fried bread below the baked eggs and parsley crisp in the rissoles, clear strong soups, strange mixtures of rice and shrimps; fresh fruit, lobster mayonnaise, and chicken served with peaches. Dishes with generations of experience behind them; we were eating a thousand years of wisdom. And the eggs! I who had once had – how long ago it seemed – fruit and an egg each morning for breakfast, now by a miracle was restored to that diet and on the morning when a wondrous omelet appeared I felt like saying a prayer of thankfulness to it.

One day at the midday meal we of the *Skaga* came to the shining table with shining faces and shining anticipations and appetites sharp as swords. As we sat down I found a strong impulse bending my head and raising my hands and putting into my mouth the old grace at table, 'Thank the Lord for this food, for Christ's sake. Amen' and then, 'Benedictus, Benedicatur'. Jokingly I mentioned it and instantly Sven, Ruth and Henery confessed to the same impulse, our graces were in different words, that was all. Joan was the only uninfluenced person, her upbringing having been less orthodox than ours. Now in a letter I had had he had said, 'I expect you with your goat, fish, paw-paw, oysters and peacock's eggs in honey will not look at beef, cutlets, omelets, and vegetables when you get back to civilization', and at that moment, the invitation not having been given, I had gone over in my mind the fortnight of wheat, peas, barley and tapioca root and curtsyed to the stodge sitting on the primus. Vegetables, omelets, beef and cutlets! They were the summit of civilization, and here they were.

Our host, the President, had been a sailor and was head of an important shipping firm in Macassar. He had that mixture of joviality, shrewdness and wit that we found in many Dutch people. His relationships with his Malay servants were jolly, informal, everything in the household ran smoothly and it was politeness and humour that greased the wheels. A manual we had about the White Man in the Tropics laid down as a maxim, 'Never joke with a native'. Perhaps the author did not consider the Malays natives, but we found many of our own race who did. The Malays are cultivated persons, laughter ripples in their eyes and is easily drawn to their mouths in a quick understanding smile; it is as if the sunshine in the air had warmed their natures too.

One evening when we were sitting round a table under the big silk-skirted electric standard lamp that grows, like a gigantic rose, one to each Macassar garden, the man selling sati came along. Sati, puppy dogs' tails, are small pieces of pork threaded on a thin wooden skewer. They are placed over a bed of live charcoal and the charcoal fanned with a grass fan till it glows. The sati are turned several times till they are ready when they are served with a small plate of chilli sauce and sectors of green cucumber.

You dip in the chilli sauce and then to quench the fire take a piece of cucumber. The sati cost five cents each. When our host paid the reckoning he told the man that formerly they had only cost three cents each.

'That is so,' the vendor admitted.

'Prices are cheaper now, you should charge less.'

'Ah, but Tuan, I put more meat on them!'

'I see how it is. Before, you carried a tray on your head, now you have a tricycle with an electric light, soon you will be selling your sati from an auto.' Everyone was pleased with this piece of raillery.

The President had never forgotten his early days at sea. He had a great passion for the sea, his rooms were hung with pictures of ships. 'The Germans can paint the sea better than anyone,' and point by point he showed us how they could, 'but the English write best about the sea'. He had a library of sea books to prove that. 'The technical phrases of the English for handling sails are superb, they are themselves poetry, they are not to be found so precise and beautiful in any other language. Where could you have such phrases as bend and set fore royal stunsails; raise weather fore clue garnets, haul forward maintop bowline and brace round mainyard; up mainsail in crossjack and mizen stay-sail, main royal and flying jib; send main top gallant and royal stunsail booms aloft?'

Sven added the strophe to his diapason of the sea. They got on well together, they knew ropes and rigs as children at school learn the multiplication table, by handling them. On our voyage we might learn a little of the sea, a few of its moods, its smiles and frowns, the palpitations of light over its surface and the vigour of the trade winds; we should learn to know one ship, every pulsation in her dead and yet living timbers, her temperament in any wind; every piece of her would become part of us, if we were to be put on her again at any time in the future our bodies would accommodate themselves to her angularities, would grasp and bend and twist without thinking, out of the intense familiarity that long living in a confined space makes, but we should never know ships as these men knew them. They chanted a liturgy of ships and voyages and for me grandfather's ghost swung up dry out of the sea, stroking its short white beard and asking, 'What is the difference between a barque and a barquentine? You should know that, I've told you before. Go over your masts again.' It was my sea catechism. (I had on a blue linen dress with a sailor collar that had anchors in the corners and the bosun's whistle he had given me hung on a yellow cord.) But grandfather had never got into his speech the metaphors the President delighted us with, 'Cutting the tow-rope', for breaking an engagement, 'The stern cabins' for the servant's quarters, 'The cut of the poop deck' for the rear view of a Dutch lady, 'the chain locker'; 'a cork fender' for a cushion, lots of absurdities.

On Saturday morning, we, economic irresponsibles, watched him drive off to his office. The days had names again. At sea they might as well have been numbers, the numbers of cook-days, but now they had whisked back to their old week-day importance, and for a moment I was back on another sunshiny veranda, looking good-bye, but not waving, waving was too surburban, to someone who hurried down the hill, late as usual, the paper tucked under one arm, glasses twinkling for a moment when he turned where the road dropped, while the sea beyond Merewether shone like a freshly-washed willow-pattern plate and the sky was frisky with clouds and even the sparrows chirped louder than on week mornings because it was Saturday and I had the day to spend exactly as I wished. This day in Macassar was just such a Saturday, except that the sparrows were brighter, the tropics had put green jewels in their dusty brown plumage, and instead of a black cat with green eyes a white one with blue eyes played on the path. I had come home to Saturday and the exquisite sensation of leading an everyday existence. I wrote. I poured forth turgidities in a twelve-page letter without a paragraph and frequently I stopped to admire the furniture. I listened with pleasure to the telephone ringing and almost I answered it. Once or twice I got up and opened and shut the door for the fun of being able to do it. Doors that shut were marvellous. The inspired creations of men, doors with hinges and handles, rooms, verandas, halls. I had a ridiculous feeling of gratitude to the chairs and taps, to the mirror and my desk with its pretty red and blue cross-stitched runner. I wanted to let that runner know that I liked its pattern very much.

I said to someone to whom I was introduced and on whose chairs I sat, 'What wonderful canework in these chairs. Are they made here?' and I gave them a friendly stroke while the bewildered lady said of the chairs that to her were the acme of the commonplace, 'These chairs? Oh they belong to the pension, I don't know where they were made,' and her thought said, 'What a strange woman, she must be very stupid to think these ordinary chairs are such fine things.'

Saturday night closed as it always used to close, as this sweet and ordinary day had to close, with a cinema. Not a good picture, posturing people simulating false emotions, lost to all natural dignity, following hypocritical conventions of feeling like the rules of a game, and providing such an object lesson in the stupidity of the 'superior' race that the President objected to it as demoralizing for the 'coloured' spectators who tittered now and then. I only wondered that they did not burst into booing outright. All the same it was good to pour oneself into evening dress, to wear pretty, light clothing, to discard the stiff khaki shorts that one had grown used to as inevitable, as part of oneself, and that wrapped one's limbs up as if they had been uninteresting brown paper parcels – ruefully – parcels that contained a large leg of mutton. It was good to lend Joan a diminutive thing that I was fond of and that I had stitched with such leisurely pleasure long before, in the before time ages when I had been a woman doing a little chic embroidery in the late afternoon, and after the loan to hear, from the next room, laughter and expostulation.

The next day was Sunday and it too had the sense of being Sunday about it, when the sun is clear, the sky hot and shiny and there is a feeling of bright calm and holiness, of a joint ready to be put in the kitchen oven and mint sauce for dinner.

At six o'clock in the morning we were off, on a picnic. We were sailing *Skaga* with some of the Yacht Club wives and children aboard over to Pulo Moreaux, a little island with bathing boxes just opposite Macassar Harbour. The President sailed his own boat across and watched us closely as we made ready and set off. We tried to do the thing properly, to show that after all these months of practice we could get away smartly and neatly without a hitch, all helping. We managed well, but the wind, what there was, was so light that *Skaga* was just able to lollop across the green straits, like a draught horse shaking its ears at a crop of lucerne while the skiffs showed us their heels and sailed circles round us. By ten there was no more wind but the *Skaga* was safely anchored and 'At Home'.

Everybody dived off her, swam round her, looked inside her and left wet patches wherever they sat. We showed off her paces, her gear and her gadgets. Yachtsmen in turn solemnly put their heads into the 'chain locker' and admired her stout shoulders. They felt her ribs and measured them, they looked at the stepping of the mast, they kicked at the canvas collar the Swede had sewed for it, they almost made her open her mouth and show her teeth. Everybody was satisfied, she was a grand boat. We made morning coffee and sported like porpoises in the water. Porpoises are fat. So were we and our Dutch visitors too were large and very amiable.

How many Sunday mornings had I known like this, on blue Lake Macquarie, doing nothing but getting sunburnt? There had been at one time the Ark, a craft that had suited its name and that in its youth had been used as a ferry. My brother owned it and dreamed of converting it into – what? A yacht-houseboat for week-ending? A kind of bus under canvas? Something of the sort. It was a tub. Every time we took her out the wind dropped and she needed a bagful of wind to blow her along. One Boxing Day we had the whole family aboard, mother, aunts with babies and parasols, even father under cover of a newspaper, and for long hours we were left windless off Bolton Point while the family amiability dripped away, like the butter from the sandwiches. The Ark was 'disposed of' after that; the Paternal Presence had been invited with conversion money in our thoughts, and the conversion money was not forthcoming . . . Now *Skaga* played us the same kind of trick. With lunch-time looming ahead and people thinking of showers, homes and the two to four afternoon rest she got stuck. Low tide.

We pushed, shoved, shouted, tied ropes to the jetty and tried to get her stern off, towed at her nose with one of the launches, ran up the staysail and put it down again and all she did in response to our efforts was to grunt and settle farther in the sand. All these nautical gentlemen present and this had happened! They had chosen the exact anchorage for us but no one was in command and everyone it appeared had waited for someone else to mention that the tide was running out *fast*.

Did it matter? Not at all. Did our Dutch friends desert us? Not at all. A launch skipped like a mosquito across the water, telephone messages told wives, house-boys, mothers, to keep the mint sauce on the ice. Very soon maccan for everybody appeared out of 'tucker-tins'. I do not know the Dutch name for them but that is what workmen in Australia call those tiers of enamel receptacles slotted one above the other on a metal handle. Such maccan. Dutch food, Malay food and Chinese food, and, as our hosts wanted us to try everything it ended for us of the *Skaga* in a regular League of Nations and in the jumble Ruth decided to give Fletcherism the go-by.

She and I were sharing a room and a big bed and that night as we lay, thankfully stretched out before sleeping and almost tasting the smoothness of the linen sheet, we talked. About the trip and what lay ahead and what we should do afterwards. I had had word that it was no longer necessary to fulfil my academic task in London and that I was free to continue the voyage or choose to do what I pleased. I had several adventurous plans for Ruth and I to combine in but she hesitated. She would stay with the boat. I would still be leaving at Singapore. Leaving cuts all knots. But nevertheless we had been getting on better, all of us, didn't she think?

She did not think so. In fact she had reason for *knowing* differently. We might seem to be getting on better but Joan had said . . . What Joan had said still meant, 'Never. Never again.' Never like a heavy hammer blow right on the heart.

Ruth had spoken for me. She had asked, 'Aren't you too hard? Don't you think so yourself? Isn't it unnecessary, such treatment?' For her part she knew where I had been 'weak' and Joan wrong . . . It was long and involved but the only outcome was that I knew that the old hurt still smarted in me. And I thought I had got over it.

I had thought she was getting over it too. I had thought that now without trying to I was climbing tangentially to the circle of her friendly respect. In that I had been wrong. I had made another mistake. We had both been dissembling, both anxious to keep up appearances, to make Singapore a united crew, and we had each known that dissimulation in the other, from one meal to the next, from moment to moment between meals. But I had thought the dissimulation was becoming the reality and that our strong common purpose was uniting us – and I had been wrong. I had been wrong a second time about the quality of her feeling, as I had been at a loss to understand what was happening to her in the first ten days out of Newcastle. She would always be the inscrutable Joan for me.

Why did she not speak? Why did she always leave me to wonder and not know? Perhaps Ruth was wrong? Perhaps Joan had dropped that devastating remark casually from her Olympus and Ruth had built it up into an inexorable barrier. Had she not confessed that her own friendship with Joan was not as satisfying as she had expected it to be? That the elusive 'Noli me tangere' had brushed her aside too? Perhaps her disappointment had wished to emphasize that steeper barrier between Joan and me, between the pivot and the outer circle? Ruth was the inner circle and I could take her word for Joan's attitude. She was positive enough. To try to talk about it again to Joan would be too painful. It ought to be done but I should not do it. I should not do it till I could be certain of my self-control, and I was not certain. I could never risk falling into tears before her again. To open up a matter with her became an act of aggression and to aggress would be to put the aggressor in the wrong instantly, as I had been put in the row. 'So stupid, so unnecessary,' her every silence said plainer than words, 'to aggress with plain speaking; life must be more subtle than that.' To myself I agreed with her, ridiculous to fight something that retreated and was never there, though its presence could be felt. The Borg. She must speak to me about it, not I to her again, or all my laboriously acquired self-value would be lost, swept away.

Thus the talk with Ruth brought Monday, and Monday began a new week. The completely happy week-end was over. Mail, an invitation, the picnic, the enlargement of living ashore, had been a many-roofed pagoda of happiness piercing the sky. Under its eaves silver bells had rung little tunes with every vagrant wind, for every fresh glimpse of Macassar, every feeling of being civilized and at home had brought delight, but the new week trailed worries as well as joys, at sea there was peace, the inevitable necessity of going on, but the problems every port brought could not be evaded, not even in exciting Macassar.

CHAPTER XXIX

SHALL I GO ON?

MONDAY began with a pleasure excursion to a waterfall, Bintang Moerang, about thirty-six miles away. It was a silent departure, each of us and the host chewing the cud of thought. His car was not large enough to take us all in comfort and so we went in a large hired car which at once made us think of money. I had forgotten money and it came as a shock to remember that two in the front and four in the back would be a crowd and that over-crowding mattered. It was Monday and when did a week-end end? We wished Henery could be explicit, it would be hard to relinquish this week-end but we must be stern, there were some things more important than being comfortable. Our impover-ished condition suddenly showed itself like a frayed shirt-cuff. We pushed it back out of our thoughts but we knew it might shoot down again at any moment.

We raced out under avenues of trees between the neat Dutch villas. Street sweepers with bundles of willow switches swept up the leaves into tiny dust-pans that housemaids might use. Under the lattice of sunlight a steady stream of traffic was coming in to market, little ponies so laden with fodder that they looked like moving haystacks, nothing showed beneath the long coarse grass, freshly-scythed, save their ears and tails. Ponderous carts with unbound wooden wheels were drawn by 'caribous', cattle that were descended from the water buffalo, dun in colour, with straight high-spreading wicked horns, savage eyes, clumsy heads and big feet splayed out by drawing heavy loads on hard road-ways. They liked best to splash along in the red dust on either side of the road.

Marketmen were carrying loads in baskets slung from poles across the shoulders; they brought charcoal, vegetables and grain and faggots of firewood from the mountains. Durians, protected by wicker-work or rags, hung from the trees outside the Malay houses by the road, ramshackle bamboo houses with the characteristic Polynesian crossed poles tied at the ridge of the roof and perched aslant on crooked piles like long-legged insects above the paddy fields. It was the dry season, everything was brown, the colour of Australian wheat country after the harvest. Driving before seven o'clock the rush of air was cool and fresh, but quickly it grew hotter, the road more open and the avenues of trees were left behind. An irrigation canal ran beside us; in it buffalo and little boys were wallowing together in the mud, the boys were not frightened of the fierce beasts, they pelted them with mud and pushed them away.

We passed through our first inland town with a police barracks and native soldiers drilling. Here the chauffeur bought his lunch, instead of paper it was parcelled in a green banana leaf neatly made into a bag and pinned with a bamboo splinter.

The road had been level and all the countryside flat, but at length a solitary needle-sharp hillock stood like a signpost beside the way. Once it had been a rock jutting from the ocean bed, for at one time all this coastal plain of the Celebes was sea bottom. Soon we reached the old coastline, now thirty miles inland, a low line of limestone hills rising abruptly from the plain in a steep wall. They were not high but their shapes were varied and the oddities of the jungle-wreathed caverns at their base made them fantastic and top-heavy, for the limestone showed clearly in the scooped-out hollows below, while above these creamy sea-domed caves soil had gathered in a black canopy of earth and trees had grown, their trunks parallel to the cliff face, making a screen to the precipice.

Behind this bastion of the old land the country was entirely changed; low jungle-covered hills tossed in confusion without rhythm or order like waves caught in the first flurry of a storm at sea. The road wound into a shallow valley, the bed of an old river that formerly had debouched into the sea at this point.

There was still a river, Malay families were bathing in a dam that held it back, their sarongs full of rich colour, reds, purples and greens.

We left the car and walked into the intense green shadow of the valley floor. Butterflies, the size of saucers, lemon yellows, black swallowtails, black and red mandarins, and big crimson dragon-flies, fluttered about. We crawled through a small hole into caverns and by an underground river into more small caves, but we did not marvel at them sufficiently, we were familiar with far vaster caverns, those at Jenolan, N.S.W., and our delight did not have the ring of enthusiasm about it till we came to an enchanted lake, deep and dark blue, completely surrounded by unclimbable cliffs.

To go farther we had to swim, in fresh water that made our limbs unexpectedly heavy, each stroke demanding more effort, taking us a shorter way, our bodies gross in the butterfly quietness. No sunlight ever fell on the water, the cliffs shut it out, the sky above was high and pale blue, we floated and stared up at it or swam sidestroke, making eddies but not splashing. On the farther side a tree with large creamy blossoms perfumed like clematis overhung the water and dipped willowy branches into it, I shook them as I trod water beneath and down fell a rain of blossom and leaves on the surface and with them big striped bees, honey-gorged drunkards who scrambled on the floating flowers and rafted themselves ashore, kicking furry legs and capsizing now and then. It was a place reluctantly to leave and not to forget.

When we left it the day was in full heat, the metalled road, shining like a corkscrew, zig-zagged into a gorge and opened a narrow way inland; it was the main road through the Celebes. Presently we got out and climbed by a foot-track to a week-end house, built Malay fashion, the eyrie of an eagle overlooking the sea of hills.

When we had rested and drunk we went on a little and then turned back. The heat licked at our faces like flames, we were all very dozy. Except for the darkest of glasses that froze the light coming through them I could not have kept my eyes open in the glare. Looking through them was like swimming underwater through the light-shrieking air, they kept the water of the enchanted lake still about us.

Apropos of the butterflies Joan had said they reminded her of the soul of one of her friends, an elderly shy lady we both knew. She was gentle and fluttery, always apprehensive of making some mistake, and she habitually wore soft gauzy black and white dresses. I liked the comparison and weighed it with pleasure, it was so seldom Joan made any contribution to the delight of a scene, and as I was wondering why it should give me so much pleasure I realized that it made Joan human, kinder; to hear her praise any female acquaintance was a novelty. In our set, perhaps because of her features, her cropped hair and the way she smoked a cigarette, Joan had always been accepted as having a 'masculine' mind, something better than the 'feminine' brand, and her judgments of women had always been pretty fierce and now that seemed to me oddly feminine, though before I had thought it quite natural, a proof of superiority. Miaou. I was getting bitter. For the first time I was looking at her through dark spectacles, with another set of eyes.

Ruth, Sven and I were given the freedom of the city, that is we got bicycles and began to explore for ourselves. A Dutch lady, Marietje, whose acquaintance I had made, negotiated the loan of one for me from a Chinese cycle store. As she was a good customer the proprietor chose the best and newest mount in his shop for me and then, when he saw me wamble away, first this side and then that, he called loudly on his gods to protect both of us, and especially the bicycle. Marietje, just before dusk, took us to see the Chinese Tomb.

Many cycles swept out along the broad boulevards of Macassar. Youths in sarongs tighter than skirts tucked them up and rode thought-free, and on men's bicycles. Two gallants on wheels, their glossy black hair carefully waved in place, sauntered along.

SHALL I GO ON?

At the end of any journey they made girls would be waiting, but
at the moment they did not care about girls, they had each other,
and rode together, one with an arm outstretched touching his
friend's shoulder and the friend strumming on a large guitar,
scorning handlebars altogether. It was a cycling trick that roused
my admiration. I looked round to see how they managed the
corner and the glance was my undoing; I ran into and unseated
the man ahead of me, he had a crate of chickens on the back of
his cycle and after the accident there was a good deal of confusion
and chicken noise. The crate was upside down on the roadway
but not broken and neither presumably were the chickens, for
when I got up wondering how much I should have to pay, the
chicken-owner's friends were laughing at him and he apologized
for being in the way! I like Malays, they have the grand manner,
they can hold up a bicycle like an impressario taking a curtain
with a prima donna. Sven came back to extricate me from the
feathers and as we pedalled along he gave me a running lecture
on brakes.

An elderly and extremely respectable Chinese lady holding a
closed umbrella and wearing steel-rimmed spectacles was riding
pillion behind her husband and reproved me with a sharp look of
censure, for she had witnessed the accident from behind and knew
who was to blame, her looks said so. Her grey hair was scraped
tightly back, she sat side-saddle, and looked very Methodist and
incorrigibly correct, she would never have gone out without
gloves had gloves been the right thing in Macassar – which they
were not. She did not like the way my skirt fluttered and my front
wheel wobbled. I badly wanted to tell her that in my country
grandmothers did not ride pillion on a push bike, and that I
did not feel in the least reproved, but all I did was to give her a
very wide berth as we rode by. She might not have had the grand
manner.

Riding out like this in a group, all abreast, made me think of
upcountry Sundays at home, when everybody rode to church,
seven miles in, and tied the horses up to the fence and then after

the sermon cantered home together, ten or twelve of us in twos and threes talking. Marietje was plump and a good sort, she liked chocolate. She showed me how to manage my skirt and how to blow my nose without falling off. We felt we were part of the life of Macassar flowing by. The air had been hot and stifling, a barrier to be pushed through, now with dusk it was light and alluring, scented and warm, gay as coloured muslin. We made arrangements for other excursions; Marietje was to show me the High School and give me a letter to the Commandant of the fort, one of the most ancient in the East.

She dined with us that evening and we made some social calls with our host, but a constraint had fallen on us. When we were left alone we were silent, it was the most damaging evidence against us, we had to manufacture conversation between our-selves, when our host was about. Ruth felt guilty about it. 'He comes into the room and finds us dumb as mummies, it's dreadful,' said she. She too had just received a blow. In one of her heart-to-heart talks with Joan it had come out that Henery could not stand her, had only put up with her from the beginning by exercising the greatest control, had once indeed declared that he would not go on with her, and Joan had wept at that and he had promised to try and it had blown over. Joan weeping! That was news, but it had been long ago, long before I had come aboard and offered a better target. Ruth was miserable now. She hadn't thought it was as bad as all that, she had never guessed at the time that she was so repugnant. So there we were, on a voyage that might have looped like the arc of a rainbow, off the humdrum earth to the other side of the world, a most wretched set of people tied together by circumstance, our antagonisms jangling like fire alarms when we encountered, having to be careful with each other as if our tempers and dislikes were marked, 'Fragile with care; Polite side up.' It gave me an ironic satisfaction to think about it, Henery and Sven, Dona and Joan, Ruth and Henery. It was as involved as the plot of a Restoration melodrama, and as sense-less, we moved in a circle of antipathies, nothing could be simple. At times we attracted each other and then for incoherent reasons were repelled, as molecules that move with such complexity that it seems to be at random. Everything said had first to be sterilized, for speech had become like surgical instruments, that might cut if not handled properly and must first be freed from any germ of cross reference as we went through the social operation together.

For the first time I didn't want to go on. I wondered if I ought not to leave. Little had been said about the winds but we knew they were getting unreliable and Sven was champing a bit. Henery laid down a month as the outside limit of duration of the next, the longest open sea stage, about eleven hundred miles, from Macassar to Singapore.

A month, the equator to cross, the winds uncertain, provisions low and, for all of us, underneath our relationship this curious sub-stratum of unfriendliness, or conflcting self interest, or wounded vanity or a conglomerate of all three.

Something ought to be said.

Money was the difficulty in the re-provisioning. Ruth and I had money and uses for it. It had to see us a good distance yet. We had earned that money and we knew what earning meant. Joan had never had to earn money as we had. The world when I left the boat was an economic dragon that had to be throttled. Sven was in rather the same position. Boat funds just about did not exist by this time. We always thought we were on our last penny but Henery always seemed to have a halfpenny up his sleeve. It was a matter of pride to all of us that we managed without family help, though the two girls thought a husband wasn't quite family and ought to be invoked while fathers . . . fathers were sacrosanct.

I screwed up my courage to suggest to Henery a loan from me to boat funds, I did not feel friendly enough to make a gift – I was leaving my share of the boat – and I wanted it to be understood as a loan. But nothing came of it. I told myself, 'Very well, that settles it. You can stand starvation too. Joan thinks there is

355

a positive merit in being Spartan and hard. She thinks you place too much importance on food, and it's true, you do. But if you quit now and they have a hard time – and they are likely to – you will be irretrievably the soft one, who could stand the pleasant parts of the voyage but not the bitter parts, and you'll hate yourself afterwards. You'll have to see this through, though you know it is folly. You'll have to show Joan that you can be brave without talking bravery, though getting into a situation that requires bravery is just damn silly.'

Not an estimable motive to act from, to plunge into conscious unwisdom through fear of being snubbed again, to have one's emotions trample down one's intelligence . . . My letters from Macassar were long and perplexed, badly I wanted advice.

There was almost a softening in Joan at this time, she had flung the remark about the butterfly at me and I had the feeling that she was waiting for me to speak on the state of things between us. She said as she went through my room to her own, 'It's funny that what we think has to go through Ruth,' and indeed the whole system of closeted conferences, Ruth, Henery and Joan, Ruth and Joan, Ruth and Dona, had been ludicrous. There was a hesitancy in her voice, Joan the absolute hesitating. I said in the same voice, 'Queer, and not necessary,' not breathing, thinking the moment had come at last between us – and I waited, fiercely I waited pleadingly, but she expected me to speak and I would not, the episode with Henery had hardened me and I had Ruth's statement, she must begin. I must never be weak again in front of Joan, and the last two days had racked me a little, crying hot-eyed with Ruth in bed. She would not say any more and went on her way. The last opportunity was past.

CHAPTER XXX

PROA HARBOUR – MACASSAR

RUTH and I visited the High School and saw again the high piles of exercise books waiting to be corrected, the familiar sad botanical specimens drooping in a glass jar on a dusty cupboard, heard again the sound of conjugation learning, the verbs slipping like worn coins over a counter. We went and came away rejoicing. So discharged prisoners might go back and watch their former companions working with pick and shovel still breaking stones by the wayside. Our appetites for enjoying freedom were sharpened.

Sometimes on board, to sauce a sunset, we used to talk about school-teaching till the others got bored. We used to groan over the examination papers we had once to mark and the returns we had had to do, all the close, neatly-written red and black figures on reports for fuel used, bursars, infectious diseases, quarterly attend-ances, and what it felt like not to be sure of a date or how to spell a word when an inspector was in the room. Inspectors. With their long noses seeking faults. We used to sit them up on the gunwale and make Aunt Sallies of them and knock them over-board to drown. They were dead and behind us. There was one we had both hated, with a cold green eye and a mouth like a shark's and a way of sneaking in on one . . . Joan could never understand our exuberance when we drowned this gentleman or why we so often resuscitated him just to have the pleasure of drowning him again.

I went round the fort, Fort Rotterdam, originally Portuguese, the Dutch had taken it in 1617 and enlarged it. It was the biggest ancient fort in the East I was to see, five-cornered, enclosing about four acres of land, built on flat land near the harbour and at one time protected by a moat, now only discernible at the rear. It was still used for military and administrative offices and for recruiting purposes. It was especially interesting because it was so comprehensive, the complete trading post of the seventeenth century, mother of all the little forts scattered round the Spice Islands. It had held the entire life of the first adventuring traders, their factories and storehouses had been behind the broad ramparts along with the garrison and quarters for officers and men, doctor and parson. Core and inner citadel of the old fort was the church, simple and austere in the Dutch manner, beautifully proportioned, and below it cellars suitable for storing gunpowder, 'Trust in God and keep your powder dry', a good Protestant motto. On the harbour side its windows were narrow slits, angled against the ricocheting of bullets and provided with iron shutters. I was to see in the ruined Church of St. John in Malacca an old Portuguese church that the Dutch had used as a fort, loop-holed round what had once been the eastern window, and the tomb of St. Francis Xavier underfoot. In their turn the British had fired on it and destroyed it. Religion, Trade and Empire, they had been enemies and allies out here.

In one corner of the fort was a street of houses for the married troops. It was only a few feet wide, 'Little Amsterdam' Marietje called it, it reminded her of Dutch paintings of the period. On the landward side were the barred cells for the prisoners but now the hinges of the doors were rusty and the cumbersome keys were, like the fort, obsolete. From the ramparts all the shipping at anchor was visible, *Skaga* looked very small, the Commandant could not believe that we had come from Sydney in it. The Professor was with me as we went over this fort; once he had made me do a lot of dull and tiresome work going over the notebooks of one of these 'master factors', the first India Merchants, and now I could hardly shake him off, he wanted to photograph, measure and investigate everything. He got me into trouble with the Commandant wanting to see a dusty attic, up some ladders very prejudicial to starched linen and gold braid. 'It is dangerous up there,' said the official.

'Dangerous?'

'There are meece.' This in a grave voice.

'Meece?'

'Ja.'

'Meece?' and then the Professor understood, he was not in the least afraid of mice. 'Be a Brave Young Woman,' he whispered and pushed me up, but the attic revealed nothing, no dangerous meece, not even a view.

The fish markets of Macassar had been written about in so lyrical a way that I wanted to see them, so Sven and I cycled there at the best time, just after sun-up when the fishing boats had been unloaded and the markets were full of dealers and servants shopping, anxious to get the pick of the catch. To us the display was a poor one; giant prawn, the kind that are fried in flakes and go in a rice tafel, and a hammer-head shark with an eye on either end of the hammer, were the most unusual specimens. Everyone sold what he had been fortunate enough to catch, little and big fish haphazardly. We were disappointed, but it was no use pretending to imitate an appreciation we did not feel. Perhaps it was an off morning for fish, or perhaps we were blasé, we had seen and hooked and speared so many unusual ones ourselves that we did not bring fresh minds to the display. Moreover we had a sense of smell. An old stall-holder gave Sven a handful of live prawns and it was such a motion of friendliness that I made him carry them for a little way, though he was most loath and swung them by the feelers as if they had been contagious.

The vegetable market close by pleased us much more, it was gratifying to all the senses, a harvest festival of the land. The splendid purples of egg-fruit, the long New Guinea beans, vegetable blunderbusses; the cream and brown of eggs, the freshness of pineapples just picked, green-crusted breadfruit, split mangosteens, green mangoes, pale young maize, the red of chillis and tomatoes, cabbages like immense pearls. They were all smooth and clean and dewy, like attractive young women waiting to be embraced. I had to drag Sven away. It was breakfast time; he was hungry.

359

On Wednesday, Ruth, Sven and I met at the Chinese tomb. It was out of the town close to the sea, built on an artificial hill in the centre of a whispering grove of coco-nuts and with several ponds in front of it. They too had been constructed. The dead Chinese had been an aesthete as well as rich, he had had to have everything, sea, groves, a lake and a hill. There were Confucian courtesies everywhere. Small summerhouses were built out over the ponds and the civilities of the view included many kerosene tins, used as flower pots, each sporting frizzled curlicues of tin among its meagre greenery. By cunningly striping them with turquoise blue and white Chinese art had managed to transform these proletarian ornaments into something pleasing, but all the same, to me they grinned incongruously among the marble; they were the kind of thing one sees on the veranda of a ramshackle pub out back in Australia. The tomb was handsome, the grey granite carved in a wide border round its three sides.

Important Chinese tombs are three-sided open temples with porticos and flights of steps before them. Carved monkeys clambered along contorted boughs, Chinese madonnas adored their babies; gods and men, houses, flowers, insects and pagodas flourished here and each small face, whether of man, beast or mythological character was distinct and endued with personality, each was as important as the other, that was the delight of it, a bee was as imposing as a war lord. A painter was re-decorating the tomb, re-lacquering in brilliant enamels the faded figures. On his tray among fine brushes, books of gold leaf and pans of umber were tins of ripolin and stove blacking, a curious mixture of ancient and modern. He was an artist, where he had been busy the faded text of the sculpture blossomed into a fairy-tale, a jewelled brightness. His two assistants held pots and prepared the surface for the master's brush.

In the lily ponds before the tombs stood two miniature mountains encrusted with toy palaces, soldiers, horses, travellers, lizards, forests, heroes and dragons. A path wound from the base to the temple at the top, passing under frowning cliffs a few inches high, by ravines and into grottos; but it was a legend that we found no one to explain. The day was hot, we lay under the trees and lunched frugally off a few coco-nuts. Ruth wanted k'lapa muda to drink but a little Malay boy explained that the trees growing near the tomb did not have milk, he had to go to the very edge of the grove to get a good one. Did the Chinese resting below, enjoying the peace he had planted, know anything of that? Or was it just that the trees were old?

Ruth had an appointment made for her by Henery with a shipping man at half-past two. She didn't know exactly why she was to go, but there might be something hanging to it, he might be that vague thing, 'useful', and Henery had impressed on her the necessity of seeing him, for he had specially asked to meet the other ladies – that was us. She begged me to go with her but I wanted her to let it slide or to handle it herself, she got out of social duties whenever she could. Finally we all went, hot, dishevelled, with the feeling of pieces of grass and grass seeds sticking to us, the grass round the tomb had been deceptive, full of little burrs.

We dismounted in front of an enormous and handsome building, all marble and plate glass, propped our cycles up by the kerb and went in. Vast rooms, wide counters, and hundreds of clerks who looked up with interest as we were shown to the innermost sanctum, the holy of holies. A pleasant man near the forties, hair going grey at the sides, fattish, blue eyes that twinkled and English that got inverted. Iced ginger beer. Deference all around him. Cablegrams brought in on silver salvers. Busy. Time means money. Good heavens, what were we doing here? We who did not value time and who had no money? We had strayed into a business battleground like a couple of kittens, mangy kittens. I felt the grass burrs prickling me. Tell a few anecdotes quickly and get away or the very clerks would start laughing. The raft episode and the sea-boots. It hadn't seemed so funny at the time. He waved away secretaries and brought out our medals again, Brave Young Women, and he put the

providoring department at Ruth's disposal, the comparador
would send down whatever she needed. She explained carefully
that she did not want to spend more than two guilders fifty (6s.)
and began to make out a list as if we were in a market. This was
dreadful! It was calling on a boot factory employing thousands in
order to buy a shoe lace for a one-legged man. How happy to be
like Ruth, naive about things. I felt our call was unnecessary,
Henery had been in again and arranged that the Tuan Bazaar,
the Important Person, come aboard that evening to see the boat
and drive us out afterwards. Ruth felt a little double-crossed but
proud, she had made him useful!

It was Wednesday and our week-end with the President had
ended that day, we had been towed into the proa harbour, an
extraordinarily interesting place, a small deep inlet, the size of a
pond, ambuscaded by wharves and the backs of ship chandlers'
and agents' premises, rattan and copra tonkongs. Most of the
trade in the Celebes, far up all the little sungeis, is done by proa
transport and the produce of the islands brought back to Macassar
for export, we had seen these trading proas up the river near
Maros. Inside the proa harbour they were thicker than cars at a
great sports event, but without the orderliness of parking lines.
Their masts made a bare forest, they lay stem to stern, packed
tightly, two and three deep; the centre of the pond was nothing
but a narrow lane up which newcomers paddled and manœuvred
for a berth. The water was dark brown and polluted, what was
pumped out of Ajax was less disagreeable than what flowed in.
No wind could get in the proa harbour, the big warehouses shut
it out, so the heat and the smells were deplorable. All the day a
crowd stood on the wharf above and stared at everything we did.
This was the closest we ever got to life in the East; we rubbed
gunwales with it all day and at night too.

Yet it was fascinating. Some of the proas were shallow and light
with deckhouses of bamboo and a great carrying capacity, many
were much larger than we were, like galleons, double-decked aft,
most curious boats, said to have been built on the pattern of the

first Portuguese visitors to the East, a pattern that has faded out in Europe but remained in the Celebes. They were rigged with mainsail and mizen, inner and outer jib, forestaysail and topgallant sails rigged on the gaff of the mainsail and mizen. Sometimes they had a trysail between the mainsail and mizen.

All the sails were patched, it might have seemed with an eye to the colour effect, black, brown and white and some a deep rusty red. One sail was made in three broad stripes, black, red and yellow, like a flag. The hulls were gaily painted, blue or green, or pitched a shiny black. There were no utility greys or slates and no yachtsman's white either. We could not restrain our delight at these old ships or the supple men like monkeys who were their crews. All day there was life in the proa harbour, coolies carrying baskets, bundles and bags; quarrels; all the multifarious wharf activities. Just by us a sailmaker was making a new suit of sails. There was no sail plan pinned on a board, instead ropes were laid on the earth, pegged down and the cutting out done from a thick roll of canvas on the spot. The sailmaker's assistants sat crosslegged sewing and everyone who passed had a word of advice or approval to give the new sails.

Tuan Bazaar was early. In his eagerness to show the ship Henery brought him below before I had finished dressing. 'Just a moment, please.' Henery ought to have given a warning. This was home territory even if it were only the proa harbour. Tuan Bazaar scrambled awkwardly out of the hatch. In a few minutes the inspection was made, the celebrated timbers shown, the water tanks explained, the mast sounded. Had *Skaga* been a Chinese boat with eyes painted on either side of the nose, she would have winked one of them.

Tuan Bazaar was driving us himself. With a bow and a speech he singled me out to go in the front seat, an honour, but, like a military outpost, the position of greatest danger. Soon his elbow reconnoitred my arm and side. A flank movement. 'Do not sit so far away. Please let us enjoy the drive, it is very beautiful.' 'Will you have lunch with me to-morrow? Say yes. Say yes.

Why are you so cold? One o'clock to-morrow at the club. If you sit so far away you must be frightened, only Englishwomen are prim. You are Australian. You are brave.' Had he pinned the medals on us for this? 'Lunch to-morrow at the club. Ah yes.' All this *sotto voce* with side glances and keeping up an intelligent, general conversation in a loud voice with the back seat. Cleverly done. Flattering but embarrassing. What a situation! I might have enjoyed it had it not been for Ruth and Joan ready to bring up my flirtatious instincts in evidence against me. I wanted to be friendly but prim too. He was taking my party sightseeing to some ancient tombs of the Malay rajahs, Macassar seemed to be proud of its graves. His hand dropped to my knee, as it were by accident, confidentially. I said I liked driving fast, he took it away and we went at sixty over a soft country road between the shadows of tall bamboos.

He drove well. Presently he took us by a network of narrow roads and native tracks where we had to go slowly. The Malays had gathered up dry leaves and rubbish from under the bamboos and had lit many fires to drive away the mosquitoes. Some caribou lurched on the road, heavy, lumbering, stupid, their big eyes rolling with fright and their straight long horns tossing wildly. We honked and pulled up and they careered into a ditch beside the road. There was a moon but she was insignificant and only showed us the dim outlines of the rice fields as we passed. The villagers in a hamlet stared at us as we waited for a buffalo cart to back aside. We were we and they were they and both of us were incredibly remote and alien for all we stared so hard at each other, we in the bright car travelling so quickly, discontented even with speed and going without object, why else was the hand and elbow begging so insistently a caress from a stranger? They on their side part of the night and the jungle, still absorbed with elemental things, rice and night and a shelter. Soon they would wrap themselves in their sarongs and sleep on their grass mats in the gloom of their dark houses, the fires under the trees would die and when they fell into slumber deep and dark as the shadows of the trees the earth where those people lived would lose consciousness of man. Even in New Guinea, far up the Merauke river, I had not felt the primitive sensation of earth and of man who toiled by day and died nightly in sleep as I did here among these Malay agriculturists. The Kai-kai had been hunters, savages whose dogs would keep barking and who got restless like their animals and prowled round on sly love affairs or for magic purposes or for dancing in the moonlight, who were simple and cunning as children, not like these Malay tillers who stared and stared with a peasant hostility.

We passed a native house being built, the framework was completed and at the foot of every upright slow-burning torches had been lit, to drive away ghosts, said the Tuan Bazaar. When one built here one had to placate nature for all life was a long slow struggle against malevolent and insidious forces.

He offered to put his car and chauffeur at our disposal for the next morning, so that we might see the tombs in daylight. I tried to have the proposal turned down but the back seat was gibbeting and accepted. The back seat could be conveniently deaf and blind and the front seat was demanding payment. Lunch to-morrow? I said yes. It might be interesting and a lunch, a civilized lunch, was not to be sneered at when one was anchored in the proa harbour.

It was too hot to go to sleep when we got back. Sven, Ruth and I had been promising ourselves a ride in a gharrie, diminutive carriages drawn by fat ponies, ten hands high. They were rubber-tyred little buggies, with fringed white covers, many tassels and bobbets, much glittering brasswork, a loud gong to give traffic signals, bells wherever they would go on the harness, lamps big enough for a Lord Mayor's coach and long whips nodding like plumes, their handles so long that they could never have been used in those pantomime equipages. Indeed we found out that they were fixtures, not meant to be used save as the insignia of office, the longer the whip, the better the class of gharrie, the higher the charge per hour.

Ruth drew out of the gharrie expedition, she had become morbid over money, sixty cents an hour seemed a lot to her. She had more money than any of us but she felt tottering on the brink of bankruptcy. Our frayed cuffs had become a precipice to her. It was our last night in Macassar, the next day we were going to Pulo Moreaux to scrape the boat, we might never meet a gharrie again . . . Sven and I set off for our jaunt.

When we got in it the gharrie almost capsized. We sat opposite each other, our knees touching, the driver on his perch in front. The whole vehicle was so lightly poised that did we lean sideways it see-sawed and threatened to jerk the rolypoly cream pony off his feet. 'Galan Galan', directed Sven, 'Anywhere.'

We did some shopping, films and tooth paste, the Chinese shops were open though it was nearly ten. Then we clop-clopped our way along the boulevards, our gong clanging at every crossing like a fire engine and the bells on the harness tinkling. At first we were self-conscious at the clatter and imagined everyone was looking at us and then we got exhilarated, we had dared to steal this adventure together. It was more fun being poor and in a gharrie than dashing about in a high-powered car. Soon we had enough. We were tired. We walked down the long wharf by the harbour-master's office; on the proas were dim lights; circles of card players; the sounds of stealthy movements and of men asleep. The wharf was black with cockroaches, big ones four inches long. They were so thick it was hard not to step on them. They were industriously scuttling to and fro, ominous as the shadows of murderers, their wing cases making a hard scraping on the stones, a frenellation as of wire against wood. We hoped they would not board us, their presence raised a nausea in me, the cockroaches we had were puny, small in stature, not offensive compared with these juicy monsters.

We stood on the windward side of the wharf for a little, Sven's arm round my waist. Meeting for the first time had changed to leaving in a fortnight. We talked. Two nights in the proa harbour were sufficient, we were short of fresh water and we could not use salt for bucketing, it was too dirty. There was no freedom on deck. We must get Henery away the following afternoon. We only had to take water aboard, get a few pounds of rice and some sugar and visit the tombs, but Henery had said he *liked* the proa harbour, that was ominous, and he had mentioned having another chat to the harbour-master. A chat! We might resign ourselves. It was no use putting forward a suggestion, his mind always flashed to rebuttal before consideration. The best method was to wait and see which way the cat jumped, it might jump the way we wanted. The objective was Pulo Moreaux at sunset.

Next morning the Tuan Bazaar was as good as his word, baskets of fresh vegetables, limes, bananas and fruit arrived from the comparador. 'Fancy getting all that for two fifty,' said Ruth with awe, 'that is the advantage of shopping wholesale. It just shows what a profit those cheats in the markets get out of us.' Well . . . er . . . exactly so.

The chauffeur and the car appeared. We went out to the tombs of the rajahs, a collection of whitewashed brick buildings near a modern cemetery and close to a mosque with nothing in its design to recommend it. The roofs of the tombs swelled upwards like white turnips. Inside each mausoleum were eight or nine coffins, family groups, the rajah, the heir apparent, wives, infant princes and aunties all together. At both ends of each coffin stood lacy wooden monuments embellished in vermilion and green on the gold leaf and inscribed with the decorative Arabic script.

I dressed with care for lunch.

The Tuan Bazaar brought a friend to share the pahit and apologized that he would have to leave me, but he would call for me and drive me back afterwards. The Don Juan of the moonlight had disappeared and the very busy business man emerged. Boards of directors, freights, imports, time-tables were stamped on his hot forehead – a wife and circumspection too. I was relieved, the Lorelei was not a role I cared to play. In a long mirror I saw myself, the blue muslin was an attractive dress, a bit girlish but pretty and it hung well. 'You are so slim,' he was to say and that was grand hearing – even though I knew that comparisons were odious, when one recollected the Dutch ladies out East, who suffer from the excellence and the butteriness of Dutch cooking.

On his return business did not seem so urgent. He dropped the friend and told the syce to drive to – of all places the Chinese Tomb! For the fourth time I was going to the Chinese Tomb. The workmen were still busy enamelling. Tuan Bazaar was disappointed, he complained that they spoiled the beauty of the scene . . . he did not have his emotions well regulated, that business man. Business men were foreign to my experience and sea ladies to his. He became very complimentary and curious. Why did I choose to go on 'that so uncomfortable little boat' from Macassar to Singapore at this time of the year? He made predictions that were gloomy enough. (What would he have said had he known the state of our provisions and the engine?) In a generous and quixotic moment – he was a man of impulses, at least where women were concerned – he offered me a berth on one of his company's ships that was sailing in the early hours of the next morning. I was surprised but not tempted, I discovered that I had already made up my mind and that I did not want to change it. There might be a string in the mouth of this gift horse, but I did not think so, though to be sure I did not know the gentlemanly East. His naive unconcern for the rest of us was amusing, he had painted an ugly fate for all of us and he expected me to pack up and leave them to it! I knew then how closely, in spite of our disagreements, we were bound together. The appositeness of the arrival of this offer only strengthened my resolution to go on. It came as a sign and portent to proceed. Chance had offered me the opportunity of not going on in order to force me to make a real decision.

Seeing that I had quite made up my mind he kissed me, lusciously, workmen or no workmen, and as I kissed this unconscious instrument of fate I wanted to laugh and say, 'Te morituri salutant', but I did not say it. I was enough of a sailor to know that. We were very gay as we drove back, one is always gay when

368

one has made up one's mind. I learnt a new use for the topee, one holds hands, hard, under it, raises it to the lips, moves it about, and turns a bland Dutch face to the syce's back, as if every syce had not eyes in the back of his head as well as a rear-vision mirror! And because this Dutchman was so utterly without a sense of the ludicrous I liked him.

At the boat Sven, Ruth and Joan were waiting, Henery was in the harbour-master's office. Everything was in profound disorder, it was very hot. 'Well?' asked Sven, the others were curious but said nothing.

'Call me Bob, hold my hand, take a first-class berth to Singapore and write to me when you get there.'

'A free berth?' Ruth was staggered. How had I done it?

'I didn't go into details but I think so.'

Why hadn't I taken it? She could not understand it at all. Hadn't I even inquired about a stewardess's job after Singapore? The idea of becoming a stewardess for the rest of the trip to England had been in my thoughts, it seemed easy, very adventurous and a decided economy; I, too, was getting money-morbid, these things are catching.

Joan allowed a quick flicker of interest, I had a suspicion that my prestige was growing with her. She appreciated that precisely because one could call a shipping magnate by his first name debarred one from asking for a stewardess's job. But Ruth wanted everything set down on a blackboard in white chalk. 'Will you write to him?'

'No. Why should I? We'll never see each other again.'

The others had had a bad time. Ruth had muddled appointments with a dentist and the President, a car had been involved and she had used Sven as a messenger-boy, it had all been very complicated and unnecessary and he had been snubbed, yet she did not see that she had asked him to do anything unpleasant. They were not feeling happy. Then in the midday heat Henery, Joan and Ruth had set out for the Chinese Tomb because Joan had not seen it, she could not cycle, and Ruth and Henery wanted photographs of it. They had taken a gharrie and squeezed in after haggling over the price. Then Ruth forgot the direction, Henery had no word for tomb in his vocabulary and 'Orang mati' (dead man) only bewildered the driver, who got lost, Henery thought on purpose. They got out and had a final dispute over the price and only paid when the driver unharnessed his pony and a crowd collected and showed signs of following them to the tomb. Ruth was upset by the fuss. After that they had difficulty in getting a conveyance back and walked most of the way. Joan got a blistered heel – she was feeling done up. And Sven, who was minding the boat, had had to take water aboard alone. There had been no meals . . . I was the only one who had enjoyed the day.

Now after four Henery came along for tea and remarked casually, 'I think we'll be able to get across the harbour to-morrow at ten, the harbour-master's gone home and the clerk doesn't know about anything for me.' (Anything was the supplement just issued of the sailing directions for the coast of Java. We had the last year's directions and we were not going near the coast of Java.) 'In any case,' this settled everything, 'the wind will drop in an hour and we can't get across without a tow.' He went off again.

Another night in the proa harbour! No bath, no swim. Did Joan want another night in the proa harbour? No. Did Ruth want a swim? Yes. She and I set off, ostensibly to say good-bye to our first host, the President, but adroitly to circumvent Henery. I had the *succès d'estime* upon me. Dear Mr. President, with his blessed love of comfort. Two ladies had only to regret the heat and another night in the proa harbour and to express a wish to swim and in twenty minutes a fast launch was towing us across to Pulo Moreaux.

To swim and be clean, to wash every trace of proa brown harbour dust off the decks and be able to sit or lie on them. We swam and had supper. The great liner on which I had been offered a berth had come in, a floating grand hotel of a ship. She stayed a few hours, lit like a skyscraper above the mirroring placid water, and then went out. I had no regrets.

We had anchored close in to be able to scrape the hull. In the night *Skaga* fell suddenly right over to starboard, we had not propped her, and for six hours we existed with the boat at an absurd angle; things hanging from hooks stood out rigidly from the walls. It is odd to live askew from the perpendicular, it gave us a new slant on life, an insect view.

We stayed at Pulo Moreaux two days, scraping but not pitching the boat. Not a month before we had done that at Pulo Babi and barnacles had flourished on the pitch, they were larger than we had ever known them. Also during our ten days lying still at Macassar green weed, fine as hair, had grown over the hull.

To get the papers from the harbour-master Henery borrowed the mandoer's canoe, called a lippa-lippa here. Our koeli-koeli was not seaworthy enough for the voyage; it was quite an adventure for him in the heat. He came back at the end of the day, towed. The President again.

Ruth and Sven and I went into the matter of provisions. Ruth was really worried. So was Sven, the bully beef man. There were fewer dried peas and beans than Joan had thought, only half a biscuit tin of each. The rice that had been bought was of poor quality, 5 cents a catti, floury and with weevils already in it. So on our own initiative we decided to buy 20 more pounds of rice at 7 cents a catti, some coco-nuts, fish for bait and more kadjong idju for sprouting. Even then . . .

She and I got a lift across in a launch, some survey officers had come to bathe; we had become the complete opportunists.

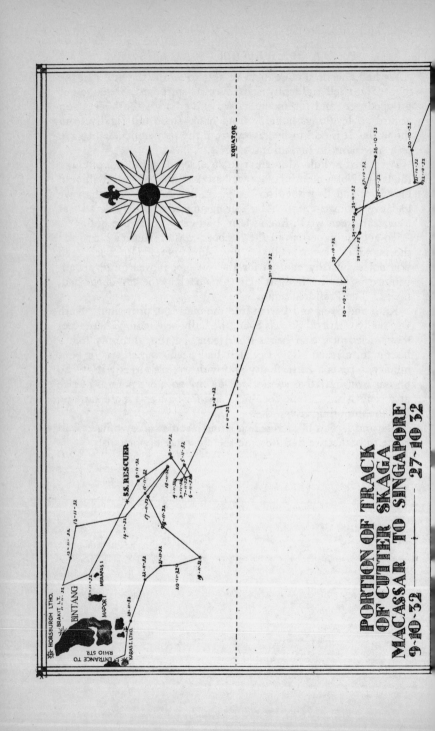

PORTION OF TRACK
OF CUTTER SKAGA
MACASSAR TO SINGAPORE
9-10-32 ——— · ——— 27-10-32

CHAPTER XXXI

THE LAST STAGE

WE left Pulo Moreaux on Sunday morning, October 9th, on a very light breeze. Some of the Yacht Club members astir early caught up with us and gave us a last handshake. Friendly people. We were hungry and ate lots of rice. The vegetables and fruit from the Tuan Bazaar were almost finished but we were careful not to use the limes extravagantly. It was a lazy, hot blue morning with the sense of a long trip ahead.

In the afternoon a good southerly sprang up and we sailed along nicely, the sky low, pregnant with wind, *Skaga* cantering easily through the green seas, pulling steadily on the tiller, putting the miles behind her. The wind kept on through the night and all the next day and the next night too. On the third day it continued but was not so strong. We were all quiet and busy reading. On the last night at Pulo Moreaux men from a big British cargo boat had come over to the islet to swim and had taken us back to dinner in their mess. They had been nine months out from England, trading between Africa, the Dutch East and the Philippines, two or three days in each port, not long enough to get to know anybody. Engineers, the doctor, the junior officers, were all very lonely. We had sung songs, 'Drink to me only', 'John Peel', 'Men of Harlech', 'Tit Willow', 'Ye Banks and Braes' – the sentimental ones were popular – Joan had played for them and Sven had sung as loudly as any. There had been a Welshman with a good tenor voice; a red-haired Scots youth, the doctor who liked modern poetry and a tall dark young electrician, 'You don't know what it means to us to have Englishwomen aboard'. We were Australians but they counted us as Englishwomen. When it was time for us to leave the smoking-room was crowded, and we had pockets crammed with addresses, 'Do call and see my people.' 'We'll be home after Christmas.' 'Maybe you'll need a pilot in the London fog.' Laughter and banter. They had piled books on us, rifling the library and their private hoards and now, in spite of the continual motion, we read and hardly stirred from our bunks except to cook or take watches.

On the fourth day we did over a hundred miles again by noon. We were getting along as if the wind were blowing to a timetable. Because we were travelling fast we caught a mackerel. Sven made a clear soup out of its backbone and head, a Swedish soup.

By noon on the fifth day ninety-eight more miles were behind us, we had only six hundred and twenty-eight left to do and the wind was still favourable. We hoisted the squaresail and we ate all we wanted to; it seemed that Henery had been right, we should do the trip in a fortnight or less and the worrying the rest of us had done over provisions and lack of wind had been over-emphatic. Singapore beckoned close ahead. Ruth startled us by announcing that she was leaving there; her previous intention had been to spend four months with Joan and Henery waiting for the change of monsoon and then to accompany them round the Cape of Good Hope to England. She had been brooding for days, but no one had known what was in her mind; the decision came as a shock. From the beginning it had been arranged that Sven was going only as far as Singapore but Joan had always been sure of Ruth going on. Now she looked worried but took the blow, as she took everything, silently. Ruth began to learn Russian (there was a grammar on board) and to sort out her clothes ready for departure.

The sixth day out was one of dry intense heat, the wind held but was not so good, we did eighty-two miles with five hundred and forty-six to go. We were sore with sitting long hours at the tiller and the heat and the diet had brought us out in spots. We had been living on dried peas; they made Ruth and Sven very ill and gave me indigestion. At night there was a golden moon with a big circle round it and the air was so warm that sitting at the tiller at midnight a single garment was enough.

Another day, my cook-day. Ruth and Sven were still ill from the peas. I made gruel for Ruth, we had found the remains of a tin of groats bought in the early days when no one had thought of famine. There was not enough flour for any more dampers, even had we had sufficient kerosene to cook them. I made a concoction of bully beef and barley for the rest of us and steamed some of the weevily wheat. The wind had died down but we got a short squall and a thunderstorm with enough water in it to wet our skins. At night it was brilliant moonlight with no wind at all so we lowered the sails and lay on the deckhouse. I fell heavily asleep, a sleep that was uncomfortable, exhausted and brought no sense of rest on waking. At midnight I helped the steersman hoist the mainsail, there was a light breeze; in the seventh twenty-four hours out we had done twenty-seven miles, and had got into latitude 2° 58′ south.

Ruth's unwellness hung about her, she could do little and was peevish, the gruel was the only food she cared for, but there was nothing definitely wrong. Joan also was not very well. She rested a lot. A rash of hard pimples had come out over her shoulders and arms; exposure and diet were to blame. We did not know it then but we women had been getting anaemic, the good food in Macassar had helped us but now we relapsed quickly. We had other symptoms. As well lethargy, a continual semi-sleepiness, was creeping on us. I tried to resist it, I wanted to work. I had a whim to feel water over me, to move freely in cool depths. We were frightened to swim because of sharks and sea snakes. I got Sven to hold my ankles and plunge me head first up and down overboard, it shook the laziness out of me. The two of them watched. Caprice had no place aboard the *Skaga*. Joan's unspoken verdict was: 'Quite mad', while Ruth suspected this was some subtle ruse to lure Sven to ruin. Luring Sven! At times her eyes could go gimlet hard and see nothing.

We were getting on edge again. The sea that usually soothed

out all our troubles was a panacea that had failed to act. The wind had gone and trifles could show which way our tempers blew. At a meal I asked for a lime, Henery selected a bad one and threw it at me; it spattered. It was more surprising because we were all as a rule so invariably polite. We could not have lived together so long, our emotions inflamed as they were, had we not been. Then Ruth thought he slighted her over the hypo-ing of some prints, and Sven got annoyed with Ruth. He was cook; it made his temper short; he would not sit contentedly on the slide in the galley, knees touching the chin, stirring occasionally and reading as the rest of us did, but stooped bent double over his cooking. The galley was only four feet high, the blood ran to his head . . . Ruth did not fancy his style of supper; a pea and onion soup with a trifle of salmon to follow, and she had been smelling it for a long time as she lay in her bunk; she craved more of the gruel that I had been making for her, but I was on watch; so taking advantage of a temporary absence from the galley she broke the etiquette of the kitchen by boiling water for a hot water bottle, making a pot of porridge and removing his cherished soup from the primus and letting it go out without a word of explanation. Joan and I both ate of her gruel, and liked it, it was a luxury, but Sven, when informed casually by Ruth that she thought his primus was out, did nothing but growl subterraneanly about plates smeared with 'whitewash' and explain loudly to Henery that they would have to wait till eight o'clock for their meal. The accessories after the fact of this crime sat silent, guiltily white-washed inside. Poor Sven. He had a habit of tutting with his tongue: 'tut, t . . . tut,' when any small thing went wrong. It sounded as if he were very very cross, and meant – nothing. He did it when the vessel rolled as he was taking a sight, or when he got out of his bunk and put his foot in a messy plate that someone had left on the galley floor or when the sun shone on the chrono-meter or when Henery would not tighten a brace to his liking. A lot of repressions came out in his tutting and every time he did it Henery smiled at Joan.

We were each of us ridiculous in our fashion: Sven's tutting, Ruth's Fletcherism, Henery's 'er-er'-ing and the way he came up on deck and sniffed at the weather, taking an observation through his nose, my ritual toilet before evening, calamine lotion, lip-stick, a change of shirt, though Ruth's eyes often asked: 'For whose benefit?' and I could not have explained to her that the portrait on the wall kept a level brown-eyed regard on my appearance because he knew how just lazy and untidy I could be. And Joan? She had taste in her small actions, to me they were cadenzas practised flawlessly; I could never criticize them and by irony in that company I could best of all appreciate them. Perhaps her careful abstinence from committing any folly or doing anything that was not hall-marked and guaranteed sterling was the only thing that made her at all insensible, foolish; or the way she let her spirit wince at the rest of us, for living so closely together exaggerated blemishes like staring too long in a shaving mirror.

We had another tropical storm but after it the wind quickly died and its only aftermath was in the clouds at sunset. There were four distinct layers. All round the horizon were grey and snow-piled battlements, huge heavy wool-packs, then a floating veil of thin black cloud with detached black wisps sailing fast and close to the earth. Behind them came an array of gold and white beauty-parlour clouds, burnished blondes neatly rounded, with no loose ends in their coiffures, huddled together like sheep with corrugated gilt fleeces, princesses in metal lamé, beneath their feet stretched long shining angel pavements, strata effects, roadways to a heavenly Ritz where harps played foxtrots. Infinitely far behind, high up and small, were little puffs of white cloud like the smoke from the firing of grape shot in old military prints, little trails of soft ethereal vapour. All the cloud family were on parade. Some rolled and twisted and skated across the sky and others were still and weighty with their own dignity, jowled uncles and bearded aunts of the party, close to the seats of honour in the north where the goatish imbecility of extreme old age was throned. All this movement in the sky and no wind at all on the sea. There was wind up there, going in the right direction too. Why could it not come down to us, blow us along?

It had stopped being a blue sea and off the coast of Borneo had turned muddy, not so thick and yellow with mud as in the shallow Torres Straits but a dulled and lifeless green whose only beauty was in moments of storm when a steely light came from behind dark clouds, caught sideways in the surface and turned it to a white-capped emerald green fury that soon passed. We were to have many of these fifteen-minute squalls, usually one a day, often two or three, but they did not help us, we moved violently for a short time, that was all; they were nothing but explosions of wind attracted from the upper air by low pressure below.

We did not make any headway for two days. The islands of Serutu, Little Buan and Carimata were still ten miles away. They were deep ultramarine blue, breast-shaped, their outlines always softened by a haze. Carimata was over three thousand feet high, rising in pinnacles on the lower slopes and bearing a perpetual wreath of white cloud round the high peak. Sven kept taking bearings of them to encourage us past them but our position hardly altered. In four hours we moved one and a half miles east and half a mile north – the course was NNW. 'Thank God we are going north,' said Sven, grateful for small mercies, but four hours later we were farther east and not so far north.

A watch from two to five that afternoon was intensely hot, the wind very light so that the reef points kept up their continual musketry fire, rattle, rattle, rat-a-plan plan, plan on the canvas and the boom lashed impotently to and fro on the length of the kicking strap like a savage dog ramping on his chain. It was so hot that I kept pouring sea water down my back though I was fully clothed in shirt and shorts. We had four hundred miles to go. The night came, black as pitch, a darkness so thick that it might be felt, no stars and a very small world. It was like being shut up in a round oven, a flat shelf of sea and a mottle-steel meat-cover dome of sky. On my watch I read poetry to myself with the hurricane lamp beside the tiller. The merry-go-round of watches turned faster at night. It seemed no time at all from stretching in thankfulness after a long hard sit than one was routed out of bed and began it all over again, the terrible rattle of the reef-points and the flap, flap, flapping of the sail like the beating of the tired wings of a big bird and at every flap a double bombardment of twitching ropes.

I lashed the tiller but had to sit by. I felt that a vessel might bear down on us out of the cloud oven in which we lay steaming, but none came. It was a dreamy watch. There was an uneasy feeling in the air, the masses of black cloud piled up ahead and they cast shadows on the less impenetrable blackness below. It was so dark that until I saw the shadows I would have said that no shadow could have been cast. I was steering for the light on Serutu but could not often see it. Vivid sheets of lightning flared across the horizon, the boat would not steer but went sideways and backwards. The binnacle smelt evilly and as usual its little door was off the hinge and skilfully tied on so that the crack was sufficiently wide to let in enough air to keep it alight but not enough to blow it out. This was a delicate adjustment. Often one had to open and close the little door when the light on the compass card showed signs of suffocation.

Suddenly the wind, before from the south-west, whipped round to the north-east. I called Sven, it was five minutes to three. He came up and undid the kicking strap, I let her gybe too quickly, the big block flung across like a thunderbolt, the sheet running through it grazed my cheek. I had ducked automatically, just in time.

The course was NW. by N. $\frac{1}{2}$ N. She got on it. I had just gone below when there was a sudden fury in the wind, the boat rose and fell under us as if we were galloping on horse-back, rain came down in a flopping shower. We put our heads cautiously out of the hatch, things carelessly left about were sliding over the table and floor. Sven was at the tiller, rain streaming down his rough-hewn face and pouring off the old felt hat as from a broken guttering on a roof. 'Eight knots,' said Henery.

'Two and a half on the course,' said Sven. The wind had moved to north, two and a half knots felt grand to us but that burst of wind only lasted fifteen minutes. It took most of next day for the swell to die down. Serutu was still there, there was hardly a trace of wind, the sails kept up their hullabaloo.

Had we had a net we could have caught fish. They were about eight inches long, not remarkable for any beauty of colour and rather inelegant, broad, vulgarly-shaped fish, nevertheless they looked very good to eat. Henery fired a shot-gun into a shoal of them, but without success. Our floating baits they scorned as they swarmed about the boat, chased by sharks below and hunted by dense clouds of sea birds above. The birds were busiest when the fish were harried by their marine enemies; then they leapt and splashed back into the water in a mad scurrying mass, plunging away from the sharks. The noise of their going was like the rush of a strong wind.

Some sucker fish, like one we had caught at Percy Islands, had been accompanying us for days, hooked on by the strong sucker on the tops of their heads or swimming behind ready to pick up any scraps; they ate everything but rice: like us they did not care for it. They swam about six feet below the surface and it seemed because of the foot-like oval sucker on top of their heads that they were swimming upside down. Sven, who thought that if we caught them our luck might improve, spent some time fishing for them with a lump of dough and got one. Henery got one as well. In the water they looked pale green and elusive but out of the water they were an unattractive slaty grey with a protruding and bullying lower jaw; they had a most unpleasant stench and a tough hide instead of scales; they were killed and thrown back and after their blood was washed away the deck still stank of them. Our luck did not change.

At night I developed films because exposed films spoil quickly in the tropics. The lowest temperature I could get was 82°F., so it was risky work and a great labour. It meant combating heat and annoyance, seizing a time when there was little movement and when the others were happy on deck. It meant manipulating by touch basins, water, trays of chemicals in complete darkness and wrestling with blankets and drawing-pins that had crooked legs. We had no red light, in any case we could not use any light for'ard. It was going again into the belly of the whale and the victory was only a disciplinary one for films have a deceptive appearance when viewed black and wet against lamplight. They looked good, one got excited, and morning brought disillusion-ment, revealing them dull and mediocre. Poems were like that too. At night when they were written they seemed crisp, sharp, exactly stated, unalterable, and in the morning they did not say enough, they were not perfect.

We dawdled on. At night a passenger ship passed us, its lights bright and Chinese pipes sounding from the afterdeck. Civiliza-tion and the machine age were going by ; we raised a coo-ee. There was no answer but we felt cheered. Perhaps the officer on watch had remarked of us: 'A strange Malay craft'.

We left the light of Serutu behind at last. Never was beacon passed so thankfully. On the eleventh day we had travelled thirty-two miles, bringing the average speed of the trip since Macassar to 1.33 knots. We were in lat. 1° 28′ south and long. 107° 59′ east, and had only three hundred and seventeen miles to go. Not so bad, we had not been out a fortnight yet; but the night was a black cloud-cap, a hanging judgment on optimism.

We lay on deck enjoying the coolness after the heat of the day. I had written 'Star Dust', 'Night Bucketing' and 'Feeling Superior' and was thinking about them. 'Star Dust' was im-portant, it had crystallized a lot of aspirations, it knew futility, but it was myself becoming aware of being alone. 'Feeling Superior', outcome of a momentary intolerance, the unconscious singing itself, a relief, a protest against all the silent emanation of her dislike; it had months of feeling behind it. Had it broken me free from my antagonism, set me above the old self that could be irritated and tormented, yearning after the moon, after something that might never have existed save in my imagination? As long as I let the survival of those feelings worry me I should be chained.

For the first time I knew that if I had been obsessed and embittered by the withdrawal of her friendliness she, in her turn, had been held in heavier chains by her own antipathy. My tortured feelings had been evoked by her, were reflected from her, how blind and strong then must hers have been? They had held not only me but her also in bondage. In her life on board I was the other figure at the perihelion of her orbit, forcing her round. She had had to obey the compulsion of her own hate. I had not been free, but neither was she. That accounted for the violence of her aloofness, her nurturing of Henery, for the many false judgments. Now as her physical and mental vigour slackened I was the first to be released, to break the compulsion. I was escaping, not by leaving, that would have been no solution, but by setting things down. Having written what I felt I no longer felt it any more. I was out of the constraint of her emotions. The long battle was almost over. I was laying down my arms, I had been beaten, I no longer wanted her regard. In that fruit of defeat I had won, I had conquered myself. Everything seemed easy, simple – but I must keep on working. I must write and not think. I found an old MS., the first chapters of a child's story that I had brought on board to finish if there should be time. Now there was plenty of time.

We woke late to a rainy morning and the tiller lashed. There was no wind. We spent a long time in agreeable infantile remembrances of wet days when we were youngsters. Our pasts had become inextricably bound together, I had never met Sven's aunt but by now I knew her quite well, the kind of blouses she wore, the way she did her hair, I knew her so well that I thought she would find a sister-in-law of mine companionable; letters were written, they met, liked each other and became friends. The pleasure we continually took in these recollections of childhood belonged to a dangerous psychic state, analogous to the lethargy that was robbing our limbs of any desire to move. Ruth, who was least well, was full of them and her conversation abounded in childish words, 'bities', 'pricnick', 'the pottie', 'nippers' for 'pliers'. The same simple transpositions kept on amusing her, 'barnacle' for 'binnacle', 'weasel' for 'weevil', 'misty Mick' for 'mystic'. Secretly she too longed to be comforted, to be out of this unsatisfactory present into a contented past, a very far past. There were so many things I found childish about her, her ignorance of the ordinary could be appealing on shore, the fantasy of a real existence, but at sea it became an appalling lack of general information. Then the way she seized on an idea and held it up like a new flag in the advancement of knowledge though in reality it might be a very tattered old banner, and she could always explain the obvious with zest. But I also enjoyed these childish recollections; I liked the way we talked about home as I liked the silvery greyness of this new day and the metallic lustre and colourlessness of the sea.

Two more days, more rain, and on the second day a wind that lasted two or three hours and got us twelve miles east and one mile south of our previous noon position – and we were trying to go north! Also it brought up the misery of a heavy swell. We lowered the mainsail and endured the heat. Sven ground peas and beans and made a soup and as we drank it under the brazen sky the perspiration rolled off our bodies as if it would wash all impurities away.

Another windless day, the fourteenth out. A strong current was running against us though the chart said it should be with us. It was difficult to take a shot of the sun because of the clouds. In spite of hatfuls of wind we were again six miles south. Sven wondered if something were wrong with the tangent screw of his sextant, or the chronometer, or my reading of the chronometer. The boat would not steer. In my one to three early morning watch, the sheet close hauled, the wind at W. by N., the course NW. by N. I could not keep her within two points even with the tiller hard over, and the breeze seemed fair enough. Food and water problems assailed me. I was quite miserable. When Sven came up he reassured me, he had spent the afternoon checking up his sextant, proving that it had not been tampered with, that its readings were correct.

The fifteenth day. Satisfactory morning and noon sights had put us in 1° 025′ S. and 107° 34′ E. Though in two days we had done thirty-four miles we still had three hundred to do, our general drift at this time was to the west.

Dinner that day was one of Henery's misconceptions, a grey and pink slop with splotches of purple. I had been steering above him for a couple of hours so I felt critical. The pink was from our last tin of camp pie, by itself I liked it well, the grey from a paste of flour, onion and uncured mace (relic of Banda), and the purple from some defunct ubi kaiou that he had found in the paint locker (Amboina those). There were grey peas in it too – no meal could escape peas – they were still very hard and as they dried they wore white overcoats from the bi-carbonate of soda designed to soften them. I ate a helping taking care to pick out the ubi kaiou against which I had always had a prejudice. As I ate I wondered mildly how Henery, who described himself on his passport as an artist, could tolerate such a colour scheme. To my surprise, for my thought had been secret, he began to talk about Cezanne and complementary composition. He was proud of the look of his dinner, he enjoyed it and Joan said – dear me how tastes could differ – that it was 'quite pretty'. They had second helpings. An hour later it was still a work of art, a culinary fugue, with the wind instruments dominant.

The new policy of setting every malice down meant that if I felt critical of Henery I had to put it in a pome, so I made a cook-day doggerel that grew until I saw the whole trip as a gastro-nomic pilgrimage, an adventuring through oysters and paw-paw, cassowary and goat, to rice and barley.

Having put down everyone in caricature I had to show it, as woman is a praise-loving animal. Sven always praised everything, which sometimes felt like no praise at all, but he really enjoyed this, it bristled with rhymes, and attracted by the jingle Joan asked to see it and used some of it in an article; writing it kept me busy and contented for two days.

Sometimes, after a particularly beautiful sunset, when calm

golden pools of light spilled upwards into a clear sky, or the west
had burnt bushfire red and been consumed by the darkness, when
the night had come, beaded with stars so large and bright that they
cast individual tracks on the ink that was the sea, I would try to
repeat poetry that I had once known better than my prayers and
I could not. The poems ran together and got muddled. It was
so long since anyone had read poetry to me. 'Out of the golden
remote wild west where the sea without shore is' . . . but I could
go no further. 'I am shut out of mine own heart', and I wanted to
go on, 'because my love is far from me'. I did not *know* if that were
right or not. 'This is no time to talk of right and wrong' . . . I
could not even say, 'On such a night as this . . .' properly.
Snatches, tags and fragments mocked me. At different times I
hankered for special poetry and I had but one book on board. I
wanted the fire dark assonances of Humbert Wolfe, I wanted his
fancy, I wanted Yeats. Edward Thomas, quiet and of the country.
Robert Frost with his little wild ponies. There was no Shakespeare
on board, I wanted to get back the multitudinous seas incarnadine
roll to my tongue. Sven had a Bible, I borrowed it to read about
Absolom.

I was missing so much. The realization of all I was missing
swept over me at times; the dark eyes, that could glow like garnets
with enthusiasm, the delicate, tender touch, the smoothness of his
back, the grace of his clever small hands. I began to dream again
these warm and languorous tropic nights when the wind blew
freshly over one's cheek; deceptively it blew, it was not strong
enough to fill the sails, it was just gentle enough to simulate a
breeze, to make one think about poetry reading, it was ready to
puff into silken, not canvas sails, into satin sails, satin sheets. Would
he think now of me, were he there, that I had lost all happiness?

Red lightning flickered above a bank of clouds in the west,
black fingerprints of cloud stretched up the sky to snatch at the
stars, probably another sumatra, a wind squall, coming.

I had a cycle of hot watches. There was no awning of any kind.
I sewed two of the lap-laps over mother's green umbrella, their

peaked edges hung down and made a pavilion breaking the glare. As well I wore a big hat and dark glasses, life at the tiller would have been insupportable without. Ruth made a mask for her face, with holes to see through and elastic round the back of the head. All of us, except Sven, thought it no shame to use the umbrella. It was one indignity we could not bring him to. He would not shelter under a 'round-sail.' Sven preferred to fry. He and Henery were burnt to a rich chocolate, almost black. I wore long sleeves; I could not bear the sun; the heat withered our flesh, we shrank as we sat. The water in the tanks, stored well below the waterline, was a warm fluid that did not appease our thirst.

Sea snakes came about us. They were thin and supple as whip-lashes, about three feet long, their backs striped, their bellies white. They swam on the surface sinuously and when frightened they nose-dived straight down. Ruth put her hand over the side of the boat and disturbed a big one, over five feet long, lying in the shadow. We believed them to be most venomous. Another we caught swimming, its head arched above the water, in its mouth a small fish tightly gripped that it was suffocating in the air, though Henery lashed at it with a cord it refused to let go.

We could not catch any fish. We tried and tried again. As we drifted the lines we towed astern draggled to starboard and then stretched ahead of us. Two empty tins and a bottle that we threw overboard floated too, keeping us company for hours. We sand-wiched a slab of bully beef between pieces of white and red rag and a couple of big fish, beauties, four feet long, with high intel-lectual foreheads and emerald spots on their sides, played round us for a long time, sniffing occasionally at the bait and ironically catching with ease their own meal of smaller fish before our very eyes.

On the seventeenth day an inventory of stores showed rice, a few beans and kadjongs and eleven small tins of beef or salmon left. There was a tin of olives in brine, a handful or two of prunes, some sugar and less than a quarter of a pound of tea. No limes, no coffee, no milk, a few soup powders and some poor spice.

Water was getting low but we were not short. We had rationed it to a quart each a day for washing purposes. To economize I tried cooking rice and beans in salt instead of salted water, but it was no economy, we were all so thirsty afterwards.

The children's story was growing, I was doing a chapter a day, but we were wearing thin emotionally being rubbed too often together. I did not know how thin till a little thing brought up a flare of emotion.

Henery had not spoken to me all day, the common counter of conversation had not been passed among us more than six times, when I found a bird in the bows, about the size of a starling but a pretty little fellow, with blue-black wings and head, apricot under the bill, a white breast and a line of white spots down to the tail. It seemed sick. We gave it water and cooked rice but it did not touch them. At night, when the others had done sentimentalizing, I put my hand over it and felt great tenderness towards it. It pecked once with its beak in the palm of my hand and that pleased me. It pleased me out of all proportion. When I opened my hand it flew across to the squaresail yard resting on the deck. I regretted that I had caused it the effort and said, half apologetically to Ruth who was watching me as she washed up on deck: 'It's all right, it hasn't gone, it's on the other side of the boat'.

She said in her dogmatic, contentious voice: 'Did you do that on purpose?' very hard. I was violently angry. Did she imagine that I would willingly hurt the poor thing? Did she think I was so hard-hearted? That hers was the only tender heart on board? I looked at her too angry to speak. 'Don't look at me so balefully,' she said.

Henery at the tiller said to Ruth, 'If looks could kill, you'd be dead now.' Some quality in the situation had given it a peculiar relish for him. A storm like a cold wind blew through my soul. I hated him.

I said to Ruth: 'Do you imagine I wanted to hurt the bird?' and went below for her explanations were not an apology but a self-righteous attack. I found myself trembling with anger, pure anger, I who was always too amused to feel anger. I wanted to hit Henery right on the nose, he had shut one eye and looked down it. It took an effort to control myself.

Sven, who knew a little of what I felt, said quietly: 'They are not the only people in the world'. Nothing more. As the obvious sanity of this sank in it brought me back to my balance. It was hard to feel any world beyond the boat. He had a knack of putting his finger on the right spot. I had the greater knowledge, but he had the greater wisdom.

The twentieth day. Thunderstorms moved about us but did not touch us, they passed like frowns over the sky. Two broke at the same time, one to port, another to starboard, and yet we were not caught in either. They joined and made, ahead of us, a dark archway across the sky from which rain poured, a bow of rain.

Ruth, who had never enjoyed it, took to smoking. She began with the remains of a packet of cigarettes bought in Thursday Island, hopelessly mildewed and disinterred in the search for provisions. She went on to a packet of bird's eye that Sven had and then contemplated carving a pipe and smoking the trade stuff but did not get so far. Joan and Henery had plenty of their favourite strong wet Virginia but cigarette papers were few, they substituted tissue paper that had been wrapped round my evening dress, it smelt of moth-balls and perfume. Matches were scarce and the petrol lighter would not work.

Late in the afternoon we got a sharp thunderstorm. The clouds hung low and menacing for a long time, then the wind came and raised waves, crested lips full of scorn pouting at the sky. A sheet of falling water raced over the sea, the wall of its advance raised a white froth as it struck the surface; it beat down in a savage fury, in a spleen of spray, again and again, lashing with puny knotted flails at the wrinkled grey hide of the prehistoric, plethoric sea, the rhinoceros-humped behemoth sea, as if it wanted to punish the cunning unassailable heart of the monster below, whose breathing still surged through beaten-down but unflattened lips, ranks of cruel full lips, licking to swallow, swelling under chastisement, unobliterated by the hail of blows.

We raced up the for'ard hatch into the rain. It stung like icy splinters. We caught what we could in the flap of the canvas deck cover and the spare mainsail, scooping it up in buckets and passing it below until the water tanks were full. Our first rain-catching. The water had no taste, no insinuation of anything beside itself, it was fresh and good.

The tiller was stiff, a phosphorescent wave broke like a wide smile across the bows, the wake was a wagging tail behind us, showers of spray mingled with the rain. The slap of the water against the sides and all the gurgling talking noises that a boat makes as she moves were invigorating, familiar. We had missed them, nothing better than a ripple had touched us for a week. The storm lasted several hours, after it came a whole day during which the swell died down. If a puff of wind blew we were not sanguine enough to expect it to last.

The bird had died. In death its attitude was still appealing, its head on one side, wings spread ready to flutter into flight.

The noon sight had put us two miles west of where we had been five days before.

Another night; misted, water and sky merging, black with grey, currents of water vapour swirling upwards, curls of smoke from a gigantic pipe. There was almost enough wind to fill the sails, at times she actually held to her course. We must not risk losing any feeble advantage, so we could not put the sails down but they were almost useless, fretful and jangling.

I had the 3.0 a.m. to 5.30 a.m. watch, the tiller was lashed. It seemed an eternity. What was eternity? It was a greyness, a circle of rain-swept sea, a cold drizzle of water, a perpetual pattering of reef-points on the sail like the concussion of minutes within the hour. There was no wind, no progression of events. Space was abolished, there was only greyness, myself in a small effulgence of light, the hand that wrote not I; time could not move, could not leave footprints where there was nothing to receive them, that was the essence of timelessness, this grey circuit of being was for ever, it was eternity. We did not move.

BECALMED

I

Glassy clear the air, of brittle bright glass the sky,
the sea is a sheet of flat blue blotting-paper.
We are all as still as the specimens in a museum,
for the boat is a butterfly,
a lop-winged white butterfly
that the mast pins immovable
to a blotting-paper ocean
in this glass case of Time.

II

Why should the sails worry?
Why should they agitate themselves and fret
that the wind comes not near them?
Should they not say: 'Let us rest,
let us have leisure and hang motionless,
waiting for the lifting breath of the wind.'

But no, they are tormented by inactivity,
they are restless dreams of unfulfilled desire,
they lash about in a purposeless frenzy,
worn thin by the unremitting flagellation
of the reef points.

III

The reef points and their shadows
dance a savage hula-hula
in the black moonlight.
Oh the misery of perpetual motion
standing still.
What devils have to be exorcized from us
that we suffer this torment,
this nerve-racking rain of canvas blows?

Is the Moon a satanic emissary
and the reef points her agents?

Let us foil them,
haul down,
make fast,
stabilize
the lunatic mainsail.

IV

On the mirror-smooth water
floats a sleeping swan at sunset;
it makes no track
tidelessly drifting, drifting back.
Swan feathers litter the sky,
swansdown,
fluffy white tails, Persian cloud kittens.

Here is a catspaw of wind
disturbing the water.
Let it strike the bent bowed neck of the swan,
kill the somnambulant bird and break its reflection.

But nothing happens,
only a cat and mouse play of light and air,
the swan drifts backwards, always, ever back,
meaningless its mirror-written meandering track.

CHAPTER XXXII

DRIFTING

WE measured the kerosene. There was a little over a gallon, and food for perhaps eight days. The kerosene, used carefully, would last as long; we needed it for cooking and for the lamps. We found six small candles. We had turned out every locker, every cranny of the boat in our search for edibles that might have been put away and forgotten. Joan discovered a tin and a half of cocoa and a bottle of lime juice, I a dozen dried plums and a bottle of vanilla essence. There was plenty of room for storing things now, the food lockers were empty, they boasted only containers.

An oil tanker, going from Bali Papan to Singapore, passed at dawn, a long way from us. Henery fired five shots and let off two of our red distress signal flares, they burned a sickly pink in the coming light. The tanker did not notice them or us, she went on. In the ensuing days Ruth and Joan made two signal flags, N.C. the international appeal for help at sea.

The sea had not changed; it remained mirror smooth. Banks of white clouds were like mountains of snow on the horizon, their reflections combed wool below them. Everything was incredibly still; the clarity of the air, the shine and the reflection of shining, from sea to sky and from sky to sea found no word in my vocabulary to fit it; glitter, glimmer, sheen, luminous, radiance, incandescent, white-hot, were not true, they suggested a movement of light within itself and there was none of that, there was rather a transparency of light and air bound in a permanent state of being stiffly brilliant, starched with heat. The shadow of the ship smouldered blue in the glassiness. Little striped fish that had been with us for a long time darted about, doubtless they imagined we were a convenient rock for the barnacles were thick again and quite large. A crab that belonged to us Sven said he recognized

from Pulo Moreaux and swore that since it had been with us it
had grown bigger. He cut a barnacle off and tried some surface
fishing with it for bait. No luck. Ruth suggested a barnacle
stew. We had all been dreaming of food, Henery dreamt of meat,
veal cutlets, Joan of lettuce and mashed potato with butter on it,
Ruth dreamt she saw me eating apricots under a tree in a garden.
I had a long circumstantial shopping dream that ended in oranges
and Sven said he dreamed of hot cross buns with currants in them
and sugar on the top; he had a bearish taste for buns, filling things,
he so often felt empty.

The noon position put us another five miles south.

In the afternoon a dark cloud came about a mile from the starboard beam and from it hung a long gossamer thread waving
about like a thick black clotted cobweb. It dangled to and fro as
if grappling for something. Out of the sea rose a shorter dark
whorl of water to meet it. A waterspout. The two whorls did not
join. There was evidently a series of local low-pressure areas
around us for a long sheet of black cloud reached out of the
southern sky and plainly touched the sea. It slowly approached,
travelling on the surface of the water. The incipient waterspout
was travelling faster than the cloud and away from us. The upper
part of it lifted a little. As the waterspout moved in front of the
black sheet of cloud its lower half was visible as a white cylinder
of vapour while the upper half moved on without it, still black.
Farther away to port, where we had not been watching, a second
waterspout had completed itself and hung, a thin black ribbon,
from sky to sea. We marvelled but were not apprehensive. They
seemed a spectacle not a danger. To go up in a waterspout would
be an interesting finish, something to break the monotony of
being becalmed.

Soon a storm pounced down on us, exciting, exhilarating and
harmless. It brought wind from the wrong quarter. We flopped on
our weary way. The first becalming out from Macassar was over.

It was October 31st, the sky was clouded but the light harsh, the
glare from the sea cruel and the humidity oppressive. We were

living on one meal a day of rice, trimmed with shreds of beef and minute choppings of onion. We had a precious little paper bag a quarter full of little brown eastern ones, the size of garlic. Twice a day, morning and evening we had a hot drink, cocoa in the morning and waterish soup in the evening. There might be a little rice in the mornings too, we poured vanilla water or cocoa over it. We had rationed rice to six, five and then four small cups per day between us. If this wind, light as it was, held, we would be in Singapore in six days. We could manage till then.

We had got to 24' south and were impatient to cross the equator. It seemed a high boundary fence barbed with heat, an invisible mountain range, a magnetic barrier blocking our way north.

The clouds after a red sunset made me think we were in for a bad storm. There was still a light wind but the air was stretched beneath it as if it were tightly held in place and ready to snap. A cloud spread low on the horizon astern, a bar sinister across the calm, it grew to the semblance of three pointing fingers, 'Hail to thee, Thane of Cawdor', then it changed to three black shrouded old women. Fates, the more malevolent because they rose, approached and spread their cloaks across the sky by sorcery, contrary to the direction of the wind. Thunder growled, we had had lightning before, but distant lightning unaccompanied by thunder. Just behind me, so that my hand on the tiller brushed it, was the iron hawse on which the block ran. Electrocution. I summoned Sven. He came from the cabin where they had just lighted half a candle, the ration for the evening. He looked at the sky, not recognizing the sinister old women there, unimpressed by the luridity of everything. 'Won't be much,' he said, and went back to finish his book before the candle guttered out. I counted the moments to my relief and called Joan promptly at eight, I was anxious to lose the responsibility for the storm. She sat down and under her habitual composure seemed nervous. I did not blame her. A few minutes later I saw Henery sitting beside her, he had read her emotions more accurately than Sven had mine. The sympathy of marriage. Presently, because of the uncanny look of things, we lowered the mainsail. A squall came, but nothing much, the usual five minute bluster that once had seemed so terrifying, but that we had learnt to take as a weather cocktail each evening.

The wind held. We were 4' south and had the satisfying sense of at last getting somewhere, even if slowly. Our course was WNW. It would take us nineteen miles before we crossed the equator. There was a drizzle of rain that might have fallen anywhere in the world, from Hobart to London. It was cold; I wore my flannel waistcoat, so much for the torrid zone of the school geography. I had planned a private ceremony for crossing the equator, a mock heroic farewell to adventuring; I was going to drop overboard my old clothes, those ragamuffinly garments that had seen so much queer service; civilization should not have the chance to be ashamed of those veterans. 'Take that, old world, put it round your middle and keep warm.' 'Rock in an easy-chair, old sea, here are some slippers.' 'This was once a bathing-suit, you might like to stage a drowning with it on some beach resort.' If we were once over the equator hope could raise a flutter of wings in the heart and whisper: 'With luck six days to Singapore. Six days to Singapore.'

Two floating islands passed us, masses of logs and soil with a palm tree or two standing up rakishly askew, at a distance they made the floating island seem like a junk. 'Boat on the port bow', Henery had reported on first seeing it. These destitute orphans of the land are often washed down from the rivers of Borneo, a menace to shipping till they break up. A coco-nut and a beam of timber passed us, going south.

The wind almost died away. We had a distressing night. The course was west by north. The current kept her jammed against the wind, doing nothing. We needed the jib in these light airs to bring her head round but the jib-boom had gone at Dobo. In Ruth's watch the boom went over and she sailed south for an hour, she would not wear round. Ruth was full of clamour about it, the men left it for a while, and then changed to the mainsail and got us on the course again with a two-knot breeze that later died away. We were two days more trying to put our patient old forefoot across the equator. There was an inane futility about trying to get across it. The boat was a spot of dust, a dusty atom with five puny parasites on the waistband of the world, the jolly rubicund world, twinkling in a seul-pas on his invisible dance floor, the plane of the ecliptic, while the sun, His Father the Sun, Le Roi Soleil of the universe, beamed with approval, charmed with the lustiness, the obedience, the sunny nature of this offspring cast off in space. But we, infinitesimal, a dust spot on the bellyband of the world, only wished the earth baby had wind, wind on the stomach, and would hiccup us northward, a paltry hundred miles to Singapore.

In a little vomit of wind we got a shark on the spinner, a young shark about four feet six long. Should we eat him? The iodine value of fresh fish. The testimony of Hartog, Dampier, Cook, La Perouse, all in favour. Hadn't we heard that hotels in summer served it up as schnapper? Of course one only saw it in fillets then, not as a very ugly customer expiring on deck with a face like a certain inspector. Cannabalism even of enemies . . . was not justified. But this was such an adolescent scavenger, too young to have eaten human flesh. Try it.

So Henery cleaned him, cut off his fins and hung them in the bows, shark-fin soup ahead, and fried a great deal of him. It tasted like – like ling, even, if one used imagination and avoided dark patches, like a chicken caught on the wing in Lent. Ruth and Joan could not stomach theirs, it needed a lot of historical training, or knowledge of Swedish stockfish, or raging hunger to *enjoy* shark. Henery boiled some for the next day and made a shark soup; from bow to stern the air was impregnated with shark for two days. It hung about, till the fins disappeared, 'gale at sea', reported Joan.

Had it been a bigger shark we might have nailed a fin to the mast, sailors did that Sven said to bring good luck, but such a small fin would be no use, it had to be a good-sized one. Ticking the mast was no use either, we had tried that, soberly; one might as well try everything, even superstition and prayer. I spent part of a night-watch making up the long-winded, flowery extempore kind of prayer Sunday school superintendents had regaled me with in youth, but I got interested in my own words and that was no good. I thought if I could try praying simply it might help. I got Sven to help me one night, we knelt together – I had not kneeled so since the day of my marriage – but it was no use, prayer was out-moded or we had lost the technique.

We were having a small dessert spoon of lime-juice a day. 'Imitation cordial' the label said, 'In accordance with provisions of the Pure Foods Act . . .' That was a nasty trick the lime-juice had played on us. We made something that looked like tea, an infusion of cloves with a drop or two of the vanilla extract. It was almost palatable. We had made two tablespoons of tea last us a fortnight, never pouring out the leaves, but collecting them and putting them back and adding each day one or two new ones or a skerrick of tea dust.

We got very hungry on the night watches. Formerly there had been prunes or a piece of coco-nut to gnaw, even at one time, it seemed a long long way behind, we had taken up biscuits when we went on watch and made ourselves early morning cups of tea. The 5.30 a.m. to 8.0 a.m. watch was the hungriest. We rattled and rumbled, the last meal was always soup at six p.m. Sven and Ruth and Henery took to chewing candlegrease, they saved every scrap and kept it carefully. They had to fight the cockroaches for parked remains. The cockroaches were having a lean time. We saw more of the survivors, the warriors, they looked pale and wan and had no respect for place any longer. Formerly they had kept to their station in life but now they drowned themselves in the beakers as we were drinking and tried to eat the kapok in the pillows as we slept. A pure white grandfather of a blattidae, who had spent all his life in the bilges and was blind, put in an appearance. There was a regular traffic route for them at night up the back of the steering cockpit across the deck to the hatch. They liked toe nails and cold cream. It added a hunting zest to mid-night watches. Someone, probably Sven, caught one four inches long with antennae double that, a migrant from Macassar, and left the corpse prominently displayed. We admired the trophy.

It took a great effort to do anything, our limbs were heavy and we were lassitudinous; yet I could not sleep. I had not done my exercises for weeks. Sven said he felt like a 'gorilla, all the strength gone to his arms and tottery in the legs'. Henery said he felt 'dead weak'. My back ached. Ruth looked worse.

From noon on the 1st till noon on the 2nd November we did fourteen miles and crossed the equator; we were now 2′ north. Our average speed for the whole trip from Macassar had dropped to 0.58 knots. Sven still troubled to work it out and put it up on his little chit near the barometer each day, but the average daily speed gave us a heartache, often it did not exist or was in the wrong direction, a minus quantity. The settlement of Rio, one hundred and thirty miles from Singapore, was forty miles distant. We had enough petrol and oil aboard to take us forty to sixty miles in these calm seas. Would the engine go? We ought to try it. The engine sat at the bottom of our thoughts like a troll in his pool. Would Henery try to make it go? He was the only one who knew anything about it, he had bought it, it was his baby. Had the battery been seen to in Macassar?

We got a head wind that tempered the heat though we made little progress. The engine remained under cover.

Next day we caught a fish, as we pulled in the line our hopes were high. 'A mackerel, let it be a mackerel please God.' That was a real prayer, the kind of prayer I used to make when I kept goal in hockey. 'Let me get this one, God.' The fish did not fight, it came sulkily. We got it on deck. Another blasted shark! The disappointment. We killed it and put it overboard.

November 4th and 5th. The sea a brilliant green, flat and hot, a salty meadow without end. More waterspouts, the closest one one and a half miles astern. It was complete, the long thin dark funnel from the clouds meeting the uprising eddies from the sea like a black glass tube plunged into a cauldron of inky steam and trying to suck it up. The tube moved faster than the cauldron, contact from sky to sea was broken, a lump of sea hung, suspended in the air by a rope from the clouds and then the rope broke, the lump of sea tumbled down, we saw it fall, the black pendant still hung raggedly above and moved away out of sight. Another began to form ahead and went dangling. The air was breathless with suspense while these aborted catastrophes were trying to happen.

Next day we found brown dust on the top of the water, had it been spoken out of the whirlwind like an echo to remind us of land? It looked like dust but Ruth thought it might be the spawn of some sea creatures. We strained some up in muslin, it was too fine for our microscope to help us. 'Full of vitamin,' Ruth declared. 'Everything young and growing is. We ought to be able to eat it'. It only tasted salty.

Noon. Again. Fourteen miles east of where we ought to be. The currents were stronger than we thought, pulling us off the steamer track, eastward. Only one hundred and thirty-three miles from Singapore, it was hard to imagine it, only thirteen hours in a very ordinary steamer. No tooth paste left; only a sliver of soap, Joan's, to wash with; no soap for washing clothes; no face cream; no more lime-juice. The imitation vanilla done. Not even any spice or nutmeg left to make rice less ricey.

Drifting once more. Another day. Two miles south and seven east. Exactly a month from setting out. In the last five days we had done forty-five miles and despite continuous steering only five in the last twenty-four hours.

Ruth was a very bad colour and she kept mentioning beri-beri. The symptoms were lassitude, aches and pains, swelling in the limbs. She had them all; but such things as beri-beri didn't happen to people like us, only coolies . . . Easy symptoms to be hysterically imitated.

Sven and Henery pored over charts. So did we but the matter was in their hands. What would be the best plan? To give up the course, sail straight west and make for the Linga Islands? Till a wind blew we could not go anywhere.

We ate rice mixed with wheat, in the centre of each grain a

weevil bent double embryo fashion. 'Husks are good for you,' said Ruth. We thought so, too; we were the prodigals who had not reached home.

Kerosene for four more days, it had lasted better than we had hoped. After it was done we could burn odd pieces of timber and the grating that Sven and I had found at West Molle. We should have fuel longer than food. We were fair about food, the cook measured the rice out by spoonful, so many all round. We looked away politely when it came to our turns, as if we did not care in the least. The tiny olives were counted around and the one or two onions. We were disappointed if we did not get a good food dream at night. I had a three course meal one sleep. Soup, minestone, a large plate of vegetables and beef, cabbage and roast potatoes, a kind of school dinner, and while I was still engaged on the meat a large blackberry tart appeared on the table. I had not got up to that when Joan waked me talking to Ruth in a loud voice. I had a sense of deprivation all day, my thoughts kept going back to the tart I had not had the chance to taste. All our feeling had run down like tired clocks. Animosity takes energy. It was too hot to hate.

I think my worst moment was on a hot two to five afternoon watch when perspiration glued me to the deck, when the light fell across the tired retina with the flicking of canes and the mainsail flapped drearily. My predecessors had had the tiller lashed but Sven had said to me when I took over that it wasn't good enough, we ought to get a bit more out of every puff. So I hung on and steered. There was a swell, the tiller kicked. She wouldn't hold any course, I got two different fingers jammed against the combing, each of them twice. My shoulder got wrenched with the jarring and twisted, my left wrist was almost useless, it was never nearly as good as the right. A puff. Sven swung the boom over and held it out to catch the wind but a swell caught us at that moment, the sail was out of control and flung back, I was just rising again from ducking out of the way of the gybe and got a blow on the side of my head that made me sit quiet for a long time.

I nursed my fingers and steered with a foot on the tiller. Let Sven criticize that.

Then I tried to fish, one must do something beside sit and sit and listen to the gear grumbling and the world falling to pieces about one. It was twenty fathoms and a sandy bottom, I might get a fish; but after rigging extra sinkers and changing the style of hook all I got was an unholy tangle in the first five minutes. I spent forty minutes more trying to get the tangle out. No luck at that either. Anyone who ventured from the strip of shadow for'ard to the inferno aft to get a drink I begged for one too. At twenty past four I thought Sven might put the mainsail down, if the mainsail were down the agony would end. There was no wind. 'Oh yes there was wind'. I knew he wanted to shave before he came on watch at five, he did not get much time to himself. At five to five he came up and looked round. 'Better put the sail down and make things tidy,' he said nonchalantly. Oh the brute! the brute!

At five o'clock I thrust the tiller at him, 'Take it,' I snapped. The staysail was drawing a little. The end of three hours' purgatory had come. I crawled on to my bunk, narrow and hot and uncomfortable, sleeping on it was lying down for a night's rest on a railway seat. Lower the cubby curtain. I felt shattered, made of thin living china that had cracked all over and that had to renew itself, cement itself together out of a too-meagre vitality. I cried for self-pity in a nobody-loves-me rage. The fatigue of being still alive. A phrase came from a letter. 'What shall he do then? Go berserk, says he, smashing the typewriter.' Typewriters and spectacles and a cool study opening on a veranda by the sea.

Soon I could get up and wash off the traces of tears. I hoped no one had seen me. Ruth's soup, weak but hot with some rice and sprouted kadjong in it for divertisement encouraged me still further. I was able to admire the sunset.

A quiet night with the sail down. In our respective watches we rested, awake ready for an emergency, but wrapped in a blanket by the tiller. A grey and misty night. An infinitude of stars above. No wind.

DRIFTING

Often we watch sea-snakes,
banded brown and yellow,
basking on the surface.
But the pythons of the sea,
the grim dragons of the underworld,
are the currents.
We are in the jaws of one now;
slowly it is sucking us Eastward,
outward into the China Sea,
where no land is nor any boat.
Ultimately it will swallow
us and the boat and our words.

Oh for some Perseus of a wind,
dark-helmeted,
to conquer the dragon!

THE AGE OF REASON

Each evening we gaze at the sunset
and remark the ribbons of cloud,
the wool-packs and fish-scales and streamers of cloud,
scanty combed hair on the forehead of night.
We speculate on the chance of wind,
desperately we hope for wind,
and beseech our private superstitions to send wind,
a great wind from the south-east.
But we live in the age of Reason,
its cynical reply, a head wind,
light as far-away laughter.

NIGHT THOUGHTS

I want to shout out. Over the grey water,
Beyond the ring of the moon in the grey sky,
Through the heavy curtains of grey air,
I want to shout 'Help!'
Only the one word, 'Help!'
'Beloved, oh, help.'

We are shut out as Lazarus,
On the threshold of plenty,
Send help, a little help,
By your charity – aid.

But the age of miracles is over,
I do not believe in prayer.
Nobody could hear me
over the grey water, beyond the ring of the moon,
home in Australia,
nobody could hear.

My unuttered cry chokes me,
the air is a grey pall,
as well to cry on the name of the wind.

CHAPTER XXXIII

RESCUED: AND AGAIN DRIFTING

THINGS were getting serious but not so serious, at any moment a blithe wind might come that would carry us to Singapore. Our friend the south-easter. Had we left Macassar a day or two earlier he might have blown us all the way; but it was no use thinking of that now. There must be some fairy-tale way of cajoling him, of coaxing this wind horse to work for us and not jingle off in a sulk. Take some straw from one of our mattresses and tie it to the mast? In twenty-four hours two miles to the north.

The heavy burden of silent collective suggestion made Henery decide to get out the engine. He and Joan worked on it in the hot sun, cleaning the plugs. Ruth and I wiped off the vaseline and oil with which it had been smeared to protect it from rust. Suspicious places in the wiring were bound again with insulating tape. The two men got it on the out-board bracket and thrust at the disk to start it. Again and again. It turned but nothing happened. Again, once more. Give her another try. Another look at the wiring. More turning. Sven thrust. Nothing. Then Henery tried again and took, as Ruth said he would, the skin off his knuckles. The engine kicked twice, two small explosions. That was all, two abortive coughs. The skeleton went back into its cupboard, rattling its parts as it went. It would have been a surprise had they made it go.

In the bright moonlight that night Ruth and I fished, still in twenty fathoms. She caught a fish, a pathetically small fish not six inches long. We talked about fasting. She said we could go for a month on water alone, I did not think a month, not after our prolonged low diet. She said, 'People die of fright not starvation,' and I did not contradict her but surreptitiously I felt my fattier parts and determined I could fast longer than Ruth. I knew nothing of fasting but I remembered Marco Polo's Tibetan sheep, they lived on their tails in the winter.

I felt pessimistic, relieved that I had made a will, it was a tidy habit, like folding one's pyjamas after sleeping. I wanted to know why Sven was so quietly confident, 'In for a deuce of a time but it will be all right,' he said. He twisted this way and that, till at last I pinned him down, his mother's prayers would not be wasted, 'She prays every night for me.' . . . All the mothers praying, 'For those in peril on the sea . . .' as good an anchor cable as anything else in mid-ocean.

The next morning's 8 a.m. longitude put us eight miles farther east. East, the eternal drift.

We had no playing cards on board. Ruth amused herself cutting out a pack from stiff paper, substituting bread, cups of tea, butter and chops for the Ace, King, Queen and Jack; and pears, apples, plums and bananas for the four suits. She drew every card, it gave her great pleasure and took two days. When it was finished I played a hand of rummy with her, no one else wanted to or would play. One had to remember that it was the chop of pears one was after or the tea of plums or the butter of bananas, it was unsatisfactory, as a system or a meal. We had only the one game. Our rules were different.

Ten and a half miles farther east. 'She has a will of her own,' said Sven, and 'Sailing under sealed orders', was his joke. He began to tell of ships with hoodoos. The course then was west, or west by south, to bring us into the range of the nearest light. As she would not do it Sven wanted to go north-west by west on a course where we would come to a steamer track, be able to get help and not waste what wind there was fighting the current. This course would take us east and north of the Rhio Archipelago. There was a long argument between the two men, it boiled down to, 'You are not being consistent, and Where we made a mistake.'

On the other hand, 'You have to go as best you can and change your plans according to conditions, you can't do it like a book when you've got no engine. The wind takes you, you have to make what use you can of it.' The wind takes you . . . The wind. If only there were wind.

The decision was come to, to try north-west by west for three days and then if it failed to make for some islands, the Tambelans, in the China Sea where steamers sometimes called, and where presumably there was a settlement. We had no sailing directions for them, only the authority of the chart.

The decision had an enlivening effect, Henery and Sven put a light chain on ropes and worked it up and down under the keel to free us from weed and barnacles. We leaned over the gunwale and scraped at the barnacles on the sides as far as we could, hundreds of them tumbled off into deep water like swollen grains of rice. Should a wind come we were ready to move.

On Wednesday, November 9th, my cook-day, I woke up with a dream vividly before me. It was of a big gum tree, dead. On a rotting piece jutting out above my head sat an extremely large black crow. I was standing near the tree. The bird unnerved me. I tried to frighten it off. Kim was suddenly by my side. We each had short lengths of rather frayed poor rope which we held in both hands and twirled and beat up and down like whips to frighten the bird. It did not pounce as we expected but sat on, we continued to beat, and I woke up. Was the tree that of life, withering, and the bird death, of which I was afraid? Single-handed I could do nothing but he was there to help, as I had been hoping. Would my letters from Macassar make him worry *soon*? An aeroplane would locate us in a few hours.

Those miracles only happen in dreams but we had a miracle on board. Our last tray of kadjong idju had sprouted better than any before. We grew it in darkness on a moistened pad of sacking. It was ready when the tips began to turn green. We had left this trayful till inch-long green leaves had sprouted and white rootlets had pushed up the seeds, smaller than peas and held them two inches above the tray, like the heads of birds, the leaves just open-ing, the beaks ready to chirp. The brown seed-covers had split and folded back like wings leaving the kadjong chicken-yellow and marked with purple. The trayful of sprouted seeds was a flock of ibis on the point of flying away. To prisoners anywhere growth is a miracle. We ate the kadjong reluctantly and talked of gardens. I wrote a garden poem.

The washing up after breakfast was simple, five plates, a pail of clean salt water and six grains of rice in the bottom of it. 'Leave one for Mr. Manners,' said grandmother. The last olives were gone. We had saved the stones and crunched them up with our teeth. The candle-grease was done. The ink was almost dried up. It had been watered down till it was so weak it fainted away on the paper. The Child story was at chapter 17. It kept me busy.

Wind. How our ideas of wind had changed. Wind. We would dignify any whispering of air by that name now, our souls were sensitive to wind, after this a breeze would never be altogether commonplace. Wind. What was wind? The theories were all very well where wind was, but where it was not? Here was a circle of sea where winds did not exist. It there was any it went vertical, a balloon could fill with it and go straight up. Winds and currents were inscrutable things, for all Henery's expensively printed four-colour wind charts.

I took pains with the barley for lunch. The last barley and the last kadjong and the last onion, but there was still about three pounds of rice and kerosene for two days. The cheap little cabin light stood disconsolate, it had not been filled for many nights. We had bought it in Macassar, it had a Swiss mountain scene painted on its tin reflector, a chalet, green meadows, snow and red cows. Similar lamps attract the tropical moths in many Malay homes under the coco-nut trees. Snow, green meadows, red cows.

Against the sides of the boat came the slap of water, the ex-hilaration communicated itself through the boat to us. We were moving. The gradual growing of a whisper of air into something that could be called a breeze. Sven called from the tiller, 'It's getting steadier; I think it will last.' How eager he sounded. It lasted and something else happened. A steamer. We saw a steamer at about three o'clock the same afternoon.

Henery ran up the signal flags, the ensign inverted and the tiny yellow and blue code flags, 'Ship in distress'. They fluttered in the wind. Would they be seen? The steamer was going to pass fairly close, they were outwards bound from Singapore. Henery fired six rounds of shot. We were to leeward of them. We dropped the mainsail and raised it again. The steamer changed course, slowed, went astern, it was stopping. Was it stopping? It was stopping! Bless the fraternity of the sea. The second officer on watch had noted the inverted ensign.

When we were close enough the skipper, dark and Dutch, called from the bridge in English, 'What you want, boys?' A stentorian call.

'Food. Out of provisions,' we replied, our voices thin in the wind. 'Come alongside.' He was jovial.

We manœuvred, they manœuvred, ropes were flung, fell short, flung again, not made fast quickly; flung, caught and the hawser dragged aboard, twisted round the mast and over the sampson post, once, twice. How she strained. Now we were dancing up and down beside the big cargo boat. Henery scrambled on board.

We were steaming along with them, half speed to them but galloping to us. Waves broke on both sides of our deck, we were almost swamped. The entire crew of the Dutch boat turned out to see us. Women! The 'boys' were women. Australians in a little boat and out of provisions. Someone came in a dressing-gown. Another held out a carafe of water, if we were starving we must be dying of thirst as well. The water was so cold beads of moisture formed on the glass even in the hot sun. Cold water. We got it aboard. We had not known there could be anything so cold in the world.

Henery took photographs. News value. Sven got a time check for the chronometer and their position. Malay boys carried tins and sacks down and tossed and slung them aboard. We said good-bye to our deliverers and cast off. The transaction had taken over an hour. Good-bye. We will never forget you – The Rescuer. We sat down to sort out the spoils.

100 Egyptian cigarettes – for the ladies (a gift from the first officer, he of the dressing-gown)
cigarette papers
matches
shag tobacco
10 six-lb. tins of beef (Australian beef at that)
20 lbs. of sugar
50 lbs. of flour
100 lbs. of rice
12 or more large tins of sardines in tomato sauce
3 gallons of kerosene
1 lb. of butter resting like a lovely flower on a big block of ice

And the wind, the wind still held! Our second becalming was over. We were going up outside the Rhio Archipelago on the way to Singapore. Sven was pleased with his position, six miles west of where he had put us. Not bad for our chronometer.

We had a whisky-soda to celebrate the rescue. That was a widely separated trinity of gifts, the General's whisky, soda water from the picnic at Pulo Moreaux, and ice from the Rescuer in mid-ocean. A toast to the Rescuer! But two sips upset me. I felt sick. Black Wednesday rushed out of its hole. I gave mine away.

It was always my fortune to be cook on auspicious occasions, and this needed something very special, we had weak soup, prepared before with the last kadjongs in it and now laced with good strong bully beef, hot scones buttered, I say it again, buttered scones, and sardines and caramel dumplings, very sweet. By eight o'clock we had finished and were as full as puppies and could dare to take laxatives. The tin reflector of the little lamp shone brightly, the red cows mooed in their green meadow, if they had snow on their mountains we had ice in our galley, ice carefully swaddled in sacking, I ran a small piece all over my skin, letting the coldness nibble me. We had done twenty-seven miles in the twenty-four hours.

The next day was our thirty-second out. It gave us grey skies, a spectacular squall, a threatening waterspout and the first sight of land since Serutu, Pulo Mapor, an interesting rocky little island clothed in woods; we hoped to walk on it to stretch our cramped legs and to get some fresh provisions. Actually the rescue had left us no better off for vitamins. The Rescuer had not been able to spare us any fruit or vegetables and in the excitement tea had been forgotten and salt, baking powder and soap, but we had plenty of rice, flour and beef, we should not starve. The sense of filled larders made us all jolly and confident.

There was a big swell coming from the Straits of Malacca after the wind of yesterday and the squall raised another, smaller one, across and on top of it. One pitched us forwards, the other swung us sideways. Gradually the smaller, steeper swell overcame and supplanted the big slow one. We were doing five knots, we should not stand in for Pulo Mapor because it would be difficult on a lee shore; we should use the wind and forge ahead. Singapore to-morrow? The day after to-morrow?

More days. Calms and patches of wind. Sixty-eight miles to Singapore. What were sixty-eight miles? Not a day's journey. We had often done more than that in a day, with a wind, granted just a little wind.

There was a brilliant moon again, stars and the moon, clouds and the wind. At night at the tiller I had cheerful imaginings, murmured hummings that were almost songs, letters, Singapore, buttered toast, Holy Ghost, winning post, taking care, beloved Brer, curly hair; conceits that expanded out of a vacuum of mind and made the flat-footed hours walk faster; Space and Time were scissors that snipped out of eternity the now of existence; *Skaga* a bloodhound smelling out the course, keeping her nose to it, heading up to Singapore. Singapore. Singapore.

Then more drifting, crawling west by day and drifting east by night, eleven miles east, the next night four miles south and ten east. Two days gone. Ruth a dreadful colour, a sickly dark yellow, Joan green under her tan, splotches on all of us, the whites of our eyes yellow, the lids inflamed with the light. Ruth flared up at Sven and Sven afterwards asked her if she wanted him to 'blow into the sails for her' and then was sorry and sat out her dreary watch for her, but she was too angry to be grateful. Joan and I easy with each other, saying nothing. The boat enlarged for me in tranquillity as the head seems to swell in extreme fatigue so that miles of space measured mentally separated a place in the sun from one in the shade, the galley from the cockpit, the cabin floor from the double bunk, me from everybody else. Henery was being mysterious about an article and plans, there were long colloquies in the cabin, my name floated up. Rice and rice and rice. No limit on the rice.

Rice and sugar, and then a big plate of rice with a solitary sardine laid out in state on top of it. Sardine soup. Henery had gone mad on rationing, he said that one tin of sardines ought to do the lot of us a whole day and he had his and Joan's cook-day running in which to carry out the experiment. Sven and I mutinied, but we had learnt discretion, we made a secret sabotage without a pang of conscience. We saved some rice from our evening portion, abstracted a tin of sardines and had a collation at one o'clock in the morning when we changed watches. We juggled guiltily with plates, forks and the tin-opener, terrified of making the least sound that would bring up a gorgon from below. We ate conspiratorily, in silence, with a stolen enjoyment. I can see Sven now as he sat on the rail and scraped the last vestige of fish and the last drop of oil from the tin. The moonlight was a strong drink, pale yellow, intoxicating, heavily fortified with spirit. We dipped the plates in the sea, making no sound. I went below like a cat, a little drunk with the moonlight, and licking at invisible fishy whiskers, should Ruth stir, she must surely smell the thievery on me.

Now the very next morning Henery, wearing his Admiral's hat, counted the tins of sardines and mentioned the score several times.

Had he heard us? Did he miss one? We did not confess. It was our single gesture of protest.

We were almost in sight of the light on the north-east of the Rhio Archipelago, almost ready for the last alteration of course, the home stretch up the Straits of Singapore. Sven was on tiptoe, tense with trying to get round before the wind fell, for it showed signs of dropping altogether.

And then came our third becalming, four days and four nights of it, drifting. We drifted seventy-seven miles south and east. Eight days after our rescue we were back on the same circle of sea, on the same piece of the map that had gone crazy with noon positions and courses laid down, a patchwork quilt of a chart; we were back, a mile or two to the east and a little to the south.

Yet we had been at the tiller most of the time. Oh the futility of those long hot valueless watches, the exasperation of continual disappointment.

What should we do when the wind did come? Try again the outside course or the inner one through the Rhio Strait? Sven was for the inner one. Admittedly we should have to go south in order to get west but once inside the shallow strait we could anchor when there was no wind and we wouldn't go drifting to the devil.

Whatever the argument they always took opposite sides. The other side was, 'If we had done this . . . You said before . . . If the wind comes here we'll be better off . . .' A blaming chain of argument and the 'I at least am keeping my temper' tone.

'It mightn't come.' Hand in pocket, fidgeting.

'The chart says . . .' Those expensive four-coloured 'gibbets'.

'We almost did it before, got nearly to the light and it died out . . . We can't risk it. It's not fair to the girls. Look at Ruth.' Passionate cry, 'Look at Ruth.'

Polite controversy for two days, then at midnight, all of us sleeping on deck, the explosion, a 'bloody' flung sky-high, rousing the women from sleep. Oh well, let them wrangle it out, the chart, common sense and the pilot book against 'ifs' and the World

Weather Bureau. And we had been managing so well; considering everything we had all been paragons. Perhaps if there had been a little more swearing and the high command not quite so ladylike we might have got on better.

Something fundamental had been touched in this dispute. 'You can't get away with that, calling me a —— so no one else can hear it and wearing a kid glove on your tongue afterwards.' It went on a long time, it had begun near fighting point and fell into argument. Quite softly, argument.

The women said nothing to each other, nor to them, though we were all awake. We were involved in the argument, two of us had made up our minds what we wanted done but the quarrel was not ours, we were out of it. Had Joan, too, the tiredness, the pit of the stomach feeling that did not care what happened?

Next day it had been settled, we were to go on the inside course. There had been an apology.

An oil tanker bound for Singapore passed us, five hours off for them, for us how many more days? Ruth wanted to ask for a tow. Would they charge salvage? 'Yes, and jerk the mast out of us into the bargain.' Even so Henery held up a rope but they did not take the hint. They could not have guessed what had been happening to us.

Yet another day, November 17th. A head wind but strong enough to steer WNW., which was good. Using the glasses and what we thought was imagination Sven discerned the two high peaks of Linga Islands, fifty miles away. He had been watching them for the hour after dawn before he broke the news and he broke it cheerfully, importantly, as if we had accomplished something, as if the real world beckoned us out of the maze, but even through the glasses they looked like clouds to me and I could not stretch my sympathies sufficiently to make them come important, it did not seem that we should ever come to land. I was too listless to work. The story languished, poems languished, articles – we had to do them to make money – not touched. Joan had begun hers, The Rescue, in capitals.

I day-dreamed of how we should greet each other when I returned. 'Hullo,' publicly and a look that meant we should keep our kiss till later. The garden freshly trimmed in my honour but a bare look about it, as if it had not been loved. Nelly glad to see me and the afternoon tea ready and that special cake, foam cake wasn't it? – she had learnt to make before I had gone away. Phantasies. Suppose he met me in Sydney and we had to spend the night in an hotel? Food again. A cup of tea. Hot weak China tea just as I liked it.

Then I did two articles in a rush, the words tumbled out and they had a news slant in them though they told nothing. I felt pleased with them but I wanted tea, tea, tea. Surely a person who had been working so hard deserved a cup of tea?

Another day, the two men on particularly good terms, being helpful and extra polite to each other. The rest of us were in good humours. Joan and I confessed that we had a tendency to scowl at the rice on our plates, as if it could help itself being there. The mountains, four thousand feet high and very plain at sunset were still fifty miles off. A dead calm. I skipped a little but my legs were flabby, the muscles uncontrolled. In the evening dolphins came about us.

The day after, November 20th, began with a storm. We travelled twenty-one miles south and west in the twenty-four hours and the net gain for the day was five miles. Which was really an achievement. This was the possibility that had excited Sven when he had seen the Linga Islands at dawn two days before. He had felt his feet on dry land then while I was still at sea and lost in dreams.

Five miles gained and I had done two articles and started another. I was out of notepaper, Ruth gave me a few sheets of hers but the boat had none to spare so I used the only kind of which we had plenty, one thing on board that we had not had to ration.

We were gradually winning our way towards Rhio Strait, fighting every inch of the way in a boat that was as obstinate as a full-rigged ship and that in these light airs with the jib missing would only sail six points off the wind. Another eleven miles south and west, the total distance made good five miles, in two days ten miles nearer.

The sun beat down; in the galley during the hottest watches we had a constant companion, a book written for adolescents, printed by a religious organization, circulated among the islands by a missionary society and then appropriated from a church library by a disreputable scallawag at Thursday Island. He had carried a bald parrot on his shoulder wherever he went, it boasted one or two feathers and an extensive and scandalous vocabulary, and he had presented us with a big fish and this book. It was a good book, we all enjoyed it. It was called *Heroes of the Arctic*.

I had another important dream, quite an ordinary school anxiety dream it appeared to be at first sight. I had at last finished the textbooks on psychology that I had put on board to be read and as an exercise in dream analysis I began to interpret it. It held symbolism, condensation, word association, a double, nay a triple composite person in it. It grew absorbing, better than a detective story; I spent every spare minute of two or three days on it and it grew to twenty-three tightly written pages. All the intimate secrets, the sordid worries of the past eight years of my life were being turned inside out like the lining of a dirty pocket. The dream interpretation made my diaries that I had thought were absolutely frank a mere whitewashed sepulchre of the soul. Ruth got interested, she started one, too, it had a lot about her illness in it, the Rescuer's provisions were not agreeing with us. What Joan thought about or wrote I never knew, she still lived in a pearl-lined oyster shell, but did not cast any pearls.

Sven disapproved of writing so much about one dream, he suspected, what was true, that I had made an exploration into places where he could never come, he knew that the end of the matter, the long toying with the idea of infidelity was over too. I had come to a decision that I thought had been decided before, but it had only been a gesture, now it was fixed.

Leaving home had flung me into the moon, into a wild, dead

and cold world, but the discipline had been good, the penalty in health, the nervous irritation due to little sleep, the slackness from inactivity, the arduous watches, the continual presence of others were things that would pass away; but I had forced myself to work and I had experienced, that would stand. The interpretation would stand too. It was a confession and it should be posted.

The interpretation was finished and I sat at the tiller. Food came. It was rice, rice with sugar and rice with the flavour of sardine, two helpings, and a soggy dough cooked in the pan. After it I became deathly sick. I could have died without caring. I took a teaspoonful of raw whisky and it made me feel better, but I was dull and flat as a Sunday School text and had no more vitality in me than a printed card hanging on a wall. I was without reason miserable. Sven notched up another score in the tally of his grievance against psycho-analysis, it had been used against him and now it had got me. Indeed it might have been the devastating result of a pure conscience after the catharsis of a dream interpretation that made me feel so dull and full of an unknown grief. Perhaps it might be jollier to be uninterpreted and full of flirtatious inclinations?

For the last twenty-four hours we had done nine miles and had got to a more westerly position than we had ever before achieved, 104° 55′ east. Singapore was only 103° 56′ east, but we were working into a position from which we could get within the Rhio Strait. We could see again our old friend the little round hummock of Merapos, passed on the day of wind and the rescue, and the big island of Linga was larger, calling to us like a mother hurrying her children home. After all these weeks we suddenly smelt land, to me it was seaweedy, a distinct odour of shore and seaweed but the others declared it smelt of decaying verdure and forest. In any case it was good, different from the sea-smell.

The sea was light green, indicating shallower water. We sounded in eighteen fathoms, the bottom had changed, now it was thick mud sucking at the lead. We could feel the tug before it lifted. The next day, November 23rd, it was sixteen fathoms and the sea a sparkling green, full of hope; the sunlight put mauve shadows in the troughs of the waves.

We passed Jim Bazaar island and saw four steamers far ahead in the entrance to the strait. Having islands in view, being close to land, and the skipping nature of the clouds and the water made the day resemble the happy sailing of Barrier times. The wind held lightly till we were almost round the point of Telang when the tide racing out between the two islands to the north caught us and we could make no head against it. We decided to go on the other tack till the tide turned. We missed stays once and wore round the second time. It was off a lee shore so we found a shallow spot, eight fathoms, and put out the heavy anchor, Moses, from 2–5 p.m. Then at 7 p.m. the south-easter we had been hoping for so long came up and at last we entered Rhio Strait – and Sven could have a cigarette. Since we had been caught in the third becalming and missed getting in to Singapore Strait he had sworn not to smoke till Rhio. Only sixty-two miles to Singapore!

Thursday, November 24th. We were two miles within Rhio Strait proper, in the previous twenty-four hours we had done seventeen miles. I climbed to the top of the mast twice. It was something I had always wanted to do and had never done. Joan had never wanted to and in front of her I had been too mortified to try. Now it was quite easy. How silly not to have tried before! We made Great Karos, an island on the western side of the Strait, near Little Karos where there is a lighthouse.

Fisherboys came out and sold us fish. Our first fresh food. We went ashore in a sampan. Trees, sand, and fishing nets spread out; big coppers for boiling down; a house that was also the village store. Tea, matches, tinned milk, duck eggs, coco-nut oil, soap and some cigarette papers. A walk on a narrow path through scratched patches of cultivation. Flowers by the wayside. Blush bouvardia, Chelsea Gem lantana, wild laciandra, cultivated hibiscus, a straggling rose the size of a florin, an attenuated balsam. Breadfruit tied up in old pyjamas, unwieldy heavy fruit

417

growing close to the trunk, like lumpy green laundry bags full of clothes.

A Malay shipwright was making a proa. He did not build the frame first and put the planks on afterwards but with wooden pins nailed the planks together above the keel, keeping them in position with a series of Spanish windlasses – Henery told me that, Spanish windlasses. The stem and stern posts went on afterwards. He had shaped the stringers and was putting the midships one in when we arrived. Henery was very nautical in Malay. A venerable old man wearing a beard, a smoking cap, a sarong and one sandal made out of a piece of motor tyre came up and held me in a long conversation about his sore foot, where we had come from and a lot more that I did not understand. I answered him with 'Tiddah's', polite 'Ohs' of surprise and 'Is that so?' and affirmative grunts in what were apparently the appropriate places, for he seemed very satisfied with the conversation as if he had gained a lot of information. Just what had I told him, I wondered.

I was very tired. I could hardly drag one leg after the other, yet we had not gone far. Ruth and Joan were full of exclamations of delight. We wanted fruit and tried many houses, Malay houses cool and comfortable, one of them sported a new corrugated iron roof, ugly beside the atap thatch of the others. Nobody wished to sell fruit. 'Tid'ada', 'There is none.' I saw a woman with a large paw-paw, molten ripe, broken, just picked up as it fell from the tree. I went across, uttering a yelp to those behind like a hunting dog on the trail and she disappeared inside her house. 'Paya-paya?' I inquired from the male householder who appeared from beneath the house among a convoy of ducks and hens.

'Tid'ada' was the reply, though I could hear his wife listening inside and the juice of the coveted paw-paw dripping on the matting.

If the children were alone when they saw us they ran away, so did the women, they could have scuttled into their houses no faster if the demons of the forest were on their heels. We saw a bunch of bananas hanging on a tree before a little house in the jungle and a beautiful woman standing at her window looking out, like a softly coloured Malay Virgin, her draperies folded over her head and the window framing her still and graceful pose so that she looked exactly like a picture above an altar. I inquired several times about the pisang, pointing to them and smiling to give her confidence, but she might indeed have been a picture so still was she. I thought she was deaf and dumb at the least, not even her eyes moved. Then Sven spoke, 'Brapa pisang?' and his male voice conjured from her as from a ventriloquist's doll a tiny squeaking answer in an incredible voice for a grown woman, the voice of a frightened puppet. She spoke, as a set speech, at length. Her mouth spoiled the illusion of the Raphael Madonna, her teeth were few and betel-stained, the opened mouth horrible. All the fruit five of us could buy was one small pineapple and two bananas.

My mind was too worn to enjoy anything. I had experienced too much, this first island after weeks of sea was too great for my comprehension. A blade of grass cut the top of my foot, the barest scratch. A drop of dirty water from a puddle was splashed on it, it festered, deepened, grew and did not clear up for many months, not till I got to a cold climate. I was so weary I paddled out before the others to the boat.

Beneath the koeli-koeli long sea grass waved. The *Skaga* seemed larger than it was, the mast taller; the islands hung like clouds in the air. It was just before sunset. The coco-nut trees on the shore lifted their proud and ragged heads higher into the sky, grown gigantic under the hallucination of evening, stretching up at the end of a long day before the black repose of night.

Another day. Perfect. Sunlight and shadow, green seas mottled with darkness, foam-crested waves, land, dark green and verdant on either hand, sudden small islands appearing and being passed by, a pale cloud-sprinkled sky full of motion to match the water; the kind of sailing day I liked best. Though we had a head wind and were tacking the tide helped us. By four o'clock in the afternoon we had done twelve miles and anchored again as the tide left us. It runs in from each entrance of Rhio Strait, curves round in the big bay of Rhio and then, turning, departs again by both exits. Opposite was the Chinese town of Rhio and on the same bank farther north a petrol station where tankers called to load.

Night, sailing on again, so many leading lights that after our weeks on the empty China Sea we felt we were in the heart of a populated country. Steamer lights green and as they swung round, red. Difficult navigation, a narrow strait, a head wind, shipping in the channel, unlighted fishing stakes far out from shore, the possibility of the wind dropping and leaving us on a lee shore, the net gain of the whole night a few miles.

Another day. We anchored off a little island called Chemara while the tide ebbed. I paddled ashore for a swim. In the afternoon we were off again, beating along.

The last night. We had got into Singapore Strait, we had intended to anchor on the northern side and wait till morning, but a fair breeze sprang up, so, using the squaresail and drifting with the tide we kept on. The black sea, the velvet sky, the large stars and a soft wind; we went smoothly as if we were skating on a black mirror. The glory of such sailing is in the silence of the motion.

It was a night of incident. I slept on deck in my rug. Ruth called me for the one to three watch. Within five minutes the wind had freshened, changed by two or three points and got on the wrong side of the sail. It was always a nuisance with the squaresail up to get round. I was particularly anxious not to call Sven, he had had no rest the night before and none during the day. He came up, however, sceptical of the 'change of wind' but it had changed; I was exonerated.

We sailed serenely for some time and then there came a lurch, a thump and a shuddering roll. I was hurled from one side of the cockpit to the other and Ruth flung off the deckhouse. She thought it was a tide rip we had met, I that we had bumped some floating logs but Sven popped up again and declared what it was, the wash from a steamer passing a long way off.

Another steamer passed, closer, her lights a looped necklace against the sky, the aft masthead light the highest. How mysterious it all was, the silent purposiveness of the steamer and our slow sailing that by reason of the great difference of speed seemed to have no purpose. But we had a purpose for all that, this was the end of it, the end of a slow five thousand miles. We were limping in.

The sheet lightning that had floodlit the sky from time to time changed to forked. Clouds covered the stars. The sky looked ominous. Ten to three, I should have to call Sven up again to see this. He came, looked at the sky and summoned Henery. They prepared to change the squaresail for the mainsail, but while they were loosening the braces a squall of wind hit us unexpectedly like a smack in the face from an open hand. They got it down in a pother of canvas and spray and hoisted the mainsail. The wind shifted. 'Put her about.' She heeled over under me. I headed her up so they could tighten the halyards. The wind changed again, I put her about again, at the same time the storm proper broke, an icy deluge. For the last time wet to the skin.

Before dawn another alarm, Sven this time. A junk without lights had almost run us down. We sheered off with a few yards between us. Their tremendous sails above our heads blotted out the pale morning sky. There was a glimpse of huge logs lashed down on her decks and figures like porcelain toys in the rigging, quite still in that instant of vision. Her bowsprit stuck up comically from the bows. She was swallowed up in obscurity.

Sunday morning, November 27th. Singapore like a dream in the dawn; tall buildings, steamers, junks. One came sailing down on us, as big as a schooner, but with a blunt prow and a square high poop, so clumsy and ugly that we laughed in derision, a headsail shaped like a box and a mainsail so thin you could see the sky through its cane slats. Each section of the matting of which it was made was stretched on a bamboo rib from the mast and could be furled separately. It was so new to us. It looked as if a crudely shaped packing-case with portion of a gigantic umbrella for a sail had put to sea. But when it turned on the other tack and we saw the height of the masts and the curve of the sails as they bellied with the wind aft we realized that it was built for speed, that these clumsy-looking sails had a rakish set and could sail fast with a light wind.

Drifting in. Tacking about, heat, white light, sunshine. Had we arrived? Was this Singapore, end of our journey? We flew no flag, not even the yacht club burgee, the stick had broken, it had been kept rolled up in the repository, under Sven's mattress. We were not making a grand entrance, we were merely getting there.

Out came a launch, a white launch with white men in white suits and white unhealthy faces in which the eyes were blue and curious. Three Norwegians, one of them a captain. 'Where do you come from?'

'Australia. Sydney.'

'The ship's Swedish built,' he declared.

We admitted it.

He turned to his son, 'I told you,' he said and explained to us, 'I saw it from my balcony. I knew at once it was from the North Sea and he as good as said his father was a fool.'

Laughter. We were glad to be greeted.

'Got an engine?'

'No.'

'Like a tow to an anchorage?'

Of course we would.

Ashore.

Rickshaws, a bewilderment of races and strange tongues. Chinese streets, slit-eyed babies, sampans thatched like hayricks in the dirty river, barges hooded like farm wagons. Money changers, washing on sticks across narrow streets. Things in shops. Sikh caretakers asleep on rope mattresses on the footpaths in front of the doors they guarded. Trolly buses. Seven months since we had seen a tram. Sven was showing Ruth and me the town. Unaccustomed shoes were tight on us, clothes stifled us.

RESCUED: AND AGAIN DRIFTING

The Raffles memorial. Sunday and the last port made. No mail, not till to-morrow. Would you like an ice-cream, girls? An ice-cream! A slow smile spread across our faces. Three grins went in by themselves to eat ice-cream. The bodies were not there, they had got lost at sea.

CHAPTER XXXIV

IT IS GOOD-BYE

I HELD a scrap of paper in my hand, a cablegram from home. 'Do not risk the Indian Ocean.' How I wished I could, that they would feel friendly enough to say, 'Do you want to? Don't you want to go on?'

If we could have taken the risk together again. But no. Wisdom, not the wisdom that fears risks but that central wisdom that persists in us beneath desire, said no; told me not to crave even the asking. Her integral hardness was still there, that deliberate withdrawal from communication.

In the weeks we all spent together in Singapore after the be-calming, knowing that we were going to separate but not compre-hending what separation meant, weeks of meeting people, scraping the boat and being entertained, I was null and void. I did what anyone wanted me to and I had no purpose, I rushed around being busy over trifles. I had not yet realized that I was free to do whatever I wanted to. A long adventure such as ours does not end suddenly, on a high emotional note. It dies slowly and there are obsequies afterwards. In life, as in death, arrangements have to be made, and this voyage ended as it began, with a series of leave-takings.

Sven was the first to go. The opportunity came suddenly, a week or two before Christmas; a Swedish captain offered him a passage to North China where there was a war on and where navigators were needed after the ice broke up at Chinwangtao. It was fixed up at a party in the evening. 'I sail to-morrow morn-ing at eleven,' he said.

Dear Sven. To-morrow morning at eleven. It had had to come. There was the last packing of the big green sea-bag, the last sorting out of possessions and the closing of suitcases. Ruth and I went to see him off. A group of men, shipping agents and the diehards of the port were on the wharf and curious about us.

The painful moments approaching separation. Sven so mahogany bronzed, his face so deeply lined, the eyes puckered at the corners with the look of far distances in them, the shoulders broad under the well-fitting linen suit; Sven, so dependable, so vulnerable, so cheery. How well we knew him. Yet the day before a woman had surprised me by saying, 'He's good-looking, isn't he?' Good-looking. It had never occurred to me that he was good-looking, I had always thought of another type as being handsome. Now as he went away I noticed for the first time his good looks, those of bone beneath the flesh, a firm jaw, vigour, resolution and an honest open happiness. He was still a boy. He had loved to do things for *Skaga*, for any of us. I had never asked Henery to do anything, but Sven, he had always been there, ready, willing, the most unselfish and the most capable of the lot of us . . . we had taken it for granted, treated him . . . I felt myself shabby within, looking at Sven.

It was time to leave. The siren was blowing, they would be lowering the gangway in a few minutes. Ruth must kiss him, she must. It was up to her, that puritan anathema against kissing must break down. She did. That only kiss. Then his lips brushed mine, for an instant. His starched linen crackled round me. Good-bye, Sven. Perhaps I was wrong and you were right. Perhaps you and I could have made it a more gallant adventure together. Arms softer than water, stars singing a melody through the south-east wind. But what are shipmates, Sven? Not only people who do things together but who feel things together. And what is a crew, Sven? It is more than two. And superiority, Sven? Superiority is maggots.

We were on the wharf. 'I'm glad I came down to see him off,' said Ruth, suddenly emphatic. She was a compass needle magnetized between Joan and me and she swung my way just then.

'Do you know,' asked a little man breathlessly, a clerkly shipping agent, 'There are brigands aboard. We have just been warned.

Sixty of the hundred and forty deck passengers are armed and will try to seize the ship.'

The vessel turned in the fairway. Up on the bridge at the very end where it was open stood Sven. Slowly he raised his arms. He gave the all clear signal. We signalled it back, 'All clear. Full steam ahead. Good luck.' He had gone on a new voyage, the voyage of the *Skaga* was really over now.

Ruth went next, a day or two before Christmas, she had got herself a passage in return for minding a baby. If the mother of the infant had known that the provisional child-minder had our piratical background and was now bound for Moscow, with meta-phorically, a knife between the teeth, she might have shut the safety-pin with a click and banned the free way to England; as it was she let Ruth invite me to dinner the night before their departure. The ship was full of commonplace people doing a round trip of the world, worrying about tips and blaming the hotel accommodation; business men who had made second-rate bargains and who worked out the margin of social profit on every new acquaintance they made, civil servants going on leave with their health impaired, young things making naughty eyes. 'Can she pake a cherry-pie, Pilly Poy, Pilly Poy?' Sven's voice sang faintly on the way to China. The dining saloon with its flowers, table lamps and hurrying stewards seemed stuffy. Rice and sar-dines under moonlight yellow as a Pernod or that first mackerel at Percy Islands, they were meals to be recollected, and, for all its courses, this dinner was just eating.

We went for her last look round Singapore, unescorted to an eastern Luna Park where we did not see another European. We watched a Malay play, a romantic melodrama with long speeches and love-making. Afterwards we learnt from the placards that it was *Twelfth Night*, but neither of us, who had taught *Twelfth Night* for examinations till we knew every line of it, had recognized it. We saw Hindoo dancers and snake charmers and had a guinea-pig swallowed for us. Not to lose any profit they tapped the back of the cobra's neck and he obligingly returned the guinea pig, wet but still living. We sat out a few scenes in a classical Chinese play, the costumes were stiff enough to stand by themselves, the action was mostly in the opening of fans with occasional bits of violent brigandage at which the audience applauded. We heard Japanese geishas sing Italian light opera and we bought toys and trifles, things to amuse the baby. Ruth said she was frightened it might howl all the way to England. We ate sati by a fountain trimmed with coloured electric lights and we drank coffee in a Chinese den at closing time. Money meanness had dropped from us, we were breaking up, she was going away. We enjoyed ourselves in the haphazard way of sailors ashore, for the last time we were sailors ashore, and when it was very late we took rickshaws by dark alleys to her boat and then to mine, adventuring it till the end.

Next morning I was just in time to see her ship depart. She stood by the rail smiling. How brown she was among those other women, how brawny her arms, how care-free and independent her every casual gesture, and how inappropriately her freshly-ironed ribbons and muslins sat upon her, they belonged to her before-time life, the shore life, we were different women now, ribbons and muslins did not suit us. As the ship turned she made me a grimace and held up the baby. Her face was a brown mask high up among pink and white daubings. I watched till I could no longer distinguish it.

And myself? Someone advised me to go inland in Malaya to see the country and the life on the rubber estates and someone else told me to go to Japan where the yen was down and it was cold and I could recuperate, and a third person got me the promise of a baby to mind on the way to England. There are always friendly practical women who know what is best for one. Because I was quite open to suggestion and without a will of my own I did all three, in that order, looking at a few forts on the way, as a last pilgrimage for the Professor, Malacca, Lukut, Macao and the relics of Will Adams in Nagasaki.

As for Joan and Henery I saw them for a few minutes when I returned from my inland trip and before I went to Japan. Joan's elder sister had come from Australia to see them and they were going for a motoring holiday together. I found them in the street just before they left; the engine of the car was running and they did not turn it off.

I was enthusiastic about the country, gushing, effervescing at seeing them again. I had been away and forgotten the *Skaga* feelings and now Joan looked at me sceptically, what levitation had raised this lightness of heart in me? I could feel the old obfuscation creeping down stage. She looked at me with her eyes the colour of prune kernels and they wondered a little, 'What had Dona been up to now?' She smiled with her lips, her Mona Lisa smile buttoned down a little at one side. Her eyelids drooped heavily, that moment I saw her as an aestheticized sphinx with long earrings, the perspective of the face pulled down. Joan the inscrutable who did not know how to surrender, who imposed on the bubble of every manifestation of the spirit a cast-iron hardness, who wanted to pull into cohesion and make permanent the flux of passing events.

Were we of different substances then? Incompatibles by nature? When I think of her I think of grey steel, highly polished, I think of the bow of a battle cruiser that cuts sharply through the water with an elegant hard line, the line of a thinly-marked eyebrow lifted a little in surprise. Compared with the cold purpose of her steel I am glass, that can glitter and reflect sunlight and shadow more quickly, that can cast back an image, and be easily seen through; that carries within its transparency a good many flaws that have been there from the beginning and will remain; the whole character, slighter, brittle, more easily smashed. But one's own substance again, not someone else's.

Henery came out of the swinging doors, he was in a hurry, carrying pencils and papers and making arrangements, his white helmet pushed back, the sun shone on his fair hair, that golden mane of the lion of Aquitane, appanage of England. At his approach the engine of the car turned more quickly, cutting short good-byes. Good-bye. Good-bye . . . without looking back.

IT IS GOOD-BYE

A few days later I left for Japan on a big liner and was a passenger, a new experience for me, an experience with two sides to it. It taught me the last lesson, my sea adventure was quite over.

BOUND FOR JAPAN

Dear old intimacy of the sea
Gone, gone, for ever.
Instead of a friendly compass and my hand on the tiller
A bridge marked 'Private',
Plenty of gold braid, seven-course dinners, souvenir menus,
Stewards innumerable . . . deck tennis
Making conversation, cards, dancing and scandal . . .
Which has nothing to do with the sea,
Gloriously keeping us in bondage
Every minute of the day and night.
Oh Humanity is degraded by comfort,
How I loathe this travelling first class.

REVERSE

Formos Channel and
Waves so big that even this elephant of a boat
Pitches on its mountain path of sea,
Wallowing under showers of icy spray.
The north-east monsoon
Is a hearty Chinese Arctic devil saying: 'Pist-Pist-Pist',
From a frigid immensity of space. . . .
Much better to snuggle bed-socked under six blankets
Then take a four-hour turn on the bridge.

When I got back to Singapore I expected to see *Skaga*, but she was not there. I looked in vain for her solid stumpy mast, her broad maternal duck-like shape, green among the white swans of the Yacht Club anchorage, her low gunwale, cut-off stern, her snub nose and her makeshift awning suspended loosely on bamboo poles. She was not there and so I could not say farewell, which was perhaps just as well for she was never a sentimentalist. And saying farewell so often means forgetting. But none of us could ever forget *Skaga*. She was the great adventurer, she would not rot while Swedish oak held, she had behind her the long years of the North Sea pilot service, and then the venturesome trip out through the hot Panama, over the two oceans, on board her the two men who grew to hate each other. And we, Australians. Did she hold us in her timbers? Were we now part of her, us and our failure that had been so near success, our so-near achievement of the almost perfect that just missed and that in missing lost all the things we might have had, the gladness, the frankness, the co-operation, just gone? We had salvaged a measure of success, we had got to port and there had been no bloody noses, but we had been wrecked all the same. Exasperation we had known, painful politeness and endurance; above all endurance. Did the ship hold that?

Joan and Henery did not continue the trip and I learnt recently that *Skaga* had been sold to two men whom I do not know but they must be young and adventurous or they would not have bought her, she is not a common ship, a harbour-loving, lake-loving pleasure ship, but an ugly duckling that can sail like a swan. *Skaga*. Will she still go home through the toss of tumultuous seas to die at last in the yard of some breaker-up in Sweden? Perhaps she will wear out in use and not be worth breaking up when she gets there.

We were all contemporaries, but she was the youngest of us, her birthday came last, her heart was the stoutest, she is the only one of us who is still going on.

The journey of the heart is over, ended the sorrowful year,
and into the beginning of new things creeps effort crying itself,
struggling to stand upright like a child grasping a chair
only to fall ridiculous bumping its bottom and not understanding
                                                            why,

but rising again and growing with every failure
into the ability of running. Solitary I have pursued events
                                    that we made together,
re-seized them when they would have escaped and been done
                                            with for ever.
They were too important to let slip and to have done with for ever.

It may be that in retrospect significance accumulates,
shows high lights and low like a film held against a lamp
registering details that have to be sponged from the memory
before the shape of things as they were emerges with the highest
                                            value of living.

That we did not know we were living highly matters nothing;
The sense we had that what was upon us was unique and transitory
                                    with brightness,
a comet falling hot into the sea and rising as a new mythological
                                            bird
compounded of fire and water, effort and failure, was in itself not
                                    self-contradictory.

For what was not done let nobody take the blame; blame is a
                        weed that takes no cultivation
and grows in cemeteries from which new life does not spring.
I cannot think that out of what we have done something will not
                                            grow,
deeds that have been fecund with emotion spawn other attempts,

and the resolution to go on is itself a victory, the gestation from
                              which a new life may be born.
I speak as a communist of the spirit in the travail of a
                              dialectical re-birth,
in a campaign of determining out of the errors of the past
                              a perfection that may yet be,
that inexorable must-be of the stars over the driftage
                              of unpiloted thought.

We were wrecked and we came to harm and now I travel
                              another sea
where the charts are more immense and the wind of a new
                              endeavour sweeps;
it is a bigger adventure that confronts us, abandoned
                              the individual barque,
the petty superiority of one personality over another, the private
                              property of fine feelings.

Never again do I want to feel the emotions of defeat
knowing that the self and the mind's work approximate to a zero
                              written small and unsupported
nor can I become a second time one of two positive roots
                              in a simple equation of living
rather would I be one of a long series added in progression,
                              each part not without value,

raised to a higher power by the enthusiasm of working together
                              for a purpose whatever it is;
one coral polyp that living and dying makes part of a strong wall,
a reef sheltering a tranquil future for a world consecrated to
                              happiness.
No hedonism is sufficient that can co-exist with the suffering of
                              another.